THE

WEPT OF WISH-TON-WISH.

A TALE.

BY J. FENIMORE COOPER.

"But she is dead to him, to all;
Her lute hangs silent on the wall,
And on the stairs, and at the door,
Her fairy step is heard no more."
ROGERS.

COMPLETE IN ONE VOLUME.

NEW YORK:
PUBLISHED BY HURD AND HOUGHTON.
Cambridge: Riverside Press
1871.

WEPT OF THE WISH-TON-WISH.

TO

THE REV. J. R. C.

OF

****** PENNSYLVANIA

The kind and disinterested manner in which you have furnished the materials of the following tale, merits a public acknowledgment. As your reluctance to appear before the world, however, imposes a restraint, you must receive such evidence of gratitude, as your own prohibition will allow.

Notwithstanding there are so many striking and deeply interesting events in the early history of those from whom you derive your being, yet are there hundreds of other families in this country, whose traditions, though less accurately and minutely preserved than the little narrative you have submitted to my inspection, would supply the materials of many moving tales. You have every reason to exult in your descent, for, surely, if any man may claim to be a citizen and a proprietor in the Union, it is one, that, like yourself, can point to a line of ancestors whose origin is lost in the obscurity of time. You are truly an American. In your eyes, we of a brief century or two, must appear as little more than denizens quite recently admitted to the privilege of a residence. That you may continue to enjoy peace and happiness, in that land where your fathers so long flourished, is the sincere wish of your obliged friend,

THE AUTHOR

PREFACE.

At this distant period, when Indian traditions are listened to with the interest that we lend to the events of a dark age, it is not easy to convey a vivid image of the dangers and privations that our ancestors encountered, in preparing the land we enjoy for its present state of security and abundance. It is the humble object of the tale that will be found in the succeeding pages, to perpetuate the recollection of some of the practices and events peculiar to the early days of our history.

The general character of the warfare pursued by the natives is too well known to require any preliminary observations; but it may be advisable to direct the attention of the reader, for a few moments, to those leading circumstances in the history of the times, that may have some connexion with the principal business of the legend.

The territory which now composes the three states of Massachusetts, Connecticut and Rhode-Island, is said, by the best informed of our annalists, to have been formerly occupied by four great nations of Indians, who were, as usual, subdivided into numberless dependent tribes. Of these people, the Massachusetts possessed a large portion of the land which now composes the state of that name; the Wampanoags dwelt in what was once the Colony of Plymouth, and in the northern districts of the Providence Plantations; the Narragansetts held the well-known islands of the beautiful bay which receives its name from their nation, and the more southern counties of the Plantations; while the Pequots, or as it is ordinarily written and pronounced, the Pequods, were masters of a broad region that lay along the western boundaries of the three other districts.

There is great obscurity thrown around the politv of the Indians, who usually occupied the country lying near the sea.

The Europeans, accustomed to despotic governments, very naturally supposed that the chiefs, found in possession of power, were monarchs to whom authority had been transmitted in virtue of their birth-rights They consequently gave them the name of kings.

How far this opinion of the governments of the aborigines was true remains a question, though there is certainly reason to think it less erroneous in respect to the tribes of the Atlantic states, than to those who have since been found further west, where, it is sufficiently known, that institutions exist which approach much nearer to republics than to monarchies. It may, however, have readily happened that the son, profiting by the advantages of his situation, often succeeded to the authority of the father, by the aid of influence, when the established regulations of the tribe acknowledged no hereditary claim. Let the principle of the descent of power be what it would, it is certain the experience of our ancestors proves, that, in very many instances, the child was seen to occupy the station formerly filled by the father; and, that in most of those situations of emergency, in which a people so violent were often placed, the authority he exercised was as summary as it was general. The appellation of Uncas came, like those of the Cæsars and Pharoahs, to be a sort of synonyme for chief with the Mohegans, a tribe of the Pequods, among whom several warriors of this name were known to govern in due succession. The renowned Metacom, or, as he is better known to the whites, King Philip, was certainly the son of Massassoit, the Sachem of the

Wampanoags that the emigrants found in authority when they landed on the rock of Plymouth. Miantonimoh, the daring but hapless rival of that Uncas who ruled the whole of the Pequod nation, was succeeded in authority, among the Narragansetts, by his not less heroic and enterprising son, Conanchet; and, even at a much later day, we find instances of this transmission of power, which furnish strong reasons for believing that the order of succession was in the direct line of blood.

The early annals of our history are not wanting in touching and noble examples of savage heroism. Virginia has its legend of the powerful Powhatan and his magnanimous daughter, the ill-requited Pocahontas; and the chronicles of New-England are filled with the bold designs and daring enterprises of Miantonimoh, of Metacom, and of Conanchet. All the last-named warriors proved themselves worthy of better fates, dying in a cause and in a manner, that, had it been their fortunes to have lived in a more advanced state of society, would have enrolled their names among the worthies of the age.

The first serious war, to which the settlers of New-England were exposed, was the struggle with the Pequods. This people was subdued after a fierce conflict; and from being enemies, all, who were not either slain or sent into distant slavery, were glad to become the auxiliaries of their conquerors. This contest occurred within less than twenty years after the Puritans had sought refuge in America.

There is reason to believe that Metacom foresaw the fate of his own people, in the humbled fortunes of the Pequods. Though his father had been the earliest and constant friend of the whites, it is probable that the Puritans owed some portion of this amity to a dire necessity. We are told that a terrible malady had raged among the Wampanoags but a short time before the arrival of the emigrants, and that their numbers had been fearfully reduced by its ravages. Some authors have hinted at the probability of this disease having been the yellow fever, whose visitations are known to be at uncertain, and, apparently, at very distant intervals. Whatever might have been the cause of this destruction of his people, Massassoit is believed to have been induced, by the consequences, to cultivate the alliance of a nation, who could protect him against the attacks of his ancient and less afflicted foes. But the son appears to have viewed the increasing influence of the whites with eyes more jealous than those of the father. He passed the morning of his life in maturing his great plan for the destruction of the strange race, and his later years were spent in abortive attempts to put this bold design in execution. His restless activity in plotting the confederation against the English, his fierce and ruthless manner of waging the war, his defeat, and his death, are too well known to require repetition.

There is also a wild and romantic interest thrown about the obscure history of a Frenchman of that period. This man is said to have been an officer of rank in the service of his king, and to have belonged to the privileged class which then monopolized all the dignities and emoluments of the kingdom of France. The traditions, and even the written annals of the first century of our possession of America, connect the Baron de la Castine with the Jesuits, who were thought to entertain views of converting the savages to Christianity, not unmingled with the desire of establishing a more temporal dominion over their minds. It is, however, difficult to say whether taste, or religion, or policy, or necessity, induced this nobleman to quit the saloons of Paris for the wilds of the Penobscot. It is merely known that he passed the greater part of his life on that river, in a rude fortress that was then called a palace, that he had many wives, a numerous progeny, and that he possessed a great influence over most of the tribes that dwelt in his vicinity. He is also believed to have been the instrument of furnishing the savages, who were hostile to the English, with ammunition, and with weapons of a more deadly character than those used in their earlier wars. In whatever degree he may have participated in the plan to exterminate the Puritans, death prevented him from assisting in the final effort of Metacom.

The Narragansetts are often mentioned in these pages. A few years before the period at which the tale commences, Miantonimoh had waged a ruthless war against Uncas, the Pequod or Mohegan chief. Fortune favored the latter, who, probably assisted by his civilized allies, not only overthrew the bands of the other, but succeeded in capturing the person of his enemy. The chief of the Narragansetts lost his life, through the agency of the whites, on the place that is now known by the appellation of "the Sachem's plain."

It remains only to throw a little light on the leading incidents of the war of King Philip. The first blow was struck in June, 1675, rather more than half a century after the English first landed in New-England, and just a century before blood was drawn in the contest which separated the colonies from the mother country. The scene was a settlement near the celebrated Mount Hope, in Rhode-Island, where Metacom and his father had both long held their councils. From this point, bloodshed and massacre extended along the whole frontier of New-England. Bodies of horse and foot were enrolled to meet the foe, and towns were burnt, and lives were taken by both parties, with little, and often with no respect for age, condition, or sex.

In no struggle with the native owners of the soil was the growing power of the whites placed in so great jeopardy, as in this celebrated contest with King Philip. The venerable historian of Connecticut estimates the loss of lives at nearly one-tenth of the whole number of the fighting men, and the destruction of houses and other edifices to have been in an equal proportion. One family in every eleven, throughout all New-England, was burnt out. As the colonists nearest the sea were exempt from the danger, an idea may be formed, from this calculation, of the risk and sufferings of those who dwelt in more exposed situations. The Indians did not escape without retaliation. The principal nations, already mentioned, were so much reduced as never afterwards to offer any serious resistance to the whites, who have since converted the whole of their ancient hunting-grounds into the abodes of civilized man. Metacom, Miantonimoh, and Conanchet, with their warriors, have become the heroes of song and legend, while the descendants of those who laid waste their dominions, and destroyed their race, are yielding a tardy tribute to the high daring and savage grandeur of their characters.

THE WEPT

OF

WISH-TON-WISH.

CHAPTER I.

"I may disjoin my hand, but not my faith."
SHAKSPEARE.

THE incidents of this tale must be sought in a remote period of the annals of America. A colony of self-devoted and pious refugees from religious persecution had landed on the rock of Plymouth, less than half a century before the time at which the narrative commences; and they, and their descendants, had already transformed many a broad waste of wilderness into smiling fields and cheerful villages. The labors of the emigrants had been chiefly limited to the country on the coast, which, by its proximity to the waters that rolled between them and Europe, afforded the semblance of a connexion with the land of their forefathers and the distant abodes of civilization. But enterprise, and a desire to search for still more fertile domains, together with the temptation offered by the vast and unknown regions that lay along their western and northern borders, had induced many bold adventurers to penetrate more deeply into the forests. The precise spot, to which we desire to transport the imagination of the reader, was one of these establishments of what may, not inaptly, be called the forlorn-hope, in the march of civilization through the country.

So little was then known of the great outlines of the American continent, that, when the Lords

Say and Seal, and Brooke, connected with a few associates, obtained a grant of the territory which now composes the state of Connecticut, the King of England affixed his name to a patent, which constituted them proprietors of a country that should extend from the shores of the Atlantic to those of the South Sea. Notwithstanding the apparent hopelessness of ever subduing, or of even occupying a territory like this, emigrants from the mother colony of Massachusetts were found ready to commence the Herculean labor, within fifteen years from the day when they had first put foot upon the well-known rock itself. The fort of Say-Brooke, the towns of Windsor, Hartford, and New-Haven, soon sprang into existence, and, from that period to this, the little community, which then had birth, has been steadily, calmly, and prosperously advancing in its career, a model of order and reason, and the hive from which swarms of industrious, hardy and enlightened yeomen have since spread themselves over a surface so vast, as to create an impression that they still aspire to the possession of the immense regions included in their original grant.

Among the religionists, whom disgust of persecution had early driven into the voluntary exile of the colonies, was more than an usual proportion of men of character and education. The reckless and the gay, younger sons, soldiers unemployed, and students from the inns of court, early sought advancement and adventure in the more southern provinces, where slaves offered impunity from labor, and where war, with a bolder and more stirring policy, oftener gave rise to scenes of excitement, and, of course, to the exercise of the faculties best suited to their habits and dispositions. The more grave, and the religiously-disposed, found refuge in the colonies of New-England. Thither a multitude of private gentlemen transferred their fortunes and their families, imparting a character of intelligence and a moral elevation to the country, which it has nobly sustained to the present hour.

The nature of the civil wars in England had enlisted many men of deep and sincere piety in the profession of arms. Some of them had retired to the colonies before the troubles of the mother country reached their crisis, and others continued to arrive, throughout the whole period of their existence, until the restoration; when crowds of those who had been disaffected to the house of Stuart sought the security of these distant possessions.

A stern, fanatical soldier, of the name of Heathcote, had been among the first of his class, to throw aside the sword for the implements of industry peculiar to the advancement of a newly-established country. How far the influence of a young wife may have affected his decision it is not germane to our present object to consider, though the records, from which the matter we are about to relate is gleaned, give reason to suspect that he thought his domestic harmony would not be less secure in the wilds of the new world, than among the companions with whom his earlier associations would naturally have brought him in communion.

Like himself, his consort was born of one of those families, which, taking their rise in the franklins of the times of the Edwards and Henrys, had become possessors of hereditary landed estates, that, by their gradually-increasing value, had elevated them to the station of small country gentlemen. In most other nations of Europe, they would have been rated in the class of the *petite noblesse*. But the domestic happiness of Capt. Heathcote was doomed to receive a fatal blow, from a quarter where circumstances had given him but little reason to apprehend danger. The very day he landed in the long-wished for asylum, his wife made him the father of a noble boy, a gift that she bestowed at the melancholy price of her own existence. Twenty years the senior of the woman who had followed his fortunes to these distant regions, the retired warrior had always considered it to be perfectly and absolutely within the order of things, that he himself was to be the first to pay the debt of nature. While the visions which Captain Heathcote entertained of a future world were sufficiently vivid and distinct, there is reason to think they were seen through a tolerably long vista of quiet and comfortable enjoyment in this. Though the calamity cast an additional aspect of seriousness over a character that was already more than chastened by the subtleties of sectarian doctrines, he was not of a nature to be unmanned by any vicissitude of human fortune. He lived on, useful and unbending in his habits, a pillar of strength in the way of wisdom and courage to the immediate neighborhood among whom he resided, but reluctant from temper, and from a disposition which had been shadowed by withered happiness, to enact that part in the public affairs of the little state, to which his comparative wealth and previous habits might well have entitled him to aspire. He gave his son such an education as his own resources and those of the infant colony of Massachusetts afforded, and, by a sort of delusive piety, into whose merits we have no desire to look, he thought he had also furnished a commendable evidence of his own desperate resignation to the will of Providence, in causing him to be publicly christened by the name of Content. His own baptismal appellation was Mark; as indeed had been that of most of his ancestors, for two or three centuries. When the world was a little uppermost in his thoughts, as sometimes happens with the most humbled spirits, he had even been heard to speak of a Sir Mark of his family, who had ridden a knight in the train of one of the more warlike kings of his native land.

There is some ground for believing, that the great parent of evil early looked with a malignant eye on the example of peacefulness, and of unbending morality, that the colonists of New-England were setting to the rest of Christendom. At any rate, come from what quarter they might, schisms and doctrinal contentions arose among the emigrants themselves; and men, who together had deserted the fire-sides of their forefathers in quest of religious peace, were ere long seen separating their fortunes, in order that each might enjoy, unmolested, those peculiar shades of faith, which all had the presumption, no less than the folly, to believe were necessary to propitiate the omnipotent and merciful father of the universe. If our task were one of theology, a wholesome moral on the vanity, no less than on the absurdity of the race, might be here introduced to some advantage.

When Mark Heathcote announced to the community, in which he had now sojourned more than twenty years, that he intended for a second time to establish his altars in the wilderness, in the hope that he and his household might worship God as to them seemed most right, the intelligence was received with a feeling allied to awe. Doctrine and zeal were momentarily forgotten, in the respect and attachment which had been unconsciously created by the united influence of the stern severity of his air, and of the undeniable virtues of his practice. The elders of the settlement communed with him freely and in charity; but the voice of conciliation and alliance came too late. He listened to the reasonings of the ministers, who were assembled from all the adjoining parishes, in sullen respect: and he joined in the petitions for light and instruction, that were offered up on the occasion, with the deep reverence with which he ever drew near to the footstool of the Almighty; but he did both in a temper into which too much positiveness of spiritual pride had entered, to open his heart to that sympathy and charity, which, as they are the characteristics of our mild and forbearing doctrines, should be the study of those who profess to follow their precepts. All that was seemly, and all that was usual, were done; but the purpose of the stubborn sectarian remained unchanged. His final decision is worthy of being recorded.

"My youth was wasted in ungodliness and ignorance," he said, "but in my manhood have I known the Lord. Near two-score years have I toiled for the truth, and all that weary time have I past in trimming my lamps, lest, like the foolish virgins, I should be caught unprepared; and now, when my loins are girded and my race is nearly run, shall I become a backslider and falsifier of the word? Much have I endured, as you know, in quitting the earthly mansion of my fathers, and in encountering the dangers of sea and land for the faith; and, rather than let go its hold, will I once more cheerfully devote to the howling wilderness, ease, offspring, and, should it be the will of Providence, life itself!"

The day of parting was one of unfeigned and general sorrow. Notwithstanding the austerity of the old man's character, and the nearly unbending severity of his brow, the milk of human kindness had often been seen distilling from his stern nature in acts that did not admit of misinterpretation. There was scarcely a young beginner in the laborious and ill-requited husbandry of the township he inhabited, a district at no time considered either profitable or fertile, who could not recall some secret and kind aid which had flowed from a hand that, to the world, seemed clenched in cautious and reserved frugality; nor did any of the faithful of his vicinity cast their fortunes together in wedlock, without receiving from him evidence of an interest in their worldly happiness, that was far more substantial than words.

On the morning when the vehicles, groaning with the household goods of Mark Heathcote, were seen quitting his door, and taking the road which led to the sea-side, not a human being, of sufficient age, within many miles of his residence, was absent from the interesting spectacle. The leave-taking, as usual on all serious occasions, was preceded by a hymn and prayer, and then the sternly-minded adventurer embraced his neighbors, with a mien, in which a subdued exterior struggled fearfully and strangely with emotions that, more than once, threatened to break through even the formidable barriers of his acquired manner. The inhabitants of every building on the road were in the open air, to receive and to return the parting benediction. More than once, they, who guided his teams, were commanded to halt, and all near, possessing human aspirations and human responsibility, were collected to offer petitions in favor of him who departed and of those who remained. The requests for mortal privileges were somewhat light and hasty, but the askings in behalf of intellectual and spiritual light were long, fervent, and oft-repeated. In this characteristic manner did one of the first of the emigrants to the new world make his second removal into scenes of renewed bodily suffering, privation and danger.

Neither person nor property was transferred from place to place, in this country, at the middle of the seventeenth century, with the dispatch and with the facilities of the present time. The roads were necessarily few and short, and communication by water was irregular, tardy, and far from commodius. A wide barrier of forest lying between that portion of Massachusetts-bay from which Mark Heathcote emigrated, and the spot, near the Connecticut river, to which it was his intention to proceed, he was induced to adopt the latter mode of conveyance. But a long delay intervened between the time when he commenced his short journey to the coast, and the hour when he was finally enabled to embark. During this detention he and his household sojourned among the godly-minded of the narrow peninsula, where there already existed the germ of a flourishing town, and where the spires of a noble and picturesque city now elevate themselves above so many thousand roofs.

The son did not leave the colony of his birth and the haunts of his youth, with the same unwavering obedience to the call of duty, as the father. There was a fair, a youthful, and a gentle being in the recently-established town of Boston, of an age, station, opinions, fortunes, and, what was of still greater importance, of sympathies suited to his own. Her form had long mingled with those holy images, which his stern instruction taught him to keep most familiarly before the mirror of his thoughts. It is not surprising, then, that the youth hailed the delay as propitious to his wishes, or that he turned it to the account, which the promptings of a pure affection so naturally suggested. He was united to the gentle Ruth Harding only the week before the father sailed on his second pilgrimage.

It is not our intention to dwell on the incidents of the voyage. Though the genius of an extraordinary man had discovered the world which was now beginning to fill with civilized men, navigation at that day was not brilliant in accomplishments. A passage among the shoals of Nantucket must have been one of actual danger, no less than of terror; and the ascent of the Connecticut itself was an exploit worthy of being mentioned. In due time the adventurers landed at the English fort of Hartford, where they tarried for a season, in order to obtain rest and spiritual comfort. But the peculiarity of doctrine, on which Mark Heathcote laid so much stress, was one that rendered it advisable for him to retire still further from the haunts of men. Accompanied by a few followers, he proceeded on an exploring expedition, and the end of the summer found him once more established on an estate that he had acquired by the usual simple forms practised in the colonies, and at the trifling cost for which extensive districts were then set apart as the property of individuals.

The love of the things of this life, while it certainly existed, was far from being predominant in the affections of the Puritan. He was frugal from habit and principle, more than from an undue longing after worldly wealth. He contented himself, therefore, with acquiring an estate that should be valuable, rather from its quality and beauty, than from its extent. Many such places offered themselves, between the settlements of Weathersfield and Hartford, and that imaginary line which separated the possessions of the colony he had quitted, from those of the one he joined. He made his location, as it is termed in the language of the country, near the northern boundary of the latter. This spot, by the aid of an expenditure that might have been considered lavish for the country and the age, if some lingering of taste, which even the self-denying and subdued habits of his later life had not entirely extinguished, and of great natural beauty in the distribution of land, water and wood, the emigrant contrived to convert into an abode, that was not more desirable for its retirement from the temptations of the world, than for its rural loveliness.

After this memorable act of conscientious self

devotion, years passed away in quiet, amid a species of negative prosperity. Rumors from the old world reached the ears of the tenants of this secluded settlement, months after the events to which they referred were elsewhere forgotten, and tumults and wars in the sister colonies came to their knowledge only at distant and tardy intervals. In the mean time, the limits of the colonial establishments wer gradually extending themselves, and valleys were beginning to be cleared nearer and nearer to their own. Old age had now begun to make some visible impression on the iron frame of the Captain, and the fresh color of youth and health, with which his son had entered the forest, was giving way to the brown covering produced by exposure and toil. We say of toil, for, independently of the habits and opinions of the country, which strongly reprobated idleness, even in those most gifted by fortune, the daily difficulties of their situation. the chase, and the long and intricate passages that the veteran himself was compelled to adventure in the surrounding forest, partook largely of the nature of the term we have used. Ruth continued blooming and youthful, though maternal anxiety was soon added to her other causes of care. Still, for a long season, nought occurred to excite extraordinary regrets for the step they had taken, or to create particular uneasiness in behalf of the future. The borderers, for such by their frontier position they had in truth become, heard the strange and awful tidings of the dethronement of one king, of the interregnum, as a reign of more than usual vigor and prosperity is called, and of the restoration of the son of him who is strangely enough termed a martyr. To all these eventful and unwonted chances in the fortunes of kings, Mark Heathcote listened with deep and reverential submission to the will of him, in whose eyes crowns and sceptres are merely the more costly baubles of the world. Like most of his contemporaries, who had sought shelter in the western continent, his political opinions, if not absolutely republican, had a leaning to liberty that was strongly in opposition to the doctrine of the divine rights of the monarch, while he had been too far removed from the stirring passions which had gradually excited those nearer to the throne, to lose their respect for its sanctity, and to sully its brightness with blood. When the transient and straggling visiters that, at long intervals, visited his settlement, spoke of the Protector, who for so many years ruled England with an iron hand, the eyes of the old man would gleam with sudden and singular interest; and once, when commenting after evening prayer on the vanity and the vicissitudes of this life, he acknowledged that the extraordinary individual, who was, in substance if not in name, seated on the throne of the Plantagenets, had been the boon companion and ungodly associate of many of his youthful hours. Then would follow a long, wholesome, extemporaneous homily on the idleness of setting the affections on the things of life, and a half-suppressed, but still intelligible commendation of the wiser course which had led him to raise his own tabernacle in the wilderness, instead of weakening the chances of eternal glory by striving too much for the possession of the treacherous vanities of the world.

But even the gentle and ordinarily little observant Ruth might trace the kindling of the eye, the knitting of the brow, and the flushings of his pale and furrowed cheek, as the murderous conflicts of the civil wars became the themes of the ancient soldier's discourse. There were moments when religious submission, and we had almost said religious precepts, were partially forgotten, as he explained to his attentive son and listening grandchild, the nature of the onset, or the quality and dignity of the retreat. At such times, his still nervous hand would even wield the blade, in order to instruct the latter in its uses, and many a long winter evening was passed in thus indirectly teaching an art, that was so much at variance with the mandates of his divine master. The chastened soldier, however, never forgot to close his instruction with a petition extraordinary, in the customary prayer, that no descendant of his should ever take life from a being unprepared to die, except in justifiable defence of his faith, his person, or his lawful rights. It must be admitted, that a liberal construction of the reserved privileges would leave sufficient matter, to exercise the subtlety of one subject to any extraordinary propensity to arms.

Few opportunities were however offered, in their remote situation and with their peaceful habits, for the practice of a theory that had been taught in so many lessons. Indian alarms, as they were termed, were not unfrequent, but, as yet, they had never produced more than terror in the bosoms of the gentle Ruth and her young offspring. It is true, they had heard of travellers massacred, and of families separated by captivity, but, either by a happy fortune, or by more than ordinary prudence in the settlers who were established along that immediate frontier, the knife and the tomahawk had as yet been sparingly used in the colony of Connecticut. A threatening and dangerous struggle with the Dutch, in the adjoining province of New-Netherlands, had been averted by the foresight and moderation of the rulers of the new plantations; and though a warlike and powerful native chief kept the neighboring colonies of Massachusetts and Rhode-Island in a state of constant watchfulness, from the cause just mentioned the apprehension of danger was greatly weakened in the breasts of those so remote as the individuals who composed the family of our emigrant

In this quiet manner did years glide by, the surrounding wilderness slowly retreating from the habitations of the Heathcotes, until they found themselves in the possession of as many of the comforts of life as their utter seclusion from the rest of the world could give them reason to expect.

With this preliminary explanation, we shall refer the reader to the succeeding narrative for a more minute, and we hope for a more interesting account of the incidents of a legend that may prove too homely for the tastes of those, whose imaginations seek the excitement of scenes more stirring, or of a condition of life less natural.

CHAPTER II.

> Sir, I do know you;
> And dare, upon the warrant of my art,
> Commend a dear thing to you.
>
> King Lear.

At the precise time when the action of our piece commences, a fine and fruitful season was drawing to a close. The harvests of the hay and of the smaller corns had long been over, and the younger Heathcote with his laborers had passed a day in depriving the luxuriant maize of its tops, in order to secure the nutritious blades for fodder, and to admit the sun and air to harden a grain, that is almost considered the staple production of the region he inhabited. The veteran Mark had ridden among the workmen, during their light toil, as well to enjoy a sight which promised abundance to his flocks and herds, as to throw in, on occasion, some wholesome spiritual precept, in which doctrinal subtlety was far more prominent than the rules of practice. The hirelings of his son, for he had long since yielded the management of the estate to Content, were, without an exception, young men born in the country and long use and much training had accustomed them to a blending of religious exercises with most of the employments of life. They listened, therefore, with respect, nor did an impious smile, or an impatient glance, escape the lightest-minded of their number, during his exhortations, though the homilies of the old man were neither very brief, nor particularly original. But devotion to the one great cause of their existence, austere habits, and unrelaxed industry in keeping alive a flame of zeal that had been kindled in the other hemisphere, to burn longest and brightest in this, had interwoven the practice mentioned with most of the opinions and pleasures of these metaphysical, though simple minded people. The toil went on none the less cheerily for the extraordinary accompaniment, and Content himself, by a certain glimmering of superstition, which appears to be the concomitant of excessive religious zeal, was fain to think that the sun shone more brightly on their labors, and that the earth gave forth more of its fruits, while these holy sentiments were flowing from the lips of a father whom he piously loved and deeply reverenced.

But when the sun, usually at that season, in the climate of Connecticut, a bright unshrouded orb, fell towards the tree-tops which bounded the western horizon, the old man began to grow weary with his own well-doing. He therefore finished his discourse with a wholesome admonition to the youths to complete their tasks before they quitted the field; and, turning the head of his horse, he rode slowly, and with a musing air, towards the dwellings. It is probble that for some time the thoughts of Mark were occupied with the intellectual matter he had just been handling with so much power; but when his little nag stopped of itself on a small eminence, which the crooked cow-path he was following crossed, his mind yielded to the impression of more worldly and more sensible objects. As the scene, that drew his contemplations from so many abstract theories to the realities of life, was peculiar to the country, and is more or less connected with the subject of our tale, we shall endeavor briefly to describe it.

A small tributary of the Connecticut divided the view into two nearly equal parts. The fertile flats that extended on each of its banks for more than a mile, had been early stripped of their burthen of forest, and they now lay in placid meadows, or in fields from which the grain of the season had lately disappeared, and over which the plow had already left the marks of recent tillage. The whole of the plain, which ascended gently from the rivulet towards the forest, was subdivided in inclosures, by numberless fences, constructed in the rude but substantial manner of the country. Rails, in which lightness and economy of wood had been but little consulted, lying in zigzag lines, like the approaches which the besieger makes in his cautious advance to the hostile fortress, were piled on each other, until barriers seven or eight feet in height, were interposed to the inroads of vicious cattle. In one spot, a large square vacancy had been cut into the forest, and, though numberless stumps of trees darkened its surface, as indeed they did many of the fields on the flats themselves, bright, green grain was sprouting forth, luxuriantly, from the rich and virgin soil. High against the side of an adjacent hill, that might aspire to be called a low rocky mountain, a similar invasion had been made on the dominion of the trees; but caprice or convenience had induced an abandonment of the clearing, after it had ill requited the toil of felling the timber by a single crop. In this spot, straggling, girdled, and consequently dead trees, piles of logs, and black and charred stubs, were seen deforming the beauty of a field, that would, otherwise, have been striking from its deep setting in the woods. Much of the surface of this opening, too, was now concealed by bushes of what is termed the second growth; though, here and there, places appeared, in which the luxuriant white clover, natural to the country, had followed the close grazing of the flocks. The eyes of Mark were bent, inquiringly, on this clearing, which, by an air line, might have been half a mile from the place where his horse had stopped, for the sounds of a dozen differently toned cow-bells were brought, on the still air of the evening, to his ears; from among its bushes.

The evidences of civilization were the least equivocal, however, on and around a natural elevation in the land, which arose so suddenly on the very bank of the stream, as to give to it the appearance of a work of art. Whether these mounds once existed everywhere on the face of the earth, and have disappeared before long tillage and labor, we shall not presume to conjecture; but we have reason to think that they occur much more frequently in certain parts of our own country, than in any other familiarly known to ordinary travellers; unless perhaps it may be in some of the valleys of Switzerland. The practised veteran had chosen the summit of this flattened cone, for the establishment of that species of military defence, which the situation of the country, and the character of the enemy he had to guard against, rendered advisable, as well as customary.

The dwelling was of wood, and constructed of the ordinary frame-work, with its thin covering of boards. It was long, low, and irregular; bearing marks of having been reared at different periods, as the wants of an increasing family had required additional accommodation. It stood near the verge of the natural declivity, and on that side of the hill where its base was washed by the rivulet, a rude piazza stretching along the whole of its front and overhanging the stream. Several large, irregular, and clumsy chimneys, rose out of different parts of the roofs, another proof that comfort, rather than taste, had been consulted in the disposition of the buildings. There were also two or three detached offices on the summit of the hill, placed near the dwellings, and at points most convenient for their several uses. A stranger might have remarked that they were so disposed as to form, far as they went, the different sides of a hollow square. Notwithstanding the great length of the principal building, and the disposition of the more minute and detached parts, this desirable formation would not, however, have been obtained, were it not that two rows of rude constructions in logs, from which the bark had not even been stripped, served to eke out the parts that were deficient. These primeval edifices were used to contain various domestic articles, no less than provisions; and they also furnished numerous lodging-rooms for the laborers and the inferior dependants of the farm. By the aid of a few strong and high gates of hewn timber, those parts of the buildings which had not been made to unite in the original construction, were sufficiently connected to oppose so many barriers against admission into the inner court.

But the building which was most conspicuous by its position, no less than by the singularity of its construction, stood on a low, artificial mound, in the centre of the quadrangle. It was high, hexagonal in shape, and crowned with a roof that came to a point, and from whose peak rose a towering flag-staff. The foundation was of stone; but, at the height of a man above the earth, the sides were made of massive, squared logs, firmly united by an ingenious combination of their ends, as well as by perpendicular supporters pinned closely into their sides. In this citadel, or block-house, as from its materials it was technically called, there were two different tiers of long, narrow loop-holes, but no regular windows. The rays of the setting sun, however, glittered on one or two small openings in the roof, in which glass had been set, furnishing evidence that the summit of the building was sometimes used for other purposes than those of defence.

About half-way up the sides of the eminence, on which the dwelling stood, was an unbroken line of high palisadoes, made of the bodies of young trees, firmly knit together by braces and horizontal pieces of timber, and evidently kept in a state of jealous and complete repair. The air of the whole of this frontier fortress was neat and comfortable, and, considering that the use of artillery was unknown to those forests, not unmilitary.

At no great distance from the base of the hill, stood the barns and the stables. They were surrounded by a vast range of rude but warm sheds, beneath which sheep and horned cattle were usually sheltered from the storms of the rigorous winters of the climate. The surfaces of the meadows, immediately around the out-buildings, were of a smoother and richer sward, than those in the distance, and the fences were on a far more artificial, and perhaps durable, though scarcely on a more serviceable plan. A large orchard of some ten or fifteen years' growth, too, added greatly to the air of improvement, which put this smiling valley in such strong and pleasing contrast to the endless and nearly-untenanted woods by which it was environed.

Of the interminable forest, it is not necessary to speak. With the solitary exception on the mountain-side, and of here and there a wind-row, along which the trees had been uprooted, by the furious blasts that sometimes sweep off acres of our trees in a minute, the eye could find no other object to study in the vast setting of this quiet rural picture, but the seemingly endless maze of wilderness. The broken surface of the land, however, limited the view to an horizon of no great extent, though the art of man could scarcely devise colors so vivid, or so gay, as those which were afforded by the brilliant hues of the foliage. The keen, biting frosts, known at the close of a New-England autumn, had already touched the broad and fringed leaves of the maples, and the sudden and secret process had been wrought upon all the other varieties of the forest, producing that magical effect, which can be nowhere seen, except in regions in which nature is so bountiful and luxuriant in summer, and so sudden and so stern in the change of the seasons.

Over this picture of prosperity and peace, the eye of old Mark Heathcote wandered with a keen degree of worldly prudence. The melancholy sounds of the various toned bells, ringing hollow and plaintively among the arches of the woods, gave him reason to believe that the herds of the family were returning, voluntarily, from their unlimited forest pasturage. His grandson, a fine spirited boy of some fourteen years, was approaching through the fields The youngster drove before him a small flock, which domestic necessity compelled the family to keep at great occasional loss, and at a heavy expense of time and trouble; both of which could alone protect them from the ravages of the beasts of prey. A species of half-witted serving-lad, whom charity had induced the old man to harbor among his dependants was seen issuing from the woods, nearly in a line with the neglected clearing on the mountain-side. The latter advanced, shouting and urging before him a drove of colts, as shaggy, as wayward, and nearly as untamed as himself.

"How now, weak one," said the Puritan, with a severe eye, as the two lads approached him, with their several charges, from different directions, and nearly at the same instant; "how now, sirrah! dost worry the cattle in this gait, when the eyes of the prudent are turned from thee? Do as thou wouldst be done by, is a just and healthful admonition, that the learned and the simple, the weak and the strong of mind, should alike recall to their thoughts and their practice. I do not know that an over-driven colt will be at all more apt to make a gentle and useful beast in its prime, than one treated with kindness and care."

"I believe the evil one has got into all the kine, no less than into the foals," sullenly returned the lad; "I've called to them in anger, and I've spoken to them as if they had been my natural kin, and yet neither fair word nor foul tongue will bring them to hearken to advice. There is something frightful in the woods this very sun-down, master; or colts that I have driven the summer through, would not be apt to give this unfair treatment to one they ought to know to be their friend."

"Thy sheep are counted, Mark?" resumed the grandfather, turning towards his descendant with a less austere, but always an authoritative brow; 'thy mother hath need of every fleece, to provide covering for thee and others like thee; thou knowest, child, that the creatures are few, and our winters weary and cold."

"My mother's loom shall never be idle from carelessness of mine," returned the confident boy; "but counting and wishing cannot make seven-and-thirty fleeces, where there are only six-and-thirty backs to carry them. I have been an hour among the briars and bushes of the hill logging, looking for the lost wether, and yet neither lock, hoof, hide, nor horn, is there to say what hath befallen the animal."

"Thou hast lost a sheep!--this carelessness will cause thy mother to grieve."

"Grandfather, I have been no idler. Since the last hunt, the flock hath been allowed to browse the woods; for no man, in all that week, saw wolf, panther, or bear, though the country was up, from the great river to the outer settlements of the colony. The biggest four-footed animal, that lost its hide in the muster, was a thin-ribbed deer, and the stoutest battle given, was between wild Whittal Ring, here, and a wood-chuck that kept him at arm's-length, for the better part of an afternoon."

"Thy tale may be true, but it neither finds that which is lost, nor completeth the number of thy mother's flock. Hast thou ridden carefully throughout the clearing? It is not long, since I saw the animals grazing in that quarter. What hast thou twisting in thy fingers, in that wasteful and unthankful manner, Whittal?"

"What would make a winter blanket, if there was enough of it! wool! and wool, too, that came from the thigh of old Straight-Horns; else have I forgotten a leg, that gives the longest and coarsest hair at the shearing."

"That truly seemeth a lock from the animal that is wanting," exclaimed the other boy. "There is no other creature in the flock, with fleece so coarse and shaggy. Where found you the handful, Whittal Ring?"

"Growing on the branch of a thorn. Queer fruit this, masters, to be seen where young plums ought to ripen!"

"Go, go," interrupted the old man; "thou idlest, and mispendest the time in vain talk. Go, fold thy flock, Mark; and do thou, weak-one, house thy charge with less uproar than is wont. We should remember that the voice is given to man, firstly, that he may improve the blessing in thanksgivings and pe titions; secondly, to communicate such gifts as may be imparted to himself, and which it is his bounden duty to attempt to impart to others; and then, thirdly, to declare his natural wants and inclinations."

With this admonition, which probably proceeded from a secret consciousness in the Puritan that he had permitted a momentary cloud of selfishness to obscure the brightness of his faith, the party separated. The grandson and the hireling took their several ways to the folds, while old Mark himself slowly continued his course towards the dwellings. It was near enough to the hours of darkness, to render the preparations we have mentioned prudent; still, no urgency called for particular haste, in the return of the veteran to the shelter and protection of his own comfortable and secure abode. He therefore loitered along the path, occasionally stopping to look into the prospects of the young crops, that were beginning to spring up in readiness for the coming year, and at times bending his gaze around the whole of his limited horizon, like one who had the habit of exceeding and unremitted care.

One of these numerous pauses promised to be much longer than usual. Instead of keeping his understanding eye on the grain, the look of the old man appeared fastened, as by a charm, on some distant and obscure object. Doubt and uncertainty, for many minutes, seemed to mingle in his gaze. But all hesitation had apparently disappeared, as his lips severed, and he spoke, perhaps unconsciously to himself, aloud.

"It is no deception," were the low words, "but a living and an accountable creature of the Lord's. Many a day has passed since such a sight hath been witnessed in this vale; but my eye greatly deceives me, or yonder cometh one ready to ask for hospitality, and, peradventure, for Christian and brotherly communion."

The sight of the aged emigrant had not deceived him. One, who appeared a wayworn and weary traveller, had indeed ridden out of the forest, at a point where a path, that was easier to be traced by the blazed trees that lay along its route, than by any marks on the earth itself, issued into the cleared land. The progress of the stranger had, at first, been so wary and slow, as to bear the manner of exceeding and mysterious caution. The blind road, along which he must have ridden not only far but hard, or night had certainly overtaken him in the woods, led to one of the distant settlements that lay near to the fertile banks of the Connecticut. Few ever followed its windings, but they who had especial affairs, or extraordinary communion, in the way of religious friendships, with the proprietors of the Wish-Ton-Wish, as, in commemoration of the first bird that had been seen by the emigrants, the valley of the Heathcotes was called.

Once fairly in view, any doubt or apprehension, that the stranger might at first have entertained, disappeared. He rode boldly and steadily forward, until he drew a rein that his impoverished and weary beast gladly obeyed, within a few feet of the proprietor of the valley, whose gaze had never ceased to watch his movements, from the instant when the other first came within view. Before speaking, the stranger, a man whose head was getting gray, apparently as much with hardship as with time, and one whose great weight would have proved a grievous burthen, in a long ride, to even a better-conditioned beast than the ill-favored provincial hack he had ridden, dismounted, and threw the bridle loose upon the drooping neck of the animal. The latter, without a moment's delay, and with a greediness that denoted long abstinence, profited by its liberty, to crop the herbage where it stood.

"I cannot be mistaken, when I suppose that I

have at length reached the valley of the Wish-Ton Wish," the visiter said, touching a soiled and slouched beaver that more than half concealed his features. The question was put in an English that bespoke a descent from those who dwell in the midland counties of the mother country, rather than in that intonation which is still to be traced, equally in the western portions of England and in the eastern states of the Union. Notwithstanding the purity of his accent, there was enough in the form of his speech to denote a severe compliance with the fashion of the religionists of the times. He used that measured and methodical tone, which was, singularly enough, believed to distinguish an entire absence of affectation in language.

"Thou hast reached the dwelling of him thou seekest; one who is a submissive sojourner in the wilderness of the world, and an humble servitor in the outer temple."

"This then is Mark Heathcote!" repeated the stranger in tones of interest, regarding the other with a look of long, and, possibly, of suspicious investigation.

"Such is the name I bear. A fitting confidence in him who knows so well how to change the wilds into the haunts of men, and much suffering, have made me the master of what thou seest. Whether thou comest to tarry a night, a week, a month, or even for a still longer season, as a brother in care, and I doubt not one who striveth for the right, I bid thee welcome."

The stranger thanked his host, by a slow inclination of the head; but the gaze, which began to partake a little of the look of recognition, was still too earnest and engrossing to admit of verbal reply. On the other hand, though the old man had scanned the broad and rusty beaver, the coarse and well-worn doublet, the heavy boots and, in short, the whole attire of his visiter, in which he saw no vain conformity to idle fashions to condemn, it was evident that personal recollection had not the smallest influence in quickening his hospitality.

"Thou hast arrived happily," continued the Puritan: "had night overtaken thee in the forest, unless much practised in the shifts of our young woodsmen, hunger, frost, and a supperless bed of brush, would have given thee motive to think more of the body than is either profitable or seemly."

The stranger might possibly have known the embarrassment of these several hardships; for the quick and unconscious glance he threw over his soiled dress, should have betrayed some familiarity already, with the privations to which his host alluded. As neither of them, however, seemed disposed to waste further time on matters of such light moment, the traveller put an arm through the bridle of his horse, and, in obedience to an invitation from the owner of the dwelling, they took their way towards the fortified edifice on the natural mound.

The task of furnishing litter and provender to the jaded beast was performed by Whittal Ring under the inspection, and, at times, under the instructions, of its owner and his host, both of whom appeared to take a kind and commendable interest in the comfort of a faithful hack, that had evidently suffered long and much in the service of its master. When this duty was discharged, the old man and his unknown guest entered the house together; the frank and unpretending hospitality of a country like that they were in, rendering suspicion or hesitation qualities that were unknown to the reception of a man of white blood; more especially if he spoke the language of the island, which was then first sending out its swarms, to subdue and possess so large a portion of a continent that nearly divides the earth in moieties.

CHAPTER III.

"This is most strange: your father's in some passion
That works him strongly."

TEMPEST.

A FEW hours made a great change in the occupations of the different members of our simple and secluded family The kine had yielded their nightly tribute; the oxen had been released from the yoke, and were now secure beneath their sheds; the sheep were in their folds, safe from the assaults of the prowling wolf; and care had been taken to see that every thing possessing life was gathered within the particular defences that were provided for its security and comfort. But while all this caution was used in behalf of living things, the utmost indifference prevailed on the subject of that species of movable property, which, elsewhere, would have been guarded with, at least, an equal jealousy. The homely fabrics of the looms of Ruth lay on their bleaching-ground, to drink in the night-dew; and plows, harrows, carts, saddles, and other similar articles, were left in situations so exposed, as to prove that the hand of man had occupations so numerous and so urgent, as to render it inconvenient to bestow labor where it was not considered absolutely necessary.

Content himself was the last to quit the fields and the out-buildings. When he reached the postern in the palisadoes, he stopped to call to those abov him, in order to learn if any yet lingered without the wooden barriers. The answer being in the negative, he entered, and drawing-to the small but heavy gate, he secured it with bar, bolt, and lock, carefully and jealously, with his own hand. As this was no more than a nightly and necessary precaution, the affairs of the family received no interruption. The meal of the hour was soon ended; and conversation, with those light toils which are peculiar to the long evenings of the fall and winter in families on the frontier, succeeded as fitting employments to close the business of a laborious and well-spent day.

Notwithstanding the entire simplicity which marked the opinions and usages of the colonists at that period, and the great equality of condition which even to this hour distinguishes the particular community of which we write, choice and inclination drew some natural distinctions in the ordinary intercourse of the inmates of the Heathcote family. A fire so bright and cheerful blazed on an enormous hearth in a sort of upper kitchen, as to render candles or torches unnecessary. Around it were seated six or seven hardy and athletic young men, some drawing coarse tools carefully through the curvatures of ox-bows, others scraping down the helves of axes, or perhaps fashioning sticks of birch into homely but convenient brooms. A demure, side-looking young woman kept her great wheel in motion; while one or two others were passing from room to room, with the notable and stirring industry of handmaidens, busied in the more familiar cares of the household. A door communicated with an inner and superior apartment. Here was a smaller but an equally cheerful fire, a floor which had recently been swept, while that without had been freshly sprinkled with river sand; candles of tallow, on a table of cherry-wood from the neighboring forest; walls that were wainscoted in the black oak of the country, and a few other articles, of a fashion so antique, and of ornaments so ingenious and rich, as to announce that they had been transported from beyond sea. Above the mantel were suspended the armorial bearings of the Heathcotes and the Hardings, elaborately emblazoned in tent-stitch.

The principal personages of the family were seated around the latter hearth, while a straggler from the other room, of more than usual curiosity, had placed himself among them, marking the distinction in ranks, or rather in situation, merely by the extraordinary care which he took that none of the scrapings should litter the spotless oaken floor.

Until this period of the evening, the duties of hospitality and the observances of religion had prevented familiar discourse. But the offices of the housewife were now ended for the night, the handmaidens had all retired to their wheels, and, as the bustle of a busy and more stirring domestic industry ceased, the cold and self-restrained silence which had hitherto only been broken by distant and brief observations of courtesy, or by some wholesome allusion to the lost and probationary condition of man, seemed to invite an intercourse of a more general character.

"You entered my clearing by the southern path," commenced Mark Heathcote, addressing himself to his guest with sufficient courtesy, "and needs must bring tidings from the towns on the river side. Has aught been done by our councillors, at home, in the matter that pertaineth so closely to the well-being of this colony?"

"You would have me say whether he that now sitteth on the throne of England, hath listened to the petitions of his people in this province, and hath granted them protection against the abuses which might so readily flow out of his own ill-advised will or out of the violence and injustice of his successors?"

"We will render unto Cæsar the things that are Cæsar's; and speak reverently of men having authority. I would fain know whether the agent sent by our people hath gained the ears of those who counsel the prince, and obtained that which he sought?"

"He hath done more," returned the stranger, with singular asperity; "he hath even gained the ear of the Lord's Anointed."

"Then is Charles of better mind, and of stronger justice, than report hath spoken. We were told that light manners and unprofitable companions had led him to think more of the vanities of the world, and less of the wants of those over whom he hath been called by Providence to rule, than is meet for one that sitteth on a high place. I rejoice that the arguments of the man we sent have prevailed over more evil promptings, and that peace and freedom of conscience are likely to be the fruits of the undertaking. In what manner hath he seen fit to order the future government of this people?"

"Much as it hath ever stood; by their own ordinances. Winthrop hath returned, and is the bearer of a Royal Charter, which granteth all the rights long claimed and practised. None now dwell under the Crown of Britain with fewer offensive demands on their consciences, or with lighter calls on their political duties, than the men of Connecticut."

"It is fitting that thanks should be rendered therefor, where thanks are most due," said the Puritan, folding his hands on his bosom, and sitting for a moment with closed eyes, like one who communed with an unseen being. "Is it known by what manner of argument the Lord moved the heart of the Prince to hearken to our wants; or was it an open and manifest token of his power?"

"I think it must needs have been the latter," rejoined the visiter, with a manner that grew still more caustic and emphatic. "The bauble, that was the visible agent, could not have weighed greatly with one so proudly seated before the eyes of men."

Until this point in the discourse, Content and

Ruth, with their offspring, and the two or three other individuals who composed the audience, had listened with the demure gravity which characterized the manners of the country. The language, united with the ill-concealed sarcasm conveyed by the countenance, no less than the emphasis, of the speaker, caused them now to raise their eyes, as by a common impulse. The word "bauble" was audibly and curiously repeated. But the look of cold irony had already passed from the features of the stranger, and it had given place to a stern and fixed austerity, that imparted a character of grimness to his hard and sun-burnt visage. Still he betrayed no disposition to shrink from the subject, but, after regarding his auditors with a glance in which pride and suspicion were strongly blended, he resumed the discourse.

"It is known," he added, "that the grandfather of him the good people of these settlements have commissioned to bear their wants over sea, lived in the favor of the man who last sat upon the throne of England; and a rumor goeth forth, that the Stuart, in a moment of princely condescension, once decked the finger of his subject, with a ring wrought in a curious fashion. It was a token of the love which a monarch may bear a man."

"Such gifts are beacons of friendship, but may not be used as gay and sinful ornaments," observed Mark, while the other paused like one who wished none of the bitterness of his allusions to be lost.

"It matters not whether the bauble lay in the coffers of the Winthrops, or has long been glittering before the eyes of the faithful, in the Bay, since it hath finally proved to be a jewel of price," continued the stranger. "It is said, in secret, that this ring hath returned to the finger of a Stuart, and it is openly proclaimed that Connecticut hath a Charter!"

Content and his wife regarded each other in melancholy amazement. Such an evidence of wanton levity and of unworthiness of motive, in one who was intrusted with the gift of earthly government, pained their simple and upright minds; while old Mark, of still more decided and exaggerated ideas of spiritual perfection, distinctly groaned aloud The stranger took a sensible pleasure in this testimony of their abhorrence of so gross and so unworthy a venality, though he saw no occasion to heighten its effect by further speech. When his host stood erect, and, in a voice that was accustomed to obedience, he called on his family to join, in behalf of the reckless ruler of the land of their fathers, in a petition to him who alone could soften the hearts of Princes, he also arose from his seat. But even in this act of devotion, the stranger bore the air of one who wished to do pleasure to his entertainers, rather than to obtain that which was asked.

The prayer, though short, was pointed, fervent, and sufficiently personal. The wheels in the outer room ceased their hum, and a general movement denoted that all there had arisen to join in the office; while one or two of their number, impelled by deeper piety or stronger interest, drew near to the open door between the rooms, in order to listen. With this singular but characteristic interruption, that particular branch of the discourse, which had given rise to it, altogether ceased.

"And have we reason to dread a rising of the savages on the borders?" asked Content, when he found that the moved spirit of his father was not yet sufficiently calmed, to return to the examination of temporal things; "one who brought wares from the towns below, a few months since, recited reasons to fear a movement among the red men."

The subject had not sufficient interest to open the ears of the stranger. He was deaf, or he chose to affect deafness, to the interrogatory. Laying his two large and weather-worn, though still muscular hands, on a visage that was much darkened by exposure, he appeared to shut out the objects of the world, while he communed deeply, and, as would seem by a slight tremor, that shook even his powerful frame, terribly, with his own thoughts.

"We have many to whom our hearts strongly cling, to heighten the smallest symptom of alarm from that quarter," added the tender and anxious mother, her eye glancing at the uplifted countenances of two little girls, who, busied with their light needle-work, sate on stools at her feet. "But I rejoice to see, that one who hath journeyed from parts where the minds of the savages must be better understood, hath not feared to do it unarmed."

The traveller slowly uncovered his features, and the glance that his eye shot over the face of the last speaker, was not without a gentle and interested expression. Instantly recovering his composure, he arose, and, turning to the double leathern sack, which had been borne on the crupper of his nag, and which now lay at no great distance from his seat, he drew a pair of horseman's pistols from two well-contrived pockets in its sides, and laid them deliberately on the table.

"Though little disposed to seek an encounter with any bearing the image of man," he said, "I have not neglected the usual precautions of those who enter the wilderness. Here are weapons that, in steady hands, might easily take life, or, at need preserve it."

The young Mark drew near with boyish curiosity, and while one finger ventured to touch a lock, as he stole a conscious glance of wrong-doing towards his mother, he said, with as much of contempt in his air, as the schooling of his manners would allow—

"An Indian arrow would make a surer aim, than a bore as short as this! When the trainer from the

Hartford town, struck the wild-cat on the hill clearing, he sent the bullet from a five-foot barrel; besides, this short-sighted gun would be a dull weapon in a hug against the keen-edged knife, that the wicked Wampanoag is known to carry."—

"Boy, thy years are few, and thy boldness of speech marvellous," sternly interrupted his parent in the second degree.

The stranger manifested no displeasure at the confident language of the lad. Encouraging him with a look, which plainly proclaimed that martial qualities in no degree lessened the stripling in his favor, he observed that—

"The youth who is not afraid to think of the fight, or to reason on its chances, will lead to a manhood of spirit and independence. A hundred thousand striplings like this, might have spared Winthrop his jewel, and the Stuart the shame of yielding to so vain and so trivial a bribe. But thou mayst also see, child, that had we come to the death-hug, the wicked Wampanoag might have found a blade as keen as his own."

The stranger, while speaking, loosened a few strings of his doublet, and thrust a hand into his bosom. The action enabled more than one eye to catch a momentary glimpse of a weapon of the same description, but of a size much smaller than those he had already so freely exhibited. As he immediately withdrew the member, and again closed the garment with studied care, no one presumed to advert to the circumstance, but all turned their attention to the long sharp hunting-knife that he deposited by the side of the pistols, as he concluded. Mark ventured to open its blade, but he turned away with sudden consciousness, when he found that a few fibres of coarse, shaggy wool, that were drawn from the loosened joint, adhered to his fingers.

"Straight-Horns has been against a bush sharper than the thorn!" exclaimed Whittal Ring, who had been at hand, and who watched with childish admiration the smallest proceedings of the different individuals. "A steel for the back of the blade, a few dried leaves and broken sticks, with such a carver, would soon make roast and broiled of the old bell-wether himself. I know that the hair of all my colts is sorrel, and I counted five at sun-down, which is just as many as went loping through the underbrush when I loosened them from the hopples in the morning; but six-and-thirty backs can never carry seven-and-thirty growing fleeces of unsheared wool. Master knows that, for he is a scholar and can count a hundred!"

The allusion to the fate of the lost sheep was so plain, as to admit of no misinterpretation of the meaning of the witless speaker. Animals of that class were of the last importance to the comfort of the settlers, and there was not probably one within hearing of Whittal Ring, that was at all ignorant of the import of his words. Indeed, the loud chuckle and the open and deriding manner with which the lad himself held above his head the hairy fibres that he had snatched from young Mark, allowed of no concealment, had it been desirable.

"This feeble-gifted youth would hint, that thy knife hath proved its edge on a wether that is missing from our flock, since the animals went on their mountain range, in the morning," said the host, calmly; though even he bent his eye to the floor, as he waited for an answer to a remark, direct as the one his sense of justice, and his indomitable love of right, had prompted.

The stranger demanded, in a voice that lost none of its depth or firmness, "Is hunger a crime, that hey who dwell so far from the haunts of selfishness, isit it with their anger?"

"The foot of Christian man never approached the gates of Wish-Ton-Wish to be turned away in uncharitableness, but that which is freely given should not be taken in licentiousness. From off the hill where my flock is wont to graze, it is easy, through many an opening of the forest, to see these roofs; and it would have been better that the body should languish, than that a grievous sin should be placed on that immortal spirit which is already too deeply laden, unless thou art far more happy than others of the fallen race of Adam."

"Mark Heathcote," said the accused, and ever with an unwavering tone, "look further at those weapons, which, if a guilty man, I have weakly placed within thy power. Thou wilt find more there to wonder at, than a few straggling hairs, that the spinner would cast from her as too coarse for service."

"It is long since I found pleasure in handling the weapons of strife; may it be longer to the time when they shall be needed in this abode of peace. These are instruments of death, resembling those used in my youth, by cavaliers that rode in the levies of the first Charles, and of his pusillanimous father. There were worldly pride and great vanity, with much and damning ungodliness, in the wars that I have seen, my children; and yet the carnal man found pleasure in the stirrings of those graceless days! Come hither, younker; thou hast often sought to know the manner in which the horsemen are wont to lead into the combat, when the broad-mouthed artillery and pattering leaden hail have cleared a passage for th struggle of horse to horse, and man to man. Much of the justification of these combats must depend on the inward spirit, and on the temper of him that striketh at the life of fellow-sinner; but righteous Joshua, it is known, contended with the heathen throughout a supernatural dav: and therefore always humbly confiding that our cause is just, I will open to thy young mind the uses of a weapon that hath never before been seen in these forests."

"I have hefted many a heavier piece than this," said young Mark, frowning equally with the exertion and with the instigations of his aspiring spirit, as he held out the ponderous weapon in a single hand; "we have guns that might tame a wolf with greater certainty than any barrel of a bore less than my own height. Tell, me grand'ther; at what distance do the mounted warriors, you so often name, take their sight?"

But the power of speech appeared suddenly to have deserted the aged veteran. He had interrupted his own discourse, and now, instead of answering the interrogatory of the boy, his eye wandered slowly and with a look of painful doubt from the weapon, that he still held before him, to the countenance of the stranger. The latter continued erect, like one courting a strict and meaning examination of his person. This dumb-show could not fail to attract the observation of Content. Rising from his seat, with that quiet but authoritative manner which is still seen in the domestic government of the people of the region where he dwelt, he beckoned to all present to quit the apartment. Ruth and her daughters, the hirelings, the ill-gifted Whittal, and even the reluctant Mark, preceded him to the door, which he closed with respectful care; and then the whole of the wondering party mingled with those of the outer room, leaving the one they had quitted to the sole possession of the aged chief of the settlement, and to his still unknown and mysterious guest.

Many anxious, and to those who were excluded seemingly interminable minutes passed, and, the secret interview appeared to draw no nearer its close That deep reverence, which the years, paternity, and character of the grandfather had inspired, prevented all from approaching the quarter of the apartment nearest to the room they had left; but a silence, still as the grave, did all that silence could do, to enlighten their minds in a matter of so much general interest. The deep, smothered sentences of the speakers were often heard, each dwelling with steadiness and propriety on his particular theme, but no sound that conveyed meaning to the minds of those without passed the envious walls. At length, the voice of old Mark became more than usually audible; and then Content arose, with a gesture to those around him to imitate his example. The young men threw aside the subjects of their light employments, the maidens left the wheels which had not been turned for many minutes, and the whole party disposed themselves in the decent and simple attitude of prayer. For the third time that evening was the voice of the Puritan heard, pouring out his spirit in a communion with that being on whom it was his practice to repose all his worldly cares. But, though long accustomed to all the peculiar forms of utterance by which their father ordinarily expressed his pious emotions, neither Content nor his attentive partner was enabled to decide on the nature of the feeling that was now uppermost. At times, it appeared to be the language of thanksgiving, and at others it assumed more of the imploring sounds of deprecation and petition; in short, it was so varied, and, though tranquil, so equivocal, if such a term may be applied to so serious a subject, as completely to baffle every conjecture.

Long and weary minutes passed after the voice had entirely ceased, and yet no summons was given to the expecting family, nor did any sound proceed from the inner room, which the respectful son was emboldened to construe into an evidence that he might presume to enter At length, apprehension began to mingle with conjectures, and then the husband and wife communed apart, in whispers. The misgivings and doubt of the former soon manifested themselves in still more apparent forms. He arose, and was seen pacing the wide apartment, gradually approaching nearer to the partition which separated the two rooms, evidently prepared to retire beyond the limits of hearing, the moment he should detect any proofs that his uneasiness was without a sufficient cause. Still no sound proceeded from the inner room. The breathless silence which had so shortly before reigned where he was, appeared to be suddenly transferred to the spot in which he was vainly endeavoring to detect the smallest proof of human existence. Again he returned to Ruth, and again they consulted, in low voices, as to the step that filial duty seemed to require at their hands.

"We were not bidden to withdraw," said his gentle companion; "why not rejoin our parent, now that time has been given to understand the subject which so evidently disturbed his mind?"

Content, at length, yielded to this opinion. With that cautious discretion which distinguishes his people, he motioned to the family to follow, in order that no unnecessary exclusion should give rise to conjectures, or excite suspicions, for which, after all. the circumstances might prove no justification. Notwithstanding the subdued manners of the age and country, curiosity, and perhaps a better feeling, had become so intense, as to cause all present to obey this silent mandate, by moving as swiftly towards the open door as a never-yielding decency of demeanor would permit.

Old Mark Heathcote occupied the chair in which he had been left, with that calm and unbending gravity of eye and features which were then thought indispensable to a fitting sobriety of spirit. But the stranger had disappeared. There were two or three outlets by which the room, and even the house, might be quitted, without the knowledge of those who had so long waited for admission; and the first impression led the family to expect the re-appearance of the absent man through one of these exterior passages. Content, however, read in the expression of his father's eye, that the moment of confidence, if it were ever to arrive, had not yet come; and, so admirable and perfect was the domestic discipline of this family, that the questions which the son did not see fit to propound, no one of inferior condition, or lesser age, might presume to agitate. With the person of the stranger, every evidence of his recent visit had also vanished.

Mark missed the weapon that had excited his admiration; Whittal looked in vain for the hunting-knife, which had betrayed the fate of the wether; Mrs. Heathcote saw, by a hasty glance of the eye, that the leathern sacks, which she had borne in mind ought to be transferred to the sleeping apartment of their guest, were gone; and a mild and playful image of herself, who bore her name no less than most of those features which had rendered her own youth more than usually attractive, sought, without success, a massive silver spur, of curious and antique workmanship, which she had been permitted to handle until the moment when the family had been commanded to withdraw.

The night had now worn later than the hour at which it was usual for people of habits so simple to be out of their beds. The grandfather lighted a taper, and, after bestowing the usual blessing on those around him, with an air as calm as if nothing had occurred, he prepared to retire into his own room. And yet, matter of interest seemed to linger on his mind. Even on the threshold of the door, he turned, and, for an instant, all expected some explanation of a circumstance which began to wear no little of the aspect of an exciting and painful mystery. But their hopes were raised only to be disappointed.

"My thoughts have not kept the passage of the time," he said. "In what hour of the night are we, my son?"

He was told that it was already past the usual moment of sleep.

"No matter; that which Providence hath bestowed for our comfort and support, should not be lightly and unthankfully disregarded. Take thou the beast I am wont to ride, thyself, Content, and follow the path which leadeth to the mountain clearing; bring away that which shall meet thine eye, near the first turning of the route toward the river towns. We have got into the last quarter of the year, and in order that our industry may not flag, and that all may be stirring with the sun, let the remainder of the household seek their rest."

Content saw, by the manner of his father, that no departure from the strict letter of these instructions was admissible. He closed the door after his retiring form, and then, by a quiet gesture of authority, indicated to his dependants that they were expected to withdraw. The maidens of Ruth led the children to their chambers, and in a few more minutes, none remained in the outer apartment, already so often named, but the obedient son, with his anxious and affectionate consort.

"I will be thy companion, husband," Ruth half-whisperingly commenced, so soon as the little domestic preparations for leaving the fires and securing the doors were ended. "I like not that thou shouldst go into the forest alone, at so late an hour of the night."

"One will be with me, there, who never deserteth

those who rely on his protection. Besides, my Ruth, what is there to apprehend in a wilderness like this? The beasts have been lately hunted from the hills, and, excepting those who dwell under our own roof, there is not one within a long day's ride."

"We know not! Where is the stranger that came within our doors as the sun was setting?"

"As thou sayest, we know not. My father is not minded to open his lips on the subject of this traveller, and surely we are not now to learn the lessons of obedience and self-denial."

"It would, notwithstanding, be a great easing to the spirit to hear at least the name of him who hath eaten of our bread, and joined in our family worship, though he were immediately to pass away for ever from before the sight."

"That may he have done, already!" returned the less curious and more self-restrained husband. "My father will not that we inquire."

"And yet there can be little sin in knowing the condition of one whose fortunes and movements can excite neither our envy nor our strife. I would that we had tarried for a closer mingling in the prayers; it was not seemly to desert a guest who, it would appear, had need of an especial up-offering in his behalf."

"Our spirits joined in the asking, though our ears were shut to the matter of his wants. But it will be needful that I should be afoot with the young men, in the morning, and a mile of measurement would not reach to the turning, in the path to the river towns Go with me to the postern, and look to the fastenings; I will not keep thee long on thy watch."

Content and his wife now quitted the dwelling, by the only door that was left unbarred. Lighted by a moon that was full, though clouded they passed a gateway between two of the outer buildings, and descended to the palisadoes. The bars and bolts of the little postern were removed, and in a few minutes, the former, mounted on the back of his father's own horse, was galloping briskly along the path which led into the part of the forest he was directed to seek.

While the husband was thus proceeding, in obedience to orders that he never hesitated to obey his faithful wife withdrew within the shelter of the wooden defences. More in compliance with a precaution that was become habitual, than from any present causes of suspicion, she drew a single bolt and remained at the postern, anxiously awaiting the result of a movement that was as unaccountable as it was extraordinary.

CHAPTER IV.

> "I' the name of something holy, sir, why stand you
> In this strange stare?"
>
> TEMPEST.

As a girl, Ruth Harding had been one of the mildest and gentlest of the human race. Though new impulses had been given to her naturally kind affections by the attachments of a wife and mother, her disposition suffered no change by marriage. Obedient, disinterested, and devoted to those she loved, as her parents had known her, so, by the experience of many years, had she proved to Content. In the midst of the utmost equanimity of temper and of deportment, her watchful solicitude in behalf of the few who formed the limited circle of her existence, never slumbered. It dwelt unpretendingly but active in her gentle bosom, like a great and moving principle of life. Though circumstances had placed her on a remote and exposed frontier, where time had not been given for the several customary divisions of employments, she was unchanged in habits, in feelings, and in character. The affluence of her husband had elevated her above the necessity of burthensome toil; and, while she had encountered the dangers of the wilderness, and neglected none of the duties of her active station, she had escaped most of those injurious consequences which are a little apt to impair the peculiar loveliness of woman. Notwithstanding the exposure of a border life, she remained feminine, attractive, and singularly youthful.

The reader will readily imagine the state of mind, with which such a being watched the distant form of a husband, engaged in a duty like that we have described. Notwithstanding the influence of long habit, the forest was rarely approached, after night-fall, by the boldest woodsman, without some secret consciousness that he encountered a positive danger. It was the hour when its roaming and hungry tenants were known to be most in motion; and the rustling of a leaf, or the snapping of a dried twig beneath the light tread of the smallest animal, was apt to conjure images of the voracious and fire-eyed panther, or perhaps of a lurking biped, which, though more artful, was known to be scarcely less savage. It is true, that hundreds experienced the uneasiness of such sensations, who were never fated to undergo the realities of the fearful pictures. Still, facts were not wanting to supply sufficient motive for a grave and reasonable apprehension.

Histories of combats with beasts of prey, and of massacres by roving and lawless Indians, were the moving legends of the border. Thrones might be subverted, and kingdoms lost and won, in distant Europe, and less should be said of the events, by those who dwelt in these woods, than of one scene of peculiar and striking forest incident, that called for the exercise of the stout courage and the keen intelligence of a settler. Such a tale passed from mouth to mouth, with the eagerness of powerful personal interest, and many were already transmitted from parent to child, in the form of tradition, until, as in more artificial communities, graver improbabilities creep into the doubtful pages of history, exaggeration became too closely blended with truth, ever again to be separated.

Under the influence of these feelings, and perhaps prompted by his never-failing discretion, Content had thrown a well-tried piece over his shoulder; and when he rose the ascent on which his father had met the stranger, Ruth caught a glimpse of his form, bending on the neck of his horse, and gliding through the misty light of the hour, resembling one of those fancied images of wayward and hard-riding sprites, of which the tales of the eastern continent are so fond of speaking.

Then followed anxious moments, during which neither sight nor hearing could in the least aid the conjectures of the attentive wife. She listened without breathing, and once or twice she thought the blows of hoofs, falling on the earth harder and quicker than common, might be distinguished; but it was only as Content mounted the sudden ascent of the hill-side, that he was again seen, for a brief instant, while dashing swiftly into the cover of the woods.

Though Ruth had been familiar with the cares of the frontier, perhaps she had never known a moment more intensely painful than that, when the form of her husband became blended with the dark trunks of the trees. The time was to her impatience longer than usual, and under the excitement of a feverish inquietude, that had no definite ob ject, she removed the single bolt that held the postern closed, and passed entirely without the stockade. To her oppressed senses, the palisadoes appeared to place limits to her vision. Still, weary minute passed after minute, without bringing relief. During these anxious moments, she became more than usually conscious of the insulated situation in which he and all who were dearest to her heart were placed. The feelings of a wife prevailed. Quitting the side of the acclivity, she began to walk slowly along the path her husband had taken, until apprehension insensibly urged her into a quicker movement. She had paused only when she stood nearly in the centre of the clearing, on the eminence where her father had halted that evening to contemplate the growing improvement of his estate.

Here her steps were suddenly arrested, for she thought a form was issuing from the forest, at that interesting spot which her eyes had never ceased to watch. It proved to be no more than the passing shadow of a cloud denser than common, which threw the body of its darkness on the trees, and a portion of its outline on the ground near the margin of the wood. Just at this instant, the recollection that she had incautiously left the postern open flashed upon her mind, and, with feelings divided between husband and children, she commenced her return, in order to repair a neglect, to which habit, no less than prudence, imparted a high degree of culpability. The eyes of the mother, for the feelings of that sacred character were now powerfully uppermost, were fastened on the ground, as she eagerly picked her way along the uneven surface; and, so engrossed was her mind by the omission of duty with which she was severely reproaching herself, that they drank in objects without conveying distinct or intelligible images to her brain.

Notwithstanding the one engrossing thought of

the moment, something met her eye that caused even the vacant organ to recoil, and every fibre in her frame to tremble with terror. There was a moment in which delirium nearly heightened terror to madness. Reflection came only when Ruth had reached the distance of many feet from the spot where this startling object had half-unconsciously crossed her vision. Then for a single and a fearful instant she paused, like one who debated on the course she ought to follow. Maternal love prevailed, and the deer of her own woods scarcely bounds with greater agility, than the mother of the sleeping and defenceless family now fled towards the dwellings. Panting and breathless she gained the postern, which was closed, with hands that performed their office more by instinct than in obedience to thought, and doubly and trebly barred.

For the first time in some minutes, Ruth now breathed distinctly and without pain. She strove to rally her thoughts, in order to deliberate on the course that prudence and her duty to Content, who was still exposed to the danger she had herself escaped, prescribed. Her first impulse was to give the established signal that was to recall the laborers from the field, or to awake the sleepers, in the event of an alarm; but better reflection told her that such a step might prove fatal to him who balanced in her affections against the rest of the world The struggle in her mind only ended, as she clearly and unequivocally caught a view of her husband, issuing from the forest, at the very point where he had entered. The return path unfortunately led directly past the spot where such sudden terror had seized her mind. She would have given worlds to have known how to apprize him of a danger with which her own imagination was full, without communicating the warning to other and terrible ears. The night was still, and though the distance was considerable, it was not so great as to render the chances of success desperate. Scarcely knowing what she did, and yet preserving, by a sort of instinctive prudence, the caution which constant exposure weaves into all our habits, the trembling woman made the effort.

"Husband! husband!" she cried, commencing plaintively, but her voice rising with the energy of excitement. "Husband, ride swiftly; our little Ruth lyeth in the agony. For her life and thine, ride at thy horse's speed. Seek not the stables, but come with all haste to the postern; it shall be open to thee."

This was certainly a fearful summons for a father's ear, and there is little doubt that, had the feeble powers of Ruth succeeded in conveying the words as far as she had wished, they would have produced the desired effect. But in vain did she call; her weak tones, though raised on the notes of the keenest apprehension, could not force their way across so wide a space. And yet, had she reason to think they were not entirely lost, for once her husband paused and seemed to listen, and once he quickened the pace of his horse; though neither of these proofs of intelligence was followed by any further signs of his having understood the alarm.

Content was now upon the hillock itself. If Ruth breathed at all during its passage, it was more imperceptibly than the gentlest respiration of the sleeping infant. But when she saw him trotting with unconscious security along the path on the side next the dwellings, her impatience broke through all restraint, and throwing open the postern, she renewed her cries, in a voice that was no longer useless. The clattering of the unshodden hoof was again rapid, and in another minute her husband galloped unharmed to her side.

"Enter!" said the nearly dizzy wife, seizing the

bridle and leading the horse within the palisadoes. "Enter, husband, for the love of all that is thine; enter, and be thankful."

"What meaneth this terror, Ruth?" demanded Content, in as much displeasure, perhaps, as he could manifest to one so gentle, for a weakness betrayed in his own behalf; "is thy confidence in him whose eye never closeth, and who equally watcheth the life of man and that of the falling sparrow, lost?"

Ruth was deaf. With hurried hands she drew the fastenings, let fall the bars, and turned a key which forced a triple-bolted lock to perform its office. Not till then did she feel either safe herself, or at liberty to render thanks for the safety of him, over whose danger she had so lately watched, in agony.

"Why this care? Hast forgotten that the horse will suffer hunger, at this distance from the rack and manger?"

"Better that he starve, than hair of thine should come to harm."

"Nay, nay, Ruth; dost not remember that the beast is the favorite of my father, who will ill brook his passing a night within the palisadoes?"

"Husband, you err; there is one in the fields!"

"Is there place, where one is not?"

"But I have seen creature of mortal birth, and creature too that hath no claim on thee, or thine, and who trespasseth on our peace, no less than on our natural rights, to be where he lurketh."

"Go to; thou art not used to be so late from thy pillow, my poor Ruth; sleep hath come over thee, whilst standing on thy watch. Some cloud hath left its shadow on the fields, or, truly, it may be that the hunt did not drive the beasts as far from the clearing as we had thought. Come; since thou wilt cling to my side, lay hand on the bridle of the horse, while I ease him of his burthen."

As Content coolly proceeded to the task he had mentioned, the thoughts of his wife were momentarily diverted from their other sources of uneasiness, by the object which lay on the crupper of the nag and which, until now, had entirely escaped her observation.

"Here is, indeed, the animal this day missing from our flock!" she exclaimed, as the carcass of a sheep fell heavily on the ground.

"Ay; and killed with exceeding judgment, if not aptly dressed to our hands. Mutton will not be wanting for the husking-feast, and the stalled creature whose days were counted may live another season."

"And where didst find the slaughtered beast?"

"On the limb of a growing hickory. Eben Dudley, with all his sleight in butchering, and in setting forth the excellence of his meats, could not have left an animal hanging from the branch of a sapling, with greater knowledge of his craft. Thou seest, but a single meal is missing from the carcass, and that thy fleece is unharmed."

"This is not the work of a Pequod!" exclaimed Ruth, surprised at her own discovery; "the red men do their mischief with less care."

"Nor has the tooth of wolf opened the veins of poor Straight-Horns. Here has been judgment in the slaughtering, as well as prudence in consumption of the food. The hand that cut so lightly, had intention of a second visit."

"And our father bid thee seek the creature where it was found! Husband, I fear some heavy judgment for the sins of the parents, is likely to befall the children."

"The babes are quietly in their slumbers, and, thus far, little wrong hath been done us. I'll cast the halter from the stalled animal ere I sleep, and Straight-Horns shall content us for the husking. We may have mutton less savory, for this evil chance, but the number of thy flock will be unaltered."

"And where is he, who hath mingled in our prayers, and hath eaten of our bread; he who counselled so long in secret with our father, and who hath now vanished from among us, like a vision?"

"That indeed is a question not readily to be answered," returned Content, who had hitherto maintained a cheerful air, in order to appease what he was fain to believe a causeless terror in the bosom of his partner, but who was induced by this question to drop his head like one that sought reasons within the repository of his own thoughts. "It mattereth not, Ruth Heathcote; the ordering of the affair is in the hands of a man of many years and great experience; should his aged wisdom fail, do we not know that one even wiser than he, hath us in his keeping? I will return the beast to his rack, and when we shall have jointly asked favor of eyes that never sleep, we will go in confidence to our rest."

"Husband, thou quittest not the palisadoes again this night," said Ruth, arresting the hand that had already drawn a bolt, ere she spoke. "I have a warning of evil."

"I would the stranger had found some other shelter in which to pass his short resting season. That he hath made free with my flock, and that he hath administered to his hunger at some cost, when a single asking would have made him welcome to the best that the owner of the Wish-Ton-Wish can command, are truths that may not be denied. Still is he mortal man, as a goodly appetite hath proven, even should our belief in Providence so far waver as to harbor doubts of its unwillingness to suffer beings of injustice to wander in our forms and substance. I tell thee, Ruth, that the nag will be needed for to-morrow's service, and that our father will give but ill thanks should we leave it to make a bed on this cold hill-side. Go to thy rest and to thy prayers, trembler; I will close the postern with all care. Fear not; the stranger is of human wants, and his agency to do evil must needs be limited by human power."

"I fear none of white blood, nor of Christian parentage: the murderous heathen is in our fields."

"Thou dreamest, Ruth!"

"'Tis not a dream. I have seen the glowing eye-balls of a savage. Sleep was little like to come over me, when set upon a watch like this. I thought me that the errand was of unknown character, and that our father was exceedingly aged, and that perchance his senses might be duped, and how an obedient son ought not to be exposed.—Thou knowest, Heathcote, that I could not look upon the danger of my children's father with indifference, and I followed to the nut-tree hillock."

"To the nut-tree! It was not prudent in thee—but the postern?"

"It was open; for were the key turned, who was there to admit us quickly, had haste been needed?" returned Ruth, momentarily averting her face to conceal the flush excited by conscious delinquency. "Though I failed in caution, 'twas for thy safety, Heathcote. But on that hillock, and in the hollow left by a fallen tree, lies concealed a heathen!"

"I passed the nut-wood in going to the shambles of our strange butcher, and I drew the rein to give breath to the nag near it, as we returned with the burthen. It cannot be; some creature of the forest hath alarmed thee."

"Ay! creature, formed, fashioned gifted like ourselves, in all but color of the skin and blessing of the faith."

"This is strange delusion! If there were enemy at hand, would men subtle as those you fear, suffer the master of the dwelling, and truly I may say it without vain-glory, one as likely as another to struggle stoutly for his own, to escape, when an ill-timed visit to the woods had delivered him unresisting into their hands? Go, go, good Ruth; thou mayst have seen a blackened log—perchance the frosts have left a fire-fly untouched, or it may be that some prowling bear has scented out the sweets of thy lately-gathered hives."

Ruth again laid her hand firmly on the arm ot her husband, who had withdrawn another bolt, and, looking him steadily in the face, she answered by saying solemnly, and with touching pathos—

"Think'st thou, husband, that a mother's eye could be deceived?"

It might have been that the allusion to the tender beings whose fate depended on his care, or that the deeply serious, though mild and gentle manner of his consort, produced some fresher impression on the mind of Content. Instead of undoing the fastenings of the postern as he had intended, he deliberately drew its bolts again and paused to think.

"If it produce no other benefit than to quiet thy fears, good Ruth," he said, after a moment of reflection, "a little caution will be well repaid. Stay you, then, here, where the hillock may be watched, while I go wake a couple of the people. With stout Eben Dudley and experienced Reuben Ring to back me, my father's horse may surely be stabled."

Ruth contentedly assumed a task that she was quite equal to perform with intelligence and zeal. "Hie thee to the laborers' chambers, for I see a light still burning in the room of those you seek," was the answer she gave to a proposal that at least quieted the intenseness of her fears for him in whose behalf they had so lately been excited nearly to agony.

"It shall be quickly done; nay, stand not thus openly between the beams, wife. Thou mayst place thyself, here, at the doublings of the wood, beneath the loop, where harm would scarcely reach thee, though shot from artillery were to crush the timber."

With this admonition to be wary of a danger that he had so recently affected to despise, Content departed on his errand. The two laborers he had mentioned by name, were youths of mould and strength, and they were well inured to toil, no less than to the particular privations and dangers of a border life. Like most men of their years and condition, they were practised too in the wiles of Indian cunning; and though the Province of Connecticut, compared to other settlements, had suffered but little in this species of murderous warfare, they both had martial feats and perilous experiences of their own to recount, during the light labors of the long winter evenings.

Content crossed the court with a quick step; for, notwithstanding his steady unbelief, the image of his gentle wife posted on her outer watch hurried his movements. The rap he gave at the door, on reaching the apartment of those he sought, was loud as it was sudden.

"Who calls?" demanded a deep-toned and firm voice from within, at the first blow of the knuckles on the plank.

"Quit thy beds quickly, and come forth with the arms appointed for a sally."

"That is soon done," answered a stout woodsman, throwing open the door and standing before Content in the garments he had worn throughout the day. "We were just dreaming that the night was not to pass without a summons to the loops."

"Hast seen aught?"

"Our eyes were not shut, more than those of others; we saw him enter that no man hath seen depart."

"Come, fellow; Whittal Ring would scarce give wiser speech than this cunning reply of thine. My wife is at the postern, and it is fit we go to relieve her watch. Thou wilt not forget the horns of powder, since it would not tell to our credit, were there service for the pieces, and we lacking in wherewithal to give them a second discharge."

The hirelings obeyed, and, as little time was necessary to arm those who never slept without weapons and ammunition within reach of their hands, Content was speedily followed by his dependants. Ruth was found at her post, but when urged by her husband to declare what had passed in his absence, she was compelled to admit that, though the moon had come forth brighter and clearer from behind the clouds, she had seen nothing to add to her alarm.

"We will then lead the beast to his stall, and close our duty by setting a single watcher for the rest of the night," said the husband. "Reuben shall keep the postern, while Eben and I will have a care for my father's nag, not forgetting the carcass for the husking-feast. Dost hear, deaf Dudley?—cast the mutton upon the crupper of the beast, and follow to the stables."

"Here has been no common workman at my office," said the blunt Eben, who, though an ordinary farm-laborer, according to an usage still very generally prevalent in the country, was also skilful in the craft of the butcher. "I have brought many a wether to his end, but this is the first sheep, within all my experience, that hath kept the fleece while a portion of the body has been in the pot! Lie there, poor Straight-Horns, if quiet thou canst lie after such strange butchery. Reuben, I paid thee, as the sun rose, a Spanish piece in silver, for the trifle of debt that lay between us, in behalf of the good turn thou didst the shoes, which were none the better for the last hunt in the hills. Hast ever that pistareen about thee?"

This question, which was put in a lowered tone, and only to the ear of the party concerned, was answered in the affirmative.

"Give it me, lad; in the morning, thou shalt be paid, with usurer's interest."

Another summons from Content, who had now led the nag loaded with the carcass of the sheep without the postern, cut short the secret conference. Eben Dudley, having received the coin, hastened to follow. But the distance to the out-buildings was sufficient to enable him to effect his mysterious purpose without discovery. Whilst Content endeavored to calm the apprehensions of his wife, who still persisted in sharing his danger, by such reasons as he could on the instant command, the credulous Dudley placed the thin piece of silver between his teeth, and, with a pressure that denoted the prodigious force of his jaws, caused it to assume a beaten and rounded shape. He then slily dropped the battered coin into the muzzle of his gun, taking care to secure its presence, until he himself should send it on its disenchanting message, by a wad torn from the lining of part of his vestments. Supported by this redoubtable auxiliary, the superstitious but still courageous borderer followed his companion, whistling a low air that equally denoted his indifference to danger of an ordinary nature, and his sensibility to impressions of a less earthly character.

They who dwell in the older districts of America.

where art and labor have united for generations to clear the earth of its inequalities, and to remove the vestiges of a state of nature, can form but little idea of the thousand objects that may exist in a clearing, to startle the imagination of one who has admitted alarm, when seen in the doubtful light of even a cloudless moon. Still less can they who have never quitted the old world, and who, having only seen, can only imagine fields smooth as the surface of tranquil water, picture the effect produced by those lingering remnants, which may be likened to so many mouldering monuments of the fallen forest scattered at such an hour over a broad surface of open land. Accustomed as they were to the sight, Content and his partner, excited by their fears, fancied each dark and distant stump a savage; and they passed no angle in the high and heavy fences without throwing a jealous glance to see that some enemy did not lie stretched within its shadows.

Still no new motive for apprehension arose, during the brief period that the two adventurers were employed in administering to the comfort of the Puritan's steed. The task was ended, the carcass of the slaughtered Straight-Horns had been secured, and Ruth was already urging her husband to return, when their attention was drawn to the attitude and mien of their companion.

"The man hath departed as he came," said Eben Dudley, who stood shaking his head in open doubt, before an empty stall; "here is no beast, though with these eyes did I see the half-wit bring hither a well-filled measure of speckled oats, to feed the nag. He who favored us with his presence at the supper and the thanksgiving, hath tired of his company before the hour of rest had come."

"The horse is truly wanting," said Content: "the man must needs be in exceeding haste, to have ridden into the forest as the night grew deepest, and when the longest summer day would scarce bring a better hack than that he rode to another Christian dwelling. There is reason for this industry, but it is enough that it concerns us not. We will now seek our rest, in the certainty that one watcheth our slumbers whose vigilance can never fail."

Though man could not trust himself to sleep in that country without the security of bars and bolts, we have already had occasion to say that property was guarded with but little care. The stable-door was merely closed by a wooden latch, and the party returned from this short sortie, with steps that were a little quickened by a sense of an uneasiness that beset them in forms suited to their several characters. But shelter was at hand, and it was speedily regained.

"Thou hast seen nothing?" said Content to Reuben Ring, who had been chosen for his quick eye, and a sagacity that was as remarkable as was his brother's impotency; "thou hast seen nothing at thy watch?"

"Nought unusual; and yet I like not yonder billet of wood, near to the fence against the knoll. If it were not so plainly a half-burnt log, one might fancy there is life in it. But when fancy is at work, the sight is keen. Once or twice I have thought it seemed to be rolling towards the brook; I am not, even now, certain that when first seen it did not lie eight or ten feet higher against the bank."

"It may be a living thing!"

"On the faith of a woodman's eye, it well may be," said Eben Dudley; "but should it be haunted by a legion of wicked spirits, one may bring it to quiet from the loop at the nearest corner. Stand aside, Madam Heathcote," for the character and wealth of the proprietors of the valley, gave Ruth a claim to this term of respect among the laborers; "let me thrust the piece through the—stop, there is an especial charm in the gun, which it might be sinful to waste on such a creature. It may be no more than some sweet-toothed bear. I will answer for the charge at my own cost, if thou wilt lend me thy musket, Reuben Ring."

"It shall not be," said his master; "one known to my father hath this night entered our dwelling and fed at our board; if he hath departed in a way but little wont among those of this Colony, yet hath he done no great wrong. I will go nigh, and exam ine with less risk of error."

There was, in this proposal, too much of that spirit of right-doing which governed all of those simple regions, to meet serious opposition. Content, supported by Eben Dudley, again quitted the postern, and proceeded directly, though still not without sufficient caution, towards the point where the suspicious object lay. A bend in the fence had first brought it into view, for previously to reaching that point, its apparent direction might for some distance have been taken under shelter of the shadows of the rails, which, at the immediate spot where it was seen, were turned suddenly in a line with the eyes of the spectators. It seemed as if the movements of those who approached were watched; for the instant they left the defences, the dark object was assuredly motionless; even the keen eye of Reuben Ring beginning to doubt whether some deception of vision had not led him, after all, to mistake a billet of wood for a creature of life.

But Content and his companion were not induced to change their determination. Even when within fifty feet of the object, though the moon fell full and brightly upon the surface, its character baffled conjecture. One affirmed it was the end of a charred log, many of which still lay scattered about the fields, and the other believed it some cringing animal of the woods. Twice Content raised his piece to fire, and as often did he let it fall, in reluctance to do injury to even a quadruped of whose character he was ignorant. It is more than probable that his less considerate, and but half-obedient companion would have decided the question soon after leaving he postern, had not the peculiar contents of his musket rendered him delicate of its uses.

"Look to thy weapons," said the former, loosening his own hunting-knife in its sheath. "We will draw near, and make certainty of what is doubtful."

They did so, and the gun of Dudley was thrust rudely into the side of the object of their distrust, before it again betrayed life or motion. Then, indeed, as if further disguise was useless, an Indian lad, of some fifteen years, rose deliberately to his feet, and stood before them in the sullen dignity of a captured warrior. Content hastily seized the stripling by an arm, and followed by Eben, who occasionally quickened the footsteps of the prisoner by an impetus obtained from the breech of his own musket, they hurriedly returned within the defences.

"My life against that of Straight-Horns, which is now of no great value," said Dudley, as he pushed the last bolt of the fastenings into its socket, "we hear no more of this red skin's companions to-night I never knew an Indian raise his whoop, when a scout had fallen into the hands of the enemy."

"This may be true," returned the other, "and yet must a sleeping household be guarded. We may be brought to rely on the overlooking favor of Providence, working with the means of our own manhood, ere the sun shall arise."

Content was a man of few words, but one of exceeding steadiness and resolution in moments of need. He was perfectly aware that an Indian youth, like him he had captured, would not have been found in that place, and under the circumstances in which he was actually taken, without a design of sufficient magnitude to justify the hazard. The tender age of the stripling, too, forbade the belief that he was unaccompanied. But he silently agreed with his laboring man that the capture would probably cause the attack, if any such were meditated, to be deferred. He therefore instructed his wife to withdraw into her chamber, while he took measures to defend the dwelling in the last emergency. Without giving any unnecessary alarm, a measure that would have produced less effect on an enemy without, than the imposing stillness which now reigned within the defences, he ordered two or three more of the stoutest of his dependants to be summoned to the palisadoes. A keen scrutiny was made into the state of all the different outlets of the place; muskets were carefully examined; charges were given to be watchful, and regular sentinels were stationed within the shadows of the buildings, at points where, unseen themselves, they could look out in safety upon the fields.

Content then took his captive, with whom he had made no attempt to exchange a syllable, and led him to the block-house: The door which communicated with the basement of this building was always open, in readiness for refuge in the event of any sudden alarm. He entered, caused the lad to mount by a ladder to the floor above, and then withdrawing the means of retreat, he turned the key without, in perfect confidence that his prisoner was secure.

Notwithstanding all this care, morning had nearly dawned before the prudent father and husband sought his pillow. His steadiness however had prevented the apprehensions, which kept his own eyes and those of his gentle partner so long open, from extending beyond the few whose services were, in such an emergency, deemed indispensable to safety. Towards the last watches of the night, only, did the images of the scenes through which they had just passed, become dim and confused, and then both husband and wife slept soundly, and happily without disturbance.

CHAPTER V.

"Are you so brave? I'll have you talked with anon."

CORIOLANUS.

THE axe and the brand had been early and effectually used, immediately around the dwelling of the Heathcotes. A double object had been gained by removing most of the vestiges of the forest from the vicinity of the buildings: the necessary improvements were executed with greater facility, and, a consideration of no small importance, the cover, which the American savage is known to seek in his attacks, was thrown to a distance that greatly diminished the danger of a surprise.

Favored by the advantage which had been obtained by this foresight, and by the brilliancy of a night that soon emulated the brightness of day, the duty of Eben Dudley and of his associate on the watch was rendered easy of accomplishment. Indeed, so secure did they become towards morning, chiefly on account of the capture of the Indian lad, that more than once, eyes, that should have been differently employed, yielded to the drowsiness of the hour and to habit, or were only opened at intervals that left their owners in some doubt as to the passage of the intermediate time. But no sooner did the signs of day approach, than, agreeably to their instructions, the watchers sought their beds, and for an hour or two, they slept soundly and without fear

When his father had closed the prayers of the

morning, Content, in the midst of the assembled family, communicated as many of the incidents of the past night as in his judgment seemed necessary. His discretion limited the narrative to the capture of the native youth, and to the manner in which he had ordered the watch for the security of the family On the subject of his own excursion to the forest, and all connected therewith, he was guardedly silent.

It is unnecessary to relate the manner in which this startling information was received. The cold and reserved brow of the Puritan became still more thoughtful; the young men looked grave, but resolute; the maidens of the household grew pale, shuddered, and whispered hurriedly together; while the little Ruth, and a female child of nearly her own age, named Martha, clung close to the side of the mistress of the family, who, having nothing new to learn, had taught herself to assume the appearance of a resolution she was far from feeling.

The first visitation which befell the listeners, after their eager ears had drunk in the intelligence Content so briefly imparted, was a renewal of the spiritual strivings of his father in the form of prayer. A particular petition was put up in quest of light on their future proceedings, for mercy on all men, for a better mind to those who wandered through the wilderness seeking victims of their wrath, for the gifts of grace on the heathen, and finally for victory over all their carnal enemies, let them come whence or in what aspect they might.

Fortified by these additional exercises, old Mark next made himself the master of all the signs and evidences of the approach of danger, by a more rigid and minute inquiry into the visible circumstances of the arrest of the young savage. Content received a merited and grateful reward for his prudence, in the approbation of one whom he still continued to revere with a mental dependence little less than that with which he had leaned on his father's wisdom in the days of his childhood.

"Thou hast done well and wisely," said his father; "but more remaineth to be performed by thy wisdom and fortitude. We have had tidings that the heathen near the Providence Plantations are unquiet, and that they are lending their minds to wicked counsellors. We are not to sleep in too much security, because a forest journey of a few days lies between their villages and our own clearing. Bring forth the captive; I will question him on the matter of this visit."

Until now, so much did the fears of all turn towards the enemies who were believed to be lurking near, that little thought had been bestowed on the prisoner in the block-house. Content, who well knew the invincible resolution, no less than the art of an Indian, had forborne to question him when taken; for he believed the time to be better suited to vigilant action, than to interrogatories that the character of the boy was likely to render perfectly useless. He now proceeded, however, with an interest that began to quicken as circumstances rendered its indulgence less unsuitable, to seek his captive, in order to bring him before the searching ordeal of his father's authority.

The key of the lower door of the block-house hung where it had been deposited; the ladder was replaced, and Content mounted quietly to the apartment where he had placed his captive. The room was the lowest of three that the building contained, all being above that which might be termed its basement. The latter, having no aperture but its door, was a dark, hexagonal space, partly filled with such articles as might be needed in the event of an alarm, and which, at the same time, were frequently required for the purposes of domestic use. In the centre of the area was a deep well, so fitted and protected by a wall of stone, as to admit of water being drawn into the rooms above. The door itself was of massive hewn timber. The squared logs of the upper stories projected a little beyond the stone-work of the basement, the second tier of the timbers containing a few loops out of which missiles might be discharged down wards, on any assailants that approached nearer than should be deemed safe for the security of the basement. As has been stated, the two principal stories were perforated with long narrow slits through the timber, which answered the double purposes of windows and loop-holes. Though the apartments were so evidently arranged for defence, the plain domestic furniture they contained was suited to the wants of the family, should they be driven to the building for refuge. There was also an apartment in the roof, or attic, as already mentioned; but it scarcely entered into the more important uses of the block-house. Still the advantage which it received from its elevation was not overlooked. A small cannon, of a kind once known and much used under the name of grasshoppers, had been raised to the place, and time had been, when it was rightly considered as of the last importance to the safety of the inmates of the dwelling. For some years its muzzle had been seen, by all the straggling aborigines who visited the valley, frowning through one of those openings which were now converted into glazed windows; and there is reason to think, that the reputation which the little piece of ordnance thus silently obtained, had a powerful agency in so long preserving unmolested the peace of the valley.

The word unmolested is perhaps too strong. More than one alarm had in fact occurred, though no positive acts of violence had ever been committed within the limits which the Puritan claimed as his own. On only one occasion, however, did matters proceed so far that the veteran had been induced to take his post in this warlike attic; where, there is little doubt, had occasion further offered for his services, he would have made a suitable display of his knowledge in the science of gunnery. But the simple history of the Wish-Ton-Wish had furnished another evidence of a political truth, which cannot be too often presented to the attention of our countrymen; we mean that the best preservative of peace is preparation for war. In the case before us, the hostile attitude assumed by old Mark and his dependants had effected all that was desirable, without proceeding to the extremity of shedding blood. Such peaceful triumphs were far more in accordance with the present principles of the Puritan, than it would have been with the reckless temper which had governed his youth. In the quaint and fanatical humor of the times, he had held a family thanksgiving around the instrument of their security, and from that moment the room itself became a favorite resorting-place for the old soldier. Thither he often mounted, even in the hours of deep night, to indulge in those secret spiritual exercises which formed the chiefest solace, and seemingly, indeed, the great employment of his life. In consequence of this habit, the attic of the block-house came in time to be considered sacred to the uses of the master of the valley. The care and thought of Content had gradually supplied it with many conveniences that might contribute to the personal comfort of his father, while the spirit was engaged in these mental conflicts. At length, the old man was known to use the mattress, that among other things it now contained, and to pass the time between the setting and rising of the sun in its solitude. The aperture originally cut for the exhibition of the grasshopper had been glazed; and no article of comfort, which was once caused to mount the difficult ladder that led to the chamber, was ever seen to descend.

There was something in the austere sanctity of old Mark Heathcote, that was favorable to the practices of an anchorite. The youths of the dwelling regarded his unbending brow, and the undisturbed gravity of the eye it shadowed, with a respect akin to awe. Had the genuine benevolence of his character been less tried, or had he mingled in active life at a later period, it might readily have been his fate to have shared in the persecution which his countrymen heaped on those who were believed to deal with influences it is thought impious to exercise. Under actual circumstances, however, the sentiment went no farther than a deep and universal reverence, that left its object, and the neglected little piece of artillery, to the quiet possession of an apartment, to invade which would have been deemed an act bordering on sacrilege.

The business of Content, on the occasion which caused his present visit to the edifice whose history and description we have thought it expedient thus to give at some length, led him no farther than to the lowest of its more military apartments. On raising the trap, for the first time a feeling of doubt came over him, as to the propriety of having left the boy so long unsolaced by words of kindness, or by deed of charity. It was appeased by observing that his concern was awakened in behalf of one whose spirit was quite equal to sustain greater trials.

The young Indian stood before one of tne loops, looking out upon that distant forest in which he had so lately roamed at liberty, with a gaze too riveted to turn aside even at the interruption occasioned by the presence of his captor.

"Come from thy prison, child," said Content, in the tones of mildness; "whatever may have been thy motive in lurking around this dwelling, thou art human, and must know human wants; come forth, and receive food: none here will harm thee."

The language of commiseration is universal. Though the words of the speaker were evidently unintelligible to him for whose ears they were intended, their import was conveyed in the kindness of the accents. The eyes of the boy turned slowly from the view of the woods, and he looked his captor long and steadily in the face. Content now indeed discovered that he had spoken in a language that was unknown to his captive, and he endeavored by gestures of kindness to invite the lad to follow. He was silently and quietly obeyed. On reaching the court, however, the prudence of a border proprietor in some degree overcame his feelings of compassion.

"Bring hither yon tether," he said to Whittal Ring, who at the moment was passing towards the stables; "here is one wild as the most untamed of thy colts. Man is of our nature and of our spirit, let him be of what color it may have pleased Providence to stamp his features; but he who would have a young savage in his keeping on the morrow, must look sharply to his limbs to-day."

The lad submitted quietly, until a turn of the rope was passed around one of his arms; but when Content was fain to complete the work by bringing the other limb into the same state of subjection, the boy glided from his grasp, and cast the fetter from him in disdain. This act of decided resistance was, however, followed by no effort to escape. The moment his person was released from a confinement which he probably considered as implying distrust of his ability to endure pain with the fortitude of a warrior, the lad turned quietly and proudly to his captor, and, with an eye in which scorn and haughtiness were alike glowing, seemed to defy the fulness of his anger.

"Be it so," resumed the equal-minded Content "if thou likest not the bonds, which, notwithstanding the pride of man, are often healthful to the body, keep then the use of thy limbs, and see that they do no mischief. Whittal, look thou to the postern and remember it is forbidden to go afield, until my father hath had this heathen under examination. The cub is seldom found far from the cunning of the aged bear."

He then made a sign to the boy to follow, and proceeded to the apartment where his father, surrounded by most of the family, awaited their coming. Uncompromising domestic discipline was one of the striking characteristics of the sway of the Puritans. That austerity of manner which was thought to mark a sense of a fallen and probationary state, was early taught; for, among a people who deemed all mirth a sinful levity, the practice of self-command would readily come to be esteemed the basis of virtue. But, whatever might have been the peculiar merit of Mark Heathcote and his household in this particular, it was likely to be exceeded by the exhibition of the same quality in the youth who had so strangely become their captive.

We have already said, that this child of the woods might have seen some fifteen years. Though he had shot upwards like a vigorous and thrifty plant, and with the freedom of a thriving sapling in his native forests, rearing its branches towards the light, his stature had not yet reached that of man. In height, form, and attitudes, he was a model of active, natural, and graceful boyhood. But, while his limbs were so fair in their proportions, they were scarcely muscular; still, every movement exhibited a freedom and ease which announced the grace of childhood, without the smallest evidence of that restraint which creeps into our air as the factitious feelings of later life begin to assert their influence. The smooth, rounded trunk of the mountain ash is not more upright and free from blemish, than was the figure of the boy, who moved into the curious circle that opened for his entrance and closed against his retreat, with the steadiness of one who came to bestow instead of appearing to receive judgment.

"I will question him," said old Mark Heathcote, attentively regarding the keen and settled eye that met his long, stern gaze as steadily as a less intelligent creature of the woods would return the look of man. "I will question him; and perchance fear will wring from his lips a confession of the evil that he and his have meditated against me and mine."

"I think he is ignorant of our forms of speech," returned Content; "for the words of neither kindness nor anger will force him to a change of feature "

"It is then meet that we commence by asking him, who hath the secret to open all hearts, to be our assistant." The Puritan then raised his voice in a short and exceedingly particular petition, in which he implored the Ruler of the Universe to interpret his meaning, in the forthcoming examination, in a manner that, had his request been granted, would have savored not a little of the miraculous. With this preparation, he proceeded directly to his task. But neither questions, signs, nor prayer, produced the slightest visible effect. The boy gazed at the rigid and austere countenance of his interrogator, while the words were issuing from his lips; but, the instant they ceased, his searching and quick eye rolled over the different curious faces by which he was hemmed in, as if he trusted more to the sense of sight than that of hearing, for the information he naturally sought concerning his future lot. It was found impossible to obtain from him gesture or sound that should betray either the purport of his questionable visit, his own personal appellation, or that of his tribe.

"I have been among the red skins of the Providence Plantations," Eben Dudley at length ventured to observe; "and their language, though but a crooked and irrational jargon, is not unknown to me. With the leave of all present," he continued regarding the Puritan in a manner to betray that this general term meant him alone, "with the leave of all present, I will put it to the younker in such a fashion that he will be glad to answer."

Receiving a look of assent, the borderer uttered certain uncouth and guttural sounds, which, notwithstanding they entirely failed of their effect, he stoutly maintained were the ordinary terms of salutation among the people to whom the prisoner was supposed to belong.

"I know him to be a Narragansett," continued Eben, reddening with vexation at his defeat, and throwing a glance of no peculiar amity at the youth who had so palpably refuted his claim to skill in the Indian tongues; "you see he hath the shells of the sea-side worked into the bordering of his moccasons; and besides this sign, which is certain as that night hath its stars, he beareth the look of a chief that was slain by the Pequods, at the wish of us Christians, after an affair in which, whether it was well done or ill done, I did some part of the work myself."

"And how call you that chief?" demanded Mark.

"Why, he had various names, according to the business he was on. To some he was known as the Leaping Panther, for he was a man of an extraordinary jump; and others again used to style him Pepperage, since there was a saying that neither bullet nor sword could enter his body: though th was a mistake, as his death hath fully proven. But his real name, according to the uses and sounds of his own people, was My Anthony Mow."

"My Anthony Mow!"

"Yes: My, meaning that he was their chief; Anthony, being the given name; and Mow, that of the breed of which he came;" rejoined Eben with confidence, satisfied that he had finally produced a sufficiently sonorous appellative and a perfectly lucid etymology. But criticism was diverted from its aim by the action of the prisoner, as these equivocal sounds struck his ear. Ruth recoiled, and clasped her little namesake closer to her side, when she saw the dazzling brightness of his glowing eyes, and the sudden and expressive dilation of his nostrils. For a moment, his lips were compressed with more than the usual force of Indian gravity, and then they slightly severed. A low, soft, and as even the startled matron was obliged to confess, a plaintive sound issued from between them, repeating mournfully—

"Miantonimoh!"

The word was uttered with a distinct, but deeply guttural enunciation.

"The child mourneth for its parent," exclaimed the sensitive mother. "The hand that slew the warrior may have done an evil deed!"

"I see the evident and foreordering will of a wise Providence in this," said Mark Heathcote with solemnity. "The youth hath been deprived of one who might have enticed him still deeper into the bond of the heathen, and hither hath he been led in order to be placed upon the straight and narrow path He shall become a dweller among mine, and we wil strive against the evil of his mind until instruction shall prevail. Let him be fed and nurtured, equally with the things of life and the things of the world; for who knoweth that which is designed in his behalf?"

If there were more of faith than of rational conclusion in this opinion of the old Puritan, there was no external evidence to contradict it. While the examination of the boy was going on in the dwelling, a keen scrutiny had taken place in the out-buildings, and in the adjacent fields. Those engaged in this duty soon returned, to say that not the smallest trace of an ambush was visible about the place; and as the captive himself had no weapons of hostility, even Ruth began to hope that the mysterious conceptions of her father on the subject were not entirely delusive. The captive was now fed, and old Mark was on the point of making a proper beginning in the task he had so gladly assumed, by an up-offering of thanks, when Whittal Ring broke rudely into the room, and disturbed the solemnity of his preparations, by a sudden and boisterous outcry.

"Away with scythe and sickle," shouted the witling; "it's many a day since the fields of Wish-Ton-Wish have been trodden down by horsemen in buff jerkins, or ambushed by creeping Wampanoags."

"There is danger at hand!" exclaimed the sensitive Ruth. "Husband, the warning was timely."

"Here are truly some riding from the forest, and drawing nigh to the dwelling; but as they are seemingly men of our kind and faith, we have need rather of rejoicing than terror. They bear the air of messengers from the River."

Mark Heathcote listened with surprise, and perhaps with a momentary uneasiness; but all emotion passed away on the instant, for one so disciplined in mind rarely permitted any outward exposure of his secret thoughts. The Puritan calmly issued an order to replace the prisoner in the block-house, assigning the upper of the two principal floors for his keeping; and then he prepared himself to receive guests that were little wont to disturb the quiet of his secluded valley He was still in the act of giving forth the necessary mandates, when the tramp of horses was heard in the court, and he was summoned to the door to greet his unknown visiters.

"We have reached Wish-Ton-Wish, and the dwelling of Captain Mark Heathcote," said one, who appeared, by his air and better attire, to be the principal of four that composed the party.

"By the favor of Providence; I call myself the unworthy owner of this place of refuge."

"Then a subject so loyal, and a man who hath so long proved himself faithful in the wilderness, will not turn from his door the agents of his Anointed Master."

"There is one greater than any of earth, who hath taught us to leave the latch free. I pray you to alight, and to partake of that we can offer."

With this courteous but quaint explanation, the horsemen dismounted; and, giving their steeds into the keeping of the laborers of the farm, they entered the dwelling.

While the maidens of Ruth were preparing a repast suited to the hour and to the quality of the guests, Mark and his son had abundant opportunity to examine the appearance of the strangers. They were men who seemed to wear visages peculiarly adapted to the characters of their entertainers being in truth so singularly demure and grave in aspect, as to excite some suspicion of their being newly-converted zealots to the mortifying customs of the Colony. Notwithstanding their extraordinary gravity, and contrary to the usages of those regions, too, they bore about their persons certain evidence of being used to the fashions of the other hemisphere. The pistols attached to their saddle-bows, and other accoutrements of a warlike aspect, would perhaps have attracted no observation, had they not been accompanied by a fashion in the doublet, the hat, and the boot, that denoted a greater intercourse with the mother country, than was usual among the less sophisticated natives of those regions. None traversed the forests without the means of defence but, on the other hand, few wore the hostile implements with so much of a worldly air, or with so many minor particularities of some recent caprice in fashion. As they had however announced themselves to be officers of the King, they, who of necessity must be chiefly concerned in the object of their visit, patiently awaited the pleasure of the strangers, to learn why duty had called them so far from all the more ordinary haunts of men: for, like the native owners of the soil, the self-restrained religionists appeared to reckon an indiscreet haste in any thing, among the more unmanly weaknesses. Nothing for the first half-hour of their visit escaped the guarded lips of men evidently well skilled in their present duty, which might lead to a clue of its purport. The morning meal passed almost without discourse, and one of the party had arisen with the professed object of looking to their steeds, before he, who seemed the chief, led the conversation to a subject, that by its political bearing might, in some degree, be supposed to have a remote connexion with the principal object of his journey to that sequestered valley.

"Have the tidings of the gracious boon that hath lately flowed from the favor of the King, reached this distant settlement?" asked the principal personage, one that wore a far less military air than a younger companion, who, by his confident mien, appeared to be the second in authority.

"To what boon hath thy words import?" demanded the Puritan, turning a glance of the eye at his son and daughter, together with the others in hearing, as if to admonish them to be prudent.

"I speak of the Royal Charter by which the

people on the banks of the Connecticut, and they of the Colony of New-Haven, are henceforth permitted to unite in government; granting them liberty of conscience, and great freedom of self-control."

"Such a gift were worthy of a King! Hath Charles done this?"

"That hath he, and much more that is fitting in a kind and royal mind. The realm is finally freed from the abuses of usurpers, and power now resteth in the hands of a race long set apart for its privileges."

"It is to be wished that practice shall render them expert and sage in its uses," rejoined Mark, somewhat drily.

"It is a merry Prince! and one but little given to the study and exercises of his martyred father; but he hath great cunning in discourse, and few around his dread person have keener wit or more ready tongue."

Mark bowed his head in silence, seemingly little disposed to push the discussion of his earthly master's qualities to a conclusion that might prove offensive to so loyal an admirer. One inclining to suspicion would have seen, or thought he saw certain equivocal glances from the stranger, while he was thus lauding the vivacious qualities of the restored monarch, which should denote a desire to detect how far the eulogiums might be grateful to his host. He acquiesced however in the wishes of the Puritan, though whether understandingly, or without design, it would have been difficult to say nd submitted to change the discourse.

"It is likely, by thy presence, that tidings hav reached the Colonies from home," said Content, who understood, by the severe and reserved expression of his father's features, that it was a fitting time for him to interpose.

"There is one arrived in the Bay, within the

month, by means of a King's frigate; but no trader hath yet passed between the countries, except the ship which maketh the annual voyage from Bristol to Boston."

"And he who hath arrived—doth he come in authority?" demanded Mark; "or is he merely another servant of the Lord, seeking to rear his tabernacle in the wilderness?"

"Thou shalt know the nature of his errand," returned the stranger, casting a glance of malicious intelligence obliquely towards his companions, at the same time that he arose and placed in the hand of his host a commission which evidently bore the Seal of State. "It is expected that all aid will be given to one bearing this warranty, by a subject of a loyalty so approved as that of Captain Mark Heathcote."

CHAPTER VI.

> "But, by your leave,
> I am an officer of state, and come
> To speak with——"
>
> CORIOLANUS.

NOTWITHSTANDING the sharp look which the Messenger of the Crown deliberately and now openly fastened on the master of Wish-Ton-Wish, while the latter was reading the instrument that was placed before his eyes, there was no evidence of uneasiness to be detected in the unmoved features of the latter. Mark Heathcote had too long schooled his passions, to suffer an unseemly manifestation of surprise to escape him; and he was by nature a man of far too much nerve, to betray alarm at any trifling exhibition of danger. Returning the parch ment to the other, he said with unmoved calmness to his son—

"We must open wide the doors of Wish-Ton-Wish. Here is one charged with authority to look into the secrets of all the dwellings of the colony.' Then, turning with dignity to the agent of the Crown, he added, "Thou hadst better commence thy duty in season, for we are many and occupy much space."

The face of the stranger flushed a little, it might have been with shame for the vocation in which he had come so far, or it might have been in resentment at so direct a hint that the sooner his disagreeable office should be ended, the better it would please his host. Still, he betrayed no intention of shrinking from its performance. On the contrary, discarding somewhat of that subdued manner which he had probably thought it politic to assume, while sounding the opinions of one so rigid, he broke out rather suddenly in the exhibition of a humor somewhat better suited to the tastes of him he served.

"Come then," he cried, winking at his companions, "since doors are opened, it would speak ill of our breeding should we refuse to enter. Captain Heathcote has been a soldier, and he knows how to excuse a traveller's freedom. Surely one who has tasted of the pleasures of the camp, must weary at times of this sylvan life!"

"The stedfast in faith weary not, though the road be long and the wayfaring grievous."

"Hum—'tis pity that the journeying between merry England and these Colonies is not more brisk. I do not presume to instruct a gentleman who is my senior, and peradventure my better; but opportunity is everything in a man's fortunes. It were charity to let you know, worthy sir, that opinions have changed at home: it is full a twelvemonth since I have heard a line of the Psalms, or a verse of St. Paul quoted, in discourse; at least by men who are at all esteemed for their discretion."

"This change in the fashion of speech may better suit thy earthly than thy heavenly master," said Mark Heathcote, sternly.

"Well, well, that peace may exist between us, we will not bandy words about a text more or less, if we may escape the sermon," rejoined the stranger, no longer affecting restraint, but laughing with sufficient freedom at his own conceit; a species of enjoyment in which his companions mingled with great good-will, and without much deference to the humor of those under whose roof they found themselves.

A small glowing spot appeared on the pale cheek of the Puritan, and disappeared again, like some transient deception produced by the play of light. Even the meek eye of Content kindled at the insult; but, like his father, the practice of self-denial, and a never-slumbering consciousness of his own imperfections, smothered the momentary exhibition of displeasure.

"If thou hast authority to look into the secret places of our habitations, do thy office," he said, with a peculiarity of tone which served to remind the other, that though he bore the commission of the Stuart, he was in an extremity of his Empire, where even the authority of a King lost some of its value.

Affecting to be, and possibly in reality conscious of his indiscretion, the stranger hastily disposed himself to the execution of his duty.

"It would be a great and a pain-saving movement," he said, "were we to assemble the household in one apartment The government at home would be glad to hear something of the quality of its lieges in this distant quarter. Thou hast doubtless a bell to summon the flock at stated periods."

"Our people are yet near the dwelling," returned Content: "if it be thy pleasure, none shall be absent from the search."

Gathering from the eye of the other that he was serious in this wish, the quiet Colonist proceeded to the gate, and, placing a shell to his mouth, blew one of those blasts that are so often heard in the forests summoning families to their homes, and which are alike used as the signals of peaceful recall, or of alarm. The sound soon brought all within hearing to the court, whither the Puritan and his unpleasant guests now repaired as to the spot best suited to the purposes of the latter.

"Hallam," said the principal personage of the four visiters, addressing him who might once have been, if he were not still, some subaltern in the forces of the Crown, for he was attired in a manner that bespoke him but a half-disguised dragoon, "I leave thee to entertain this goodly assemblage. Thou mayst pass the time in discoursing on the vanities of the world, of which I believe few are better qualified to speak understandingly than thyself, or a few words of admonition to hold fast to the faith would come with fitting weight from thy lips. But look to it, that none of thy flock wander; for here must every creature of them remain, stationary as the indiscreet partner of Lot, till I have cast an eye into all the cunning places of their abode. So set wit at work, and show thy breeding as an entertainer."

After this irreverent charge to his subordinate the speaker signified to Content and his father, that he and his remaining attendant would proceed to a more minute examination of the premises.

When Mark Heathcote saw that the man who had so rudely broken in upon the peaceful habits of his family was ready to proceed, he advanced steadily in his front, like one who boldly invited inquiry, and by a grave gesture desired him to follow. The stranger, perhaps as much from habit as from any settled design, first cast a free glance around at the bevy of fluttered maidens, leered even upon the modest and meek-eyed Ruth herself, and then took the direction indicated by him who had so unhesitatingly assumed the office of a guide.

The object of this examination still remained a secret between those who made it, and the Puritan, who had probably found its motive in the written warranty which had been submitted to his inspection. That it proceeded from fitting authority, none might doubt; and that it was in some manner connected with the events that were known to have wrought so sudden and so great a change in the government of the mother country, all believed probable. Notwithstanding the seeming mystery of the procedure, the search was not the less rigid. Few habitations of any size or pretension were erected in those times, which did not contain certain secret places, where valuables and even persons might be concealed, at need. The strangers displayed great familiarity with the nature and ordinary positions of these private recesses. Not a chest, a closet, or even a drawer of size, escaped their vigilance; nor was there a plank that sounded hollow, but the master of the valley was called on to explain the cause. In one or two instances, boards were wrested violently from their fastenings, and the cavities beneath were explored, with a wariness that increased as the investigation proceeded without success.

The strangers appeared irritated by their failure. An hour passed in the keenest scrutiny, and nothing had transpired which brought them any nearer to their object. That they had commenced the search with more than usually confident anticipations of a favorable result, might have been gathered from the boldness of tone assumed by their chief, and the pointed personal allusions in which, from time to time, he indulged, often too freely, and always at some expense to the loyalty of the Heathcotes. But when he had completed the circuit of the buildings, having entered all parts from their cellars to the garrets, his spleen became so strong as, in some degree, to get the better of a certain parade of discretion, which he had hitherto managed to maintain in the midst of all his levity.

"Hast seen nothing, Mr. Hallam?" he demanded of the individual left on watch, as they crossed the court in retiring from the last of the out-buildings; "or have those traces which led us to this distant settlement proved false? Captain Heathcote, you have seen that we come not without sufficient warranty, and it is in my power to say we come not without sufficient——"

Checking himself as if about to utter more than was prudent, he suddenly cast an eye on the block-house, and demanded its uses.

"It is, as thou seest, a building erected for the purposes of defence," replied Mark; "one to which, in the event of an inroad of the savages, the family may fly for refuge."

"Ah! these citadels are not unknown to me. I have met with others during my journey, but none so formidable or so military as this. It hath a soldier for its governor, and should hold out for a reasonable siege. Being a place of pretension, we will look closer into its mystery."

He then signified an intention to close the search by an examination of this edifice. Content unhesitatingly threw open its door, and invited him to enter.

"On the word of one who, though now engaged in a more peaceful calling, has been a campaigner in his time, 'twould be no child's-play to carry this tower without artillery. Had thy spies given notice of our approach, Captain Heathcote, the entrance might have been more difficult than we now find it. We have a ladder, here! Where the means of mounting are found, there must be something to tempt one to ascend. I will taste your forest air from an upper room."

"You will find the apartment above, like this below, merely provided for the security of the unoffending dwellers of the habitations," said Content; while he quietly arranged the ladder before the trap, and then led the way himself to the floor above.

"Here have we loops for the musketoons," cried the stranger, looking about him, understandingly, "and reasonable defences against shot. Thou hast not forgotten thy art, Captain Heathcote, and I consider myself fortunate in having entered thy fortress by surprise, or I should rather say, in amity, since the peace is not yet broken between us. But why have we so much of household gear in a place so evidently equipped for war?"

"Thou forgettest that women and children may be driven to this block for a residence," replied Content. "It would show little discretion to neglect matters that might be useful to their wants."

"Is there trouble with the savages?" demanded the stranger, a little quickly; "the gossips of the Colony bade us fear nothing on that head."

"One cannot say at what hour creatures trained in their wild natures may choose to rise. The dwellers on the borders therefore never neglect a fitting caution."

"Hist!" interrupted the stranger; "I hear a footstep above. Ha! the scent will prove true at last! Hilloa, Master Hallam!" he cried from one of the loops, "let thy statues of salt dissolve, and come hither to the tower. Here is work for a regiment;

for well do we know the nature of that we are to deal with."

The sentinel in the court shouted to his companion in the stables, and then, openly and boisterously exulting in the prospects of a final success to a search which had hitherto given them useless employment throughout many a long day and weary ride, they rushed together to the block-house.

"Now, worthy lieges of a gracious master," said the leader, when he perceived himself backed by all his armed followers, and speaking with the air of a man flushed with success, "now quickly provide the means of mounting to the upper story. I have thrice heard the tread of man, moving across that floor; though it hath been light and wary, the planks are tell-tales, and have not had their schooling."

Content heard the request, which was uttered sufficiently in the manner of an order, perfectly unmoved. Without betraying either hesitation or concern, he disposed himself to comply. Drawing the light ladder through the trap below, he placed it against the one above him, and ascending he raised the door. He then returned to the floor beneath, making a quiet gesture to imply that they who chose might mount. But the strangers regarded each other with very visible doubts. Neither of the inferiors seemed disposed to precede his chief, and the latter evidently hesitated as to the order in which it was meet to make the necessary advance.

"Is there no other manner of mounting, but by this narrow ascent?" he asked.

"None. Thou wilt find the ladder secure, and of no difficult height. It is intended for the use of women and children."

"Ay," muttered the officer, "but your women and children are not called upon to confront the devil in a human form. Fellows, are thy weapons in serviceable condition? Here may be need of spirit, ere we get our—Hist! by the Divine Right of our Gracious Master! there is truly one stirring above. Harkee, my friend; thou knowest the road so well, we will choose to follow thy conduct."

Content, who seldom permitted ordinary events to disturb the equanimity of his temper, quietly assented, and led the way up the ladder. like one who saw no ground for apprehension in the undertaking. The agent of the crown sprang after him, taking care to keep as near as possible to the person of his leader, and calling to his inferiors to lose no time in backing him with their support. The whole mounted through the trap, with an alacrity nothing short of that with which they would have pressed through a dangerous breach; nor did either of the four take time to survey the lodgment he had made, until the whole party was standing in array, with hands grasping the handles of their pistols, or seeking as it were instinctively the hilts of their broadswords.

"By the dark visage of the Stuart!" exclaimed the principal personage, after satisfying himself by a long and disappointed gaze, that what he said was true, "here is nought but an unarmed savage boy!"

"Didst expect to meet else?" demanded the still unmoved Content.

"Hum—that which we expected to meet is sufficiently known to the quaint old gentleman below, and to our own good wisdom. If thou doubtest of our right to look into thy very hearts, warranty for that we do can be forthcoming. King Charles hath little cause to be tender of his mercies to the dwellers of these Colonies, who lent but too willing ears to the whinings and hypocrisies of the wolves in sheeps' clothing, of whom old England hath now so happily gotten rid. Thy buildings shall again be rummaged from the bricks of the chimney-tops to the corner-stone in thy cellars, unless deceit and rebellious cunning shall be abandoned, and the truth proclaimed with the openness and fairness of bold-speaking Englishmen."

"I know not what is called the fairness of bold-speaking Englishmen, since fairness of speech is not a quality of one people, or of one land; but well I do know that deceit is sinful, and little of it, I humbly trust, is practised in this settlement. I am ignorant of what is sought, and therefore it cannot be that I meditate treachery."

"Thou hearest, Hallam; he reasoneth on a matter that toucheth the peace and safety of the King!" cried the other, his arrogance of manner increasing with the anger of disappointment. "But why is this dark-skinned boy a prisoner? dost dare to constitute thyself a sovereign over the natives of this continent, and affect to have shackles and dungeons for such as meet thy displeasure?"

"The lad is in truth a captive; but he has been taken in defence of life, and hath little to complain of, more than loss of freedom."

"I will inquire deeply into this proceeding. Though commissioned on an errand of different interest, yet, as one trusted in a matter of moment, I take upon me the office of protecting every oppressed subject of the Crown. There may grow discoveries out of this practice, Hallam, fit to go before the Council itself."

"Thou wilt find but little here, worthy of the time and attention of those burthened with the care of a nation," returned Content. "The youthful heathen was found lurking near our habitations, the past night; and he is kept where thou seest, that he may not carry the tidings of our condition to his people, who are doubtless outlying in the forest, waiting for the fit moment to work their evil."

"How meanest thou?" hastily exclaimed the other, "at hand, in the forest, didst say?"

"There can be little doubt. One young as this would scarce be found distant from the warriors of his tribe; and that the more especially, as he was taken in the commission of an ambush."

"I hope thy people are not without good provision of arms, and other sufficient muniments of resistance. I trust the palisadoes are firm, and the posterns ingeniously defended."

"We look with a diligent eye to our safety, for it is well known to us dwellers on the borders that there is little security but in untiring watchfulness. The young men were at the gates until the morning, and we did intend to make a strong scouting into the woods as the day advanced, in order to look for those signs that may lead us to conclusions on the number and purposes of those by whom we are environed, had not thy visit called us to other duties."

"And why so tardy in speaking of this intent?" demanded the agent of the King, leading the way down the ladder with suspicious haste. "It is a commendable prudence, and must not be delayed. I take upon me the responsibleness of commanding that all proper care be had in defence of the weaker subjects of the Crown who are here collected. Are our roadsters well replenished, Hallam? Duty, as thou sayest, is an imperative master; it recalls us more into the heart of the Colony. I would it might shortly point the way to Europe!" he muttered as he reached the ground. "Go, fellows; see to our beasts, and let them be speedily prepared for departure."

The attendants, though men of sufficient spirit in open war, and when it was to be exercised in a fashion to which they were accustomed, had, like other mortals, a wholesome deference for unknown and terrific-looking danger. It is a well-known truth, and one that has been proved by the experience of two centuries, that while the European soldier has ever been readiest to have recourse to the assistance of the terrible warrior of the American forest, he has, in nearly every instance, when retaliation or accident has made him the object instead of the spectator of the ruthless nature of his warfare, betrayed the most salutary, and frequently the most abject and ludicrous apprehension of the prowess of his ally. While Content therefore looked so steadily, though still seriously, at the peculiar danger in which he was placed, the four strangers seemingly saw all of its horrors without any of the known means of avoiding them. Their chief quickly abandoned the insolence of office, and the tone of disappointment, for a mien of greater courtesy; and, as policy is often seen suddenly to change the sentiments of even more pretending personages, when interests assume a new aspect, so did his language rapidly take a character of conciliation and courtesy.

The handmaidens were no longer leered at; the mistress of the dwelling was treated with marked deference; and the air of deep respect with which even the principal of the party addressed the aged Puritan, bordered on an exhibition of commendable reverence. Something was said, in the way of apology, for the disagreeable obligations of duty, and of a difference between a manner that was assumed to answer secret purposes, and that which nature and a sense of right would dictate: but neither Mark nor his son appeared to have sufficient interest in the motives of their visiters, to put them to the trouble of repeating explanations that were as awkward to those who uttered them, as they were unnecessary to those who listened.

So far from offering any further obstacle to the movements of the family, the borderers were seriously urged to pursue their previous intentions of thoroughly examining the woods. The dwelling was accordingly intrusted, under the orders of the Puritan, to the keeping of about half the laborers, assisted by the Europeans, who clung with instinctive attachment to the possession of the block-house; their leader repeatedly and rightly enough declaring that though ready at all times to risk life on a plain, he had an unconquerable distaste to putting it in jeopardy in a thicket. Attended by Eben Dudley, Reuben Ring, and two other stout youths, all well though lightly armed, Content then left the palisadoes, and took his way towards the forest. They entered the woods at the nearest point, always marching with the caution and vigilance that a sense of the true nature of the risk they ran would inspire, and much practice only could properly direct.

The manner of the search was as simple as it was likely to prove effectual. The scouts commenced a circuit around the clearing, extending their line as far as might be done without cutting off support, and each man lending his senses attentively to the signs of the trail, or of the lairs, of those dangerous enemies, who they had reason to think were outlying in their neighborhood. But, like the recent search in the buildings, the scouting was for a long time attended by no results. Many weary miles were passed slowly over, and more than half their task was ended, and no sign of being having life was met, except the very visible trail of their four guests, and the tracks of a single horse along the path leading to the settlements from the quarter by which the visiter of the previous night had been known to approach. No comments were made by any of the party, as each in succession struck and crossed this path, nearly at the same instant; but a low call from Reuben Ring which soon after met their ears, caused them to assemble in a body at the spot whence the summons had proceeded.

"Here are signs of one passing *from* the clearing," said the quick-eyed woodsman, "and of one too that is not numbered among the family of Wish-Ton-Wish; since his beast hath had a shodden hoof, a mark which belongeth to no animal of ours."

"We will follow," said Content, immediately striking in upon a straggling trail, that by many unequivocal signs had been left by some animal which had passed that way not many hours before. Their search, however, soon grew to a close. Ere they had gone any great distance, they came upon the half-demolished carcass of a dead horse. There was no mistaking the proprietor.of this unfortunate animal. Though some beast, or rather beasts of prey, had fed plentifully on the body, which was still fresh and had scarcely yet done bleeding, it was plain, by the remains of the torn equipments, as well as by the color and size of the animal, that it was no other than the hack ridden by the unknown and mysterious guest, who, after sharing in the worship and in the evening meal of the family of the Wish-Ton-Wish, had so strangely and so suddenly disappeared. The leathern sack, the weapons which had so singularly riveted the gaze of old Mark, and indeed all but the carcass and a ruined saddle, were gone; but what was left, sufficiently served to identify the animal.

"Here has been the tooth of wolf,' said Eben Dudley, stooping to examine into the nature of a ragged wound in the neck; 'and here, too, has been cut of knife; but whether by the hand of a red skin, it exceedeth my art to say."

Each individual of the party now bent curiously over the wound; but the results of their inquiries went no further than to prove that it was undeniably the horse of the stranger, that had forfeited its life. To the fate of its master, however, there was not the slightest clue. Abandoning the investigation, after a long and fruitless examination, they proceeded to finish the circuit of the clearing. Night had approached ere the fatiguing task was accomplished. As Ruth stood at the postern waiting anxiously for their return, she saw by the countenance of her husband, that while nothing had transpired to give any grounds of additional alarm, no satisfactory testimony had been obtained to explain the nature of the painful doubts, with which, as a tender and sensitive mother, she had been distressed throughout the day.

CHAPTER VII.

"Is there not milking-time,
When you go to bed, or kiln-hole,
To whistle off these secrets; but you must be
Tattling before all our guests?"

WINTER'S TALE

LONG experience hath shown that the white man, when placed in situations to acquire such knowledge, readily becomes the master of most of that peculiar skill for which the North American Indian is so remarkable, and which enables him, among other things, to detect the signs of a forest trail, with a quickness and an accuracy of intelligence that amount nearly to an instinct. The fears of the family were therefore greatly quieted by the reports of the scouts, all of whom agreed in the opinion that no party of savages, that could be at all dangerous to a force like their own, was lying near the valley; and some of whom, the loudest of which number being stout Eben Dudley, boldly offered to answer for the security of those who depended on their vigilance, with their own lives These assurances had, beyond a doubt, a soothing influence on the apprehensions of Ruth and her handmaidens; but they somewhat failed of their effect, with those unwelcome visiters who still continued to cumber Wish-Ton-Wish with their presence. Though they had evidently abandoned all ideas connected with the original object of their visit, they spoke not of departure. On the contrary as night approached, their chief entered into council with old Mark Heathcote, and made certain propositions for the security of his dwelling, which the Puritan saw no reason to oppose.

A regular watch was, in consequence, set, and maintained till morning, at the palisadoes. The different members of the family retired to their usual places of rest, tranquil in appearance, if not in entire confidence of peace; and the military messengers took post in the lower of the two fighting apartments of the citadel. With this simple, and to the strangers particularly satisfactory arrangement, the hours of darkness passed away in quiet; morning returning to the secluded valley, as it had so often done before, with its loveliness unimpaired by violence or tumult.

In the same peaceful manner did the sun set successively three several times, and as often did it arise on the abode of the Heathcotes, without further sign of danger, or motive of alarm. With the passage of time, the agents of the Stuart gradually regained their confidence. Still they never neglected to withdraw within the protection of the block house with the retiring light; a post which the sub ordinate named Hallam, more than once gravely observed, they were, by their disciplined and military habits, singularly qualified to maintain. Though the Puritan secretly chafed under this protracted visit, habitual self-denial, and a manner so long subdued, enabled him to conceal his disgust. For the first two days after the alarm, the deportment of his guests was unexceptionable. All their faculties appeared to be engrossed with keen and anxious watchings of the forest, out of which it would seem they expected momentarily to see issue a band of ferocious and ruthless savages: but symptoms of returning levity began to be apparent, as confidence and a feeling of security increased, with the quiet passage of the hours.

It was on the evening of the third day from that on which they had made their appearance in the settlement, that the man called Hallam was seen strolling, for the first time, through the postern so often named, and taking a direction which led towards the out-buildings. His air was less distrustful than it had been for many a weary hour, and his step proportionably confident and assuming. Instead of wearing, as he had been wont, a pair of heavy horseman's pistols at his girdle, he had even laid aside his broadsword, and appeared more in the guise of one who sought his personal ease, than in that cumbersome and martial attire which all of his party, until now, had deemed it prudent to maintain. He cast his glance cursorily over the fields of the Heathcotes, as they glowed under the soft light of a setting sun; nor did his eye even refuse to wander vacantly along the outline of that forest, which his imagination had so lately been peopling with beings of a fierce and ruthless nature.

The hour was one when rustic economy brings the

labors of the day to a close. Among those who were more than usually active at that busy moment, was a handmaiden of Ruth, whose clear sweet voice was heard, in one of the inclosures, occasionally rising on the notes of a spiritual song, and as often sinking to a nearly inaudible hum, as she extracted from a favorite animal liberal portions of its nightly tribute to the dairy of her mistress. To that inclosure the stranger, as it were by accident, suffered his sauntering footsteps to stroll, seemingly as much in admiration of the sleek herd as of any other of its comely tenants.

"From what thrush hast taken lessons, my pretty maid, that I mistook thy notes for one of the sweetest songsters of thy woods?" he asked, trusting his person to the support of the pen in an attitude of easy superiority. "One might fancy it a robin, or a wren, trolling out his evening song, instead of human voice rising and falling in every-day psalmody."

"The birds of our forest rarely speak," returned the girl; "and the one among them which has most to say, does it like those who are called gentlemen, when they set wit to work to please the ear of simple country maidens."

"And in what fashion may that be?"

"Mockery."

"Ah! I have heard of the creature's skill. It is said to be a compound of the harmony of all other forest songsters; and yet I see little resemblance to the honest language of a soldier, in its manner of utterance."

"It speaketh without much meaning; and oftener to cheat the ear, than in honest reason."

"Thou forgettest that which I told thee in the morning, child. It would seem that they who named thee, have no great cause to exult in their judgment of character, since Unbelief would better describe thy disposition, than Faith."

"It may be, that they who named me little knew how great must be credulity, to give ear to all I have been required to credit."

"Thou canst have no difficulty in admitting that thou art comely, since the eye itself will support thy belief; nor can one of so quick speech fail to know that her wit is sharper than common. Thus far, I admit, the name of Faith will not surely belie thy character."

"If Eben Dudley hear thee use such vanity-stirring discourse," returned the half-pleased girl, "he might give thee less credit for wit than thou seemest willing to yield to others. I hear his heavy foot among the cattle, and ere long we shall be sure to see a face that hath little more of lightness to boast."

"This Eben Dudley is a personage of no mean importance, I find!" muttered the other, continuing his walk, as the borderer named made his appearance at another entrance of the pen. The glances exchanged between them were far from friendly, though the woodsman permitted the stranger to pass without any oral expression of displeasure.

"The skittish heifer is getting gentle at last, Faith Ring," said the borderer; casting the but of his musket on the ground with a violence that left a deep impression on the faded sward at his feet. "That brindled ox, old Logger, is not more willing to come into his yoke, than is the four-year-old to yield her milk."

"The creature has been getting kind, since you taught the manner to tame its humor," returned the dairy girl, in a voice that, spite of every effort of maiden pride, betrayed something of the flurry of her spirits, while she plied her light task with violent industry.

"Umph! I hope some other of my teachings may be as well remembered; but thou art quick at the trick of learning, Faith, as is plain by the ready manner in which thou hast so shortly got the habit of discourse with a man as nimble-tongued as yon riding reprobate from over sea."

"I hope that civil listening is no proof of unseemly discourse on the part of one who hath been trained in modesty of speech, Eben Dudley. Thou hast often said, it was the bounden duty of her who was spoken to, to give ear, lest some might say she was of scornful mind, and her name for pride be better earned than that for good-nature."

"I see that more of my lessons than I had hoped are still in thy keeping. So thou listenest thus readily, Faith, because it is meet that a maiden should not be scornful!"

"Thou sayest so. Whatever ill name I may deserve, thou hast no right to count scorn among my failings."

"If I do, may I——" Eben Dudley bit his lip and checked an expression which would have given grievous offence to one whose habits of decency were as severe as those of his companion. "Thou must have heard much that was profitable to-day, Faith Ring," he added, "considering that thy ear is so open, and that thy opportunities have been great."

"I know not what thou wouldst say by speaking of my opportunities," returned the girl, bending still lower beneath the object of her industry, in order to conceal the glow which her own quick consciousness told her was burning on her cheek.

"I would say that the tale must be long, that needeth four several trials of private speech to finish."

"Four! as I hope to be believed for a girl of truth in speech or deed, this is but the third time that the stranger hath spoken to me apart, since the sun hath risen."

"If I know the number of the fingers of my hand, it is the fourth!"

"Nay, how canst thou, Eben Dudley, who hast been afield since the crowing of the cock, know what hath passed about the dwellings? It is plain that envy, or some other evil passion, causeth thee to speak angrily."

"How is it that I know! perhaps thou thinkest Faith, thy brother Reuben, only, hath the gift of sight."

"The labor must have gone on with great profit to the Captain, whilst eyes have been roving over other matters! But perhaps they kept the strong of arm for the lookers-out, and have set them of feebler bodies to the toil."

"I have not been so careless of thy life as to forget, at passing moments, to cast an eye abroad, pert-one. Whatever thou mayst think of the need, there would be fine wailings in the butteries and dairies, did the Wampanoâgs get into the clearing, and were there none to give the alarm in season."

"Truly, Eben, thy terror of the child in the block must be grievous for one of thy manhood, else wouldst thou not watch the buildings so narrowly," retorted Faith, laughing; for with the dexterity of her sex, she began to feel the superiority she was gradually obtaining in the discourse. "Thou dost not remember that we have valiant troopers, from old England, to keep the younker from doing harm. But here cometh the brave soldier himself: it will be well to ask vigilance at his hands, or this night may bring us to the tomahawk in our sleep!"

'Thou speakest of the weapon of the savages!' said the messenger, who had drawn near again with a visible willingness to share in an interview which while he had watched its progress at a distance appeared to be growing interesting. "I trust all fear is over, from that quarter."

"As you say, for *this* quarter," said Eben, adjusting his lips to a low whistle, and coolly looking up to examine the heavenly body to which he meant allusion. "But the *next* quarter may bring us a pretty piece of Indian skirmishing."

"And what hath the moon in common with an incursion of the savages? Are there those among them, who study the secrets of the stars?"

"They study deviltries and other wickedness, more than aught else. It is not easy for the mind of man to fancy horrors such as they design, when Providence has given them success in an inroad."

"But thou didst speak of the moon! In what manner is the moon leagued with their bloody plots?"

"We have her now in the full, and there is little of the night when the eye of a watcher might not see a red skin in the clearing; but a different tale may be heard, when an hour or two of jet darkness shall again fall among these woods. There will be a change shortly; it behoveth us therefore to be on our guard."

"Thou thinkest then, truly, that there are outlyers waiting for the fitting moment?" said the officer, with an interest so marked as to cause even the but-half-pacified Faith to glance an arch look at her companion, though he still had reason to distrust a wilful expression that lurked in the corner of her eyes, which threatened at each moment to contradict his relation of the sinister omens.

"There may be savages lying in the hills, at a day's journey in the forest; but they know the aim of a white man's musket too well, to be sleeping within reach of its range. It is the nature of an Indian to eat and sleep while he has time for quiet, and to fast and murder when the killing hour hath come."

"And what call you the distance to the nearest settlement on the Connecticut?" demanded the other with an air so studiously indifferent as to furnish an easy clue to the inner workings of his mind.

"Some twenty hours would bring a nimble runner to the outer habitations, granting small time for food and rest. He that is wise, however, will take bu little of the latter, until his head be safely housed within some such building as yon block, or until there shall stand between him and the forest at least a goodly row of oaken pickets."

"There is no path ridden by which travellers may avoid the forest during the darkness?"

"I know of none. He who quits Wish-Ton-Wish for the towns below, must make his pillow of the earth, or be fain to ride as long as beast can carry."

"We have truly had experience of this necessity, journeying hither. Thou thinkest, friend, the savages are in their resting time, and that they wait the coming quarter of the moon?"

"To my seeming, we shall not have them sooner, returned Eben Dudley; taking care to conceal all qualification of this opinion, if any such he entertained, by closely locking its purport in a mental reservation.

"And what season is it usual to choose for getting into the saddle, when business calls any to the settlements below?"

"We never fail to take our departure about the time the sun touches the tall pine, which stands on yonder height of the mountain. Much experience hath told us it is the safest hour; hand of time-piece is not more sure than yon tree."

"I like the night," said the other, looking about him with the air of one suddenly struck with the promising appearance of the weather. "The blackness no longer hangs about the forest, and it seems a fitting moment to push the matter. on which we are sent, nearer to its conclusion."

So saying, and probably believing that he had sufficiently concealed the motive of his decision, the uneasy dragoon walked with an air of soldierly coolness towards the dwellings, signing at the same time to one of his companions, who was regarding him from a distance, to approach.

"Now dost thou believe, witless Dudley, that the four fingers of thy clumsy hand have numbered the full amount of all that thou callest my listenings?" said Faith, when she thought no other ear but his to whom she spoke could catch her words, and at the same time laughing merrily beneath her heifer, though still speaking with a vexation she could not entirely repress.

"Have I spoken aught but truth? It is not for such as I to give lessons in journeying, to one who follows the honest trade of a man-hunter. I have said that which all who dwell in these parts know to be reasonable."

"Surely nought else. But truth is made so powerful in thy hands, that it needs be taken, like a bitter healing draught, with closed eyes and at many swallows. One who drinketh of it too freely, may well-nigh be strangled. I marvel that he who is so vigilant in providing for the cares of others, should take so little heed of those he is set to guard."

"I know not thy meaning, Faith. When was danger near the valley, and my musket wanting?"

"The good piece is truer to duty than its master Thou mayest have lawful license to sleep on thy post, for we maidens know nothing of the pleasure of the Captain in these matters; but it would be as seemly, if not as soldierly, to place the arms at the postern and thyself in the chambers, when next thou hast need of watching and sleeping in the same hour."

Dudley looked as confused as one of his mould and unbending temperament might well be, though he stubbornly refused to understand the allusion of his offended companion.

"Thou hast not discussed with the trooper from over sea in vain," he said, "since thou speakest so wisely of watches and arms."

"Truly he hath much schooled me in the matter."

"Umph! and what may be the amount of his teaching?"

"That he who sleepeth at a postern should neither talk too boldly of the enemy, nor expect maidens to put too much trust——"

"In what, Faith?"

"Thou surely knowest I mean in his watchfulness. My life on it, had one happened to pass at a later hour than common near the night-post of that gentle-spoken soldier, he would not have been found, like a sentinel of this household, in the second watch of the night that is gone, dreaming of the good things of the Madam's buttery."

"Didst truly come then, girl?" said Eben, dropping his voice, and equally manifesting his satisfaction and his shame. "But thou knowest, Faith, that the labor had fallen behind in behalf of the scouting party, and that the toil of yesterday exceeded that of our usual burthens. Nevertheless, I keep the postern again to-night, from eight to twelve and——"

"Will make a goodly rest of it, I doubt not. No he who hath been so vigilant throughout the day must needs tire of the task as night draws on. Fare thee well, wakeful Dudley; if thine eyes should open on the morrow, be thankful that the maidens have not stitched thy garments to the palisadoes!"

Notwithstanding the efforts of the young man to detain her, the light-footed girl eluded his grasp, and, bearing her burden towards the dairy, she tripped along the path with a half-averted face, in which triumph and repentance were already struggling for the possession.

In the mean time, the leader of the messengers and his military subordinate had a long and interesting conference. When it was ended, the former took his way to the apartment in which Mark Heathcote was wont to pass those portions of his time that were not occupied in his secret strivings for the faith, or in exercise without, while superintending the laborers in the fields. With some little circumlocution, which was intended to mask his real motives, the agent of the King announced his intention to take his final departure that very night.

"I felt it a duty, as one who has gained experience in arms by some practice in the wars of Europe," he said, "to tarry in thy dwelling while danger threatened from the lurking savage. It would ill become soldiers to speak of their intentions; but had the alarm in truth sounded, thou wilt give faith, when I say that the block-house would not have been lightly yielded! I shall make report to them that sent me, that in Captain Mark Heathcote, Charles hath a loyal subject, and the Constitution a firm supporter. The rumors, of a seemingly mistaken description, which have led us hither, shall be contradicted; and doubtless it will be found, that some accident hath given rise to the deception. Should there be occasion to dwell on the particulars of the late alarm, I trust the readiness of my followers to do good service to one of the King's subjects will not be overlooked."

"It is the striving of an humble spirit to speak nought evil of its fellows, and to conceal no good," returned the reserved Puritan "If thou hast found thy abode in my dwelling to thy liking, thou art welcome; and if duty or pleasure calleth thee to quit it, peace go with thee. It will be useful to unite with us in asking that thy passage through the wilderness may be unharmed; that he who watcheth over the meanest of his creatures should take thee in his especial keeping, and that the savage heathen——"

"Dost think the savage out of his villages?" demanded the messenger, with an indecorous rapidity, that cut short the enumeration of the particular blessings and dangers that his host thought it meet to include in the leave-taking prayer.

"Thou surely hast not tarried with us to aid in the defence, and yet feel it doubtful that thy services might be useful!" observed Mark Heathcote, drily.

"I would the Prince of Darkness had thee and all the other diabolicals of these woods in his own good gripe!" muttered the messenger between his teeth; and then, as if guided by a spirit that could not long be quelled, he assumed something more of his unbridled and natural air, boldly declining to join in the prayer on the plea of haste, and the necessity of his looking in person to the movements of his followers. "But this need not prevent thee, worthy Captain, from pouring out an asking in our behalf, while we are in the saddle," he concluded, 'for ourselves, there remaineth much of thy previously-bestowed pious aliment to be digested; though we doubt not, that should thy voice be raised in our behalf, while journeying along the first few leagues of the forest, the tread of the hacks would not be heavier, and, it is certainty, that we ourselves should be none the worse for the favor."

Then casting a glance of ill-concealed levity at one of his followers, who had come to say that their steeds awaited, he made the parting salutation with an air, in which the respect that one like the Puritan could scarce fail to excite, struggled with his habitual contempt for things of a serious character.

The family of Mark Heathcote, the lowest dependant included, saw these strangers depart with great inward satisfaction. Even the maidens, in whom nature, in moments weaker than common, had awakened some of the lighter vanities, were gladly rid of gallants, who could not soothe their ears with the unction of flattery, without frequently giving great offence to their severe principles, by light and irreverent allusions to things on which they themselves were accustomed to think with fitting awe. Eben Dudley could scarcely conceal the chuckle with which he saw the party bury themselves in the forest, though neither he, nor any of the more instructed in such matters, believed they incurred serious risk from their sudden enterprise.

The opinions of the scouts proved to be founded on accurate premises. That and many a subsequent night passed without alarm. The season continued to advance, and the laborers pursued their toil to its close, without another appeal to their courage, or any additional reasons for vigilance. Whittal Ring followed his colts with impunity, among the recesses of the neighboring forests; and the herds of the family went and came, as long as the weather would permit them to range the woods, in regularity and peace. The period of the alarm, and the visit of the agents of the Crown, came to be food for tradition; and during the succeeding winter, the former often furnished motive of merriment around the blazing fires that were so necessary to the country and the season.

Still there existed in the family a living memorial of the unusual incidents of that night. The captive remained, long after the events which had placed him in the power of the Heathcotes were beginning to be forgotten.

A desire to quicken the seeds of spiritual regeneration, which, however dormant they might be, old Mark Heathcote believed to exist in the whole family of man, and consequently in the young heathen as well as in others, had become a sort of ruling passion in the Puritan. The fashions and mode of thinking of the times had a strong leaning towards superstition; and it was far from difficult for a man of his ascetic habits and exaggerated doctrines, to believe that a special interposition had cast the boy into his hands, for some hidden but mighty purpose, that time in the good season would not fail to reveal.

Notwithstanding the strong coloring of fanaticism which tinged the characters of the religionists of those days, they were rarely wanting in worldly discretion. The agents they saw fit to employ, in order to aid the more hidden purposes of Providence, were in common useful and rational. Thus, while Mark never forgot to summon the lad from his prison at the hour of prayer, or to include an especial asking in behalf of the ignorant heathen in general and of this chosen youth in particular, he hesitated to believe that a manifest miracle would be exerted in his favor. That no blame might attach to the portion of duty that was confided to human means, he had recourse to the discreet agency of kindness and unremitted care. But all attempts to lure the lad into the habits of a civilized man, were completely unsuccessful. As the severity of the weather increased, the compassionate and thoughtful Ruth endeavored to induce him to adopt the garments that were found so necessary to the comfort of men who were greatly his superiors in hardihood and in strength. Clothes, decorated in a fashion suited to the taste of an Indian, were considerately provided, and entreaties and threats were both freely used, with a view to make the captive wear them. On one occasion, he was even forcibly clad by Eben Dudley; and being brought, in the unwonted guise, into the presence of old Mark, the latter offered up an especial petition that the youth might be made to feel the merits of this concession to the principles of a chastened and instructed man. But within an hour, the stout woodsman, who had been made on the occasion so active an instrument of civilization, announced to the admiring Faith that the experiment was unsuccessful; or, as Eben somewhat irreverently described the extraordinary effort of the Puritan, "the heathen hath already resumed his skin leggings and painted waist-cloth, notwithstanding the Captain has strove to pin better garments on his back, by virtue of a prayer that might have clothed the nakedness of a whole tribe." In short, the result proved, in the case of this lad, as similar experiments have since proved in so many other instances, the difficulty of tempting one trained in the freedom and ease of a savage, to consent to admit of the restraints of a state of being that is commonly thought to be so much superior. In every instance in which the youthful captive had liberty of choice, he disdainfully rejected the customs of the whites; adhering with a singular, and almost heroic pertinacity to the usages of his people and his condition.

The boy was not kept in his bondage without extraordinary care. Once, when trusted in the fields, he had openly attempted to escape; nor was the possession of his person recovered without putting the speed of Eben Dudley and Reuben Ring to a more severe trial, as was confessed by the athletic young borderers themselves, than any they had hitherto undergone. From that moment, he was never permitted to pass the palisadoes. When duty called the laborers afield, the captive was invariably secured in his prison, where, as some compensation for his confinement, he was supposed to enjoy the benefit of long and familiar communication with Mark Heathcote, who had the habit of passing many hours of each day, and, not unfrequently long portions of the night, too, within the retirement of the block-house. During the time only when the gates were closed, or when some one of strength and activity sufficient to control his movements was present, was the lad permitted to stroll, at will, among the buildings of the border fortress. This liberty he never failed to exercise, and often in a manner that overcame the affectionate Ruth with a painful excess of sensibility.

Instead of joining in the play of the other children, the young captive would stand aloof, and regard their sports with a vacant eye, or, drawing near to the palisadoes, he often passed hours in gazing wistfully at those endless forests in which he first drew breath, and which probably contained all that was most prized in the estimation of his simple judgment. Ruth, touched to the heart by this silent but expressive exhibition of suffering, endeavored in vain to win his confidence, with a view of enticing him into employments that might serve to relieve his care. The resolute but still quiet boy would not be lured into a forgetfulness of his origin. He appeared to comprehend the kind intentions of his gentle mistress, and frequently he even suffered himself to be led by the mother into the centre of her own joyous and merry offspring; but it was only to look upon their amusements with his former cold air, and to return, at the first opportunity, to his beloved site at the pickets. Still there were singular and even mysterious evidences of a growing consciousness of the nature of the discourse of which he was occasionally an auditor, that would have betrayed greater familiarity with the language and opinions of the inhabitants of the valley, than his known origin and his absolute withdrawal from communication could give reason to expect. This important and inexplicable fact was proved by the frequent and meaning glances of his dark eye, when aught was uttered in his hearing that affected, ever so remotely, his own condition; and, once or twice, by the haughty gleamings of ferocity that escaped him, when Eben Dudley was heard to vaunt the prowess of the white men in their encounters with the original owners of the country. The Puritan did not fail to note these symptoms of a budding intelligence, as the pledges of a fruit that would more than reward his pious toil; and they served to furnish a great relief to certain occasional repugnance, which all his zeal could not entirely subdue, at being the instrument of causing so much suffering to one who, after all, had inflicted no positive wrong on himself.

At the period of which we are writing, the climate of these States differed materially from that which is now known to their inhabitants. A winter in the Province of Connecticut was attended by many successive falls of snow, until the earth was entirely covered with firmly compressed masses of the frozen element. Occasional thaws and passing storms of rain, that were driven away by a return of the clear and cutting cold of the north-western gales, were wont at times to lay a covering on the ground, that was congealed to the consistency of ice, until men, and not unfrequently beasts, and sometimes sleighs, were seen moving on its surface, as on the bed of a frozen lake. During the extremity of a season like this, the hardy borderers, who could not toil in their customary pursuits, were wont to range the forest in quest of game, which, driven for food to known resorting places in the woods, then fell most easily a prey to the intelligence and skill of such men as Eben Dudley and Reuben Ring.

The youths never left the dwellings on these nunts, without exciting the most touching interest in their movements, on the part of the Indian boy. On all such occasions, he would linger at the loops of his prison throughout the day, listening intently to the reports of the distant muskets, as they resounded in the forest; and the only time, during a captivity of so many months, that he was ever seen to smile, was when he examined the grim look and muscular claws of a dead panther, that had fallen beneath the aim of Dudley, in one of these excursions to the mountains. The compassion of all the borderers was powerfully awakened in behalf of the patient and dignified young sufferer, and gladly would they have given their captive the pleasure of joining in the chase, had not the task been one that was far from easy of accomplishment. The former of the woodsmen just mentioned had even volunteered to lead him like a hound in a leash; but this was a species of degradation against which it was certain that a young Indian, ambitious of the character and jealous of the dignity of a warrior, would have openly rebelled.

The quick interest of the observant Ruth had, as it has been seen, early detected a growing intelligence in the boy. The means by which one, who never mingled in the employments, and who rarely seemed to listen to the dialogues of the family could come to comprehend the meaning of a language that is found sufficiently difficult for a scholar, were however as much of a mystery to her, as to all around her. Still, by the aid of that instinctive tact which so often enlightens the mind of woman was she certain of the fact. Profiting by this know ledge, she assumed the task of endeavoring to obtai an honorary pledge from her protegé, that, if permitted to join the hunters, he would return to the valley at the end of the day. But though the language of the woman was gentle as her own kind nature, and her entreaties that he would give some evidence of having comprehended her meaning were zealous and oft repeated, not the smallest symptom of intelligence, on this occasion, could be extracted from her pupil. Disappointed, and not without sorrow, Ruth had abandoned the compassionate design in despair, when, on a sudden, the old Puritan, who had been a silent spectator of her fruitless efforts, announced his faith in the integrity of the lad, and his intention to permit him to make one of the very next party, that should leave the habitations.

The cause of this sudden change in the hitherto stern watchfulness of Mark Heathcote was, like so many other of his impulses, a secret in his own bosom. It has just been said, that during the time Ruth was engaged in her kind and fruitless experiment to extract some evidence of intelligence from the boy, the Puritan was a close and interested observer of her efforts. He appeared to sympathize in her disappointment, but the weal of those unconverted tribes who were to be led from the darkness of their ways by the instrumentality of this youth, was far too important to admit the thought of rashly losing the vantage-ground he had gained, in the radually-expanding intellect of the boy, by running the hazard of an escape. To all appearance, the intention of permitting him to quit the defences had therefore been entirely abandoned, when old Mark so suddenly announced a change of resolution. The conjectures on the causes of this unlooked-for determination were exceedingly various. Some beieved that the Puritan had been favored with a mysterious intimation of the pleasure of Providence, in the matter; and others thought that, beginning to despair of success in his undertaking, he was willing to seek for a more visible manifestation of its purposes, by hazarding the experiment of trusting the boy to the direction of his own impulses. All appeared to be of opinion that if the lad returned, the circumstance might be set down to the intervention of a miracle. Still, with his resolution once taken, the purpose of Mark Heathcote remained unchanged. He announced this unexpected intention, after one of his long and solitary visits to the block-house, where it is possible he had held a powerful spiritual strife on the occasion; and, as the weather was exceedingly favorable for such an object, he commanded his dependants to prepare to make the sortie on the following morning.

A sudden and an uncontrollable gleam of delight flashed on the dark features of the captive, when Ruth was about to place in his hands the bow of her own son, and, by signs and words, she gave him to understand that he was to be permitted to use it in the free air of the forest. But the exhibition of pleasure disappeared as quickly as it had been betrayed. When the lad received the weapons, it was rather with the manner of a hunter accustomed to their use, than of one to whose hands they had so long been strangers. As he left the gates of Wish-Ton-Wish, the handmaidens of Ruth clustered about him, in wondering interest; for it was strange to see a youth so long guarded with jealous care, again free and unwatched. Notwithstanding their ordinary dependence on the secret lights and great wisdom of the Puritan, there was a very general impression that the lad, around whose presence there was so much that was mysterious and of interest to their own security, was now to be gazed upon for the last time. The boy himself was unmoved to the last. Still he paused, with his foot on the threshold of the dwelling, and appeared to regard Ruth and her young offspring with momentary concern. Then, assuming the calm air of an Indian warrior, he suffered his eye to grow cold and vacant, following with a nimble step the hunters who were already passing without the palisadoes.

CHAPTER VIII.

"Well, I am your theme: you have the start of me. I am dejected; I am not able to answer the Welsh flannel; ignorance itself is a plummet over me: use me as you will."

MERRY WIVES OF WINDSOR.

POETS, aided by the general longing of human nature, have given a reputation to the Spring, that it rarely merits. Though this imaginative class of writers have said so much of its balmy airs and odoriferous gales, we find it nearly everywhere the most reluctant, churlish, and fickle of the four seasons. It is the youth of the year, and, like that probationary period of life, most fitted to afford the promise of better things. There is a constant struggle between reality and hope throughout the whole of this slow-moving and treacherous period, which has an unavoidable tendency to deceive. All that is said of its grateful productions is fallacious, for the earth is as little likely to yield a generous tribute without the quickening influence of the summer heats, as man is wont to bring forth commendable fruits without the agency of a higher moral power than any he possesses in virtue of his innate propensities. On the other hand, the fall of the year, possesses a sweetness, a repose, and a consistency, which may be justly likened to the decline of a well-spent life. It is, in all countries and in every climate, the period when physical and moral causes unite to furnish the richest sources of enjoyment. If the Spring is the time of hope, Autumn is the season of fruition. There is just enough of change to give zest to the current of existence, while there is too little of vicissitude to be pregnant of disappointment. Succeeding to the nakedness of Winter, the Spring is grateful by comparison; while the glories of Autumn are enjoyed, after the genial powers of Summer have been lavishly expended.

In obedience to this great law of the earth, let poets sing and fancy as they may, the Spring and Autumn of America partake largely of the universally distinctive characters of the rival seasons. What Nature has done on this Continent, has not been done niggardly; and, while we may boast of a decline of the year that certainly rivals, and, with few exceptions, eclipses the glories of most of the climates of the old world, the opening months rarely fail of equalizing the gifts of Providence, by a very decided exhibition of all the disagreeable qualities for which they are remarkable.

More than half a year had elapsed, between the time when the Indian boy had been found lurking in the valley of the Heathcotes, and that day when he was first permitted to go into the forest, fettered by no other restraint than the moral tie which the owner of the valley either knew, or fancied, would not fail to cause him to return to a bondage he had found so irksome. It was April; but it was April as the month was known a century ago in Connecticut, and as it is even now so often found to disappoint all expectations of that capricious season of the year. The weather had returned suddenly and violently to the rigor of winter. A thaw had been succeeded by a storm of snow and sleet, and the interlude of the spring-time of blossoms had terminated with a biting gale from the north-west, which had apparently placed a permanent seal on the lingering presence of a second February.

On the morning that Content led his followers into the forest, they issued from the postern clad in coats of skin. Their lower limbs were protected by the coarse leggings which they had worn in so many previous hunts, during the past winter, if that might be called past which had returned, weakened but little of its keenness, and bearing all the outward marks of January. When last seen, Eben Dudley, the heaviest of the band, was moving firmly on the crust of the snow, with a step as sure as if he had trodden on the frozen earth itself. More than one of the maidens declared, that though they had endeavored to trace the footsteps of the hunters from the palisadoes, it would have exceeded even the sagacity of an Indian eye to follow their trail along the icy path they travelled.

Hour after hour passed, without bringing tidings from the chase. The reports of fire-arms had indeed been occasionally heard, ringing among the arches of the woods; and broken echoes were, for some hours, rolling from one recess of the hills to another. But even these signs of the presence of the hunters gradually receded with the advance of the day; and, long ere the sun had gained the meridian, and its warmth, at that advanced season not without power, was shed into the valley, the whole range of the adjoining forest lay in its ordinary dull and solemn silence.

The incident of the hunt, apart from the absence of the Indian boy, was one of too common occurrence to give birth to any particular motives of excitement. Ruth quietly busied herself among her women, and when the recollection of those who were scouring the neighboring forest came at all to her mind, it was coupled with the care with which the was providing to administer to their comforts after the fatigue of a day of extraordinary personal efforts. This was a duty never lightly performed. Her situation was one eminently fitted to foster the best affections of woman, since it admitted of few temptations to yield to other than the most natural feeling; she was, in consequence, known on all occasions to exercise them with the devotedness of her sex.

"Thy father and his companions will look on ou care with pleasure," said the thoughtful matron to her youthful image, as she directed a more than usual provision of her larder to be got in readiness for the hunters; "home is ever sweetest after toil and exposure."

"I doubt if Mark be not ready to faint with so weary a march," said the child already introduced by the name of Martha; "he is young to go into the woods, with scouters tall as great Dudley."

"And the heathen," added the little Ruth, "he is young too as Mark, though more used to the toil. It may be, mother, that he will never come to us more!"

"That would grieve our venerable parent; for thou knowest, Ruth, that he hath hopes of working on the mind of the boy, until his savage nature shall yield to the secret power. But the sun is falling behind the hill, and the evening is coming in cool as winter; go to the postern, and look out upon the fields. I would know if there be any signs of thy father and his party."

Though Ruth gave this mandate to her daughter, she did not the less neglect to exercise her own faculties in the same grateful office. While the children went, as they were ordered, to the outer gate, the matron herself ascended to the lower apartment of the block, and, from its different loops, she took a long and anxious survey of the limited prospect. The shadows of the trees, that lined the western side of the view, were already thrown far across the broad sheet of frozen snow, and the sudden chill which succeeded the disappearance of the sun announced the rapid approach of a night that promised to support the severe character of the past day. A freezing wind, which had brought with it the cold airs of the great lakes, and which had even triumphed over the more natural influence of an April sun, had however fallen, leaving a temperature not unlike that which dwells in the milder seasons of the year among the glaciers of the upper Alps.

Ruth was too long accustomed to such forest scenes, and to such a "lingering of winter in the lap of May," to feel, on their account, any additional uneasiness. But the hour had now arrived when she had reason to look for the return of the hunters. With the expectation of seeing their forms issuing from the forest, came the anxiety which is an unavoidable attendant of disappointment. The shadows continued to deepen in the valley, until the gloom thickened to the darkness of night, without bringing any tidings from those without.

When a delay, which was unusual in the members of a family circumstanced like that of the Wish-Ton-Wish, came to be coupled with various little observations that had been made during the day, it was thought that reasons for alarm were beginning, at each instant, to grow more plausible. Reports of fire-arms had been heard, at an early hour, from opposite points in the hills, and in a manner too distinct to be mistaken for echoes; a certain proof that the different members of the hunt had separated in the forest. Under such circumstances, it was not difficult for the imagination of a wife and a mother, of a sister, or of her who secretly confessed a still more tender interest in some one of the hunters, to conjure to the imagination the numberless dangers to which those who were engaged in these expeditions were known to be exposed.

"I doubt that the chase hath drawn them further from the valley than is fitting for the hour and the season," observed Ruth to her maidens, who had gathered in a group about her, at a point that overlooked as much of the cleared land around the buildings, as the darkness would allow; "the gravest man becomes thoughtless as the unreflecting child when led by the eagerness of the pursuit. It is the duty of older heads to think for those that want experience—but into what indiscreet complaints are my fears leading! It may be that my husband is even now striving to collect his party, in order to return. Hast any heard his conch sounding the recall?"

"The woods are still as the day the first echo of the axe was heard among the trees," returned Faith. "I did hear that which sounded like a strain of brawling Dudley's songs, but it proved to be no more than the lowing of one of his own oxen. Perchance the animal misseth some of its master's care."

"Whittal Ring hath looked to the beasts, and it may not be that he hath neglected to feed, among others, the creatures of Dudley. Thy mind is given to levity, Faith, in the matter of this young man. It is not seemly that one of thy years and sex should manifest so great displeasure at the name of a youth, who is of an honest nature, and of honest habits, too, though he may appear ungainly to the eye, and have so little favor with one of thy disposition."

"I did not fashion the man," said Faith, biting her lip, and tossing her head; "nor is it aught to me whether he be gainly or not. As to my favor when he asks it, the man shall not wait long to know the answer. But is not yon figure the fellow himself Madam Heathcote?—here, coming in from the eastern hill, along the orchard path. The form I mean is just here; you may see it, at this moment, turning by the bend in the brook."

"There is one of a certainty, and it should be one of our hunting party, too; and yet he doth not seem to be of a size or of a gait like that of Eben Dudley. Thou shouldst have a knowledge of thy kindred, girl; to me it seemeth thy brother."

"Truly, it may be Reuben Ring; still it hath much of the swagger of the other, though their stature be nearly equal—the manner of carrying the musket is much the same with all the borderers too—one cannot easily tell the form of man from a stump by this light—and—yet do I think it will prove to be the loitering Dudley."

"Loiterer or not, he is the first to return from this long and weary chase," said Ruth, breathing heavily, like one who regretted that the truth were so. "Go thou to the postern, and admit him, girl. I ordered bolts to be drawn, for I like not to leave a fortress defended by a female garrison, at this hour, with open gates. I will hie to the dwelling, and see to the comforts of those who are a-hungered, since it will not be long ere we shall have more of them at hand."

Faith complied, with affected indifference and sufficient delay. By the time she had reached the place of admission, a form was seen ascending the acclivity, and taking the direction which led to the same spot. In the next minute, a rude effort to enter announced an arrival without.

"Gently, Master Dudley," said the wilful girl, who held the bolt with one hand, though she maliciously delayed to remove it. "We know thou art powerful of arm, and yet the palisadoes will scarcely fall at thy touch. Here are no Sampsons to pull down the pillars on our heads. Perhaps we may not be disposed to give entrance to them who stay abroad out of all season."

"Open the postern, girl," said Eben Dudley "after which, if thou hast aught to say, we shall be better convenienced for discourse."

"It may be that thy conversation is most agreeable when heard from without. Render an account of thy backslidings, throughout this day, penitent Dudley, that I may take pity on thy weariness. But lest hunger should have overcome thy memory, I may serve to help thee to the particulars. The first of thy offences was to consume more than thy portion of the cold meats; the second was to suffer Reuben Ring to kill the deer, and for thee to claim it; and a third was the trick thou hast of listening so much to thine own voice, that even the beasts fled thee, from dislike of thy noise."

"Thou triflest unseasonably, Faith; I would speak with the Captain, without delay."

"It may be that he is better employed than to desire such company. Thou art not the only strange animal by many who hath roared at the gate of Wish-Ton-Wish."

"Have any come within the day, Faith?" demanded the borderer, with the interest such an event would be likely to create in the mind of one who habitually lived in so great retirement.

"What sayest thou to a second visit from the gentle-spoken stranger? he who favored us with so much gay discourse, the by-gone fall of the year. That would be a guest fit to receive! I warrant me his knock would not be heard a second time."

"The gallant had better beware the moon!" exclaimed Dudley, striking the but of his musket against the ice with so much force as to cause his companion to start, in alarm. "What fool's errand hath again brought him to prick his nag so deep into the forest?"

"Nay, thy wit is ever like the unbroken colt, a headstrong run-away. I said not, in full meaning that the man had come; I only invited thee to give an opinion in the event that he should arrive unexpectedly, though I am far from certain that any here ever expect to see his face again."

"This is foolish prating," returned the youth, provoked at the exhibition of jealousy into which he had been incautiously betrayed. "I tell thee to withdraw the bolt, for I have great need to speak with the Captain, or with his son."

"Thou mayst open thy mind to the first, if he will listen to what thou hast to say," returned the girl, removing the impediment to his entrance; "but thou wilt sooner get the ear of the other by remaining at the gate, since he has not yet come in from the forest."

Dudley recoiled a pace, and repeated her words in the tone of one who admitted a feeling of alarm to mingle with his surprise.

"Not in from the forest!" he said; "surely there are none abroad, now that I am home!"

"Why dost say it? I have put my jibes upon thee more in payment of ancient transgressions than for any present offence. So far from being last, thou art the first of the hunters we have yet seen. Go in to the Madam without delay, and tell her of the danger, if any there be, that we take speedy measures for oui safety."

"That would do little good, truly," muttered the borderer, like one musing. "Stay thou here, and watch the postern, Faith; I will back to the woods; for a timely word, or a signal blown from my conch, might quicken their footsteps."

What madness hath beset thee, Dudley! Thou wouldst not go into the forest again, at this hour and alone, if there be reason for fear! Come farther within the gate, man, that I may draw the bolt the Madam will wonder that we tarry here so long."

"Ha!—I hear feet moving in the meadow; I know it by the creaking of the snow; the others are not lagging."

Notwithstanding the apparent certainty of the young man, instead of going forth to meet his friends, he withdrew a step, and with his own hand drew the bolt that Faith had just desired might be fastened; taking care at the same time to let fall a swinging bar of wood, which gave additional security to the fastenings of the postern. His apprehensions, if any such had induced this caution, were however unnecessary; for ere he had time to make, or even to reflect on any further movement, admission was demanded in the well-known voice of the son of him who owned the valley. The bustle of the arrival, for with Content entered a group of companions loaded with venison, put an end to the dialogue. Faith seized the opportunity to glide away in the obscurity, in order to announce to her mistress that the hunters had returned—an office that she performed without entering at all into the particulars of her own interview with Eben Dudley.

It is needless to dwell on the satisfaction with which Ruth received her husband and son, after the uneasiness she had just suffered. Though the severe manners of the Province admitted of no violent exhibition of passing emotions, secret joy was reigning in the mild eyes and glowing about the flushed cheeks of the discreet matron, while she personally officiated in the offices of the evening meal.

The party had returned teeming with no extraordinary incidents; nor did they appear to be disturbed with any of that seriousness of air which had so unequivocally characterized the deportment of him who had preceded them. On the contrary, each had his quiet tale to relate, now perhaps at the expense of a luckless companion, and sometimes in order that no part of his own individual skill, as a hunter, should be unknown. The delay was accounted for, as similar delays are commonly explained, by distance and the temptations of an unusually successful chase. As the appetites of those who had passed the day in the exciting toil were keen and the viands tempting, the first half-hour passed quickly, as all such half-hours are wont to pass, in garrulous recitals of personal exploits, and of the hairbreadth escapes of deer, which, had fortune not been fickle, should have now been present as trophies of the skill of the hand by which they fell. It was only after personal vanity was sufficiently appeased, and when the hunger even of a border-man could achieve no more, that the hunters began to look about them with a diminished excitement, and to discuss the events of the day with a fitting calmness, and with a discretion more suited to their ordinary self-command.

"We lost the sound of thy conch, wandering Dudley, as we fell into the deep hollow of the mountain," said Content, in a pause of the discourse; "since which time, neither eye nor ear of any has had trace of thy movements, until we met thee at the postern, stationed like a looker-out on his watch."

The individual addressed had mingled in none of the gaiety of the hour. While others fed freely, or joined in the quiet joke, which could escape the lips of even men chastened as his companions, Eben Dudley had tasted sparingly of the viands. Nor had the muscles of his hard countenance once relaxed in a smile. A gravity and silence so extraordinary, in one so little accustomed to exhibit either quality, did not fail to attract attention. It was universally ascribed to the circumstance that he had returned empty-handed from the hunt: and now that one having authority had seen fit to give such a direction to the discourse, the imaginary delinquent was not permitted to escape unscathed.

"The butcher had little to do with this day's killing," said one of the young men; "as a punishment for his absence from the slaughter, he should be made to go on the hill and bring in the two bucks he will find hanging from a maple sapling near to the drinking spring. Our meat should pass through his hands in some fashion or other, else will it lack savor."

"Ever since the death of the straggling wether, the trade of Eben hath been at a stand," added another; "the down-hearted youth seems like one ready to give up his calling to the first stranger that shall ask it."

"Creatures which run at large prove better mutton than the stalled wether," continued a third; "and thereby custom was getting low before this hunt. Beyond a doubt, he has a full supply for all who shall be likely to seek venison in his stall."

Ruth observed that the countenance of her husband grew grave, at these allusions to an event he had always seemed to wish forgotten; and she interposed with a view to lead the minds of those who listened, back to matter more fitting to be discussed.

"How is this?" she exclaimed in haste; "hath the stout Dudley lost any of his craft? I have never counted with greater certainty on the riches of the table, than when he hath been sent among the hills for the fat deer, or the tender turkey. It would much grieve me to learn that he beginneth to lack the hunter's skill."

"The man is getting melancholy with over-feeding," muttered the wilful tones of one busied among the vessels, in a distant part of the room. "He taketh his exercise alone, in order that none need discover the failing. I think he be much disposed to go over sea, in order to become a trooper."

Until now, the subject of these mirthful attacks had listened like one too confident of his established reputation to feel concern; but at the sound of the last speaker's voice, he grasped the bushy covering of one entire cheek in his hand, and turning a reproachful and irritated glance at the already half-repentant eye of Faith Ring, all his natural spirit returned.

"It may be that my skill hath left me," he said, "and that I love to be alone, rather than to be troubled with the company of some that might readily be named, no reference being had to such gallants as ride up and down the colony, putting evil opinions into the thoughts of honest men's daughters; but why is Eben Dudley to bear all the small shot of your humors, when there is another who, it might seem, hath strayed even further from your trail than he?"

Eye sought eye, and each youth by hasty glances endeavored to read the countenances of all the rest in company, in order to learn who the absentee might be. The young borderers shook their heads, as the features of every well-known face were recognised, and a general exclamation of denial was about to break from their lips, when Ruth exclaimed—

"Truly, the Indian is wanting!"

So constant was the apprehension of danger from the savages, in the breasts of those who dwelt on that exposed frontier, that every man arose at the words, by a sudden and common impulse, and each individual gazed about him in a surprise that was a little akin to dismay.

"The boy was with us when we quitted the forest," said Content, after a moment of death-like stillness. "I spoke to him in commendation of his activity, and of the knowledge he had shown in beating up the secret places of the deer; though there is little reason to think my words were understood."

"And were it not sinful to take such solemn evidence in behalf of so light a matter, I could be qualified on the Book itself, that he was at my elbow as we entered the orchard," added Reuben Ring, a man renowned in that little community for the accuracy of his vision

"And I will make oath or declaration of any sort, lawful or conscientious, that he came not within the postern when it was opened by my own hand," returned Eben Dudley. "I told off the number of the party as you passed, and right sure am I that no red skin entered."

"Canst thou tell us aught of the lad?" demanded Ruth, quick to take the alarm on a subject that had so long exercised her care, and given food to her imagination.

"Nothing. With me he hath not been since the turn of the day. I have not seen the face of living man from that moment, unless in truth one of mysterious character, whom I met in the forest, may be so called."

The manner in which the woodsman spoke was too serious and too natural, not to give birth in his auditors to some of his own gravity. Perhaps the appearance of the Puritan, at that moment, aided in quieting the levity that had been uppermost in the minds of the young men; for, it is certain, that when he entered, a deeper and a general curiosity came over the countenances of all present. Content waited a moment in respectful silence, till his father had moved slowly through the circle, and then he prepared himself to look further into an affair that began to assume the appearance of matter worthy of investigation.

CHAPTER IX.

> "Last night of all,
> When yon same star, that's westward from the pole,
> Had made its course to illume that part of heaven
> Where now it burns, Marcellus, and myself
> The bell then beating one——"
> "Peace, break thee off; look, where it comes again!"
>
> HAMLET.

It is our duty, as faithful historians of the events recorded in this homely legend, to conceal no circumstance which may throw the necessary degree of light on its incidents, nor any opinion that may serve for the better instruction of the reader in the characters of its actors. In order that this obligation may be discharged with sufficient clearness and precision, it has now become necessary to make a short digression from the immediate action of the tale.

Enough has been already shown, to prove that the Heathcotes lived at a time, and in a country, where very quaint and peculiar religious dogmas had the ascendancy. At a period when visible manifestations of the goodness of Providence, not only in spiritual but in temporal gifts, were confidently expected and openly proclaimed, it is not at all surprising that more evil agencies should be thought to exercise their power in a manner that is somewhat opposed to the experience of our own age. As we have no wish, however, to make these pages the medium of a theological or metaphysical controversy, we shall deal tenderly with certain important events, that most of the writers, who were cotemporary with the facts, assert took place in the Colonies of New-England, at and about the period of which we are now writing. It is sufficiently known that the art of witchcraft, and one even still more diabolical and direct in its origin, were then believed to flourish, in that quarter of the world, to a degree that was probably in a very just proportion to the neglect with which most of the other arts of life were treated.

There is so much grave and respectable authority, to prove the existence of these evil influences, that it requires a pen hardier than any we wield, to attack them without a suitable motive. "Flashy people," says the learned and pious Cotton Mather, Doctor of Divinity and Fellow of the Royal Society, "may burlesque these things; but when hundreds of the most sober people, in a country where they have as much mother wit, certainly, as the rest of mankind, *know them to be true*, nothing but the absurd and froward spirit of Sadducism can question them." Against this grave and credited authority, we pretend to raise no question of scepticism. We submit to the testimony of such a writer as conclusive, though as credulity is sometimes found to be bounded by geograpical limits, and to possess something of a national character, it may be prudent to refer certain readers, who dwell in the other hemisphere, to the Common Law of England, on this interesting subject, as it is ingeniously expounded by Keeble and approved by the twelve judges of that highly civilized and enlightened island. With this brief reference to so grave authorities, in support of what we have now to offer, we shall return to the matter of the narrative, fully trusting that its incidents will throw some additional light on the subject of so deep and so general concern.

Content waited respectfully until his father had taken his seat, and then perceiving that the venerable Puritan had no immediate intention of moving personally in the affair, he commenced the examination of his dependant as follows; opening the matter with a seriousness that was abundantly warrant ed by the gravity of the subject itself.

"Thou hast spoken of one met in the forest," he said: "proceed with the purport of that interview, and tell us of what manner of man it was."

Thus directly interrogated, Eben Dudley disposed himself to give a full and satisfactory answer. First casting a glance around, so as to embrace every curious and eager countenance, and letting his look rest a little longer than common on a half-interested, half-incredulous, and a somewhat ironical dark eye, that was riveted on his own from a distant corner of the room, he commenced his statement as follows:

"It is known to you all," said the borderer, "that when we had gained the mountain-top, there was a division of our numbers, in such a fashion that each hunter should sweep his own range of the forest, in order that neither moose, deer, nor bear, might have reasonable chance of escape. Being of large frame and it may be of swifter foot than common, the young Captain saw fit to command Reuben Ring to flank one end of the line, and a man, who is nothing short of him in either speed, or strength, to do the same duty on the other. There was nothing particularly worthy of mention that took place on the flank I held, for the first two hours; unless indeed the fact, that three several times did I fall upon a maze of well-beaten deer-tracks, that as often led to nothing——"

"These are signs common to the woods, and they are no more than so many proofs that the animal has its sports, like any other playful creature, when not pressed by hunger or by danger," quietly observed Content.

"I pretend not to take those deceitful tracks much into the account," resumed Dudley; "but shortly after losing the sound of the conchs, I roused a noble buck from his lair beneath a thicket of hemlocks, and having the game in view, the chase led me wide-off towards the wilderness, it may have been the distance of two leagues."

"And in all that time, had you no fitting moment to strike the beast?"

"None whatever; nor, if opportunity had been given, am I bold to say that hand of mine would have been hardy enough to aim at its life."

"Was there aught in the deer, that a hunter should seek to spare it?"

"There was that in the deer, that might bring a Christian man to much serious reflection

"Deal more openly with the nature and appearance of the animal," said Content, a little less tranquil than usual; while the youths and maidens placed themselves in attitudes still more strongly denoting attention.

Dudley pondered an instant, and then he commenced a less equivocal enumeration of what he conceived to be the marvels of his tale.

"Firstly," he said, "there was no trail, neither to nor from the spot where the creature had made its lair; secondly, when roused, it took not the alarm, but leaped sportingly ahead, taking sufficient care to be beyond the range of musket, without ever becoming hid from the eye; and lastly its manner of disappearance was as worthy of mention as any other of its movements."

"And in what manner didst thou lose the creature?"

"I had gotten it upon the crest of a hillock, where true eye and steady hand might make sure of a buck of much smaller size, when—didst hear aught that might be accounted wonderful, at a season of the year when the snows are still lying on the earth?"

The auditors regarded one another curiously, each

endeavoring to recall some unwonted sound which might sustain a narrative that was fast obtaining the seducing interest of the marvellous.

"Wast sure, Charity, that the howl we heard from the forest was the yell of the beaten hound?" demanded a handmaiden of Ruth, of a blue-eyed companion, who seemed equally well disposed to contribute her share of evidence in support of any exciting legend.

"It might have been other," was the answer "though the hunters do speak of their having beaten the pup for restiveness."

"There was a tumult among the echoes, that sounded like the noises which follow the uproar of a falling tree," said Ruth, thoughtfully. "I remember to have asked if it might not be that some fierce beast had caused a general discharge of the musketry, but my father was of opinion that death had undermined some heavy oak."

"At what hour might this have happened?"

"It was past the turn of the day; for it was at the moment I bethought me of the hunger of those who had toiled since light, in the hills."

"That then was the sound I mean. It came not from falling tree, but was uttered in the air, far above all forests. Had it been heard by one better skilled in the secrets of nature——"

"He would say it thundered;" interrupted Faith Ring, who, unlike most of the other listeners, manifested little of the quality which was expressed by her name. "Truly, Eben Dudley hath done marvels in this hunt; he hath come in with a thunderbolt in his head, instead of a fat buck on his shoulders!"

"Speak reverently, girl, of that thou dost not comprehend," said Mark Heathcote, with stern authority. "Marvels are manifested equally to the ignorant and to the learned; and although vain-minded pretenders to philosophy affirm, that the warring of the elements is no more than nature working out its own purification, yet do we know, from all ancient authorities, that other manifestations are therein exhibited. Satan may have control over the magazines of the air; he can 'let off the ordnance of Heaven.' That 'the Prince of the Powers of Darkness hath as good a share in chemistry as goes to the making of Aurum Fulminans, is asserted by one of the wisest writers of our age."

From this declaration, and more particularly from the learning discovered in the Puritan's speech, there was no one so hardy as to dissent. Faith was glad to shrink back among the bevy of awe-struck maidens; while Content, after a sufficiently respectful pause, invited the woodsman, who was yet teeming with the most important part of his communication, to proceed.

"While my eye was searching for the lightning, which should in reason have attended that thunder, had it been uttered in the manner of nature, the buck had vanished; and when I rushed upon the hillock, in order to keep the game in view, a man mounting its opposite side came so suddenly upon me, that our muskets were at each other's breasts before either had time for speech."

"What manner of man was he?"

"So far as human judgment might determine, he seemed a traveller, who was endeavoring to push through the wilderness, from the towns below to the distant settlements of the Bay Province; but I account it exceeding wonderful, that the trail of a leaping buck should have brought us together in so unwonted a manner!"

"And didst thou see aught of the deer, after that encounter?"

"In the first hurry of the surprise, it did certainly appear as if an animal were bounding along the wood into a distant thicket; but it is known how readily one may be led by seeming probabilities into a false conclusion, and so I account that glimpse as delusion. No doubt, the animal, having done that which it was commissioned to perform, did then and there disappear, in the manner I have named."

"It might have been thus. And the stranger—had you discourse with him, before parting?"

"We tarried together a short hour. He related much marvellous matter of the experiences of the people, near the sea. According to the testimony of the stranger, the Powers of Darkness have been manifested in the Provinces in a hideous fashion. Numberless of the believers have been persecuted by the invisibles, and greatly have they endured suffering, both in soul and body."

"Of all this have I witnessed surprising instances, in my day," said Mark Heathcote, breaking the awful stillness that succeeded the annunciation of so heavy a visitation on the peace of the Colony, with his deep-toned and imposing voice. "Did he, with whom you conferred, enter into the particulars of the trials?"

"He spoke also of certain other signs that are thought to foretell the coming of trouble. When I named the weary chase that I had made, and the sound which came from the air, he said that these would be accounted trifles in the towns of the Bay where the thunder and its lightnings had done much evil work, the past season; Satan having especially shown his spite, by causing them to do injury to the houses of the Lord."

"There has long been reason to think that the pilgrimage of the righteous, into these wilds, will be visited by some fierce opposition of those envious natures, which, fostering evil themselves, cannot brook to look upon the toiling of such as strive to keep the narrow path. We will now resort to the only weapon it is permitted us to wield in this controversy, but which, when handled with diligence and zeal, never fails to lead to victory."

So saying, without waiting to hear more of the tale of Eben Dudley, old Mark Heathcote arose, and assuming the upright attitude usual among the people of his sect, he addressed himself to prayer. The grave and awe-struck but deeply confiding congregation imitated his example, and the lips of the Puritan had parted in the act of utterance, when a low, faltering note, like that produced by a wind instrument, rose on the outer air, and penetrated to the place where the family was assembled. A conch was suspended at the postern, in readiness to be used by any of the family whom accident or occupation should detain beyond the usual hour of closing the gates; and both by the direction and nature of this interruption, it would seem that an applicant for admission stood at the portal. The effect on the auditors was general and instantaneous. Notwithstanding the recent dialogue, the young men involuntarily sought their arms, while the startled females huddled together like a flock of trembling and timid deer.

"There is, of a certainty, a signal from without!" Content at length observed, after waiting to suffer the sounds to die away among the angles of the buildings. "Some hunter, who hath strayed from his path, claimeth hospitality."

Eben Dudley shook his head like one who dissented, but, having with all the other youths grasped his musket, he stood as undetermined as the rest concerning the course it was proper to pursue. It is uncertain how long this indecision might have continued, had no further summons been given; but he without appeared too impatient of delay to suffer much time to be lost. The conch sounded again, and with far better success than before. The blast was longer, louder, and bolder, than that which had first pierced the walls of the dwelling, rising full and rich on the air, as though one well practised in the use of the instrument had placed lips to the shell.

Content would scarcely have presumed to disobey a mandate coming from his father, had it been little in conformity with his own intentions. But second thoughts had already shown him the necessity of decision, and he was in the act of motioning to Dudley and Reuben Ring to follow, when the Puritan bade him look to the matter. Making a sign for the rest of the family to remain where they were, and arming himself with a musket which had more than once that day been proved to be of certain aim, he led the way to the postern which has already been so often mentioned.

"Who sounds at my gate?" demanded Content, when he and his followers had gained a position, under cover of a low earthen mound erected expressly for the purpose of commanding the entrance; "who summons a peaceful family, at this hour of the night, to their outer defences?"

"One who hath need of what he asketh, or he would not disturb thy quiet," was the answer. "Open the postern, Master Heathcote, without fear; it is a brother in the faith, and a subject of the same laws, that asketh the boon."

"Here is truly a Christian man without," said Content, hurrying to the postern; which, without a moment's delay, he threw freely open, saying as he did so, "enter of Heaven's mercy, and be welcome to that we have to bestow."

A tall, and, by his tread, a heavy man, wrapped in a riding-cloak, bowed to the greeting, and immediately passed beneath the low lintel. Every eye was keenly fastened on the stranger, who, after ascending the acclivity a short distance, paused, while the young men, under their master's orders, carefully and scrupulously renewed the fastenings of the gate. When bolts and bars had done their office, Content joined his guest; and after making another fruitless effort, by the feeble light which fell from the stars, to scan his person, he said, in his own meek and quiet manner—

"Thou must have great need of warmth and nourishment. The distance from this valley to the nearest habitation is wearisome, and one who hath journeyed it, in a season like this, may well be nigh fainting. Follow, and deal with that we have to bestow as freely as if it were thine own."

Although the stranger manifested none of that impatience which the heir of the Wish-Ton-Wish appeared to think one so situated might in all reason feel, thus invited he did not hesitate to comply. As he followed in the footsteps of his host, his tread, however, was leisurely and dignified; and once or twice, when the other half delayed in order to make some passing observation of courtesy, he betrayed no indiscreet anxiety to enter on those personal indulgences which might in reality prove so grateful to one who had journeyed far in an inclement season, and along a road where neither dwelling nor security invited repose.

"Here is warmth and a peaceful welcome," pursued Content, ushering his guest into the centre of a group of fearfully anxious faces. "In a little time, other matters shall be added to thy comfort."

When the stranger found himself under the glare of a powerful light, and confronted to so many curious and wondering eyes, for a single instant he hesitated. Then stepping calmly forward, he cast the short riding-cloak, which had closely muffled his features, from his shoulders, and discovered the severe eye, the stern lineaments, and the athletic form of him who had once before been known to enter the doors of Wish-Ton-Wish with little warning, and to have quitted them so mysteriously.

The Puritan had arisen, with quiet and grave courtesy, to receive his visiter; but obvious, powerful, and extraordinary interest gleamed about his usually subdued visage, when, as the features of the other were exposed to view, he recognised the person of the man who advanced to meet him.

"Mark Heathcote," said the stranger, "my visit is to thee. It may, or it may not, prove longer than the last, as thou shalt receive my tidings. Affairs of the last moment demand that there should be little delay in hearing that which I have to offer."

Notwithstanding the excess and nature of the surprise which the veteran Mark had certainly betrayed, it endured just long enough to allow those wondering eyes, which were eagerly devouring all that passed, to note its existence. Then, the subdued and characteristic manner, which in general marked his air, instantly returned, and with a quiet gesture, like that which friends use in moments of confidence and security, he beckoned to the other to follow to an inner room. The stranger complied, making a slight bow of recognition to Ruth, as he passed her on the way to the apartment chosen for an interview that was evidently intended to be private.

CHAPTER X.

"*Mar.* Shall I strike at it with my partizan.
Hor. Do, if it will not stand.
Mar. 'Tis here!
Hor. 'Tis here!
Mar. 'Tis gone!"

HAMLET.

THE time that this unexpected visiter stood uncloaked and exposed to recognition, before the eyes of the curious group in the outer room, did not much exceed a minute. Still it was long enough to allow men who rarely overlooked the smallest peculiarity of dress or air, to note some of the more distinguishing accompaniments of his attire. The heavy horseman's pistols, once before exhibited, were in his girdle, and young Mark got a glimpse of a silver-handled dagger which had pleased his eye before that night. But the passage of his grandfather and the stranger from the room prevented the boy from determining whether it was entirely of the same fashion as that, which, rather as a memorial of by-gone scenes than for any service that it might now be expected to perform, hung above the bed of the former.

"The man hath not yet parted with his arms!" exclaimed the quick-sighted youth, when he found that every other tongue continued silent. "I would he may now leave them with my grand'ther, that I may chase the skulking Wampanoag to his hiding—"

"Hot-headed boy! Thy tongue is too much given to levity," said Ruth, who had not only resumed her seat, but the light employment that had been interrupted by the blast at the gate with a calmness of mien that did not fail in some degree to reassure her maidens. "Instead of cherishing the lessons of peace that are taught thee, thy unruly thoughts are ever bent on strife."

"Is there harm in wishing to be armed with a weapon suited to my years, that I may do service in beating down the power of our enemies; and perhaps aid something, too, in affording security to my mother?"

"Thy mother hath no fears," returned the matron gravely, while grateful affection prompted a kind but furtive glance towards the high-spirited though sometimes froward lad. "Reason hath already taught me the folly of alarm, because one has knocked at our gate in the night-season. Lay aside thy arms, men; you see that my husband no longer clings to the musket. Be certain that his eye will give us warning, when there shall be danger at hand."

The unconcern of her husband was even more strikingly true, than the simple language of his wife would appear to convey. Content had not only laid aside his weapon, but he had resumed his seat near the fire, with an air as calm, as assured, and it might have seemed to one watchfully observant, as understanding, as her own. Until now, the stout Dudley had remained leaning on his piece, immovable and apparently unconscious as a statue. But, following the injunctions of one he was accustomed to obey, he placed the musket against the wall, with the care of a hunter, and then running a hand through his shaggy locks, as though the action might quicken ideas that were never remarkably active, he bluntly exclaimed—

"An armed hand is well in these forests, but an armed heel is not less wanting to him who would push a roadster from the Connecticut to the Wish-Ton-Wish, between a rising and a setting sun! The stranger no longer journeys in the saddle, as is plain by the sign that his boot beareth no spur. When he worried, by dint of hard pricking, the miserable hack that proved food for the wolves, through the forest, he had better appointments. I saw the bones of the animal no later than this day. They have been polished by fowls and frost, till the driven snow of the mountains is not whiter!"

Meaning and uneasy, but hasty glances of the eye were exchanged between Content and Ruth, as Eben Dudley thus uttered the thoughts which had been suggested by the unexpected return of the stranger.

"Go you to the look-out at the western palisadoes," said the latter; "and see if perchance the Indian may not be lurking near the dwellings, ashamed of his delay, and perchance fearful of calling us to his admission. I cannot think that the child means to desert us, with no sign of kindness, and without leave-taking."

"I will not take upon me to say, how much or how little of ceremony the youngster may fancy to be due to the master of the valley and his kin; but if not gone already, the snow will not melt more quietly in the thaw, than the lad will one day disappear. Reuben Ring, thou hast an eye for light or darkness; come forth with me, that no sign escape us. Should thy sister, Faith, make one of our party, it would not be easy for the red-skin to pass the clearing without a hail."

"Go to," hurriedly answered the female; "it is more womanly that I tarry to see to the wants of him who hath journeyed far and hard, since the rising of the sun. If the boy pass thy vigilance, wakeful Dudley, he will have little cause to fear that of others."

Though Faith so decidedly declined to make one of the party, her brother complied without reluctance. The young men were about to quit the place together; when the latch, on which the hand of Dudley was already laid, rose quietly without aid from his finger, the door opened, and the object of their intended search glided past them, and took his customary position in one of the more retired corners of the room. There was so much of the ordinary, noiseless manner of the young captive in this entrance, that for a moment they who witnessed the passage of his dark form across the apartment, were led to think the movement no more than the visit he was always permitted to make at that hour. But recollection soon came, and with it not only the suspicious circumstance of his disappearance, but the inexplicable manner of his admission within the gates.

"The pickets must be looked to!" exclaimed Dudley, the instant a second look assured him that his eyes in truth beheld him who had been missing "The place that a stripling can scale, might well admit a host."

"Truly," said Content, "this needeth explanation. Hath not the boy entered when the gate was opened for the stranger?—Here cometh one that may speak to the fact!"

"It is so," said the individual named, who re-entered from the inner room in season to hear the nature of the remark. "I found this native child near thy gate, and took upon me the office of a Christian man to bid him welcome. Certain am I, that one, kind of heart and gently disposed, like the mistress of this family, will not turn him away in anger."

"He is no stranger at our fire, or at our board," said Ruth; "had it been otherwise, thou wouldst have done well."

Eben Dudley looked incredulous. His mind had been powerfully exercised that day with visions of the marvellous, and, of a certainty, there was some reason to distrust the manner in which the re-appearance of the youth had been made.

"It will be well to look to the fastenings," he muttered, "lest others, less easy to dispose of, should follow. Now that invisible agencies are at work in the Colony, one may not sleep too soundly!"

"Then go thou to the look-out, and keep the watch, till the clock shall strike the hour of midnight;" said the Puritan, who uttered the command in a manner to show that he was in truth moved by considerations far deeper than the vague apprehensions of his dependant. "Ere sleep overcome thee, another shall be ready for the relief."

Mark Heathcote seldom spoke, but respectful silence permitted the lowest of his syllables to be audible. On the present occasion, when his voice was first heard, such a stillness came over all in presence, that he finished the sentence amid the nearly imperceptible breathings of the listeners. In this momentary but death-like quiet, there arose a blast from the conch at the gate, that might have seemed an echo of that which had so lately startled the already-excited inmates of the dwelling. At the repetition of sounds so unwonted, all sprang to their feet, but no one spoke. Content cast a hurried and inquiring glance at his father, who in his turn had anxiously sought the eye of the stranger. The latter stood firm and unmoved. One hand was clenched upon the back of the chair from which he had arisen, and the other grasped, perhaps unconsciously, the handle of one of those weapons which had attracted the attention of young Mark, and which still continued thrust through the broad leathern belt that girded his doublet.

"The sound is like that, which one little used to deal with earthly instruments might raise!" muttered one of those whose mind had been prepared, by the narrative of Dudley, to believe in any thing marvellous.

"Come from what quarter it may, it is a sum mons that must be answered;" returned Content. "Dudley, thy musket; this visit is so unwonted, that more than one hand should do the office of porter."

The borderer instantly complied, muttering between his teeth as he shook the priming deeper into the barrel of his piece, "Your over-sea gallants are quick on the trail to-night!" Then throwing the musket into the hollow of his arm, he cast a look of discontent and resentment towards Faith Ring, and was about to open the door for the passage of Content, when another blast arose on the silence without. The second touch of the shell was firmer, longer, louder, and more true, than that by which it had just been preceded.

"One might fancy the conch was speaking in mockery," observed Content, looking with meaning towards their guest. "Never did sound more resemble sound than these we have just heard, and those thou drew from the shell when asking admission."

A sudden light appeared to break in upon the intelligence of the stranger. Advancing more intc the circle, rather with the freedom of long familiarity than with the diffidence of a newly-arrived guest, he motioned for silence as he said—

"Let none move, but this stout woodsman, the young captain and myself. We will go forth, and doubt not that the safety of those within shall be regarded."

Notwithstanding the singularity of this proposal, as it appeared to excite neither surprise nor opposition in the Puritan or his son, the rest of the family offered no objection. The stranger had no sooner spoken, than he advanced near to the torch, and looked closely into the condition of his pistols. Then turning to old Mark, he continued in an under tone—

"Peradventure there will be more worldly strife than any which can flow from the agencies that stir up the unquiet spirits of the Colonies. In such an extremity, it may be well to observe a soldier's caution."

"I like not this mockery of sound," returned the Puritan; "it argueth a taunting and fiend-like temper. We have, of late, had in this Colony tragical instances of what the disappointed malice of Azazel can attempt; and it would be vain to hope that the evil agencies are not vexed with the sight of my Bethel."

Though the stranger listened to the words of his host with respect, it was plain that his thoughts dwelt on dangers of a different character. The member that still rested on the handle of his weapon, was clenched with greater firmness; and a grim, though a melancholy expression was seated about a mouth, that was compressed in a manner to denote the physical, rather than the spiritual resolution of the man. He made a sign to the two companions he had chosen, and led the way to the court.

By this time, the shades of night had materially thickened, and, although the hour was still early, a darkness had come over the valley that rendered it difficult to distinguish objects at any distance from the eye. The obscurity made it necessary that they, who now issued from the door of the dwelling, should advance with caution, lest, ere properly admonished of its presence, their persons should be exposed to some lurking danger. When the three, however, were safely established behind the thick curtain of plank and earth that covered and commanded the entrance, and where their persons, from the shoulders downward, were completely protected, alike from shot and arrow, Content demanded to know, who applied at his gates for admission at an hour when they were habitually closed for the night. Instead of receiving, as before, a ready answer, the silence was so profound, that his own words were very distinctly heard repeated, as was not uncommon at that quiet hour, among the recesses of the neighboring woods.

"Come it from Devil, or come it from man, here is treachery!" whispered the stranger after a fitting pause. "Artifice must be met by artifice; but thou art much abler to advise against the wiles of the forest, than one trained, as I have been, in the less cunning deceptions of Christian warfare."

"What think'st, Dudley?" asked Content—"Will it be well to sally, or shall we wait another signal from the conch?"

"Much dependeth on the quality of the guests expected," returned he of whom counsel was asked. 'As for the braggart gallants, that are over-valiant among the maidens, and heavy of heart when they think the screech of the jay an Indian whoop, I care not if ye beat the pickets to the earth, and call upon them to enter on the gallop. I know the manner to send them to the upper story of the block, quicker than the cluck of the turkey can muster its young; but——"

"'Tis well to be discreet in language, in a moment of such serious uncertainty!" interrupted the stranger. "We look for no gallants of the kind."

"Then will I give you a conceit that shall know the reason of the music of yon conch. Go ye two back into the house, making much conversation by the way, in order that any without may hear. When ye have entered, it shall be my task to find such a post nigh the gate, that none shall knock again, and no porter be at hand to question them in the matter of their errand."

"This soundeth better," said Content; "and that

it may be done with all safety, some others of the young men, who are accustomed to this species of artifice, shall issue by the secret door and lie in wait behind the dwellings, in order that support shall not be wanting in case of violence. Whatever else thou dost, Dudley, remember that thou dost not undo the fastenings of the postern."

"Look to the support," returned the woodsman; "should it be keen-eyed Reuben Ring, I shall feel none the less certain that good aid is at my back. The whole of that family are quick of wit and ready of invention, unless it may be the wight who hath got the form without the reason of a man."

"Thou shalt have Reuben, and none other of his kin," said Content. "Be well advised of the fastenings, and so I wish thee all fitting success, in a deception that cannot be sinful, since it aims only at our safety."

With this injunction, Content and the stranger left Dudley to the practice of his own devices, the former observing the precaution to speak aloud while returning, in order that any listeners without might be led to suppose the whole party had retired from the search, satisfied of its fruitlessness.

In the mean time, the youth left nigh the postern set about the accomplishment of the task he had undertaken, in sober earnest. Instead of descending in a direct line to the palisadoes, he also ascended, and made a circuit among the out-buildings on the margin of the acclivity. Then bending so low as to blend his form with objects on the snow, he gained an angle of the palisadoes, at a point remote from the spot he intended to watch, and, as he hoped, aided by the darkness of the hour and the shadows of the hill, completely protected from observation. When beneath the palisadoes, the sentinel crouched to the earth, creeping with extreme caution along the timber which bound their lower ends, until he found himself arrived at a species of sentry-box that was erected for the very purpose to which he now intended it should be applied. Once within the cover of this little recess, the sturdy woodsman bestowed his large frame, with as much attention to comfort and security as the circumstances would permit. Here he prepared to pass many weary minutes, before there should be further need of his services.

The reader will find no difficulty in believing that one of opinions like those of the borderer, did not enter on his silent watch without much distrust of the character of the guests that he might be called upon to receive. Enough has been shown to prove that the suspicion uppermost in his mind was, that the unwelcome agents of the government had returned on the heels of the stranger. But, notwithstanding the seeming probability of this opinion, there were secret misgivings of the earthly origin of the two last windings of the shell. All the legends, and all the most credited evidence in cases of prestigious agency, as it had been exhibited in the colonies of New-England, went to show the malignant pleasure the Evil Spirits found, in indulging their wicked mockeries, or in otherwise tormenting those who placed their support on a faith, that was believed to be so repugnant to their own ungrateful and abandoned natures. Under the impressions, naturally excited by the communication he had held with the traveller in the mountains, Eben Dudley found his mind equally divided between the expectation of seeing, at each moment, one of the men whom he had induced to quit the valley so unceremoniously, returning to obtain, surreptitiously, admission within the gate, or of being made an unwilling witness of some wicked manifestation of that power which was temporarily committed to the invisibles. In both of these expectations, however, he was fated to be disappointed Notwithstanding the strong spiritual bias of the opinions of the credulous sentinel, there was too much of the dross of temporal things in his composition, to elevate him altogether above the weakness of humanity. A mind so encumbered began to weary with its own contemplations; and, as it grew feeble with its extraordinary efforts, th dominion of matter gradually resumed its sway. Thought, instead of being clear and active, as the emergency would have seemed to require, began to grow misty. Once or twice the borderer half arose, and appeared to look about him with observation; and then, as his large frame fell heavily back into its former semi-recumbent attitude, he grew tranquil and stationary. This movement was several times repeated, at intervals of increasing length, till, at the end of an hour, forgetting alike the hunt, the troopers, and the mysterious agents of evil, the young man yielded to the fatigue of the day. The tall oaks of the adjoining forest stood not more immovable in the quiet of the tranquil hour, than his frame now leaned against the side of its narrow habitation.

How much time was thus lost in inactivity, Eben Dudley could never precisely tell. He always stoutly maintained it could not have been long, since his watch was not disturbed by the smallest of those sounds from the woods, which sometimes occur in deep night, and which may be termed the breathing of the forest in its slumbers. His first distinct recollection, was that of feeling a hand grasped with the power of a giant. Springing to his feet, the young man eagerly stretched forth an arm, saying as he did so, in words sufficiently confused—

"If the buck hath fallen by a shot in the head, I grant him to be thine, Reuben Ring; but if struck in limb or body, I claim the venison for a surer hand."

"Truly, a very just division of the spoil," returned one in an under tone, and speaking as if sounds too loud might be dangerous. "Thou givest the head of the deer for a target to Reuben Ring, and keepest the rest of the creature to thine own uses."

"Who hath sent thee, at this hour, to the postern? Dost not know that there are thought to be strangers, outlying in the fields?"

"I know that there are some, who are not strangers, in-lying on their watch!" said Faith Ring. "What shame would come upon thee, Dudley, did the Captain, and they who have been so strongly exercised in prayer within, but suspect how little care thou hast had of their safety, the while!"

"Have they come to harm? If the Captain hath held them to spiritual movements, I hope he will allow that nothing earthly hath passed this postern to disturb the exercise. As I hope to be dealt honestly by, in all matters of character, I have not once quitted the gate, since the watch was set."

"Else wouldst thou be the famousest sleep-walker in the Connecticut Colony! Why, drowsy one, conch cannot raise a louder blast than that thou soundest, when eyes are fairly shut in sleep. This may be watching, according to thy meaning of the word; but infant in its cradle is not half so ignorant of that which passeth around it, as thou hast been."

"I think, Faith Ring, that thou hast gotten to be much given to backbiting, and evil saying against friends, since the visit of the gallants from over sea."

"Out upon the gallants from over sea, and thee too, man! I am not a girl to be flouted with bold speech from one who doth not know whether he be sleeping or waking. I tell thee, thy good name would be lost in the family, did it come to the ears of the Captain, and more particularly to the knowledge of that soldier stranger, up in the dwelling, of whom even the Madam maketh so great ceremony, that thou hast been watching with a tuneful nose, an open mouth, and a sealed eye."

"If any but thee hadst said this slander of me, girl, it would go nigh to raise hot speech between us! Thy brother, Reuben Ring, knows better than to stir my temper, by such falsity of accusation."

"Thou dealest so generously by him, that he is prone to forget thy misdeeds. Truly he hath the head of the buck, while thou contentest thyself with the offals and all the less worthy parts! Go to, Dudley; thou wast in a heavy dream when I caused thee to awake."

"A pretty time have we fallen upon, when petticoats are used instead of beards and strong-armed men, to go the rounds of the sentinels, and to say who sleepeth and who is watchful! What hath brought thee so far from the exercises and so nigh the gates, Mistress Faith, now that there is no over-sea gallant to soothe thy ears with lying speech and light declarations."

"If speech not to be credited is that I seek," returned the girl, "truly the errand hath not been without its reward. What brought me hither, sooth! why, the Madam hath need of articles from the outer buttery—and—ay—and my ears led me to the postern. Thou knowest, musical Dudley, tha I have had occasion to hearken to thy watchful notes before this night. But my time is too useful to be wasted in idleness; thou art now awake, and may thank her who hath done thee a good turn with no wish to boast of it, that one of a black beard is not the laughing-stock of all the youths in the family. If thou keepest thine own counsel, the Captain may yet praise thee for a vigilant sentinel;

though Heaven forgive him the wrong he will do the truth!"

"Perhaps a little anger at unjust suspicions may have prompted more than the matter needed, Faith, when I taxed thee with the love of backbiting, and I do now recall that word; though I will ever deny that aught more, than some wandering recollection concerning the hunt of this day, hath come over my thoughts, and perhaps made me even forgetful that it was needful to be silent at the postern; and therefore, on the truth of a Christian man, I do forgive thee, the——"

But Faith was already out of sight and out of hearing. Dudley himself, who began to have certain prickings of conscience concerning the ingratitude he had manifested to one who had taken so much interest in his reputation, now bethought him seriously of that which remained to be done. He had much reason to suspect that there was less of the night before him than he had at first believed, and he became in consequence more sensible of the necessity of making some report of the events of his watch. Accordingly, he cast a scrutinizing glance around, in order to make sure that the facts should not contradict his testimony, and then, first examining the fastenings of the postern, he mounted the hill, and presented himself before the family. The members of the latter, having in truth passed most of the long interval of his absence in spiritual exercises, and in religious conversation, were not so sensible of his delay in reporting, as they might otherwise have been.

"What tidings dost thou bring us from without?" said Content, so soon as the self-relieved sentinel appeared. "Hast seen any, or hast heard that which is suspicious?"

Ere Dudley would answer, his eye did not fail to study the half-malicious expression of the countenance of her who was busy in some domestic toil, directly opposite to the place where he stood. But reading there no more than a glance of playful though smothered irony, he was encouraged to proceed in his report.

"The watch has been quiet," was the answer; "and there is little cause to keep the sleepers longer from their beds. Some vigilant eyes, like those of Reuben Ring and my own, had better be open until the morning; further than that, is there no reason for being wakeful."

Perhaps the borderer would have dwelt more at large on his own readiness to pass the remainder of the hours of rest in attending to the security of those who slept, had not another wicked glance from the dark, laughing eye of her who stood so favorably placed to observe his countenance, admonished him of the prudence of being modest in his professions.

"This alarm hath then happily passed away," said the Puritan, arising. "We will now go to our pillows in thankfulness and peace. Thy service shall not be forgotten, Dudley; for thou hast exposed thyself to seeming danger, at least, in our behalf."

"That hath he!" half-whispered Faith; "and sure am I, that we maidens will not forget his readiness to lose the sweets of sleep, in order that the feeble may not come to harm."

"Speak not of the trifle," hurriedly returned the other. "There has been some deception in the sounds, for it is now my opinion, except to summon us to the gate, that this stranger might enter—the conch hath not been touched at all to night."

"Then is it a deception which is repeated!" exclaimed Content, rising from his chair as a faint and broken blast from the shell, like that which had first announced their visiter, again struggled among the buildings, until it reached every ear in the dwelling.

"Here is warning as mysterious as it may prove portentous!" said old Mark Heathcote, when the surprise, not to say consternation of the moment had subsided. "Hast seen nothing that might justify this?"

Eben Dudley, like most of the auditors, was too much confounded to reply. All seemed to attend anxiously for the second and more powerful blast, which was to complete the imitation of the stranger's summons. It was not necessary to wait long; for in a time as near as might be, to that which had intervened between the two first peals of the horn followed another, and in a note so true, again, as to give it the semblance of an echo.

CHAPTER XI.

"I will watch to-night;
Perchance 't will walk again."

HAMLET.

"MAY not this be a warning given in mercy?" the Puritan, at all times disposed to yield credit to supernatural manifestations of the care of Providence, demanded with a solemnity that did not fail to produce its impression on most of his auditors. "The history of our Colonies is full of the evidences of these merciful interpositions."

"We will thus consider it;" returned the stranger, to whom the question seemed more particularly addressed. "The first measure shall be to seek out the danger to which it points. Let the youth they call Dudley, give me the aid of his powerful frame and manly courage; then trust the discovery of the meaning of these frequent speakings of the conch, to me."

"Surely, Submission, thou wilt not again be the first to go forth!" exclaimed Mark, in a surprise that was equally manifested by Content and Ruth, the latter of whom pressed her little image to her side as though the bare proposal presented a powerful picture of supernatural danger. "'Twill be well to think maturely on the step, ere thou runnest the hazard of such an adventure."

"Better it should be I," said Content, "who am accustomed to forest signs, and all the usual testimonials of the presence of those who may wish us harm."

"No," said he, who for the first time had been called 'Submission,' a name that savored of the religious enthusiasm of the times, and which might have been adopted as an open avowal of his readiness to bow beneath some peculiar dispensation of Providence. "This service shall be mine. Thou art both husband and father; and many are there who look to thy safety as to their rock of earthly support and comfort, while neither kindred, nor——but we will not speak of things foreign to our purpose! Thou knowest, Mark Heathcote, that peril and I are no strangers. There is little need to bid me be prudent. Come, bold woodsman; shoulder thy musket, and be ready to do credit to thy manhood, should there be reason to prove it."

"And why not Reuben Ring?" said a hurried female voice, that all knew to proceed from the lips of the sister of the youth just named. "He is quick of eye and ready of hand, in trials like these; would it not be well to succor thy party with such aid?"

"Peace, girl," meekly observed Ruth. "This matter is already in the ordering of one used to command; there needeth no counsel from thy short experience."

Faith shrunk back abashed, the flush which had mantled over her brown cheek deepening to a tint like that of blood.

Submission (we use the appellation in the absence of all others) fastened a searching glance, for a single moment, on the countenance of the girl; and then, as if his intention had not been diverted from the principal subject in hand, he rejoined coolly—

"We go as scouters and observers of that which may hereafter call for the ready assistance of this youth; but numbers would expose us to observation, without adding to our usefulness—and yet," he added, arresting his footstep, which was already turned towards the door, and looking earnestly and long at the Indian boy, "perhaps there standeth one who might much enlighten us, would he but speak!"

This remark drew every eye on the person of the captive. The lad stood the scrutiny with the undismayed and immovable composure of his race. But though his eye met the looks of those around him haughtily and in pride, it was not gleaming with any of that stern defiance which had so often been known to glitter in his glances, when he had reason to think that his fortunes, or his person, was the subject of the peculiar observation of those with whom he dwelt. On the contrary, the expression of his dark visage was rather that of amity than of hatred, and there was a moment when the look he cast upon Ruth and her offspring was visibly touched with a feeling of concern. A glance, charged with such a meaning, could not escape the quick-sighted vigilance of a mother.

"The child hath proved himself worthy to be trusted," she said; "and in the name of him who looketh into and knoweth all hearts, let him once more go forth."

Her lips became sealed, for again the conch announced the seeming impatience of those without to be admitted. The full tones of the shell thrilled on the nerves of the listeners, as though they proclaimed the coming of some great and fearful judgment.

In the midst of these often-repeated and mysterious sounds, Submission alone seemed calm and unmoved. Turning his look from the countenance of the boy, whose head had dropped upon his breast as the last notes of the conch rang among the buildings, he motioned hurriedly to Dudley to follow, and left the place.

There was, in good truth, that in the secluded situation of the valley, the darkness of the hour, and the nature of the several interruptions, which might readily awaken deep concern in the breasts of men as firm even as those who now issued into the open air, in quest of the solution of doubts that were becoming intensely painful. The stranger, or Submission, as we may in future have frequent occasion to call him, led the way in silence to a point of the eminence, without the buildings, where the eye might overlook the palisadoes that hedged the sides of the acclivity, and command a view beyond of all that the dusky and imperfect light would reveal.

It was a scene that required familiarity with a border life to be looked on, at any moment, with indifference. The broad, nearly interminable, and seemingly trackless forest lay about them, bounding the view to the narrow limits of the valley, as though it were some straitened oasis amidst an ocean of wilderness. Within the boundaries of the cleared land, objects were less indistinct; though even those nearest and most known were now seen only in the confused and gloomy outlines of night.

Across this dim prospect, Submission and his companion gazed long and cautiously.

"There is nought but motionless stumps, and fences loaded with snow," said the former, when his eye had roamed over the whole circuit of the view which lay on the side of the valley where they stood. "We must go forth, that we may look nearer to th fields."

"Thither then is the postern," said Dudley, observing that the other took a direction opposite to that which led to the gate. But a gesture of authority induced him at the next instant to restrain his voice, and to follow whither his companion chose to lead the way.

The stranger made a circuit of half the hill ere he descended to the palisadoes, at a point where lay long and massive piles of wood, which had been collected for the fuel of the family. This spot was one that overlooked the steepest acclivity of the eminence, which was in itself, just there, so difficult of ascent, as to render the provision of the pickets far less necessary than in its more even faces. Still no useful precaution for the security of the family had been neglected, even at this strong point of the works. The piles of wood were laid at such a distance from the pickets as to afford no facilities for scaling them, while, on the other hand, they formed platforms and breast-works that might have greatly added to the safety of those who should be required to defend this portion of the fortress. Taking his way directly amid the parallel piles, the stranger descended rapidly through the whole of their mazes, until he had reached the open space between the outer of the rows and the palisadoes, a space that was warily left too wide to be passed by the leap of man.

"'Tis many a day since foot of mine has been in this spot," said Eben Dudley, feeling his way along a path that his companion threaded without any apparent hesitation. "My own hand laid this outer pile, some winters since, and certain am I, that from that hour to this, man hath not touched a billet of the wood—And yet, for one who hath come from over sea, it would appear that thou hast no great difficulty in making way among the narrow lanes!"

"He that hath sight may well choose between air nd beechen logs," returned the other, stopping at the palisadoes, and in a place that was concealed from any prying eyes within the works, by triple and quadruple barriers of wood. Feeling in his girdle, he then drew forth something which Dudley was not long in discovering to be a key. While the latter, aided by the little light that fell from the heavens, was endeavoring to make the most of his eyes, Submission applied the instrument to a lock that was artfully sunk in one of the timbers, at the height of a man's breast from the ground; and giving a couple of vigorous turns, a piece of the palisado, some half a fathom long, yielded on a powerful hinge below, and, falling, made an opening sufficiently large for the passage of a human body.

"Here is a sally-port ready provided for our sortie," the stranger coolly observed, motioning to the other to precede him. When Dudley had passed, his companion followed, and the opening was then carefully closed and locked.

"Now is all fast again, and we are in the fields without raising alarm to any of mortal birth, at least," continued the guide, thrusting a hand into the folds of his doublet, as if to feel for a weapon, and preparing to descend the difficult declivity which still lay between him and the base of the hill. Eben Dudley hesitated to follow. The interview with the traveller in the mountains occurred to his heated imagination, and the visions of a prestigious agency revived with all their original force.

The whole manner and the mysterious character of his companion, was little likely to reassure a mind disturbed with such images.

"There is a rumor going in the Colony," muttered the borderer, "that the invisibles are permitted for a time to work their evil; and it may well happen that some of their ungodly members shall journey to the Wish-Ton-Wish, in lack of better employment."

"Thou sayest truly,'' replied the stranger; "but the power that allows of their wicked torments may have seen fit to provide an agent of its own, to defeat their subtleties. We will now draw nearer to the gate, in order that an eye may be kept on their malicious designs."

Submission spoke with gravity, and not without a certain manner of solemnity. Dudley yielded, though with a divided and a disturbed mind, to his suggestion. Still he followed in the footsteps of the stranger, with a caution that might well have eluded the vigilance of any agency short of that which drew its means of information from sources deeper than any of human power.

When the two watches had found a secret and suitable place, not far from the postern, they disposed themselves in silence to await the result. The out-buildings lay in deep quiet, not a sound of any sort arising from all of the many tenants they were known to contain. The lines of ragged fences; the blackened stumps, capped with little pyramids of snow; the taller and sometimes suspiciously-looking stubs; an insulated tree, and finally the broad border of forest,—were alike motionless, gloomy, and clothed in the doubtful forms of night. Still, the space around the well-secured and trebly-barred postern was vacant. A sheet of spotless snow served as a back-ground, that would have been sure to betray the presence of any object passing over its surface. Even the conch might be seen suspended from one of the timbers, as mute and inoffensive as the hour when it had been washed by the waves, on the sands of the sea-shore.

"Here will we watch for the coming of the stranger, be he commissioned by the powers of air, or be he one sent on an errand of earth;" whisper ed Submission, preparing his arms for immediat use, and disposing of his person, at the same time, in a manner most convenient to endure the weariness of a patient watch.

"I would my mind were at ease on the question of right-doing in dealing harm to one who disturbs the quiet of a border family," said Dudley, in a tone sufficiently repressed for caution; "it may be found prudent to strike the first blow, should one like an over-sea gallant, after all, be inclined to trouble us at this hour."

"In that strait, thou wilt do well to give little heed to the order of the offences," gloomily returned the other. "Should another messenger of England appear——"

He paused, for a note of the conch was heard rising gradually on the air, until the whole of the wide valley was filled with its rich and melancholy sound.

"Lip of man is not at the shell!" exclaimed the stranger, who like Dudley had made a forward movement towards the postern, the instant the blast reached his ear, and who like Dudley recoiled in an amazement that even his practised self-command could not conceal, as he undeniably perceived the truth of that his speech affirmed. "This exceedeth all former instances of marvellous visitations!"

"It is vain to pretend to raise the feeble nature of man to the level of things coming from the invisible world," returned the woodsman at his side. "In such a strait, it is seemly that sinful men should withdraw to the dwellings, where we may sustain our feebleness by the spiritual strivings of the Captain."

To this discreet proposal the stranger raised no objection. Without taking the time necessary to effect their retreat with the precaution that had been observed in their advance, the two adventurers quickly found themselves at the secret entrance through which they had so lately issued.

"Enter," said the stranger, lowering the piece of the palisado for the passage of his companion. "Enter, of a Heaven's sake! for it is truly meet that we assemble all our spiritual succor."

Dudley was in the act of complying, when a dark line, accompanied by a low rushing sound, cut the air between his head and that of his companion. At the next instant, a flint-headed arrow quivered in the timber.

"The heathen!" shouted the borderer, recovering all his manhood as the familiar danger became apparent, and throwing back a stream of fire in the direction from which the treacherous missile had come. "To the palisadoes, men! the bloody heathen is upon us!"

"The heathen!" echoed the stranger, in a deep steady, commanding voice, that had evidently often raised the warning in scenes of even greater emergency, and levelling a pistol, which brought a dark form that was gliding across the snow to one knee. "The heathen! the bloody heathen is upon us!"

As if both assailants and assailed paused, one moment of profound stillness succeeded this fierce interruption of the quiet of the night. Then the cries of the two adventurers were answered by a burst of yells from a wide circle, that nearly environed the hill. At the same moment, each dark object, in the fields, gave up a human form. The shouts were followed by a cloud of arrows, that rendered further delay without the cover of the palisadoes eminently hazardous. Dudley entered; but the passage of the stranger would have been cut off, by a leaping, whooping band that pressed fiercely on his rear, had not a broad sheet of flame, glancing from the hill directly in their swarthy and grim countenances, driven the assailants back upon their own footsteps. In another moment, the bolts of the lock were passed, and the two fugitives were in safety behind the ponderous piles of wood.

CHAPTER XII.

> "There need no ghost, my lord, come from the grave
> To tell us this."
>
> HAMLET

Although the minds of most, if not of all the inmates of the Wish-Ton-Wish, had been so powerfully exercised that night with a belief that the powers of the invisible world were about to be let loose upon them, the danger had now presented itself in a shape too palpable to admit of further doubt. The cry of 'the heathen' had been raised from every lip; even the daughter and elève of Ruth repeated it, as they fled wailing through the buildings; and, for a moment, terror and surprise appeared to involve the assailed in inextricable confusion. But the promptitude of the young men in rushing to the rescue, with the steadiness of Content, soon restored order. Even the females assumed at least the semblance of composure, the family having been too long trained to meet the exigencies of such an emergency, to be thrown entirely off its guard, for more than the first and the most appalling moments of the alarm.

The effect of the sudden repulse was such as all experience had taught the Colonists to expect, in their Indian warfare. The uproar of the onset ceased as abruptly as it had commenced, and a calmness so tranquil, and a stillness so profound, succeeded, that one who had for the first time witnessed such a scene, might readily have fancied t the effects of some wild and fearful illusion.

During these moments of general and deep silence, the two adventurers, whose retreat had probably hastened the assault by offering the temptation of an easy passage within the works, left the cover of the piles of wood, and ascended the hill to the place where Dudley knew Content was to be posted, in the event of a summons to the defences.

"Unless much inquiry hath deceived me in the nature of the heathen's craftiness," said the stranger, "we shall have breathing-time ere the onset be renewed. The experience of a soldier bids me say, that prudence now urges us to look into the number and position of our foes, that we may order our resistance with better understanding of their force."

"In what manner of way may this be done? Thou seest nought about us but the quiet and the darkness of night. Speak of the number of our enemies we cannot, and sally forth we may not, without certain destruction to all who quit the palisadoes."

"Thou forgottest that we have a hostage in the boy; he may be turned to some advantage, if our power over his person be used with discretion."

"I doubt that we deceive ourselves with a hope that is vain," returned Content, leading the way as he spoke, however, towards the court which communicated with the principal dwelling. "I have closely studied the eye of that lad, since his unaccountable entrance within the works, and little do I find there that should teach us to expect confidence

It will be happy if some secret understanding with those without, has not aided him in passing the palisadoes, and that he prove not a dangerous spy on our force and movements."

"In regard to that he hath entered the dwelling without sound of conch or aid of postern, be no disturbed," returned the stranger with composure. "Were it fitting, this mystery might be of easy explanation; but it may truly need all our sagacity to discover whether he hath connexion with our foes! The mind of a native does not give up its secrets like the surface of a vanity-feeding mirror."

The stranger spoke like a man who wrapped a portion of his thoughts in reserve, and his companion listened as one who comprehended more than it might be seemly or discreet to betray. With this secret and yet equivocal understanding of each other's meaning, they entered the dwelling, and soon found themselves in the presence of those they sought.

The constant danger of their situation had compelled the family to bring themselves within the habits of a methodical and severely-regulated order of defence. Duties were assigned, in the event of alarm, to the feeblest bodies and the faintest hearts; and during the moments which preceded the visit of her husband, Ruth had been endeavoring to commit to her female subordinates the several necessary charges that usage, and more particularly the emergency of the hour, appeared so imperiously to require.

"Hasten, Charity, to the block," she said; "and look into the condition of the buckets and the ladders, that should the heathen drive us to its shelter, provision of water, and means of retreat, be not wanting in our extremity; and hie thee, Faith, into the upper apartments, to see that no lights may direct their murderous aim at any in the chambers.

Thoughts come tardily, when the arrow or the bullet hath already taken its flight! And now, that the first assault is over, Mark, and we may hope to meet the wiles of the enemy by some prudence of our own, thou mayst go forth to thy father. It would have been tempting Providence too rashly, hadst thou rushed, unbidden and uninformed, into the first hurry of the danger. Come hither, child, and receive the blessing and prayers of thy mother: after which thou shalt, with better trust in Providence, place thy young person among the combatants, in the hope of victory. Remember that thou art now of an age to do justice to thy name and origin, and yet art thou of years too tender to be foremost in speech, and far less in action, on such a night as this."

A momentary flush, that only served to render the succeeding paleness more obvious, passed across the brow of the mother. She stooped, and imprinted a kiss on the forehead of the impatient boy, who scarcely waited to receive this act of tenderness, ere he hurried to place himself in the ranks of her defenders.

"And now," said Ruth, slowly turning her eye from the door by which the lad had disappeared, and speaking with a sort of unnatural composure, "and now will we look to the safety of those who can be of but little service, except as sentinels to sound the alarm. When thou art certain, Faith, that no neglected light is in the rooms above, take the children to the secret chamber; thence they may look upon the fields, without danger from any chance direction of the savages' aim. Thou knowest, Faith, my frequent teaching in this matter; let no sounds of alarm, nor frightful whoopings of the people without, cause thee to quit the spot; since thou wilt there be safer even than in the block, against which many missiles will doubtless be driven on account of its seeming air of strength. Timely notice shall be given of the change, should we seek its security. Thou wilt descend, only, shouldst thou see enemies scaling the palisadoes on the side which overhangs the stream; since there have we the fewest eyes to watch their movements. Remember that on the side of the out-buildings and of the fields, our force is chiefly posted; there can be less reason therefore that thou shouldst expose thy lives by endeavoring to look. too curiously, into that which passeth in the fields. Go, my children; and a heavenly Providence prove thy guardian!"

Ruth stooped to kiss the cheek that her daughter offered to the salute. The embrace was then given to the other child, who was in truth scarcely less near her heart, being the orphan daughter of one who had been as a sister in her affections. But, unlike the kiss she had impressed on the forehead of Mark, the present embraces were hasty, and evidently awakened less intense emotion. She had committed the boy to a known and positive danger, but, under the semblance of some usefulness, she sent the others to a place believed to be even less exposed, so long as the enemy could be kept without the works, than the citadel itself. Still, a feeling of deep and maternal tenderness came over her mind, as her daughter retired; and, yielding to its sudden impulse, she recalled the girl to her side.

"Thou wilt repeat the prayer for especial protection against the dangers of the wilderness," she solemnly continued. "In thy asking, fail not to remember him to whom thou owest being, and who now exposeth life, that we may be safe. Thou knowest the Christian's rock; place thy faith on its foundation."

"And they who seek to kill us," demanded the well-instructed child; "are they too of the number of those for whom he died?"

"It may not be doubted, though the manner of the dispensation be so mysterious! Barbarians in their habits, and ruthless in their enmities, they are creatures of our nature, and equally objects of his care."

Flaxen locks, that half-covered a forehead and face across which ran the most delicate tracery of veins, added lustre to a skin as spotlessly fair as if the warm breezes of that latitude had never fanned the countenance of the girl. Through this maze of ringlets, the child turned her full, clear, blue eyes, bending her looks, in wonder and in fear, on the dark visage of the captive Indian youth, who at that moment was to her a subject of secret horror. Unconscious of the interest he excited, the lad stood calm, haughty, and seemingly unobservant, cautious to let no sign of weakness or of concern escape him, in this scene of womanly emotion.

"Mother," whispered the still wondering child; "may we not let him go into the forest? I do not love to——"

"This is no time for speech. Go to thy hiding-place, my child, and remember both thy askings and the cautions I have named. Go, and heavenly care protect thy innocent head!"

Ruth again stooped, and bowing her face until the features were lost in the rich tresses of her daughter, a moment passed during which there was an eloquent silence. When she arose, a tear glistened on the cheek of the child. The latter had received the embrace more in apathy than in concern; and now, when led towards the upper rooms, she moved from the presence of her mother, it was with an eye that never bent its riveted gaze from the features of the young Indian, until the intervening walls hid him entirely from her sight.

"Thou hast been thoughtful and like thyself, my good Ruth," said Content, who at that moment entered, and who rewarded the self-command of his wife by a look of the kindest approbation. "The youths have not been more prompt in meeting the foe at the stockades, than thy maidens in looking to their less hardy duties. All is again quiet, without; and we come, now, rather for consultation, than for any purposes of strife."

"Then must we summon our father from his pos at the artillery, in the block."

"It is not needful," interrupted the stranger. "Time presses, for this calm may be too shortly succeeded by a tempest that all our power shall not quell. Bring forth the captive."

Content signed to the boy to approach, and when he was in reach of his hand, he placed him full before the stranger.

"I know not thy name, nor yet even that of thy people," commenced the latter, after a long pause in which he seemed to study deeply the countenance of the lad; "but certain am I, though a more wicked spirit may still be struggling for the mastery in thy wild mind, that nobleness of feeling is no stranger to thy bosom. Speak; hast thou aught to impart concerning the danger that besets this family? I have learned much this night from thy manner, but to be clearly understood, it is now time that thou shouldst speak in words."

The youth kept his eye fastened on that of the speaker, until the other had ended, and then he bent it slowly, but with searching observation, on the anxious countenance of Ruth. It seemed as if he balanced between his pride and his sympathies. The latter prevailed; for, conquering the deep reluctance of an Indian, he spoke openly, and for the first time, since his captivity, in the language of the hated race.

"I hear the whoops of warriors," was his calm an swer "Have the ears of the pale men been shut?'

"Thou hast spoken with the young men of thy tribe in the forest, and thou hadst knowledge of this onset?"

The youth made no reply, though the keen look of his interrogator was met steadily, and without fear. Perceiving that he had demanded more than would be answered, the stranger changed his mode of investigation, masking his inquiries with a little more of artifice.

"It may not be that a great tribe is on the bloody path!" he said; "warriors would have walked over the timbers of the palisadoes, like bending reeds! 'Tis a Pequot who hath broken faith with a Christian, and who is now abroad, prowling as a wolf in the night."

A sudden and wild expression gleamed over the swarthy features of the boy. His lips moved, and the words that issued from between them were uttered in the tones of biting scorn. Still he rather muttered than pronounced aloud—

"The Pequot is a dog!"

"It is as I had thought; the knaves are out of their villages, that the Yengeese may feed their squaws. But a Narragansett, or a Wampanoag, is a man; he scorns to lurk in the darkness. When he comes, the sun will light his path. The Pequot steals in silence, for he fears that the warriors will hear his tread."

It was not easy to detect any evidence that the captive listened, either to the commendation or the censure, with answering sympathy; for marble is not colder that were the muscles of his unmoved countenance.

The stranger studied the expression of his features in vain, and drawing so near as to lay his hand on the naked shoulder of the lad, he added—"Boy, thou hast heard much moving matter concerning the nature of our Christian faith, and thou hast been the subject of many a fervent asking; it may not be that so much good seed hath been altogether scattered by the way-side! Speak; may I again trust thee?"

"Let my father look on the snow. The print of the moccason goes and comes."

"It is true. Thus far hast thou proved honest; but when the war-whoop shall be thrilling through thy young blood, the temptation to join the warriors may be too strong. Hast any gage, any pledge, in which we may find warranty for letting thee depart?"

The boy regarded his interrogator with a look that plainly denoted ignorance of his meaning.

"I would know what thou canst leave with me, to show that our eyes shall again look upon thy face, when we have opened the gate for thy passage into the fields."

Still the gaze of the other was wondering and confused.

"When the white man goes upon the war-path and would put trust in his foe, he takes surety for his faith, by holding the life of one dear as a warranty of its truth. What canst offer, that I may know thou wilt return from the errand on which I would fain send thee?"

"The path is open."

"Open, but not certain to be used. Fear may cause thee to forget the way it leads."

The captive now understood the meaning of the other's doubts, but, as if disdaining to reply, he bent his eyes aside, and stood in one of those immovable attitudes which so often gave him the air of a piece of dark statuary.

Content and his wife had listened to this short dialogue, in a manner to prove that they possessed some secret knowledge, which lessened the wonder they might otherwise have felt, at witnessing so obvious proofs of a secret acquaintance between the speakers. Both however manifested unequivocal signs of astonishment, when they first heard English sounds issuing from the lips of the boy. There was, at least, the semblance of hope in the mediation of one who had received, and who had appeared to acknowledge, so much kindness from herself; and Ruth clung to the cheering expectation with the quickness of maternal care.

"Let the boy depart," she said. "I will be his hostage; and should he prove false, there can be less to fear in his absence than in his presence."

The obvious truth of the latter assertion probably weighed more with the stranger than the unmeaning pledge of the woman.

"There is reason in this," he resumed. "Go, then, into the fields, and say to thy people that they have mistaken the path; that, they are on, hath led them to the dwelling of a friend—Here are no Pequots. nor any of the men of the Manhattoes; but Christian Yengeese, who have long dealt with the Indian as one just man dealeth with another. Go, and when thy signal shall be heard at the gate, it shall be open to thee, for readmission."

Thus saying, the stranger motioned to the boy to follow, taking care, as they left the room together, to instruct him in all such minor matters as might assist in effecting the pacific object of the mission on which he was employed.

A few minutes of doubt and of fearful suspense succeeded this experiment. The stranger, after seeing that egress was permitted to his messenger, had returned to the dwelling, and rejoined his companions. He passed the moments in pacing the apartment, with the strides of one in whom powerful concern was strongly at work. At times, the sound of his heavy footstep ceased, and then all listened intently, in order to catch any sound that might instruct them in the nature of the scene that was passing without. In the midst of one of these pauses, a yell like that of savage delight arose in the fields. It was succeeded by the death-like and portentous calm, which had rendered the time since the momentary attack even more alarming than when the danger had a positive and known character. But all the attention the most intense anxiety could now lend, furnished no additional clue to the movement of their foes. For many minutes, the quiet of midnight reigned both within and without the defences. In the midst of this suspense, the latch of the door was lifted, and their messenger appeared with that noiseless tread and collected mien which distinguish the people of his race.

"Thou hast met the warriors of thy tribe?" hastily demanded the stranger.

"The noise did not cheat the Yengeese. It was not a girl, laughing in the woods.'

"And thou hast said to thy people, 'we are friends'?"

"The words of my father were spoken."

"And heard—Were they loud enough to enter the ears of the young men?"

The boy was silent.

"Speak," continued the stranger, elevating his form, proudly, like one ready to breast a more severe shock. "Thou hast men for thy listeners. Is the pipe of the savage filled? will he smoke in peace, or holdeth he the tomahawk in a clenched hand?'

The countenance of the boy worked with a feeling that it was not usual for an Indian to betray He bent his look, with concern, on the mild eyes of the anxious Ruth; then drawing a hand slowly from beneath the light robe that partly covered his body, he cast at the feet of the stranger a bundle of arrows, wrapped in the glossy and striped skin of the rattlesnake.

"This is warning we may not misconceive!" said

Content, raising the well-known emblem of ruthles hostility to the light, and exhibiting it before the eyes of his less-instructed companion. "Boy, what have the people of my race done, that thy warriors should seek their blood, to this extremity?"

When the boy had discharged his duty, he moved aside, and appeared unwilling to observe the effect which his message might produce on his companions. But thus questioned, all gentle feelings were near being forgotten, in the sudden force of passion. A hasty glance at Ruth quelled the emotion, and he continued calm as ever, and silent.

"Boy," repeated Content, "I ask thee why thy people seek our blood?"

The passage of the electric spark is not more subtle, nor is it scarcely more brilliant, than was the gleam that shot into the dark eye of the Indian. The organ seemed to emit rays coruscant as the glance of the serpent. His form appeared to swell with the inward strivings of the spirit, and for a moment there was every appearance of a fierce and uncontrollable burst of ferocious passion. The conquest of feeling was, however, but momentary. He regained his self-command by a surprising effort of the will, and advancing so near to him who had asked this bold question, as to lay a finger on his breast, the young savage haughtily said—

'See! this world is very wide. There is room on it for the panther and the deer. Why have the Yengeese and the red-men met?"

"We waste the precious moments in probing the stern nature of a heathen," said the stranger. "The object of his people is certain, and, with the aid of the Christian's staff, will we beat back their power. Prudence requireth at our hands, that the lad be secured; after which, will we repair to the stockades and prove ourselves men."

Against this proposal no reasonable objection

could be raised. Content was about to secure the person of his captive in a cellar, when a suggestion of his wife caused him to change his purpose. Notwithstanding the sudden and fierce mien of the youth, there had been such an intelligence created between them by looks of kindness and interest, that the mother was reluctant to abandon all hope of his aid.

"Miantonimoh!" she said, "though others distrust thy purpose, I will have confidence. Come, then, with me; and while I give thee promise of safety in thine own person, I ask at thy hands the office of a protector for my babes."

The boy made no reply; but as he passively followed his conductress to the chambers, Ruth fancied she read assurance of his faith, in the expression of his eloquent eye. At the same moment, her husband and Submission left the house, to take their stations at the palisadoes.

CHAPTER XIII.

"Thou art, my good youth, my page;
I'll be thy master: walk with me; speak freely."
CYMBELINE.

THE apartment, in which Ruth had directed the children to be placed, was in the attic, and, as already stated, on the side of the building which faced the stream that ran at the foot of the hill. It had a single projecting window, through which there was a view of the forest and of the fields on that side of the valley. Small openings in its sides admitted also of glimpses of the grounds which lay further in the rear. In addition to the covering of the roofs, and of the massive frame-work of the building, an interior partition of timber protected the place against the entrance of most missiles then known in the warfare of the country. During the infancy of the children, this room had been their sleeping apartment; nor was it abandoned for that purpose, until the additional outworks, which increased with time around the dwellings, had emboldened the family to trust themselves, at night, in situations more convenient, and which were believed to be no less equally secure against surprise.

"I know thee to be one who feeleth the obligations of a warrior," said Ruth, as she ushered her follower into the presence of the children. "Thou wilt not deceive me; the lives of these tender ones are in thy keeping. Look to them, Miantonimoh, and the Christian's God will remember thee in thine own hour of necessity!"

The boy made no reply, but in a gentle expression which was visible in his dark visage, the mother endeavored to find the pledge she sought. Then, as the youth, with the delicacy of his race, moved aside in order that they who were bound to each other by ties so near might indulge their feelings without observation, Ruth again drew near her offspring, with all the tenderness of a mother beaming in her eyes.

"Once more I bid thee not to look too curiously at the fearful strife that may arise in front of our habitations," she said. "The heathen is truly upon us, with bloody mind; young, as well as old, must now show faith in the protection of our master, and such courage as befitteth believers."

"And why is it, mother," demanded her child, "that they seek to do us harm? have we ever done evil to them?"

"I may not say. He that hath made the earth hath given it to us for our uses, and reason would seem to teach that if portions of its surface are vacant, he that needeth truly, may occupy."

"The savage!" whispered the child, nestling still nearer to the bosom of her stooping parent. "His eye glittereth like the star which hangs above the trees."

"Peace, daughter; his fierce nature broodeth over some fancied wrong!"

"Surely, we are here rightfully. I have heard my father say, that when the Lord made me a present to his arms, our valley was a tangled forest, and that much toil only has made it as it is."

I hope that what we enjoy, we enjoy rightfully! And yet it seemeth that the savage is ready to deny our claims."

"And where do these bloody enemies dwell? have they, too, valleys like this, and do the Christians break into them to shed blood, in the night?"

"They are of wild and fierce habits, Ruth, and little do they know of our manner of life. Woman is not cherished as among the people of thy father's race, for force of body is more regarded than kinder ties."

The little auditor shuddered, and when she buried her face deeper in the bosom of her parent, it was with a more quickened sense of maternal affection, and with a livelier view, than her infant perception had ever yet known, of the gentle charities of kindred. When she had spoken, the matron impressed the final kiss on the forehead of each of the children, and asking, aloud, that God might bless them, she turned to go to the performance of duties that called for the exhibition of very different qualities. Before quitting the room, however, she once more approached the boy, and, holding the light before his steady eye, she said solemnly—

"I trust my babes to the keeping of a young warrior!"

The look he returned was like the others, cold but not discouraging. A gaze of many moments elicited no reply; and Ruth prepared to quit the place, troubled by uncertainty concerning the intentions of the guardian she left with the girls, while she still trusted that the many acts of kindness which she had shown him, during his captivity, would not go without their reward. Her hand rested on the bolt of the door, in indecision. The moment was favorable to the character of the youth, for she recalled the manner of his return that night, no less than his former acts of faith, and she was about to leave the passage for his egress open, when an uproar arose on the air which filled the valley with all the hideous cries and yells of a savage onset. Drawing the bolt, the startled woman descended, without further thought, and rushed to her post, with the hurry of one who saw only the necessity of exertion in another scene.

"Stand to the timbers, Reuben Ring! Bear back the skulking murderers on their bloody followers! The pikes! Here, Dudley is opening for thy valor. The Lord have mercy on the souls of the ignorant heathen!" mingled with the reports of musketry, the whoops of the warriors, the whizzing of bullets and arrows, with all the other accompaniments of such a contest, were the fearful sounds that saluted the senses of Ruth as she issued into the court. The valley was occasionally lighted by the explosion of fire-arms, and then, at times, the horrible din prevailed in the gloom of deep darkness. Happily, in the midst of all this confusion and violence, the young men of the valley were true to their duties. An alarming attempt to scale the stockade had already been repulsed, and, the true character of two or three feints having been ascertained, the principal force of the garrison was now actively employed in resisting the main attack.

"In the name of him who is with us in every danger!" exclaimed Ruth, advancing to two figures that were so busily engaged in their own concerns, as not to heed her approach, "tell me how goes the struggle? Where are my husband and the boy? –or has it pleased Providence that any of our people should be stricken?"

"It hath pleased the Devil," returned Eben Dudley, somewhat irreverently for one of that chastened school, "to send an Indian arrow through jerkin and skin, into this arm of mine! Softly, Faith; dost think, girl, that the covering of man is like the coat of a sheep, from which the fleece may be plucked at will! I am no moulting fowl, nor is this arrow a feather of my wing. The Lord forgive the rogue for the ill turn he hath done my flesh, say I, and amen like a Christian! he will have occasion too for the mercy, seeing he hath nothing further to hope for in this world. Now, Faith, I acknowledge the debt of thy kindness, and let there be no more cutting speech between us. Thy tongue often pricketh more sorely than the Indian's arrow."

"Whose fault is it that old acquaintance hath sometimes been overlooked, in new conversations? Thou knowest that, wooed by proper speech, no maiden in the Colony is wont to render gentler answer. Dost feel uneasiness in thine arm, Dudley?"

"'Tis not tickling with a straw, to drive a flint-headed arrow to the bone! I forgive thee the matter of too much discourse with the trooper, and all the side-cuts of thy over-ambling tongue, on conditions that——"

"Out upon thee, brawler! wouldst be prating here the night long on pretence of a broken skin, and the savage at our gates? A fine character will the Madam render of thy deeds, when the other youths have beaten back the Indian, and thou loitering among the buildings!"

The discomfited borderer was about to curse in his heart the versatile humor of his mistress, when he saw, by a side-glance, that ears which had no concern in the subject, had liked to have shared in the matter of their discourse. Seizing the weapon which was leaning against the foundation of the block, he hurried past the mistress of the family, and, in another minute, his voice and his musket were again heard ringing in the uproar.

"Does he bring tidings from the palisadoes?' repeated Ruth, too anxious that the young man should return to his post, to arrest his retreat. "What saith he of the onset?"

"The savage hath suffered for his boldness, and little harm hath yet come to our people. Except that yon block of a man hath managed to put arm before the passage of an arrow, I know not that any of our people have been harmed."

"Hearken! they retire, Ruth. The yells are less near, and our young men will prevail! Go thou to thy charge among the piles of the fuel, and see that no lurker remaineth to do injury. The Lord hath remembered mercy, and it may yet arrive that this evil shall pass away from before us!"

The quick ear of Ruth had not deceived her. The tumult of the assault was gradually receding from the works, and though the flashings of the muskets and the bellowing reports that rang in the surrounding forest were not less frequent than before, it was plain that the critical moment of the onset was already past. In place of the fierce effort to carry the place by surprise, the savages had now resorted to means that were more methodical, and which, though not so appalling in appearance, were perhaps quite as certain of final success. Ruth profited by a momentary cessation in the flight of the missiles, to seek those in whose welfare she had placed her chief concern.

"Has other, than brave Dudley, suffered by this assault?" demanded the anxious wife, as she passed swiftly among a group of dusky figures that were collected in consultation, on the brow of the declivity; "has any need of such care as a woman's hand may bestow? Heathcote, thy person is unharmed!"

"Truly, one of great mercy hath watched over it, for little opportunity hath been given to look to our own safety. I fear that some of our young men have not regarded the covers with the attention that prudence requires."

"The thoughtless Mark hath not forgotten my admonitions! Boy, thou hast never lost sight of duty so far as to precede thy father?"

"One sees or thinks but little of the red-skins, when the whoop is ringing among the timbers of the palisadoes, mother," returned the boy, dashing his hand across his brow, in order that the drops of blood which were trickling from a furrow left by the passage of an arrow, might not be seen. "I have kept near my father, but whether in his front or in his rear, the darkness hath not permitted me to note."

"The lad hath behaved in a bold and seemly manner," said the stranger; "and he hath shown the metal of his grandsire's stock—ha! what is't we see gleaming among the sheds? A sortie may be needed, to save the granaries and thy folds from destruction!"

"To the barns! to the barns!" shouted two of the youths, from their several look-outs. "The brand is in the buildings!" exclaimed a maiden who discharged a similar duty under cover of the dwellings. Then followed a discharge of muskets, all of which were levelled at the glancing light that was glaring in fearful proximity to the combustible materials which filled the most of the out-buildings. A savage yell, and the sudden extinguishment of the blazing knot, announced the fatal accuracy of the aim.

"This may not be neglected!" exclaimed Content, moved to extraordinary excitement by the extremity of the danger. "Father!" he called aloud, "'tis fitting time to show our utmost strength."

A moment of suspense succeeded this summons. The whole valley was then as suddenly lighted, as if a torrent of the electric fluid had flashed across its gloomy bed; a sheet of flame glanced from the attic of the block, and then came the roar of the little piece of artillery, which had so long dwelt there in silence. The rattling of a shot among the sheds, and the rending of timber, followed. Fifty dark forms were seen, by the momentary light, gliding from among the out-buildings, in an alarm natural to their ignorance, and with an agility proportioned to their alarm. The moment was propitious. Content silently motioned to Reuben Ring; they passed the postern together, and disappeared in the direction of the barns. The period of their absence was one of intense care to Ruth, and it was not without its anxiety even to those whose nerves were better steeled. A few moments, however, served to appease these feelings; for the adventurers returned in safety, and as silently as they had quitted the defences. The trampling of feet on the crust of the snow, the neighing of horses, and the bellowing of frightened cattle, as the terrified beasts scattered about the fields, soon proclaimed the object of the risk which had just been run.

"Enter!" whispered Ruth, who held the postern with her own hand. "Enter, of Heaven's mercy! Thou hast given liberty to every hoof, that no living creature perish by the flames?"

"All; and truly not too speedily—for, see—the brand is again at work!"

Content had much reason to felicitate himself on

his expedition; for, even while he spoke, half-concealed torches, made as usual of blazing knots of pine, were again seen glancing across the fields, evidently approaching the out-buildings by such indirect and covered paths, as might protect those who bore them from the shot of the garrison. A final and common effort was made to arrest the danger. The muskets of the young men were active, and more than once did the citadel of the stern old Puritan give forth its flood of flame, in order to beat back the dangerous visitants. A few shrieks of savage disappointment and of bodily anguish, announced the success of these discharges; but, though most of those who approached the barns were either driven back in fear, or suffered for their temerity, one among them, more wary or more practised than his companions, found means to effect his object. The firing had ceased, and the besieged were congratulating themselves on success, when a sudden light glared across the fields. A sheet of flame soon came curling over the crest of a wheat-stack, and quickly wrapped the inflammable material in its fierce torrent. Against this destruction there remained no remedy. The barns and inclosures which, so lately, had been lying in the darkness of the hour, were instantly illuminated, and life would have been the penalty paid by any of either party, who should dare to trust his person within the bright glare. The borderers were soon compelled to fall back, even within the shadows of the hill, and to seek such covers as the stockades offered, in order to avoid the aim of the arrow or the bullet.

"This is a mournful spectacle to one that has harvested in charity with all men;" said Content to the trembler who convulsively grasped his arm, as the flame whirled in the currents of the heated air, and, sweeping once or twice across the roof of a shed, left a portion of its torrent creeping insidiously along the wooden covering. "The in-gathering of a blessed season is about to melt into ashes, before the brand of these accur——"

"Peace, Heathcote! What is wealth, or the fulness of thy granaries, to that which remains? Check these repinings of thy spirit, and bless God that he leaveth us our babes, and the safety of our inner roofs."

"Thou sayest truly," returned the husband, endeavoring to imitate the meek resignation of his companion. "What indeed are the gifts of the world, set in the balance against the peace of mind —ha! that evil blast of wind sealeth the destruction of our harvest! The fierce element is in the heart of the granaries."

Ruth made no reply, for though less moved by worldly cares than her husband, the frightful progress of the conflagration alarmed her with a sense of personal danger. The flames had passed from roof to roof, and meeting everywhere with fuel of the most combustible nature, the whole of the vast range of barns, sheds, granaries, cribs and out-buildings, was just breaking forth in the brightness of a torrent of fire. Until this moment, suspense, with hope on one side and apprehension on the other, had kept both parties mute spectators of the scene. But yells of triumph soon proclaimed the delight with which the Indians witnessed the completion of their fell design. The whoops followed this burst of pleasure, and a third onset was made.

The combatants now fought under a brightness which, though less natural, was scarcely less brilliant than that of noon-day. Stimulated by the prospect of success, which was offered by the conflagration, the savages rushed upon the stockade with more audacity than it was usual to display in their cautious warfare. A broad shadow was cast, by the hill and its buildings, across the fields on the side opposite to the flames, and through this belt of comparative gloom, the fiercest of the band made their way to the very palisadoes, with impunity. Their presence was announced by the yell of delight, for too many curious eyes had been drinking in the fearful beauty of the conflagration, to note their approach, until the attack had nearly proved successful. The rushes to the defence, and to the attack, were now alike quick and headlong. Volleys were useless, for the timbers offered equal security to both assailant and assailed. It was a struggle of hand to hand, in which numbers would have prevailed, had it not been the good fortune of the weaker party to act on the defensive. Blows of the knife were passed swiftly between the timbers, and occasionally the discharge of the musket, or the twanging of the bow was heard.

"Stand to the timbers, my men!" said the deep tones of the stranger, who spoke in the midst of the fierce struggle with that commanding and stirring cheerfulness that familiarity with danger can alone inspire. "Stand to the defences, and they are impassable. Ha! 'twas well meant, friend savage," he muttered between his teeth, as he parried, at some jeopardy to one hand, a thrust aimed at his throat, while with the other he seized the warrior who had inflicted the blow, and drawing his naked breast, with the power of a giant, full against the opening between the timbers, he buried his own keen blade to its haft in the body. The eyes of the victim rolled wildly, and when the iron hand which bound him to the wood, with the power of a vice, loosened its grasp, he fell motionless on the earth. This death was succeeded by the usual yell of disappointment, and the assailants disappeared, as swiftly as they had approached.

"God be praised, that we have to rejoice in this advantage!" said Content, enumerating the individuals of his force, with an anxious eye, when all were again assembled at the stand on the hill, where, favored by the glaring light, they could overlook, in comparative security, the more exposed parts of their defences. "We count our own, though I fear me, many may have suffered."

The silence and the occupations of his listeners most of whom were stanching their blood, was a sufficient answer.

"Hist, father!" said the quick-eyed and observant Mark; "one remaineth on the palisado nearest the wicket. Is it a savage? or do I see a stump, in the field beyond?"

All eyes followed the direction of the hand of the speaker, and there was seen, of a certainty, something clinging to the inner side of one of the timbers, that bore a marked resemblance to the human form. The part of the stockades, where the seeming figure clung, lay more in obscurity than the rest of the defences, and doubts as to its character were not alone confined to the quick-sighted lad who had first detected its presence.

"Who hangs upon our palisadoes?" called Eben Dudley. "Speak, that we do not harm a friend!"

The wood itself was not more immovable than the dark object, until the report of the borderer's musket was heard, and then it came tumbling to the earth like an insensible mass.

"Fallen like a stricken bear from his tree! Life was in it, or no bullet of mine could have loosened the hold!" exclaimed Dudley, a little in exultation as he saw the success of his aim.

"I will go forward, and see that he is past——"

The mouth of young Mark, was stopped by the hand of the stranger, who calmly observed—

"I will look into the fate of the heathen, myself." He was about to proceed to the spot, when the supposed dead, or wounded man, sprang to his feet, with a yell that rang in echoes along the margin of the forest, and bounded towards the cover of the buildings, with high and active leaps. Two or three muskets sent their streaks of flame across his path, but seemingly without success. Jumping in a manner to elude the certainty of their fire, the unharmed savage gave forth another yell of triumph, and disappeared among the angles of the dwellings. His cries were understood, for answering whoops were heard in the fields, and the foe without again rallied to the attack.

"This may not be neglected," said he who, more by his self-possession and air of authority, than by any known right to command, had insensibly assumed so much authority in the important business of that night. "One like this, within our walls, may quickly bring destruction on the garrison. The postern may be opened to an inroad——"

"A triple lock secures it," interrupted Content. "The key is hid where none know to seek it, other than such as are of our household."

"And happily the means of passing the private wicket are in my possession," muttered the other, in an under tone. "So far, well; but the brand! the brand! the maidens must look to the fires and lights, while the youths make good the stockade, since this assault admitteth not of further delay."

So saying, the stranger gave an example of courage by proceeding to his stand at the pickets, where, supported by his companions, he continued to defend the approaches against a discharge of arrows and bullets that was more distant, but scarcely less dangerous to the safety of those who showed themselves on the side of the acclivity, than those which had been previously showered upon the garrison.

In the mean time, Ruth summoned her assistants, and hastened to discharge the duty which had just been prescribed. Water was cast freely on all the fires, and, as the still raging conflagration continued to give far more light than was either necessary or safe, care was taken to extinguish any torch or candle that, in the hurry of alarm, might have been left to moulder in its socket, throughout the extensive range of the dwellings and the offices.

CHAPTER XIV.

> "Thou mild, sad mother—
> Quit him not so soon!
> Mother, in mercy, stay!
> Despair and death are with him; and canst thou,
> With that kind, earthward look, go leave him now?"
>
> DANA.

When these precautions were taken, the females returned to their several look-outs; and Ruth, whose duty it was in moments of danger to exercise a general superintendence, was left to her meditations and to such watchfulness as her fears might excite. Quitting the inner rooms, she approached the door that communicated with the court, and for a moment lost the recollection of her immediate cares in a view of the imposing scene by which she was surrounded.

By this time, the whole of the vast range of outbuildings, which had been constructed, as was usual in the Colonies, of the most combustible materials and with no regard to the expenditure of wood, was wrapt in fire. Notwithstanding the position of the intermediate edifices, broad flashes of light were constantly crossing the court itself, on whose surface he was able to distinguish the smallest object, while the heavens above her were glaring with a lurid red. Through the openings between the buildings of the quadrangle, the eye could look out upon the fields, where she saw every evidence of a sullen intention on the part of the savages to persevere in their object. Dark, fierce-looking, and nearly naked human forms were seen flitting from cover to cover while there was no stump nor log within arrow's-flight of the defences, that did not protect the person of a daring and indefatigable enemy. It was plain the Indians were there in hundreds, and a the assaults continued after the failure of a surprise, it was too evident that they were bent on victory, at some hazard to themselves. No usual means of adding to the horrors of the scene were neglected. Whoops and yells were incessantly ringing around the place, while the loud and often-repeated tones of a conch betrayed the artifice by which the savages had so often endeavored, in the earlier part of the night, to lure the garrison out of the palisadoes. A few scattering shot, discharged with deliberation and from every exposed point within the works, proclaimed both the coolness and the vigilance of the defendants. The little gun in the block-house was silent, for the Puritan knew too well its real power to lessen its reputation by a too frequent use The weapon was therefore reserved for those moments of pressing danger that would be sure to arrive.

On this spectacle Ruth gazed in fearful sadness The long-sustained and sylvan security of her abode was violently destroyed; and in the place of a quiet which had approached as near as may be on earth to that holy peace for which her spirit strove, she and all she most loved were suddenly confronted to the most frightful exhibition of human horrors. In such a moment, the feelings of a mother were likely to revive; and ere time was given for reflection, aided by the light of the conflagration, the matron was moving swiftly through the intricate passages of the dwelling, in quest of those whom she had placed in the security of the chambers.

"Thou hast remembered to avoid looking on the fields, my children," said the nearly breathless woman as she entered the room. "Be thankful, babes; hitherto the efforts of the savages have been vain and we still remain masters of our habitations."

"Why is the night so red? Come hither, mother thou mayest look into the wood as if the sun were shining!"

"The heathens have fired our granaries, and what thou seest is the light of the flames. But happily they cannot put brand into the dwellings, while thy father and the young men stand to their weapons. We must be grateful for this security, frail as it seemeth. Thou hast knelt, my Ruth; and hast remembered to think of thy father and brother in thy prayers."

"I will do so again, mother," whispered the child, bending to her knees, and wrapping her young features in the garments of the matron.

"Why hide thy countenance? One young and innocent as thou, may lift thine eyes to Heaven with confidence."

"Mother, I see the Indian, unless my face be hid. He looketh at me, I fear, with wish to do us harm."

"Thou art not just to Miantonimoh, child," answered Ruth, as she glanced her eye rapidly round to seek the boy, who had modestly withdrawn into a remote and shaded corner of the room. "I left him with thee for a guardian, and not as one who would wish to injure. Now think of thy God, child," imprinting a kiss on the cold, marble-like forehead of her daughter, "and have reliance in his goodness. Miantonimoh, I again leave you with a charge to be their protector," she added, quitting her daughter and advancing towards the youth.

"Mother!" shrieked the child, "come to me, or I die!"

Ruth turned from the listening captive, with the quickness of instinct. A glance showed her the jeopardy of her offspring. A naked savage, dark, powerful of frame, and fierce in the frightful masquerade of his war-paint, stood winding the silken hair of the girl in one hand, while he already held the glittering axe above a head that seemed inevitably devoted to destruction.

"Mercy! mercy!" exclaimed Ruth, hoarse with horror, and dropping to her knees, as much from inability to stand as with intent to petition. "Monster, strike me, but spare the child!"

The eyes of the Indian rolled over the person of the speaker, but it was with an expression that seemed rather to enumerate the number of his victims, than to announce any change of purpose. With a fiend-like coolness, that bespoke much knowledge of the ruthless practice, he again swung the quivering but speechless child in the air, and prepared to direct the weapon with a fell certainty of aim. The tomahawk had made its last circuit, and an instant would have decided the fate of the victim, when the captive boy stood in front of the frightful actor in this revolting scene. By a quick, forward movement of his arm, the blow was arrested. The deep guttural ejaculation, which betrays the surprise of an Indian, broke from the chest of the savage, while his hand fell to his side, and the form of the suspended girl was suffered again to touch the floor. The look and gesture with which the boy had interfered, expressed authority rather than resentment or horror. His air was calm, collected, and, as it appeared by the effect, imposing.

"Go," he said in the language of the fierce people from whom he had sprung; "the warriors of the pale men are calling thee by name."

"The snow is red with the blood of our young men," the other fiercely answered; "and not a scalp is at the belt of my people."

"These are mine," returned the boy with dignity, sweeping his arm, while speaking, in a manner to show that he extended protection to all present.

The warrior gazed about him grimly, and like one but half-convinced. He had incurred a danger too fearful, in entering the stockade, to be easily diverted from his purpose.

"Listen!" he continued, after a short pause, during which the artillery of the Puritan had again bellowed in the uproar, without. "The thunder is with the Yengeese! Our young women will look another way and call us Pequots, should there be no scalps on our pole."

For a single moment, the countenance of the boy changed, and his resolution seemed to waver. The other, who watched his eyes with longing eagerness, again seized his victim by the hair, when Ruth shrieked in the accents of despair—

"Boy! boy! if thou art not with us, God hath deserted us!"

"She is mine," burst fiercely from the lips of the lad. "Hear my words, Wompahwisset; the blood of my father is very warm within me."

The other paused, and the blow was once more suspended. The glaring eye-balls of the savage rested intently on the swelling form and stern countenance of the young hero, whose uplifted hand appeared to menace instant punishment, should he dare to disregard the mediation. The lips of the warrior severed, and the word 'Miantonimoh' was uttered as softly as if it recalled a feeling of sorrow. Then, as a sudden burst of yells rose above the roar of the conflagration, the fierce Indian turned in his tracks, and, abandoning the trembling and nearly insensible child, he bounded away like a hound loosened on a fresh scent of blood.

"Boy! boy!" murmured the mother; "heathen or Christian, there is one that will bless thee!—"

A rapid gesture of the hand interrupted the fervent expression of her gratitude. Pointing after the form of the retreating savage, the lad encircled his own head with a finger, in a manner that could not be mistaken, as he uttered steadily, but with the deep emphasis of an Indian—

"The young Pale-face has a scalp!"

Ruth heard no more. With instinctive rapidity, every feeling of her soul quickened nearly to agony, she rushed below, in order to warn Mark against the machinations of so fearful an enemy. Her step was heard but for a moment in the vacant chambers, and then the Indian boy, whose steadiness and authority had just been so signally exerted in favor of the children, resumed his attitude of meditation, as quietly as if he took no further interest in the frightful events of the night.

The situation of the garrison was now, indeed, to the last degree critical. A torrent of fire had passed from the further extremity of the out-houses to that which stood nearest to the defences, and, as building after building melted beneath its raging power, the palisadoes became heated nearly to the point of ignition. The alarm created by this imminent danger had already been given, and, when Ruth issued into the court, a female was rushing past her, seemingly on some errand of the last necessity.

"Hast seen him?" demanded the breathless mother, arresting the steps of the quick-moving girl.

"Not since the savage made his last onset, but I warrant me he may be found near the western loops, making good the works against the enemy!"

"Surely he is not foremost in the fray! Of whom speakest thou, Faith? I questioned thee of Mark

There is one, even now, raging within the pickets seeking a victim."

"Truly, I thought it had been question of—— the boy is with his father and the stranger soldier who does such deeds of valor in our behalf. I have seen no enemy within the palisadoes, Madam Heathcote, since the entry of the man who escaped, by favor of the powers of darkness, from the shot of Eben Dudley's musket."

"And is this evil like to pass from us," resumed Ruth, breathing more freely, as she learned the safety of her son; "or does Providence veil its face in anger?"

"We keep our own, though the savage hath pressed the young men to extremity. Oh! it gladdened heart to see how brave a guard Reuben Ring, and others near him, made in our behalf. I do think me, Madam Heathcote, that, after all, there is real manhood in the brawler Dudley! Truly, the youth hath done marvels in the way of exposure and resistance. Twenty times this night have I expected to see him slain."

"And he that lyeth there?" half-whispered the alarmed Ruth, pointing to a spot near them, where, aside from the movements of those who still acted in the bustle of the combat, one lay stretched on the earth—"who hath fallen?"

The cheek of Faith blanched to a whiteness that nearly equalled that of the linen, which, even in the hurry of such a scene, some friendly hand had found leisure to throw, in decent sadness, over the form.

"That!" said the faltering girl; "though hurt and bleeding, my brother Reuben surely keepeth the loop at the western angle; nor is Whittal wanting in sufficient sense to take heed of danger—This may not be the stranger, for under the covers of the postern breast-work he holdeth counsel with the young captain."

"Art certain, girl?"

"I saw them both within the minute. Would to God we could hear the shout of noisy Dudley, Madam Heathcote: his cry cheereth the heart, in a moment awful as this!"

"Lift the cloth," said Ruth with calm solemnity, "that we may know which of our friends hath been called to the great account."

Faith hesitated, and when, by a powerful effort, in which secret interest had as deep an influence as obedience, she did comply, it was with a sort of desperate resolution. On raising the linen, the eyes of the two women rested on the pallid countenance of one who had been transfixed by an iron-headed arrow. The girl dropped the linen, and in a voice that sounded like a burst of hysterical feeling, she exclaimed—

"'Tis but the youth that came lately among us! We are spared the loss of any ancient friend."

"Tis one who died for our safety. I would give largely of this world's comforts, that this calamity might not have been, or that greater leisure for the last fearful reckoning had been accorded. But we may not lose the moments in mourning. Hie thee, girl, and sound the alarm that a savage lurketh within our walls, and that he skulketh in quest of a secret blow. Bid all be wary. If the young Mark should cross thy path, speak to him twice of this danger; the child hath a froward spirit, and may not hearken to words uttered in too great hurry."

With this charge, Ruth quitted her maiden. While the latter proceeded to give the necessary notice, the other sought the spot where she had just learned there was reason to believe her husband might be found.

Content and the stranger were in fact met in

consultation over the danger which threatened destruction to their most important means of defence. The savages themselves appeared to be conscious that the flames were working in their favor; for their efforts sensibly slackened, and having already severely suffered in their attempts to annoy the garrison, they had fallen back to their covers, and awaited the moment when their practised cunning should tell them they might, with more flattering promises of success, again rally to the onset. A brief explanation served to make Ruth acquainted with the imminent jeopardy of their situation. Under a sense of a more appalling danger, she lost the recollection of her former purpose, and with a contracted and sorrowing eye, she stood like her companions, in impotent helplessness, an entranced spectator of the progress of the destruction.

"A soldier should not waste words in useless plaints," observed the stranger, folding his arms like one who was conscious that human effort could do no more, "else should I say, 'tis pity that he who drew yon line of stockade hath not remembered the uses of the ditch."

"I will summon the maidens to the wells," said Ruth.

"'Twill not avail us. The arrow would be among them, nor could mortal long endure the heat of yon glowing furnace. Thou seest that the timbers already smoke and blacken, under its fierceness."

The stranger was still speaking, when a small quivering flame played on the corners of the palisado nearest the burning pile. The element fluttered like a waving line along the edges of the heated wood, after which it spread over the whole surface of the timber, from its larger base to the pointed summit. As if this had merely been the signal of a general destruction, the flames kindled in fifty places at the same instant, and then the whole line of the stockade, nearest the conflagration, was covered with fire. A yell of triumph arose in the fields, and a flight of arrows, sailing tauntingly into the works, announced the fierce impatience of those who watched the increase of the conflagration.

"We shall be driven to our block," said Content "Assemble thy maidens, Ruth, and make speedy preparation for the last retreat."

"I go; but hazard not thy life in any vain endeavor to retard the flames. There will yet be time for all that is needful to our security."

"I know not," hurriedly observed the stranger. "Here cometh the assault in a new aspect!"

The feet of Ruth were arrested. On looking upward, she saw the object which had drawn this remark from the last speaker. A small bright ball of fire had arisen out of the fields, and, describing an arc in the air, it sailed above their heads and fell on the shingles of a building which formed part of the quadrangle of the inner court. The movement was that of an arrow thrown from a distant bow, and its way was to be traced by a long trail of light, that followed its course like a blazing meteor. This burning arrow had been sent with a cool and practised judgment. It lighted upon a portion of the combustibles that were nearly as inflammable as gunpowder, and the eye had scarcely succeeded in tracing it to its fall, ere the bright flames were seen stealing over the heated roof.

"One struggle for our habitations!" cried Content—but the hand of the stranger was placed firmly on his shoulder. At that instant, a dozen similar meteor-looking balls shot into the air, and fell in as many different places on the already half-kindled pile. Further efforts would have been useless. Relinquishing the hope of saving his property, every thought was now given to personal safety.

Ruth recovered from her short trance, and has

tened with hurried steps to perform her well-known office. Then came a few minutes of exertion, during which the females transferred all that was necessary to their subsistence, and which had not been already provided in the block, to their little citadel. The glowing light, which penetrated the darkest passages among the buildings, prevented this movement from being made without discovery. The whoop summoned their enemies to another attack: The arrows thickened in the air, and the important duty was not performed without risk, as all were obliged, in some degree, to expose their persons, while passing to and fro, loaded with necessaries. The gathering smoke, however, served in some measure for a screen; and it was not long before Content received the welcome tidings that he might command the retreat of his young men from the palisadoes. The conch sounded the necessary signal, and ere the foe had time to understand its meaning, or profit by the defenceless state of the works, every individual within them had reached the door of the block in safety. Still, there was more of hurry and confusion than altogether comported with their safety. They who were assigned to that duty, however, mounted eagerly to the loops, and stood in readiness to pour out their fire on whoever might dare to come within its reach, while a few still lingered in the court, to see that no necessary provision for resistance, or of safety, was forgotten. Ruth had been foremost in exertion, and she now stood pressing her hands to her temples, like one whose mind was bewildered by her own efforts.

"Our fallen friend!" she said. "Shall we leave his remains to be mangled by the savage?"

"Surely not; Dudley, thy hand. We will bear the body within the lower——ha! death hath struck another of our family."

The alarm with which Content made this discovery passed quickly to all in hearing. It was but too apparent, by the shape of the linen, that two bodies lay beneath its folds. Anxious and rapid looks were cast from face to face, in order to learn who was missing; and then, conscious of the hazard of further delay, Content raised the linen, in order to remove all doubts by certainty. The form of the young borderer, who was known to have fallen, was first slowly and reverently uncovered; but even the most self-restrained among the spectators started back in horror, as his robbed and reeking head showed that a savage hand had worked its ruthless will on the unresisting corpse.

"The other!" Ruth struggled to say, and it was only as her husband had half removed the linen that she could succeed in uttering the words—"Beware the other!"

The warning was not useless, for the linen waved violently as it rose under the hand of Content, and a grim Indian sprang into the very centre of the startled group. Sweeping his armed hand widely about him, the savage broke through the receding circle, and, giving forth the appalling whoop of his tribe, he bounded into the open door of the principal dwelling, so swiftly as utterly to defeat any design of pursuit. The arms of Ruth were frantically extended towards the place where he had disappeared, and she was about to rush madly on hi footsteps, when the hand of her husband stoppe the movement.

"Wouldst hazard life, to save some worthless trifle?"

"Husband, release me!" returned the woman, nearly choked with her agony—"nature hath slept within me!"

"Fear blindeth thy reason!"

The form of Ruth ceased to struggle. All the

madness, which had been glaring wildly about her eyes, disappeared in the settled look of an almost preternatural calm. Collecting the whole of her mental energy in one desperate effort of self-command, she turned to her husband, and, as her bosom swelled with the terror that seemed to stop her breath, she said in a voice that was frightful by its composure—

"If thou hast a father's heart, release me!—Our babes have been forgotten!"

The hand of Content relaxed its hold, and, in another instant, the form of his wife was lost to view on the track that had just been taken by the successful savage. This was the luckless moment chosen by the foe to push his advantage. A fierce burst of yells proclaimed the activity of the assailants, and a general discharge from the loops of the block-house sufficiently apprised those in the court that the onset of the enemy was now pushed into the very heart of the defences. All had mounted, but the few who lingered to discharge the melancholy duty to the dead. They were too few to render resistance prudent, and yet too many to think of deserting the distracted mother and her offspring without an effort.

"Enter," said Content, pointing to the door of the block. "It is my duty to share the fate of those nearest my blood."

The Stranger made no answer. Placing his powerful hands on the nearly stupified husband, he thrust his person, by an irresistible effort, within the basement of the building, and then he signed, by a quick gesture, for all around him to follow. After the last form had entered, he commanded that the fastenings of the door should be secured, remaining himself, as he believed, alone without. But when by a rapid glance he saw there was another gazing in dull awe on the features of the fallen man, it was too late to rectify the mistake. Yells were now rising out of the black smoke, that was rolling in volumes from the heated buildings, and it was plain that only a few feet divided them from their pursuers. Beckoning the man who had been excluded from the block to follow, the stern soldier rushed into the principal dwelling, which was still but little injured by the fire. Guided rather by chance than by any knowledge of the windings of the building, he soon found himself in the chambers. He was now at a loss whither to proceed. At that moment, his companion, who was no other than Whittal Ring, took the lead, and in another instant, they were at the door of the secret apartment.

"Hist!" said the stranger, raising a hand to command silence as he entered the room. "Our hope is in secrecy."

"And how may we escape without detection?" demanded the mother, pointing about her at objects illuminated by a light so powerful as to penetrate every cranny of the ill-constructed building. "The noon-day sun is scarce brighter than this dreadful fire!"

"God is in the elements! His guiding hand shall point the way. But here we may not tarry, for the flames are already on the shingles. Follow, and speak not."

Ruth pressed the children to her side, and the whole party left the apartment of the attic in a body. Their descent to a lower room was made quickly, and without discovery. But here their leader paused, for the state of things without was one to demand the utmost steadines of nerve, and great reflection.

The Indians had by this time gained command of the whole of Mark Heathcote's possessions, with the exception of the block-house; and as their first act had been to apply the brand wherever it might be wanting, the roar of the conflagration was now heard in every direction. The discharge of muskets and the whoops of the combatants, however, while they added to the horrible din of such a scene, proclaimed the unconquered resolution of those who held the citadel. A window of the room they occupied enabled the stranger to take a cautious survey of what was passing without. The court, lighted to the brilliancy of day, was empty; for the increasing heat of the fires, no less than the discharges from the loops, still kept the cautious savages to their covers. There was barely hope, that the space between the dwelling and the block-house might yet be passed in safety.

"I would I had asked that the door of the block should be held in hand," muttered Submission; "it would be death to linger an instant in that fierce light; nor have we any manner of——"

A touch was laid upon his arm, and turning, the speaker saw the dark eye of the captive boy looking steadily in his face.

"Wilt do it?" demanded the other, in a manner to show that he doubted, while he hoped.

A speaking gesture of assent was the answer, and then the form of the lad was seen gliding quietly from the room.

Another instant, and Miantonimoh appeared in the court. He walked with the deliberation that one would have shown in moments of the most entire security. A hand was raised towards the loops, as if to betoken amity, and then dropping the limb, he moved with the same slow step into the very centre of the area. Here the boy stood in the fulles glare of the conflagration, and turned his face deliberately on every side of him. The action showed that he wished to invite all eyes to examine his person. At this moment the yells ceased in the surrounding covers, proclaiming alike the common feeling that was awakened by his appearance, and the hazard that any other would have incurred by exposing himself in that fearful scene. When this act of exceeding confidence had been performed, the boy drew a pace nearer to the entrance of the block.

"Comest thou in peace, or is this another device of Indian treachery?" demanded a voice, through an opening in the door left expressly for the purposes of parley.

The boy raised the palm of one hand towards the speaker, while he laid the other with a gesture of confidence on his naked breast.

"Hast aught to offer in behalf of my wife and babes? If gold will buy their ransom, name thy price."

Miantonimoh was at no loss to comprehend the other's meaning. With the readiness of one whose faculties had been early schooled in the inventions of emergencies, he made a gesture that said even more than his figurative words, as he answered—

"Can a woman of the Pale-faces pass through wood? An Indian arrow is swifter than the foot of my mother."

"Boy, I trust thee," returned the voice from within the loop. "If thou deceivest beings so feeble and so innocent, Heaven will remember the wrong."

Miantonimoh again made a sign to show that caution must be used, and then he retired with a step calm and measured as that used in his advance. Another pause to the shouts betrayed the interest of those whose fierce eyes watched his movements in the distance.

When the young Indian had rejoined the party in the dwelling, he led them, without being observed by the lurking band that still hovered in the smoke of the surrounding buildings, to a spot that commanded a full view of their short but perilous route. At this moment the door of the block-house half-opened, and was closed again. Still the stranger hesitated, for he saw how little was the chance that all should cross the court unharmed, and to pass it by repeated trials he knew to be impossible.

"Boy," he said, "thou, who hast done thus much, may still do more. Ask mercy for these children, in some manner that may touch the hearts of thy people."

Miantonimoh shook his head, and pointing to the ghastly corpse that lay in the court, he answered coldly—

"The red-man has tasted blood."

"Then must the desperate trial be done! Think not of thy children, devoted and daring mother, but look only to thine own safety. This witless youth and I will charge ourselves with the care of the innocents."

Ruth waved him away with her hand, pressing her mute and trembling daughter to her bosom, in a manner to show that her resolution was taken. The stranger yielded, and turning to Whittal, who stood near him, seemingly as much occupied in vacant admiration of the blazing piles as in any apprehension of his own personal danger, he bade him look to the safety of the remaining child. Moving in front himself, he was about to offer Ruth such protection as the case afforded, when a window in the rear of the house was dashed inward, announcing the entrance of the enemy, and the imminent danger that their flight would be intercepted. There was no time to lose, for it was now certain that only a single room separated them from their foes. The generous nature of Ruth was roused, and catching Martha from the arms of Whittal Ring, she endeavored, by a desperate effort, in which feeling rather than any reasonable motive predominated, to envelop both the children in her robe.

"I am with ye!" whispered the agitated woman. "hush ye, hush ye, babes! thy mother is nigh!"

The stranger was very differently employed. The instant the crash of glass was heard, he rushed to the rear; and he had already grappled with the savage so often named, and who acted as guide to a dozen fierce and yelling followers.

"To the block!" shouted the steady soldier, while with a powerful arm he held his enemy in the throat of the narrow passage, stopping the approach of those in the rear by the body of his foe. "For the love of life and children, woman, to the block!"

The summons rang frightfully in the ears of Ruth, but in that moment of extreme jeopardy her presence of mind was lost. The cry was repeated, and not till then did the bewildered mother catch her daughter from the floor. With eyes still bent on the fierce struggle in her rear, she clasped the child to her heart and fled, calling on Whittal Ring to follow. The lad obeyed, and ere she had half-crossed the court, the stranger, still holding his savage shield between him and his enemies, was seen endeavoring to take the same direction. The whoops, the flight of arrows, and the discharges of musquetry, that succeeded, proclaimed the whole extent of the danger. But fear had lent unnatural vigor to the limbs of Ruth, and the gliding arrows themselves scarce sailed more swiftly through the heated air, than she darted into the open door of the block. Whittal Ring was less successful. As he crossed the court, bearing the child intrusted to his care, an arrow pierced his flesh. Stung by the pain, the witless lad turned, in anger, to chide the hand that had inflicted the injury.

"On, foolish boy!" cried the stranger, as he passed him, still making a target of the body of the savage that was writhing in his grasp. "On, for thy life, and that of the babe!"

The mandate came too late. The hand of an Indian was already on the innocent victim, and in the next instant the child was sweeping the air, while with a short yell the keen axe flourished above his head. A shot from the loops laid the monster dead in his tracks. The girl was instantly seized by another hand, and as the captor with his prize darted unharmed into the dwelling, there arose in the block a common exclamation of the name of "Miantonimoh!" Two more of the savages profited by the pause of horror that followed, to lay hands on the wounded Whittal and to drag him within the blazing building. At the same moment, the stranger cast the unresisting savage back upon the weapons of his companions. The bleeding and half-strangled Indian met the blows which had been aimed at the life of the soldier, and as he staggered and fell, his vigorous conqueror disappeared in the block. The door of the little citadel was instantly closed, and the savages, who rushed headlong against the entrance, heard the fitting of the bars which secured it against their attacks. The yell of retreat was raised, and in the next instant the court was left to he possession of the dead.

CHAPTER XV.

"Did Heaven look on,
And would not take their part?—
—: Heaven rest them now!"
MACBETH.

"WE will be thankful for this blessing," said Content, as he aided the half-unconscious Ruth to mount the ladder, yielding himself to a feeling of nature that said little against his manhood. "If we have lost one, that we loved, God hath spared our own child."

His breathless wife threw herself into a seat, and folding the treasure to her bosom, she whispered rather than said aloud—"From my soul, Heathcote, am I grateful!"

"Thou shieldest the babe from my sight," returned the father, stooping to conceal a tear that was stealing down his brown cheek, under a pretence of embracing the child—but suddenly recoiling, he added in alarm—"Ruth!"

Startled by the tone in which her husband uttered her name, the mother threw aside the folds of her dress, which still concealed the girl, and stretching her out to the length of an arm, she saw that, in the hurry of the appalling scene, the children had been exchanged, and that she had saved the life of Martha!

Notwithstanding the generous disposition of Ruth, it was impossible to repress the feeling of disappointment which came over her with the consciousness of the mistake. Nature at first had sway, and to a degree that was fearfully powerful.

"It is not our babe!" shrieked the mother, still holding the child at the length of her arm, and gazing at its innocent and terrified countenance, with an expression that Martha had never yet seen gleaming from eyes that were, in common, so soft and so indulgent.

"I am thine! I am thine!" murmured the little trembler, struggling in vain to reach the bosom that had so long cherished her infancy. "If not thine, whose am I?"

The gaze of Ruth was still wild, the workings of her features hysterical.

"Madam—Mrs. Heathcote—mother!" came timidly, and at intervals, from the lips of the orphan. Then the heart of Ruth relented. She clasped the daughter of her friend to her breast, and Nature found a temporary relief in one of those frightful exhibitions of anguish, which appear to threaten the dissolution of the link which connects the soul with the body.

"Come, daughter of John Harding," said Content, looking around him with the assumed composure of a chastened man, while natural regret struggled hard at his heart; "this has been God's pleasure; it is meet that we kiss his parental hand. Let us be thankful," he added, with a quivering lip but steady eye, "that even this mercy hath been shown. Our babe is with the Indian, but our hopes are far beyond the reach of savage malignity. We have not 'laid up treasure where moth and rust can corrupt, or where thieves may break in and steal.' It may be hat the morning shall bring means of parley, and 1aply, opportunity of ransom."

There was the glimmering of hope in this suggestion. The idea seemed to give a new direction to the thoughts of Ruth, and the change enabled the long habits of self-restraint to regain something of their former ascendancy. The fountains of her tears became dry, and, after one short and terrible struggle, she was again enabled to appear composed. But at no time during the continuance of that fearful struggle, was Ruth Heathcote again the same ready and useful agent of activity and order that she had been in the earlier events of the night.

It is scarcely necessary to remind the reader that the brief burst of parental agony which has just been related, escaped Content and his wife amid a scene in which the other actors were too much occupied by their exertions to note its exhibition. The fate of those in the block was too evidently approaching its close, to allow of any interest in such an episode to the great tragedy of the moment.

The character of the contest had in some measure changed. There was no longer any immediate apprehension from the missiles of the assailants, though danger pressed upon the besieged in a new and even in a more horrible aspect. Now and then indeed an arrow quivered in the openings of the loops, and the blunt Dudley had once a narrow escape from the passage of a bullet, which, guided by chance, or aimed by a hand surer than common, glanced through one of the narrow slits, and would have terminated the history of the borderer, had not the head it obliquely encountered, been too solid to yield even to such an assault. The attention of the garrison was chiefly called to the imminent danger of the surrounding fire. Though the probability of such an emergency as that in which the family was now placed, had certainly been foreseen, and in some degree guarded against, in the size of the area and in the construction of the block, yet it was found that the danger exceeded all former calculations.

For the basement, there was no reason to feel alarm. It was of stone, and of a thickness and a material to put at defiance any artifices that their enemy might find time to practise. Even the two upper stories were comparatively safe; for they were composed of blocks so solid as to require time to heat them, and they were consequently as little liable to combustion as wood well could be. But the roof, like all of that, and indeed, like most of the present day in America, was composed of short inflammable shingles of pine. The superior height of the tower was some little protection, but as the flames rose roaring above the buildings of the court, and waved in wide circuits around the heated area, the whole of the fragile covering of the block was often wrapped in folds of fire. The result may be anticipated. Content was first recalled from the bitterness of his parental regret, by a cry, which passed among the family, that the roof of their little citadel was in flames. One of the ordinary wells of the habitation was in the basement of the edifice, and it was fortunate that no precaution necessary to render it serviceable in an emergency like that which was now arrived, had been neglected. A well-secured shaft of stone rose through the lower apartment into the upper floor. Profiting by this happy precaution, the handmaidens of Ruth plied the buckets with diligence, while the young men cast water freely on the roof, from the windows of the attic. The latter duty, it may readily be su posed, was not performed without hazard. Flig of arrows were constantly directed against the borers, and more than one of the youths received greater or less injuries, while exposed to their annoyance. There were indeed a few minutes, during which it remained a question of grave interest how far the risk they ran was likely to be crowned with success. The excessive heat of so many fires, and the occasional contact with the flames, as they swept in eddies over the place, began to render it doubtful whether any human efforts could long arrest the evil. Even the massive and moistened logs of the body of the work began to smoke; and it was found, by experiment, that the hand could rest but a moment on their surface.

During this interval of deep suspense, all the men posted at the loops were called to aid in extinguishing the fire. Resistance was forgotten in the discharge of a duty that had become still more pressing. Ruth herself was aroused by the nature of the alarm, and all hands and all minds were arduously occupied in a toil that diverted attention from incidents which had less interest, because they were teeming less with instant destruction. Danger is known to lose its terrors by familiarity. The young borderers became reckless of their persons in the ardor of exertion, and as success began to crown their efforts, something like the levity of happier moments got the better of their concern. Stolen and curious glances were thrown around a place that had so long been kept sacred to the secret uses of the Puritan, when it was found that the flames were subdued, and that the present danger was averted. The light glared powerfully through several openings in the shingles, no less than through the windows; and every eye was enabled to scan the contents of an apartment which all had longed, though none had ever before presumed, to enter.

The Captain looketh well to the body," whisred Reuben Ring to one of his comrades, as he wiped the effects of the toil from a sun-burnt brow. 'Thou seest, Hiram, that there is good store of cheer."

"The buttery is not better stored!" returned the other, with the shrewdness and ready observation of a border-man. "It is known that he never toucheth that which the cow yields, except as it comes from the creature, and here we find of the best that the Madam's dairy can yield!"

"Surely yon buff jerkin is like to those worn by

the idle cavaliers at home! I think it be long since the Captain hath ridden forth in such a guise."

"That may be matter of ancient usage, for thou seest he hath relics of the fashion of the English troopers in this bit of steel; it is like, he holdeth deep exercise over the vanities of his youth, while recalling the times in which they were worn."

This conjecture appeared to satisfy the other, though it is probable that a sight of a fresh store of bodily aliment, which was soon after exposed in order to gain access to the roof, might have led to some further inferences, had more time been given to conjectures. But at this moment a new wail proceeded from the maidens who plied the buckets beneath.

"To the loops! to the loops, or we are lost!" was a summons that admitted of no delay. Led by the stranger, the young men rushed below, where, in truth, they found a serious demand on all their activity and courage.

The Indians were wanting in none of the sagacity which so remarkably distinguishes the warfare of this cunning race. The time spent by the family, in arresting the flames, had not been thrown away by the assailants. Profiting by the attention of those within, to efforts that were literally of the last importance, they had found means to convey burning brands to the door of the block, against which they had piled a mass of blazing combustibles, that threatened shortly to open the way into the basement of the citadel itself. In order to mask this design, and to protect their approaches, the savages had succeeded in dragging bundles of straw and other similar materials to the foot of the work, to which the fire soon communicated, and which consequently served both to increase the actual danger of the building and to distract the attention of those by whom it was defended. Although the water that fell from the roof served to retard the progress of these flames, it contributed to produce the effect of all others that was most desired by the savages The dense volumes of smoke that arose from the half-smothered fire, first apprised the females of the new danger which assailed them. When Content and the stranger reached the principal floor of their citadel, it required some little time, and no small degree of coolness, to comprehend the situation in which they were now placed. The vapor that rolled upward from the wet straw and hay had already penetrated into the apartment, and it was with no slight difficulty that they who occupied it were enabled to distinguish objects, or even to breathe.

"Here is matter to exercise our utmost fortitude," said the stranger to his constant companion. "We must look to this new device, or we come to the fate of death by fire. Summon the stoutest-hearted of thy youths, and I will lead them to a sortie, ere the evil get past a remedy."

"That were certain victory to the heathen. Thou hearest, by their yells, that 'tis no small band of scouters who beleaguer us; a tribe hath sent forth its chosen warriors to do their wickedness. Better is it that we bestir ourselves to drive them from our door, and to prevent the further annoyance of this cloud, since, to issue from the block, at this moment, would be to offer our heads to the tomahawk; and to ask mercy is as vain as to hope to move the rock with tears."

"And in what manner may we do this needful service?"

"Our muskets will still command the entrance, by means of these downward loops, and water may be yet applied through the same openings. Thought hath been had of this danger, in the disposition of the place."

"Then, of Heaven's mercy! delay not the effort."

The necessary measures were taken, instantly. Eben Dudley applied the muzzle of his piece to a oop, and discharged it downward, in the direction of the endangered door. But aim was impossible in the obscurity, and his want of success was proclaimed by a taunting shout of triumph. Then followed a flood of water, which however was scarcely of more service, since the savages had foreseen its use, and had made a provision against its effects by placing boards, and such vessels as they found scattered among the buildings, above the fire, in a manner to prevent most of the fluid from reaching its aim.

"Come hither with thy musket, Reuben Ring," said Content, hurriedly; "the wind stirreth the smoke, here; the savages still heap fuel against the wall."

The borderer complied. There were in fact moments when dark human forms were to be seen gliding in silence around the building, though the density of the vapor rendered the forms indistinct and their movements doubtful. With a cool and practised eye, the youth sought a victim; but as he discharged his musket, an object glanced near his own visage, as though the bullet had recoiled on him who had given it a very different mission. Stepping backward a little hurriedly, he saw the stranger pointing through the smoke at an arrow which still quivered in the floor above them.

"We cannot long abide these assaults," the soldier muttered; "something must be speedily devised, or we fall."

His words ceased, for a yell that appeared to lift the floor on which he stood, announced the destruction of the door and the presence of the savages in the basement of the tower. Both parties appeared momentarily confounded at this unexpected success; for while the one stood mute with astonishment and dread, the other did little more than triumph. But this inaction soon ended. The conflict was resumed, though the efforts of the assailants began to assume the confidence of victory, while, on the part of the besieged, they partook fearfully of the aspect of despair.

A few muskets were discharged, both from below and above, at the intermediate floor, but the thickness of the planks prevented the bullets from doing injury. Then commenced a struggle in which the respective qualities of the combatants were exhibited in a singularly characteristic manner. While the Indians improved their advantages beneath, with all the arts known to savage warfare, the young men resisted with that wonderful aptitude of expedient, and readiness of execution, which distinguish the American borderer.

The first attempt of the assailants was to burn the floor of the lower apartment. In order to effect this, they threw vast piles of straw into the basement. But ere the brand was applied, water had reduced the inflammable material to a black and murky pile. Still the smoke had nearly effected a conquest which the fire itself had failed to achieve. So suffocating indeed were the clouds of vapor which ascended through the crevices, that the females were compelled to seek a refuge in the attic. Here the openings in the roof, and a swift current of air, relieved them, in some degree, from its annoyance.

When it was found that the command of the well afforded the besieged the means of protecting the wood-work of the interior, an effort was made to cut off the communication with the water, by forcing a passage into the circular stone shaft, through which it was drawn into the room above. This attempt was defeated by the readiness of the youths, who soon cut holes in the floor, whence they sent down certain death on all beneath. Perhaps no part of the assault was more obstinate than that which accompanied this effort; nor did either assailants or assailed, at any time during its continuance, suffer greater personal injury. After a long and fierce struggle, the resistance was effectual, and the savages had recourse to new schemes in order to effect their ruthless object.

During the first moments of their entrance, and with a view to reap the fruits of the victory when the garrison should be more effectually subdued, most of the furniture of the dwelling had been scattered by the conquerors on the side of the hill. Among other articles, some six or seven beds had been dragged from the dormitories. These were now brought into play, as powerful instruments in the assault. They were cast, one by one, on the still burning though smothered flames, in the basement of the block, whence they sent up a cloud of their intolerable effluvia. At this trying moment, the appalling cry was heard in the block, that the well had failed! The buckets ascended as empty as they went down, and they were thrown aside as no longer useful. The savages seemed to comprehend their advantage, for they profited by the confusion that succeeded among the assailed, to feed the slumbering fires. The flames kindled fiercely, and in less than a minute they became too violent to be subdued. They were soon seen playing on the planks of the floor above. The subtle element flashed from point to point, and it was not long ere it was stealing up the outer side of the heated block itself.

The savages now knew that conquest was sure. Yells and whoopings proclaimed the fierce delight with which they witnessed the certainty of their victory. Still there was something portentous in the death-like silence with which the victims within the block awaited their fate. The whole exterior of the building was already wrapped in flames, and yet no show of further resistance, no petition for mercy, issued from its bosom. The unnatural and frightful stillness, that reigned within, was gradually communicated to those without. The cries and shouts of triumph ceased, and the crackling of the flames, or the falling of timber in the adjoining buildings, alone disturbed the awful calm. At length a solitary voice was heard in the block. Its tones were deep, solemn, and imploring. The fierce beings who surrounded the glowing pile bent forward to listen, for their quick faculties caught the first sounds that were audible. It was Mark Heathcote pouring out his spirit in prayer. The petition was fervent, but steady, and though uttered in words that were unintelligible to those without, they knew enough of the practices of the Colonists, to be aware that it was the chief of the Pale-faces holding communion with his God. Partly in awe, and partly in doubt of what might be the consequences of so mysterious an asking, the dark crowd with drew to a little distance, and silently watched the progress of the destruction. They had heard strange sayings of the power of the Deity of their invaders, and as their victims appeared suddenly to cease using any of the known means of safety, they appeared to expect, perhaps they did expect, some unequivocal manifestation of the power of the Great Spirit of the stranger.

Still no sign of pity, no relenting from the ruthless barbarity of their warfare, escaped any of the assailants. If they thought at all of the temporal fate of those who might still exist within the fiery pile, it was only to indulge in some passing regret, that the obstinacy of the defence had deprived them of the glory of bearing the usual bloody tokens of victory, in triumph to their villages. But even these peculiar and deeply-rooted feelings were for gotten, as the progress of the flames placed the hope of its indulgence beyond all possibility.

The roof of the block rekindled, and, by the light that shone through the loops, it was but too evident the interior was in a blaze. Once or twice, smothered sounds came out of the place, as if suppressed shrieks were escaping the females; but they ceased so suddenly as to leave doubts among the auditors, whether it were more than the deception of their own excited fancies. The savages had witnessed many a similar scene of human suffering, but never one before in which death was met by so unmoved a calmness. The serenity that reigned in the blazing block communicated to them a feeling of awe; and when the pile came a tumbling and blackened mass of ruins to the earth, they avoided the place, like men that dreaded the vengeance of a Deity who knew how to infuse so deep a sentiment of resignation in the breasts of his worshippers.

Though the yells of victory were again heard in the valley that night, and though the sun had arisen before the conquerors deserted the hill, but few of the band found resolution to approach the smouldering pile, where they had witnessed so impressive an exhibition of Christian fortitude. The few that did draw near, stood around the spot rather in the reverence with which an Indian visits the graves of the just, than in the fierce rejoicings with which he is known to glut his revenge over a fallen enemy

15

CHAPTER XVI.

> "What are these,
> So withered, and so wild in their attire;
> That look not like the inhabitants of earth,
> And yet are on't?"
>
> MACBETH.

THAT sternness of the season, which has already been mentioned in these pages, is never of long continuance in the month of April. A change in the wind had been noted by the hunters, even before they retired from their range among the hills; and though too seriously occupied to pay close attention to the progress of the thaw, more than one of the young men had found occasion to remark, that the final breaking up of the winter had arrived. Long ere the scene of the preceding chapter reached its height, the southern winds had mingled with the heat of the conflagration. Warm airs, that had been following the course of the Gulf Stream, were driven to the land, and, sweeping over the narrow island that at this point forms the advanced work of the continent, but a few short hours had passed before they destroyed every chilling remnant of the dominion of winter. Warm, bland, and rushing in torrents, the subtle currents penetrated the forests, melted the snows from the fields, and as all alike felt the genial influence, it appeared to bestow a renovated existence on man and beast. With morning, therefore, a landscape very different from that last placed before the mind of the reader, presented itself in the valley of the Wish-Ton-Wish.

The winter had entirely disappeared, and as the buds had begun to swell under the occasional warmth of the spring, one ignorant of the past would not have supposed that the advance of the season had been subject to so stern an interruption. But the principal and most melancholy change was in the more artificial parts of the view. Instead of those simple and happy habitations which had crowned the little eminence, there remained only a mass of blackened and charred ruins. A few abused and half-destroyed articles of household furniture lay scattered on the sides of the hill, and, here and there, a dozen palisadoes, favored by some accidental cause, had partially escaped the flames. Eight or ten massive and dreary-looking stacks of chimneys rose out of the smoking piles. In the centre of the desolation was the stone basement of the block-house, on which still stood a few gloomy masses of the timber, resembling coal. The naked and unsupported shaft of the well reared its circular pillar from the centre, looking like a dark monument of the past. The wide ruin of the out-buildings blackened one side of the clearing, and, in different places, the fences, like radii diverging from the common centre of destruction, had led off the flames into the fields. A few domestic animals ruminated in the back-ground, and even the feathered inhabitants of the barns still kept aloof, as if warned by their instinct that danger lurked around the site of their ancient abodes. In all other respects, the view was calm, and lovely as ever. The sun shone from a sky in which no cloud was visible. The blandness of the winds, and the brightness of the heavens, lent an air of animation to even the leafless forest; and the white vapor, that continued to rise from the smouldering piles, floated high over the hills, as the peaceful smoke of the cottage curled above its roof.

The ruthless band which had occasioned this sudden change was already far on the way to its villages, or, haply, it sought some other scene of blood.

A skilful eye might have traced the route these fierce creatures of the woods had taken, by fences hurled from their places, or by the carcass of some animal that had fallen, in the wantonness of victory, beneath a parting blow. Of all these wild beings, one only remained; and he appeared to linger at the spot in the indulgence of feelings that were foreign to those passions that had so recently stirred the bosoms of his comrades.

It was with a slow, noiseless step that the solitary loiterer moved about the scene of destruction. He was first seen treading, with a thoughtful air, among the ruins of the buildings that had formed the quadrangle, and then, seemingly led by an interest in the fate of those who had so miserably perished, he drew nearer to the pile in its centre. The nicest and most attentive ear could not have detected the fall of his foot, as the Indian placed it within the gloomy circle of the ruined wall; nor is the breathing of the infant less audible, than the manner in which he drew breath, while standing in a place so lately consecrated by the agony and martyrdom of a Christian family. It was the boy called Miantonimoh, seeking some melancholy memorial of those with whom he had so long dwelt in amity, if not in confidence.

One skilled in the history of savage passions might have found a clue to the workings of the mind of the youth, in the play of his speaking features. As his dark glittering eye rolled over the smouldering fragments, it seemed to search keenly for some vestige of the human form. The element however had done its work too greedily, to have left many visible memorials of its fury. An object resembling that he sought, however, caught his glance, and stepping lightly to the spot where it lay, he raised the bone of a powerful arm from the brands. The flashing of his eye, as it lighted on this sad object, was wild and exulting, like that of the savage when he first feels the fierce joy of glutted vengeance; but gentler recollections came with the gaze, and kinder feelings evidently usurped the place of the hatred he had been taught to bear a race, who were so fast sweeping his people from the earth. The relic fell from his hand, and had Ruth been there to witness the melancholy and relenting shade that clouded his swarthy features, she might have found pleasure in the certainty that all her kindness had not been wasted.

Regret soon gave place to awe. To the imagination of the Indian, it seemed as if a still voice, like that which is believed to issue from the grave, was heard in the place. Bending his body forward, he listened with the intensity and acuteness of a savage. He thought the smothered tones of Mark Heathcote were again audible, holding communion with his God. The chisel of the Grecian would have loved to delineate the attitudes and movements of the wondering boy, as he slowly and reverently withdrew from the spot. His look was riveted on the vacancy where the upper apartments of the block had stood, and where he had last seen the family, calling, in their extremity, on their Deity for aid. Imagination still painted the victims, in their burning pile. For a minute longer, during which brief space the young Indian probably expected to see some vision of the Pale-faces, did he linger near; and then, with a musing air and softened mind, he trod lightly along the path which led on the trail of his people. When his active form reached the boundary of the forest, he again paused, and taking a final gaze at the place where fortune had made him a witness to so much domestic peace and of so much sudden misery, his form was quickly swallowed in the gloom of his native woods.

The work of the savages now seemed complete. An effectual check appeared to be placed to the further progress of civilization in the ill-fated valley of the Wish-Ton-wish. Had nature been left to its own work, a few years would have covered the deserted clearing with its ancient vegetation; and half a century would have again buried the whole of its quiet glades, in the shadows of the forest. But it was otherwise decreed.

The sun had reached the meridian, and the hostile band had been gone some hours, before aught occurred likely to affect this seeming decision of Providence. To one acquainted with the recent horrors, the breathing of the airs over the ruins might have passed for the whisperings of departed spirits. In short, it appeared as if the silence of the wilderness had once more resumed its reign, when it was suddenly though slightly interrupted. A movement was made within the ruins of the block. It sounded as if billets of wood were gradually and cautiously displaced, and then a human head was reared slowly, and with marked suspicion, above the shaft of the well. The wild and unearthly air of this seeming spectre, was in keeping with the rest of the scene. A face begrimed with smoke and stained with blood, a head bound in some fragment of a soiled dress, and eyes that were glaring in a species of dull horror, were objects in unison with all the other frightful accessories of the place.

"What seest thou?" demanded a deep voice from within the walls of the shaft. "Shall we again come to our weapons, or have the agents of Moloch departed? Speak, entranced youth! what dost behold?"

"A sight to make a wolf weep!" returned Eben Dudley, raising his large frame so as to stand erect on the shaft, where he commanded a bird's-eye view of most of the desolation of the valley. "Evil though it be, we may not say that forewarning signs have been withheld. But what is the cunningest man, when mortal wisdom is weighed in the scale against the craft of devils? Come forth! Belial hath done his worst, and we have a breathing-time."

The sounds, which issued still deeper from the well, denoted the satisfaction with which this intelligence was received, no less than the alacrity with which the summons of the borderer was obeyed. Sundry blocks of wood and short pieces of plank were first passed, with care, up to the hands of Dudley, who cast them, like useless lumber, among the other ruins of the building. He then descended from his perch, and made room for others to follow.

The stranger next arose. After him came Content, the Puritan, Reuben Ring, and, in short, all the youths, with the exception of those who had unhappily fallen in the contest. After these had mounted, and each in turn had leaped to the ground, a very brief preparation served for the liberation of the more feeble of body. The readiness of border skill soon sufficed to arrange the necessary means. By the aid of chains and buckets, Ruth and the little Martha, Faith and all of the handmaidens, without even one exception, were successively drawn from the bowels of the earth, and restored to the light of day. It is scarcely necessary to say to those whom experience has best fitted to judge of such an achievement, that no great time or labor was necessary for its accomplishment.

It is not our intention to harass the feelings of the reader, further than is required by a simple narrative of the incidents of the legend. We shall therefore say nothing of the bodily pain, or of the mental alarm, by which this ingenious retreat from the flames and the tomahawk had been effected. The suffering was chiefly confined to apprehension; for as the descent was easy, so had the readiness and ingenuity of the young men found means, by the aid of articles of furniture first cast into the shaft, and by well-secured fragments of the floors properly placed across, both to render the situation of the females and children less painful than might at first be supposed, and effectually to protect them from the tumbling block. But little of the latter however, was likely to affect their safety, as the form of the building was, in itself, a sufficient security against the fall of its heavier parts.

The meeting of the family, amid the desolation of the valley, though relieved by the consciousness of having escaped a more shocking fate, may easily be imagined. The first act was to render brief but solemn thanks for their deliverance, and then, with the promptitude of people trained in hardship, their attention was given to those measures which prudence told them were yet necessary.

A few of the more active and experienced of the youths were dispatched, in order to ascertain the direction taken by the Indians, and to gain what intelligence they might concerning their future movements. The maidens hastened to collect the kine, while others searched, with heavy hearts, among the ruins, in quest of such articles of food and comfort as could be found, in order to administer to the first wants of nature.

Two hours had effected most of that which could immediately be done, in these several pursuits. The young men returned with the assurance that the trails announced the certain and final retreat of the savages. The cows had yielded their tribute and such provision had been made against hunger as circumstances would allow. The arms had been examined, and put, as far as the injuries they had received would admit, in readiness for instant service. A few hasty preparations had been made, in order to protect the females against the cool airs of the coming night; and, in short, all was done that the intelligence of a border-man could suggest, or his exceeding readiness in expedients could in so brief a space supply.

The sun began to fall towards the tops of the beeches that crowned the western outline of the view, before all these necessary arrangements were ended. It was not till then, however, that Reuben Ring, accompanied by another youth of equal activity and courage, appeared before the Puritan, equipped, as well as men in their situation might be, for a journey through the forest.

"Go," said the old religionist, when the youths presented themselves before him; "Go; carry forth the tidings of this visitation, that men come to our succor. I ask not vengeance on the deluded and heathenish imitators of the worshippers of Moloch. They have ignorantly done this evil. Let no man arm in behalf of the wrongs of one sinful and erring. Rather let them look into the secret abominations of their own hearts, in order that they crush the living worm, which, by gnawing on the seeds of a healthful hope, may yet destroy the fruits of the promise in their own souls. I would that there be profit in this example of divine displeasure. Go: make the circuit of the settlements for some fifty miles, and bid such of the neighbors as may be spared, come to our aid. They shall be welcome; and may it be long ere any of them send invitation to me or mine, to enter their clearings on the like melancholy duty. Depart, and bear in mind, that you are messengers of peace; that your errand toucheth not the feelings of vengeance, but that it is succor, in all fitting reason, and no arming of the hand to chase the savage to his retreats, that I ask of the brethren."

With this final admonition, the young men took their leaves. Still it was evident, by their frowning brows and compressed lips, that some part of its forgiving principle might be forgotten, should chance, in their journey, bring them on the trail of any wandering inhabitant of the forest. In a few minutes, they were seen passing, with swift steps, from the fields into the depths of the forest, along that path which led to the towns that lay lower on the Connecticut.

Another task still remained to be performed. In making the temporary arrangements for the shelter of the family, attention had been first paid to the block-house. The walls of the basement of this building were still standing, and it was found easy, by means of half-burnt timbers, with an occasional board that had escaped the conflagration, to cover it, in a manner that offered a temporary protection against the weather. This simple and hasty construction, with an extremely inartificial office erected around the stack of a chimney, embraced nearly all that could be done, until time and assistance should enable them to commence other dwellings. In clearing the ruins of the little tower of its rubbish, the remains of those who had perished in the fray were piously collected. The body of the youth who had died in the earlier hours of the attack, was found, but half-consumed, in the court, and the bones of two more, who fell within the block, were collected from among the ruins. It had now become a melancholy duty to consign them all to the earth, with decent solemnity.

The time selected for this sad office was just as the western horizon began to glow with that which one of our own poets has so beautifully termed, "the pomp that brings and shuts the day." The sun was in the tree-tops, and a softer or sweeter light could not have been chosen for such a ceremony. Most of the fields still lay in the soft brightness of the hour, though the forest was rapidly getting the more obscure look of night. A broad and gloomy margin was spreading from the boundary of the woods, and, here and there, a solitary tree cast its shadow on the meadows without its limits, throwing a dark ragged line, in bold relief, on the glow of the sun's rays. One, it was the dusky image of a high and waving pine, that reared its dark green pyramid of never-fading foliage nearly a hundred feet above the humbler growth of beeches, cast its shade to the side of the eminence of the block. Here the pointed extremity of the shadow was seen, stealing slowly towards the open grave,—an emblem of that oblivion in which its humble tenants were so shortly to be wrapped.

At this spot, Mark Heathcote and his remaining companions had assembled. An oaken chair, saved from the flames, was the seat of the father; and two parallel benches, formed of planks placed on stones, held the other members of the family. The grave lay between. The patriarch had taken his station at one of its ends; while the stranger, so often named in these pages, stood with folded arms and a thoughtful brow at the other. The bridle of a horse, caparisoned in that imperfect manner which the straitened means of the borderers now rendered necessary, was hanging from one of the half-burnt palisadoes, in the back-ground.

"A just, but a merciful hand hath been laid heavily on my household;" commenced the old Puritan, with the calmness of one who had long been accustomed to chasten his regrets by humility. "He that hath given freely, hath taken away; and one, that hath long smiled upon my weakness, hath now veiled his face in anger. I have known him in his power to bless; it was meet that I should see him in his displeasure. A heart that was waxing confident would have hardened in its pride. At that which hath befallen, let no man murmur. Let none imitate the speech of her who spoke foolishly: 'What! shall we receive good at the hand of God, and shall we not receive evil?' I would that the feeble-minded of the world, they that jeopard the soul on vanities, they that look with scorn on the neediness of the flesh, might behold the riches of one stedfast I would that they might know the consolation of the righteous! Let the voice of thanksgiving be heard in the wilderness. Open thy mouths in praise, that the gratitude of a penitent be not hid!"

As the deep tones of the speaker ceased, his stern eye fell upon the features of the nearest youth, and it seemed to demand an audible response to his own lofty expression of resignation. But the sacrifice exceeded the power of the individual to whom had been made this silent, but intelligible, appeal. After regarding the relics that lay at his feet, casting a wandering glance at the desolation which had swept over a place his own hand had helped to decorate, and receiving a renewed consciousness of his own bodily suffering in the shooting pain of his wounds, the young borderer averted his look, and seemed to recoil from so officious a display of submission. Observing his inability to reply, Mark continued.—

"Hath no one a voice to praise the Lord? The bands of the heathen have fallen upon my herds; the brand hath been kindled within my dwellings; my people have died by the violence of the unenlightened, and none are here to say that the Lord is just! I would that the shouts of thanksgiving should arise in my fields! I would that the song of praise should grow louder than the whoop of the savage, and that all the land might speak joyfulness!"

A long, deep, and expecting pause succeeded Then Content rejoined, in his quiet tones, speaking firmly, but with the modest utterance he rarely failed to use—

"The hand that hath held the balance is just," he said, "and we have been found wanting. He that made the wilderness blossom hath caused the ignorant and the barbarous to be the instruments of his will. He hath arrested the season of our prosperity, that we may know he is the Lord. He hath spoken in the whirlwind, but his mercy granteth that our ears shall know his voice."

As his son ceased, a gleam of satisfaction shot across the countenance of the Puritan. His eye next turned inquiringly towards Ruth, who sate among her maidens the image of womanly sorrow. Common interest seemed to still the breathing of the little assembly, and sympathy was quite as active as curiosity, when each one present suffered a glance to steal towards her benignant but pallid face. The eye of the mother was gazing earnestly, but without a tear, on the melancholy spectacle before her. It unconsciously sought, among the dried and shrivelled remnants of mortality that lay at her feet, some relic of the cherub she had lost. A shudder and struggle followed, after which her gentle voice breathed so low that those nearest her person could scarce distinguish the words—

"The Lord gave, and the Lord hath taken away: blessed be his holy name!"

"Now know I that he who hath smote me is merciful, for he chasteneth them he loveth," said Mark Heathcote, rising with dignity to address his house hold. "Our life is a life of pride. The young ar wont to wax insolent, while he of many years saith to his own heart, 'it is good to be here.' There is a fearful mystery in one who sitteth on high. The heavens are his throne, and he hath created the earth for his footstool. Let not the vanity of the weak of mind presume to understand it, for 'who that hath the breath of life, lived before the hills?' The bonds of the evil one, of Satan, and of the sons of Belial, have been loosened, that the faith of the elect may be purified, that the names of those written, since the foundations of the earth were laid, may be read in letters of pure gold. The time of man is but a moment in the reckoning of him whose life is eternity; earth the habitation of a season! The bones of the bold, of the youthful, and of the strong of yesterday, lie at our feet. None know what an hour may bring forth. In a single night my children, hath this been done. They whose voices were heard in my halls are now speechless and they who so lately rejoiced are sorrowing. Yet hath this seeming evil been ordered that good may come thereof. We are dwellers in a wild and distant land," he continued, insensibly permitting his thoughts to incline towards the more mournful details of their affliction; "our earthly home is afar off. Hither have we been led by the flaming pillar of truth, and yet the malice of the persecuters hath not forgotten to follow. One houseless, and sought like the hunted deer, is again driven to flee. We have the canopy of the stars for a roof; none may tarry longer to worship, secretly, within our walls. But the path of the faithful, though full of thorns, leadeth to quiet, and the final rest of the just man can never know alarm. He that hath borne hunger, and thirst, and the pains of the flesh, for the sake of truth, knoweth how to be satisfied; nor will the hours of bodily suffering be accounted weary to him whose goal is the peace of the righteous." The strong lineaments of the stranger grew even more than usually austere, and as the Puritan continued, the hand which rested on the handle of a pistol grasped the weapon, until the fingers seemed imbedded in the wood. He bowed, however, as if to acknowledge the personal allusion, and remained silent.

"If any mourn the early death of those who have rendered up their being, struggling, as it may be permitted, in behalf of life and dwelling," continued Mark Heathcote, regarding a female near him, "let her remember, that from the beginning of the world were his days numbered, and that not a sparrow falleth without answering the ends of wisdom. Rather let the fulfilment of things remind us of the vanity of life, that we may learn how easy it is to become immortal. If the youth hath been cut down, seemingly like unripened grass, he hath fallen by the sickle of one who knoweth best when to begin the in-gathering of the harvest to his eternal garners. Though a spirit bound unto his, as one feeble is wont to lean on the strength of man and mourn over his fall, let her sorrow be mingled with rejoicing." A convulsive sob broke out of the bosom of the handmaiden who was known to have been affianced to one of the dead, and for a moment the address of Mark was interrupted. But when silence again ensued, he continued, the subject leading him, by a transition that was natural, to allude to his own sorrows. "Death hath been no stranger in my habitation," he said. "His shaft fell heaviest, when it struck her, who, like those that have here fallen, was in the pride of her youth, and when her soul was glad with the first joy of the birth of a man-child! Thou who sittest on high!" he added, turning a glazed and tearless eye to heaven; "thou knowest how heavy was that blow, and thou hast written down the strivings of an oppressed soul. The burthen was not found too heavy for endurance. The sacrifice hath not sufficed; the world was again getting uppermost in my heart. Thou didst bestow an image of that innocence and loveliness that dwelleth in the skies, and this hast thou taken away, that we might know thy power. To this judgment we bow. If thou hast called our child to the mansions of bliss, she is wholly thine, and we presume not to complain; but if thou hast still left her to wander further in the pilgrimage of life, we confide in thy goodness. She is of a long-suffering race, and thou wilt not desert her to the blindness of the heathen. She is thine, she is wholly thine, King of Heaven! and yet hast thou permitted our hearts to yearn towards her, with the fondness of earthly love. We await some further mani festation of thy will, that we may know whether the fountains of our affection shall be dried in the certainty of her blessedness—" (scalding tears were rolling down the cheeks of the pallid and immovable mother) "or whether hope, nay, whether duty to thee calleth for the interference of those bound tc her in the tenderness of the flesh. When the blow was heaviest on the bruised spirit of a lone and solitary wanderer, in a strange and savage land, he held not back the offspring it was thy will to grant him in the place of her called to thyself; and now that the child hath become a man, he too layeth, like Abraham of old, the infant of his love, a willing offering at thy feet. Do with it as to thy never-failing wisdom seemeth best."—The words were interrupted by a heavy groan, that burst from the chest of Content. A deep silence ensued, but when the assembly ventured to throw looks of sympathy and awe at the bereaved father, they saw that he had arisen and stood gazing steadily at the speaker, as if he wondered, equally with the others, whence such a sound of suffering could have come. The Puritan renewed the subject, but his voice faltered, and for an instant, as he proceeded, his hearers were oppressed with the spectacle of an aged and dignified man shaken with grief. Conscious of his weakness, the old man ceased speaking in exhortation, and addressed himself to prayer. While thus engaged, his tones again became clear, firm and distinct, and the petition was ended in the midst of a deep and holy calm.

With the performance of this preliminary office, the simple ceremony was brought to its close. The remains were lowered, in solemn silence, into the grave, and the earth was soon replaced by the young men. Mark Heathcote then invoked aloud the blessing of God on his household, and bowing in person, as he had before done in spirit, to the will of Heaven, he motioned to the family to withdraw.

The interview that succeeded was over the resting-place of the dead. The hand of the stranger was firmly clenched in that of the Puritan, and the stern self-command of both appeared to give way, before the regrets of a friendship that had endured through so many trying scenes.

"Thou knowest that I may not tarry," said the former, as if he replied to some expressed wish of his companion. "They would make me a sacrifice to the Moloch of their vanities; and yet would I fain abide, until the weight of this heavy blow may be forgotten. I found thee in peace, and I quit thee in the depths of suffering!"

"Thou distrustest me, or thou dost injustice to thine own belief," interrupted the Puritan, with a smile, that shone on his haggard and austere visage, as the rays of the setting sun light a wintry cloud "Seemed I happier when this hand placed that of a loved bride into mine own, than thou now seest me in this wilderness, houseless, stripped of my wealth, and, God forgive the ingratitude! but I had almost said, childless? No, indeed, thou mayest not tarry, for the blood-hounds of tyranny will be on their scent; here is shelter no longer."

The eyes of both turned, by a common and melancholy feeling, towards the ruin of the block. The stranger then pressed the hand of his friend in both his own, and said in a struggling voice—

"Mark Heathcote, adieu! he that had a roof for the persecuted wanderer shall not long be houseless: neither shall the resigned for ever know sorrow."

His words sounded in the ears of his companion like the revelation of a prophecy. They again pressed their hands together, and, regarding each other with looks in which kindness could not be altogether smothered by the repulsive character of an acquired air, they parted. The Puritan slowly took his way to the dreary shelter which covered his family; while the stranger was shortly after seen urging the beast he had mounted, across the pastures of the valley, towards one of the most retired paths of the wilderness.

CHAPTER XVII.

"Together towards the village then we walked,
And of old friends and places much we talked:
And who had died, who left them, would he tell;
And who still in their father's mansion dwell."

DANA

We leave the imagination of the reader to supply an interval of several years. Before the thread of the narrative shall be resumed, it will be necessary to take another hasty view of the condition of the country in which the scene of our legend had place.

The exertions of the provincials were no longer limited to the first efforts of a colonial existence. The establishments of New-England had passed the ordeal of experiment, and were become permanent. Massachusetts was already populous; and Connecticut, the colony with which we have more immediate connexion, was sufficiently peopled to manifest a portion of that enterprise which has since made her active little community so remarkable. The effects of these increased exertions were becoming extensively visible; and we shall endeavor to set one of these changes, as distinctly as our feeble powers will allow, before the eyes of those who read these pages.

When compared with the progress of society in the other hemisphere, the condition of what is called, in America, a new settlement, becomes anomalous. There, the arts of life have been the fruits of an intelligence that has progressively accumulated with the advancement of civilization; while here, improvement is, in a great degree, the consequence of experience elsewhere acquired. Necessity, prompted by an understanding of its wants incited by a commendable spirit of emulation, and encouraged by liberty, early gave birth to those improvements which have converted a wilderness into the abodes of abundance and security, with a rapidity that wears the appearance of magic. Industry has wrought with the confidence of knowledge, and the result has been peculiar.

It is scarcely necessary to say that, in a country where the laws favor all commendable enterprise, where unnecessary artificial restrictions are unknown, and where the hand of man has not yet xhausted its efforts, the adventurer is allowed the greatest freedom of choice, in selecting the field of his enterprise. The agriculturist passes the heath and the barren, to seat himself on the river-bottom; the trader looks for the site of demand and supply and the artisan quits his native village to seek employment in situations where labor will meet its fullest reward. It is a consequence of this extraordinary freedom of election, that, while the great picture of American society has been sketched with so much boldness, a large portion of the filling-up still remains to be done. The emigrant has consulted his immediate interests; and, while no very extensive and profitable territory, throughout the whole of our immense possessions, has been wholly neglected, neither has any particular district yet attained the finish of improvement. The city is even now, seen in the wilderness, and the wilderness often continues near the city, while the latter is sending forth its swarms to distant scenes of industry. After thirty years of fostering care on the part of the government, the Capital, itself, presents its disjointed and sickly villages, in the centre of the deserted 'old-fields' of Maryland, while numberless youthful rivals are flourishing on the waters of the West, in spots where the bear has ranged and the wolf howled, long since the former has been termed a city.

Thus it is that high civilization, a state of infant existence, and positive barbarity, are often brought so near each other, within the borders of this republic. The traveller, who has passed the night in an inn that would not disgrace the oldest country in Europe, may be compelled to dine in the shantee* of a hunter; the smooth and gravelled road sometimes ends in an impassable swamp; the spires of the town are often hid by the branches of a tangled forest, and the canal leads to a seemingly barren and unprofitable mountain. He that does not return to see what another year may bring forth, commonly

* *Shanty*, or *Shantee*, is a word much used in the newer settlements. It strictly means a rude cabin of bark and brush, such as is often erected in the forest for temporary purposes. But the borderers often quaintly apply it to their own habitations. The only derivation which the writer has heard for this American word, is one that supposes it to be a corruption of *Chientè*, a term said to be used among the Canadians to express a dog-kennel.

bears away from these scenes, recollections that conduce to error. To see America with the eyes of truth, it is necessary to look often; and in order to understand the actual condition of these states, it should be remembered, that it is equally unjust to believe that all the intermediate points partake of the improvements of particular places, as to infer the want of civilization at more remote establishments, from a few unfavorable facts gleaned near the centre. By an accidental concurrence of moral and physical causes, much of that equality which distinguishes the institutions of the country is extended to the progress of society over its whole surface.

Although the impetus of improvement was not as great in the time of Mark Heathcote as in our own days, the principle of its power was actively in existence. Of this fact we shall furnish a sufficient evidence, by pursuing our intention of describing one of those changes to which allusion has already been made.

The reader will remember that the age of which we write had advanced into the last quarter of the seventeenth century. The precise moment at which the action of the tale must re-commence, was that period of the day when the gray of twilight was redeeming objects from the deep darkness with which the night draws to its close. The month was June, and the scene such as it may be necessary to describe with some particularity.

Had there been light, and had one been favorably placed to enjoy a bird's-eye view of the spot, he would have seen a broad and undulating field of leafy forest, in which the various deciduous trees of New-England were relieved by the deeper verdure of occasional masses of evergreens. In the centre of this swelling and nearly interminable outline of woods, was a valley that spread between three low mountains. Over the bottom-land, for the distance of several miles, all the signs of a settlement in a state of rapid and prosperous improvement were visible. The devious course of a deep and swift brook, that in the other hemisphere would have been termed a river, was to be traced through the meadows by its borders of willow and sumach. At a point near the centre of the valley, the waters had been arrested by a small dam; and a mill, whose wheel at that early hour was without motion, stood on the artificial mound. Near it was the site of a New-England hamlet.

The number of dwellings in the village might have been forty. They were, as usual, constructed of a firm frame-work, neatly covered with sidings of boards. There was a surprising air of equality in the general aspect of the houses; and, if there were question of any country but our own, it might be added there was an unusual appearance of comfort and abundance in even the humblest of them all. They were mostly of two low stories, the superior overhanging the inferior, by a foot or two; a mode of construction much in use in the earlier days of the Eastern Colonies. As paint was but little used at that time, none of the buildings exhibited a color different from that the wood would naturally assume, after the exposure of a few years to the weather. Each had its single chimney in the centre of the roof, and but two or three showed more than a solitary window on each side of the principal or outer door. In front of every dwelling was a small neat court, in green sward, separated from the public road by a light fence of deal. Double rows of young and vigorous elms lined each side of the wide street, while an enormous sycamore still kept possession of the spot, in its centre, which it had occupied when the white man entered the forest. Beneath the shade of this tree the inhabitants often collected, to gather tidings of each other's welfare, or to listen to some matter of interest that rumor had borne from the towns nearer the sea A narrow and little-used wheel-track ran, with a graceful and sinuous route, through the centre of the wide and grassy street. Reduced in appearance to little more than a bridle-path, it was to be traced, without the hamlet, between high fences of wood, for a mile or two, to the points where it entered the forest. Here and there, roses were pressing through the openings of the fences before the doors of the different habitations, and bushes of fragrant lilacs stood in the angles of most of the courts.

The dwellings were detached. Each occupied its own insulated plot of ground, with a garden in its rear. The out-buildings were thrown to that distance which the cheapness of land, and security from fire, rendered both easy and expedient.

The church stood in the centre of the highway, and near one end of the hamlet. In the exterior and ornaments of the important temple, the taste of the times had been fastidiously consulted, its form and simplicity furnishing no slight resemblance to the self-denying doctrines and quaint humors of the religionists who worshipped beneath its roof. The building, like all the rest, was of wood, and externally of two stories. It possessed a tower, without a spire; the former alone serving to betray its sacred character. In the construction of this edifice, especial care had been taken to eschew all deviations from direct lines and right angles. Those narrow-arched passages for the admission of light, that are elsewhere so common, were then thought, by he stern moralists of New-England, to have some mysterious connexion with her of the scarlet mantle. The priest would as soon have thought of appearing before his flock in the vanities of stole and cassock, as the congregation of admitting the repudiated ornaments into the outline of their severe architecture. Had the Genii of the Lamp suddenly exchanged the windows of the sacred edifice with those of the inn that stood nearly opposite, the closest critic of the settlement could never have detected the liberty, since, in the form, dimensions, and style of the two, there was no visible difference

A little inclosure, at no great distance from the church, and on one side of the street, had been set apart for the final resting-place of those who had finished their race on earth. It contained but a solitary grave.

The inn was to be distinguished from the surrounding buildings, by its superior size, an open horse-shed, and a sort of protruding air, with which it thrust itself on the line of the street, as if to invite the traveller to enter. A sign swung on a gallows-looking post, that, in consequence of frosty nights and warm days, had already deviated from the perpendicular. It bore a conceit that, at the first glance, might have gladdened the heart of a naturalist, with the belief that he had made the discovery of some unknown bird. The artist, however, had sufficiently provided against the consequences of so embarrassing a blunder, by considerately writing beneath the offspring of his pencil, "This is the sign of the Whip-Poor-Will;" a name, that the most unlettered traveller, in those regions, would be likely to know was vulgarly given to the Wish-Ton-Wish, or the American night-hawk.

But few relics of the forest remained immediately around the hamlet. The trees had long been felled, and sufficient time had elapsed to remove most of the vestiges of their former existence. But as the eye receded from the cluster of buildings, the signs of more recent inroads on the wilderness became apparent, until the view terminated with openings, in which piled logs and mazes of felled trees announced the recent use of the axe.

At that early day, the American husbandman like the agriculturists of most of Europe, dwelt in his village. The dread of violence from the savages had given rise to a custom similar to that which, centuries before, had been produced in the other hemisphere by the inroads of more pretending barbarians, and which, with few and distant exceptions, has deprived rural scenery of a charm that, it would seem, time and a better condition of society are slow to repair. Some remains of this ancient practice are still to be traced in the portion of the Union of which we write, where, even at this day, the farmer often quits the village to seek his scattered fields in its neighborhood. Still, as man has never been the subject of a system here, and as each individual has always had the liberty of consulting his own temper, bolder spirits early began to break through a practice, by which quite as much was lost in convenience as was gained in security. Even in the scene we have been describing, ten or twelve humble habitations were distributed among the recent clearings on the sides of the mountains, and in situations too remote to promise much security against any sudden inroad of the common enemy.

For general protection, in cases of the last extremity, however, a stockaded dwelling, not unlike that which we have had occasion to describe in our earlier pages, stood in a convenient spot near the hamlet. Its defences were stronger and more elaborate than usual, the pickets being furnished with flanking block-houses; and, in other respects, the building bore the aspect of a work equal to any resistance that might be required in the warfare of those regions. The ordinary habitation of the priest was within its gates; and hither most of the sick were timely conveyed, in order to anticipate the necessity of removals at more inconvenient moments.

It is scarcely necessary to tell the American, that heavy wooden fences subdivided the whole of this little landscape into inclosures of some eight or ten acres in extent; that, here and there, cattle and flocks were grazing without herdsmen or shepherds, and that, while the fields nearest to the dwellings were beginning to assume the appearance of a careful and improved husbandry, those more remote became gradually wilder and less cultivated, until the half-reclaimed openings, with their blackened stubs and barked trees, were blended with the gloom of the living forest. These are, more or less, the accompaniments of every rural scene, in districts of the country where time has not yet effected more than the first two stages of improvement.

At the distance of a short half-mile from the fortified house, or garrison, as by a singular corruption of terms the stockaded building was called, stood a dwelling of pretensions altogether superior to any in the hamlet. The buildings in question, though simple, were extensive; and though scarcely other than such as might belong to an agriculturist in easy circumstances, still they were remarkable, in that settlement, by the comforts which time alone could accumulate, and some of which denoted an advanced condition for a frontier family. In short, there was an air about the establishment, as in the disposition of its out-buildings, in the superior workmanship, in the materials, and in numberless other well-known circumstances, which went to show that the whole of the edifices were re-constructions. The fields near this habitation exhibited smoother surfaces than those in the distance; the fences were lighter and less rude; the stumps had absolutely disappeared, and the gardens and homestead were well planted with flourishing fruit-trees. A conical eminence arose, at a short distance, in the rear of the principal dwelling. It was covered with that beautiful and peculiar ornament of an American farm, a regular, thrifty, and luxuriant apple-orchard. Still, age had not given its full beauty to the plantation, which might have had a growth of some eight or ten years. A blackened tower of stone, which sustained the charred ruins of a superstructure of wood, though of no great height in itself, rose above the tallest of the trees, and stood a sufficient memorial of some scene of violence, in the brief history of the valley. There was also a small block-house near the habitation; but, by the air of neglect that reigned around, it was quite apparent the little work had been of a hurried construction, and of but temporary use. A few young plantations of fruit-trees were also to be seen in different parts of the valley, which was beginning to exhibit many other evidences of an improved agriculture.

So far as all these artificial changes went, they were of an English character. But it was England devoid alike of its luxury and its poverty, and with a superfluity of space that gave to the meanest habitation in the view, an air of abundance and comfort that is so often wanting about the dwellings of the comparatively rich, in countries where man is found bearing a far greater numerical proportion to the soil, than was then, or is even now the case, in the regions of which we write.

CHAPTER XVIII.

"Come hither, neighbor Sea-coal—God hath blessed you with a good name: to be a well-favored man is the gift of fortune; but to write and read comes by Nature."

MUCH ADO ABOUT NOTHING.

IT has already been said, that the hour at which the action of the tale must re-commence, was early morning. The usual coolness of night, in a country extensively covered with wood, had passed, and the warmth of a summer morning, in that low latitude, was causing the streaks of light vapor, that floated about the meadows, to rise above the trees. The feathery patches united to form a cloud that sailed away towards the summit of a distant mountain, which appeared to be a common rendezvous for all the mists that had been generated by the past hours of darkness.

Though the burnished sky announced his near approach, the sun was not yet visible. Notwithstanding the earliness of the hour, a man was already mounting a little ascent in the road, at no great distance from the southern entrance of the hamlet, and at a point where he could command a view of all the objects described in the preceding chapter. A musket thrown across his left shoulder, with the horn and pouch at his sides, together with the little wallet at his back, proclaimed him one who had either been engaged in a hunt, or in some short expedition of even a less peaceable character. His dress was of the usual material and fashion of a countryman of the age and colony, though a short broadsword, that was thrust through a wampum belt which girded his body, might have attracted observation. In all other respects, he had the air of an inhabitant of the hamlet, who had found occasion to quit his abode on some affair of pleasur or of duty, that had made no very serious demand on his time.

Whether native or stranger, few ever passed the hillock named, without pausing to gaze at the quiet loveliness of the cluster of houses that lay in full view from its summit. The individual mentioned loitered as usual, but, instead of following the line of the path, his eye rather sought some object in the direction of the fields. Moving leisurely to the nearest fence, he threw down the upper rails of a pair of bars, and beckoned to a horseman, who was picking his way across a broken bit of pasture land, to enter the highway by the passage he had opened.

"Put the spur smartly into the pacer's flank," said he who had done this act of civility, observing that the other hesitated to urge his beast across the irregular and somewhat scattered pile; "my word for it, the jade goes over them all, without touching with more than three of her four feet. Fie, doctor! there is never a cow in the Wish-Ton-Wish, but it would take the leap to be in the first at the milking."

"Softly, Ensign;" returned the timid equestrian, aying the emphasis on the final syllable of his companion's title, and pronouncing the first as if it were spelt with the third instead of the second vowel. 'Thy courage is meet for one set apart for deeds of valor, but it would be a sorrowful day when the ailing of the valley should knock at my door, and a broken limb be made the apology for want of succor. Thy efforts will not avail thee, man; for the mare hath had schooling, as well as her master. I have trained the beast to methodical habits, and she hath come to have a rooted dislike to all irregularities of movement. So, cease tugging at the rein, as if thou wouldst compel her to pass the pile in spite of her teeth, and throw down the upper bar altogether."

"A doctor in these rugged parts should be mounted on one of these ambling birds of which we read," said the other, removing the obstacle to the secure passage of his friend; "for truly a journey at night, in the paths of these clearings, is not always as safe moving as that which is said to be enjoyed by the settlers nearer sea."

"And where hast found mention of a bird of a size and velocity fit to be the bearer of the weight of a man?" demanded he who was mounted, with a vivacity that betrayed some jealousy on the subject of a monopoly of learning. I had thought there was never a book in the valley, out of mine own closet, that dealeth in these abstrusities!"

"Dost think the scriptures are strangers to us? There—thou art now in the public path, and thy journey is without danger. It is matter of marvel to many in this settlement, how thou movest about at midnight, amongst upturned roots of trees, holes, logs and stumps, without falling——"

"I have told thee, Ensign, it is by virtue of much training given to the beast. Certain am I, that neither whip nor spur would compel the animal to pass the bounds of discretion. Often have I travelled this bridle-path, without fear as in truth without danger, when sight was a sense of as little use as that of smelling."

"I was about to say, falling into thine own hands,

which would be a tumble of little less jeopardy than even that of the wicked spirits."

The medical man affected to laugh at his companion's joke; but, remembering the dignity suited to one of his calling, he immediately resumed the discourse with gravity—

"These may be matters of levity, with those who know little of the hardships that are endured in the practice of the settlements. Here have I been on yonder mountain, guided by the instinct of my horse——"

"Ha! hath there been a call at the dwelling of my brother Ring?" demanded the pedestrian, observing, by the direction of the other's eye, the road he had been travelling.

"Truly, there hath; and at the unseasonable hour that is wont, in a very unreasonable proportion of the cases of my practice."

"And Reuben numbereth another boy to the four that he could count yesterday?"

The medical man held up three of his fingers, in a significant manner, as he nodded assent.

"This putteth Faith something in arrears," returned he who has been called Ensign, and who was no other than the reader's old acquaintance Eben Dudley, preferred to that station in the train-band of the valley. "The heart of my brother Reuben will be gladdened by these tidings, when he shall return from the scout."

"There will be occasion for thankfulness, since he will find seven beneath a roof where he left but four!"

"I will close the bargain with the young captain for the mountain lot, this very day!" muttered Dudley, like one suddenly convinced of the prudence of a long-debated measure. "Seven pounds of the colony money is no usurer's price, after all, for a hundred acres of heavily-timbered land; and they in full view of a settlement where boys come three at a time!"

The equestrian stopped his horse, and regarding his companion intently and with a significant air, he answered—

"Thou hast now fallen on the clue of an important mystery, Ensign Dudley. This continent was created with a design. The fact is apparent by its riches, its climate, its magnitude, its facilities of navigation, and chiefly in that it hath been left undiscovered until the advanced condition of society hath given opportunity and encouragement to men of a certain degree of merit, to adventure in its behalf. Consider, neighbor, the wonderful progress it hath already made in the arts and in learning, in reputation and in resources, and thou wilt agree with me in the conclusion that all this hath been done with a design."

"'Twould be presuming to doubt it; for he hath indeed a short memory, to whom it shall be necessary to recall the time when this very valley was little other than a den for beasts of prey, and this beaten highway, a deer-track. Dost think that Reuben will be like to raise the whole of the recent gift?"

"With judgment, and by the blessing of Providence. The mind is active, Ensign Dudley, when the body is journeying among the forests; and much have my thoughts been exercised in this matter, whilst thou and others have been in your slumbers. Here have we the colonies in their first century, and yet thou knowest to what a pass of improvement they have arrived. They tell me the Hartford settlement is getting to be apportioned like the towns of mother England, that there is reason to think the day may come when the provinces shall have a power, and a convenience of culture and commumication, equalling that which belongeth to some parts of the venerable island itself!"

"Nay, nay, Doctor Ergot," returned the other with an incredulous smile, "that is exceeding the bounds of a discretionable expectation."

"Thou wilt remember that I said equalling to *certain* parts. I think we may justly imagine, that ere many centuries shall elapse, there may be millions counted in these regions, and truly that, too, where one seeth nought, at present, but the savage and the beast."

"I will go with any man, in this question, as far as reason will justify; but doubtless thou hast read in the books uttered by writers over sea, the matters concerning the condition of those countries, wherein it is plain that we may never hope to reach the exalted excellence they enjoy."

"Neighbor Dudley, thou seemest disposed to push an unguarded expression to extremity. I said equalling *certain* parts, meaning always, too, in certain things. Now it is known in philosophy, that the stature of man hath degenerated, and must degenerate in these regions, in obedience to established laws of nature; therefore it is meet that allowance should be made for some deficiency in less material qualities."

"It is like, then, that the better sort of the men over sea are ill-disposed to quit their country," returned the Ensign, glancing an eye of some unbelief along the muscular proportions of his own vigorous frame. "We have no less than three from the old countries in our village, here, and yet I do not find them men like to have been sought for at the building of Babel."

"This is settling a knotty and learned point by the evidence of a few shallow exceptions. I presume to tell you, Ensign Dudley, that the science, and wisdom, and philosophy of Europe, have been exceeding active in this matter; and they have proved to their own perfect satisfaction, which is the same thing as disposing of the question without appeal, that man and beast, plant and tree, hill and dale, lake and pond, sun, air, fire and water, are all wanting in some of the perfectness of the older regions. I respect a patriotic sentiment, and can carry the disposition to applaud the bounties received from the hands of a beneficent Creator a far as any man; but that which hath been demonstrated by science, or collected by learning, is placed too far beyond the objections of light-minded cavillers, to be doubted by graver faculties."

"I shall not contend against things that are proven," returned Dudley, who was quite as meek in discussion as he was powerful and active in more physical contests; "since it needs be that the learning of men in the old countries must have an exceeding excellence, in virtue of its great age. It would be a visit to remember, should some of its rare advantages be dispersed in these our own youthful regions!"

"And can it be said that our mental wants have been forgotten—that the nakedness of the mind hath been suffered to go without its comely vestment, neighbor Dudley? To me, it seemeth, that therein we have unwonted reason to rejoice, and that the equilibrium of nature is in a manner restored by the healing exercises of art. It is unseemly in an unenlightened province, to insist on qualities that have been discreetly disproven; but learning is a transferable and communicable gift, and it is meet to affirm that it is to be found here, in quantities adapted to the wants of the colony."

"I'll not gainsay it, for having been more of an adventurer in the forest than one who hath travelled in quest of sights among the settlements along the sea-shore, it may happen that many things are to be seen there, of which my poor abilities have formed no opinion."

"And are we utterly unenlightened, even in this distant valley, Ensign?" returned the leech, leaning over the neck of his horse, and addressing his companion in a mild and persuasive tone, that he had probably acquired in his extensive practice among the females of the settlement. "Are we to be classed with the heathen in knowledge, or to be accounted as the unnurtured men who are known once to have roamed through these forests in quest of their game? Without assuming any infallibility of judgment, or aspiring to any peculiarity of information, it doth not appear to my defective understanding, Master Dudley, that the progress of the settlement hath ever been checked for want of necessary foresight, nor that the growth of reason among us hath ever been stunted from any lack of mental aliment. Our councils are not barren of wisdom, Ensign, nor hath it often arrived that abstrusities have been propounded, that some one intellect, to say no more in our own favor, hath not been known to grapple with, successfully."

"That there are men, or perhaps I ought to say that there *is a man*, in the valley, who is equal to many marvels in the way of enlightened gifts——"

"I knew we should come to peaceable conclusions, Ensign Dudley," interrupted the other, rising erect in his saddle, with an air of appeased dignity; "for I have ever found you a discreet and consequent reasoner, and one who is never known to resist conviction, when truth is pressed with understanding That the men from over sea are not often so well gifted as some—we will say, for the sake of a convenient illustration, as thyself, Ensign—is placed beyond the reach of debate, since sight teacheth us that numberless exceptions may be found to all the more general and distinctive laws of nature. I think we are not likely to carry our disagreement further?"

"It is impossible to make head against one so ready with his knowledge," returned the other, well content to exist in his own person a striking exception to the inferiority of his fellows; "though it appeareth to me that my brother Ring might be chosen, as another instance of a reasonable stature a fact that thou mayst see, Doctor, by regarding him as he approaches through yon meadow. He hath been, like myself, on the scout among the mountains."

"There are many instances of physical merit among thy connexions, Master Dudley," returned the complaisant physician; "though it would seem that thy brother hath not found his companion among them. He is attended by an ill-grown, and, it may be added, an ill-favored comrade, that I know not."

"Ha! It would seem that Reuben hath fallen on the trail of savages! The man in company is certainly in paint and blanket. It may be well to pause at yonder opening, and await their coming."

As this proposition imposed no particular inconvenience, the Doctor readily assented. The two drew nigh to the place where the men, whom they saw crossing the fields in the distance, were expected to enter the highway.

But little time was lost in attendance. Ere many minutes had elapsed, Reuben Ring, accoutred and armed like the borderer already introduced in this chapter, arrived at the opening, followed by the stranger whose appearance had caused so much surprise to those who watched their approach.

"What now, Sergeant," exclaimed Dudley, when the other was within ear-shot, speaking a little in the manner of one who had legal right to propound his questions; "hast fallen on a trail of the savage, and made a captive? or hath some owl permitted one of its brood to fall from the nest across thy foot-path?"

"I believe the creature may be accounted a man," returned the successful Reuben, throwing the breech of his gun to the earth, and leaning on its long barrel, while he intently regarded the half-painted vacant, and extremely equivocal countenance of his captive. "He hath the colors of a Narragansett about the brow and eyes, and yet he faileth greatly in the form and movements."

"There are anomalies in the physicals of an Indian, as in those of other men," interrupted Doctor Ergot, with a meaning glance at Dudley. "The conclusion of our neighbor Ring may be too hasty, since paint is the fruit of art, and may be applied to any of our faces, after an established usage. But the evidences of nature are far less to be distrusted. It hath come within the province of my studies, to note the differences in formation which occur in the different families of man; and nothing is more readily to be known, to an eye skilled in these abstrusities, than the aboriginal of the tribe Narragansett Set the man more in a position of examination, neighbors, and it shall shortly be seen to which race he belongs. Thou wilt note in this little facility of investigation, Ensign, a clear evidence of most of the matters that have this morning been agitated between us. Doth the patient speak English?"

"Therein have I found some difficulty of inquiry," returned Reuben, or as he should now be, and as he was usually called, Sergeant Ring. "He hath been spoken to in the language of a Christian, no less than in that of a heathen, and as yet no reply hath been made, while he obeys commands uttered in both forms of speech."

"It mattereth not," said Ergot, dismounting and drawing near to his subject, with a look towards Dudley that should seem to court his admiration

"Happily the examination before me leaneth but little on any subtleties of speech. Let the man be placed in an attitude of ease; one in which nature may not be fettered by restraint. The conformation of the whole head is remarkably aboriginal, but the distinction of tribes is not to be sought in these general delineations. The forehead, as you see, neighbors, is retreating and narrow, the cheek-bones, as usual, high, and the olfactory member, as in all of the natives, inclining to Roman."

"Now to me it would seem that the nose of the man hath a marked upturning at the end," Dudley ventured to remark, as the other ran volubly over the general and well-known distinctive points of physical construction in an Indian.

"As an exception! Thou seest, Ensign, by this elevation of the bone, and the protuberance of the more fleshy parts, that the peculiarity is an exception. I should rather have said that the nose originally inclined to the Roman. The departure from regularity has been produced by some casualty of their warfare, such as a blow from a tomahawk, or the gash of a knife—ay! here thou seest the scar left by the weapon! It is concealed by the paint, but remove that, and you will find it hath all the form of a cicatrice of a corresponding shape. These departures from generalities have a tendency to confound pretenders; a happy circumstance, in itself, for the progress of knowledge on fixed principles. Place the subject more erect, that we may see the natural movement of the muscles. Here is an evidence of great aquatic habits in the dimensions of the foot, which go to confirm original conceptions It is a happy proof, through which, reasonable and prudent conclusions confirm the quick-sighted glances of practice. I pronounce the fellow to be a Narragansett."

"Is it then a Narragansett that hath a foot to confound a trail?" returned Eben Dudley, who had been studying the movements and attitudes of the captive with quite as much keenness, and with something more of understanding, than the leech. "Brother Ring, hast ever known an Indian leave such an out-turning foot-print on the leaves?"

"Ensign, I marvel that a man of thy discretion should dwell on a slight variety of movement, when a case exists in which the laws of nature may be traced to their sources. This training for the Indian troubles hath made thee critical in the position of a foot. I have said that the fellow is a Narragansett, and what I have uttered hath not been lightly ventured. Here is the peculiar formation of the foot, which hath been obtained in infancy, a fullness in the muscles of the breast and shoulders, from unusual exercise in an element denser than the air, and a nicer construction in——"

The physician paused, for Dudley had coolly advanced to the captive, and, raising the thin robe of deer-skin which was thrown over the whole of his superior members, he exposed the unequivocal skin of a white man. This would have proved an embarrassing refutation to one accustomed to the conflict of wits; but monopoly, in certain branches of knowledge, had produced in favor of Doctor Ergot an acknowledged superiority, that, in its effects, might be likened to the predominating influence of any other aristocracy, on those faculties that have been benumbed by its operation. His opinion changed, which is more than can be said of his countenance, for, with the readiness of invention which is so often practised in the felicitous institutions we have named, and by which the reasoning instead of regulating is adapted to the practice, he exclaimed with uplifted hands and eyes that bespoke the fullness of his admiration—

"Here have we another proof of the wonderful agency by which the changes in nature are gradually wrought! Now do we see in this Narragansett——"

"The man is white!" interrupted Dudley, tapping the naked shoulder, which he still held exposed to view.

"White, but not a tittle the less a Narragansett. Your captive, beyond a doubt, oweth his existence to Christian parentage, but accident hath thrown him early among the aboriginals, and all those parts, which were liable to change, were fast getting to assume the peculiarities of the tribe. He is one of those beautiful and connecting links in the chain of knowledge, by which science followeth up its deductions to demonstration."

"I should ill brook coming to harm for doing violence to a subject of the King," said Reuben Ring, a steady, open-faced yeoman, who thought far less of the subtleties of his companion, than of discharging his social duties in a manner fitting the character of a quiet and well-conditioned citizen. "We have had so much of stirring tidings, latterly, concerning the manner the savages conduct their warfare, that it behoveth men in place of trust to be vigilant; for," glancing his eyes towards the ruin of the distant block-house, "thou knowest, brother Dudley, that we have occasion to be watchful, in a settlement as deep in the forest as this."

"I will answer for the indemnity, Sergeant Ring," said Dudley, with an air of dignity. "I take upon myself the keeping of this stranger, and will see that he be borne, properly and in fitting season, before the authorities. In the mean time, duty hath caused us to overlook matters of moment in thy household, which it may be seemly to communicate. Abundance hath not been neglectful of thy interests, during the scout."

"What!" demanded the husband, with rather more of earnestness than was generally exhibited by one of habits as restrained as his own; "hath the woman called upon the neighbors, during my absence?"

Dudley nodded an assent.

"And shall I find another boy beneath my roof?"

Doctor Ergot nodded three times with a gravity that might have suited a communication even more weighty than the one he made.

"Thy woman rarely doth a good turn by halves, Reuben. Thou wilt find that she hath made provision for a successor to our good neighbor Ergot, since a seventh son is born in thy house."

The broad, honest face of the father flushed with joy, and then a feeling less selfish came over him. He asked, with a slight tremor in the voice, that was none the less touching for coming from the lips of one so stout of frame and firm of movement—

"And the woman?—in what manner doth Abundance bear up under the blessing?"

"Bravely," returned the leech; "go to thy dwelling, Sergeant Ring, and praise God that there is one to look to its concerns, in thy absence. He who hath received the gift of seven sons, in five years, need never be a poor nor a dependent man, in a country like this. Seven farms, added to that pretty homestead of mountain-land which thou now tillest, will render thee a patriarch in thine age, and sustain the name of Ring, hundreds of years hence, when these colonies shall become peopled and powerful, and, I say it boldly, caring not who may call me one that vaunteth out of reason, equal to some of your lofty and self-extolled kingdoms of Europe—ay, even peradventure to the mighty sovereignty of Portugal, itself! I have enumerated thy future farms at seven, for the allusion of the Ensign to the virtues of men born with natu ral propensities to the healing art, must be taken as pleasant speech, since it is a mere delusion of old wives' fancy, and it would be particularly unnecessary, here, where every reasonable situation of this nature is already occupied. Go to thy wife, Sergeant, and bid her be of good cheer; for she hath done herself, thee, and thy country, a service, and that without dabbling in pursuits foreign to her comprehension."

The sturdy yeoman, on whom this rich gift of Providence had been dispensed, raised his hat, and placing it decently before his face, he offered up a silent thanksgiving for the favor. Then, transferring his captive to the keeping of his superior and kinsman, he was soon seen striding over the fields towards his upland dwelling, with a heavy foot, though with a light heart.

In the mean time, Dudley and his companion bestowed a more particular attention on the silent and nearly motionless object of their curiosity. Though the captive appeared to be of middle age, his eye was unmeaning, his air timid and uncertain, and his form cringing and ungainly. In all these particulars, he was seen to differ from the known peculiarities of a native warrior.

Previously to departing, Reuben Ring had explained, that while traversing the woods, on that duty of watchfulness to which the state of the colony and some recent signs had given rise, this wandering person had been encountered and secured, as seemed necessary to the safety of the settlement. He had neither sought nor avoided his captor; but when questioned concerning his tribe, his motive for traversing those hills, and his future intentions, no satisfactory reply could be extracted. He had scarcely spoken, and the little that he said was uttered in a jargon between the language of his interrogator and the dialect of some barbarous nation. Though there was much in the actual state of the colonies, and in the circumstances in which this wanderer had been found, to justify his detention, little had in truth been discovered, to supply a clue either to any material facts in his history, or to any of his views in being in the immediate vicinity of the valley.

Guided only by this barren information, Dudley and his companion endeavored, as they moved towards the hamlet, to entrap their prisoner into some confession of his object, by putting their questions with a sagacity not unusual to men in remote and difficult situations, where necessity and danger are apt to keep alive all the native energies of the human mind. The answers were little connected and unintelligible, sometimes seeming to exhibit the finest subtlety of savage cunning, and at others to possess the mental helplessness of appearing the most abject fatuity.

CHAPTER XIX.

"I am not prone to weeping, as our sex
Commonly are;—
But I have
That honorable grief lodged here, which burns
Worse than tears drown."

WINTER'S TALE.

IF the pen of a compiler, like that we wield, possessed the mechanical power of the stage, it would be easy to shift the scenes of this legend as rapidly and effectively, as is required for its right understanding, and for the proper maintenance of its interest. That which cannot be done with the magical aid of machinery, must be attempted by less ambitious, and we fear by far less efficacious means

At the same early hour of the day, and at no great distance from the spot where Dudley announced his good fortune to his brother Ring, another morning meeting had place, between persons of the same blood and connexions. From the instant when the pale light, that precedes the day, was first seen in the heavens, the windows and doors of the considerable dwelling, on the opposite side of the valley, had been unbarred. Ere the glow of the sun ha gilded the sky over the outline of the eastern woods, this example of industry and providence was followed by the inmates of every house in the village, or on the surrounding hills; and, by the time the golden globe itself was visible above the trees, there was not a human being in all that settlement, of proper age and health, who was not actively afoot.

It is unnecessary to say that the dwelling particularly named was the present habitation of the household of Mark Heathcote. Though age had sapped the foundations of his strength, and had nearly dried the channels of his existence, the venerable religionist still lived. While his physical perfection had been gradually giving way before the ordinary decay of nature, the moral man was but little altered. It is even probable that his visions of futurity were less dimmed by the mists of carnal interests than when last seen, and that the spirit had gained some portion of that energy which had certainly been abstracted from the more corporeal parts of his existence. At the hour already named, the Puritan was seated in the piazza, which stretched along the whole front of a dwelling, that, however it might be deficient in architectural proportions, was not wanting in the more substantial comforts of a spacious and commodious frontier residence. In order to obtain a faithful portrait of a man so intimately connected with our tale, the reader will fancy him one who had numbered four-score and ten years, with a visage on which deep and constant mental striving had wrought many and menacing furrows, a form that trembled while it yet exhibited the ruins of powerful limb and flexible muscle, and a countenance in which ascetic reflections had engraved a severity, that was but faintly relieved by the gleamings of a natural kindness, which no acquired habits, nor any traces of metaphysical thought, could ever entirely erase. Across this picture of venerable and self-mortifying age, the first rays of the sun were now softly cast, lighting a dimmed eye and furrowed face with a look of brightness and peace. Perhaps the blandness of the expression belonged as much to the season and hour, as to the habitual character of the man. This benignancy of feature, unusual rather in its strength than in its existence, might have been heightened by the fact that his spirit had just wrought in prayer, as was usual, in the circle of his children and dependants, ere they left those retired parts of the building where they had found rest and security during the night. Of the former, none known and cherished in the domestic circle had been absent; and the ample provision that was making for the morning meal, sufficiently showed that the number of the latter had in no degree diminished since the reader was familiar with the domestic economy of his household.

Time had produced no very striking alteration in the appearance of Content. It is true that the brown hue of his features had deepened, and that his frame was beginning to lose some of its elasticity and ease of action, in the more measured movements of middle age. But the governed temperament of the individual had always kept the animal in more than usual subjection. Even his earlier days had rather exhibited the promise than the performance of the ordinary youthful qualities. Mental gravity had long before produced a corresponding physical effect. In reference to his exterior, and using the language of the painter, it would now be said, that, without having wrought any change in form and proportions, the colors had been mellowed by time. If a few hairs of gray were sprinkled, here and there, around his brow, it was as moss gathers on the stones of the edifice, rather furnishing evidence of its increased adhesion and approved stability, than denoting any symptoms of decay.

Not so with his gentle and devoted partner That softness and sweetness of air which had first touched the heart of Content was still to be seen, though it existed amid the traces of a constant and a corroding grief. The freshness of youth had departed, and in its place was visible the more lasting, and, in her case, the more affecting beauty of expression. The eye of Ruth had lost none of its gentleness, and her smile still continued kind and attractive; but the former was often painfully vacant, seeming to look inward upon those secret and withering sources of sorrow that were deeply and almost mysteriously seated in her heart; while the latter resembled the cold brightness of that planet, which illumines objects by repelling the borrowed lustre from its own bosom. The matronly form, the feminine beaming of the countenance, and the melodious voice, yet remained; but the first had been shaken till it stood on the very verge of a premature decay, the second had a mingling of anxious care in its most sympathetic movements, and the last was seldom without that fearful thrill which so deeply affects the senses, by conveying to the understanding a meaning so foreign from the words. And yet an uninterested and ordinary observer might not have seen, in the faded comeliness and blighted maturity of the matron, more than the every-day signs that betray the turn in the tide of human existence.

As befitted such a subject, the coloring of sorrow had been traced by a hand too delicate to leave the lines visible to every vulgar eye. Like the master-touches of art, her grief, as it was beyond the sympathies, so it lay beyond the ken of those whom excellence may fail to excite, or in whom absence can deaden affections. Still her feelings were true to all who had any claims on her love. The predominance of wasting grief over the more genial springs of her enjoyments, only went to prove how much greater is the influence of the generous than the selfish qualities of our nature, in a heart that is truly endowed with tenderness. It is scarce necessary to say, that this gentle and constant woman sorrowed for her child.

Had Ruth Heathcote known that the girl ceased to live, it would not have been difficult for one of her faith to have deposited her regrets by the side of hopes that were so justifiable, in the grave of the innocent. But the living death to which her offspring might be condemned, was rarely absent from her thoughts. She listened to the maxims of resignation, which were heard flowing from lips she loved with the fondness of a woman and the meekness of a Christian; and then, even while the holy lessons were still sounding in her attentive organs, the workings of an unconquerable nature led her insidiously back to the sorrow of a mother.

The imagination of this devoted and feminine being had never possessed an undue control over her reason Her visions of happiness with the man whom her judgment not less than her inclination approved, had been such as experience and religion might justify. But she was now fated to learn there is a fearful poetry in sorrow, which can sketch with a grace and an imaginative power that no feebler efforts of a heated fancy may ever equal. She heard the sweet breathing of her slumbering infant in the whispering of the summer airs; its plaints came to her ears amid the howlings of the gale; while the eager question and fond reply were mixed up with the most ordinary intercourse of her own household. To her the laugh of childish happiness that often came on the still air of evening from the hamlet, sounded like the voice of mourning; and scarce an infantile sport met her eye, that did not bring with it a pang of anguish. Twice, since the events of the inroad, had she been a mother; and, as if an eternal blight were doomed to destroy her hopes, the little creatures to whom she had given birth, slept, side by side, near the base of the ruined block. Thither she often went, but it was rather to be the victim of those cruel images of her fancy, than as a mourner. Her visions of the dead were calm and even consolatory, but if ever her thoughts mounted to the abodes of eternal peace, and her feeble fancy essayed to embody the forms of the blessed, her mental eye sought her who was not, rather than those who were believed to be secure in their felicity. Wasting and delusory as were these glimpses of the mind, there were others far more harrowing, because they presented themselves with more of the coarse and certain features of the world. It was the common, and perhaps it was the better, opinion of the inhabitants of the valley, that death had early sealed the fate of those who had fallen into the hands of the savages on the occasion of the inroad. Such a result was in conformity with the known practices and ruthless passions of the conquerors, who seldom spared life, unless to render revenge more cruelly refined, or to bring consolation to some bereaved mother of the tribe, by offering a substitute for the dead in the person of a captive. There was relief, to picture the face of the laughing cherub in the clouds, or to listen to its light footstep in the empty halls of the dwelling; for in these illusive images of the brain, suffering was confined to her own bosom. But when stern reality usurped the place of fancy, and she saw her living daughter shivering in the wintry blasts or sinking beneath the fierce heats of the climate, cheerless in the desolation of female servitude, and suffering meekly the lot of physical weakness beneath a savage master, she endured that anguish which was gradually exhausting the springs of life.

Though the father was not altogether exempt from similar sorrow, it beset him less ceaselessly He knew how to struggle with the workings of his mind, as best became a man. Though strongly impressed with the belief that the captives had early been put beyond the reach of suffering, he had neglected no duty, which tenderness to his sorrowing partner, parental love, or Christian duty, could require at his hands.

The Indians had retired on the crust of the snow, and with the thaw every foot-print, or sign, by which such wary foes might be traced, had vanished. It remained matter of doubt to what tribe or even to what nation, the marauders belonged. The peace of the colony had not yet been openly broken, and the inroad had been rather a violent and fierce symptom of the evils that were contemplated, than the actual commencement of the ruthless hostilities which had since ravaged the frontier. But while policy had kept the colonists quiet, private affection omitted no rational means of effecting the restoration of the sufferers, in the event of their having been spared.

Scouts had passed among the conspiring and but half-peaceable tribes, nearest to the settlement, and rewards and menaces had both been liberally used, in order to ascertain the character of the savages who had laid waste the valley, as well as the more interesting fortunes of their hapless victims. Every expedient to detect the truth had failed. The Narragansetts affirmed that their constant enemies the Mohicans, acting with their customary treachery, had plundered their English friends while the Mohicans vehemently threw back the imputation on the Narragansetts. At other times, some Indians affected to make dark allusions to the hostile feelings of fierce warriors, who, under the name of the Five Nations, were known to reside within the limits of the Dutch colony of New-Netherlands, and to dwell upon the jealousy of the Pale-faces who spoke a language different from that of the Yengeese. In short, inquiry had produced no result; and Content, when he did permit his fancy to represent his daughter as still living, was forced to admit to himself the probability that she might be buried far in the ocean of wilderness which then covered most of the surface of this continent.

Once, indeed, a rumor of an exciting nature had reached the family. An itinerant trader, bound from the wilds of the interior to a mart on the seashore, had entered the valley. He brought with him a report, that a child, answering in some respects to the appearance which might now be supposed to belong to her who was lost, was living among the savages, on the banks of the smaller lakes of the adjoining colony. The distance to this spot was great; the path led through a thousand dangers, and the result was far from certain. Yet it quickened hopes which had long been dormant. Ruth never urged any request that might involve serious hazard to her husband, and for many months the latter had even ceased to speak on the subject. Still, nature was working powerfully within him. His eyes, at all times reflecting and calm, grew more thoughtful; deeper lines of care gathered about his brow; and at length, melancholy took possession of a countenance which was usually so placid.

It was at this precise period, that Eben Dudley chose to urge the suit, he had always pressed after his own desultory fashion, on the decision of Faith. One of those well-ordered accidents, which, from time to time, had brought the girl and the young borderer in private conversation, enabled him to effect his design with sufficient clearness. Faith heard him without betraying any of her ordinary waywardness, and answered with as little prevarication as the subject seemed to demand.

"This is well, Eben Dudley," she said, "and it is no more than an honest girl hath a right to hear, from one who hath taken as many means as thou to get into her favor. But he who would have his life tormented by me, hath a solemn duty to do, ere I listen to his wishes."

"I have been in the lower towns and studied their manner of life, and I have been upon the scouts of the colony, to keep the Indians in their wigwams," returned her suitor, endeavoring to recount the feats of manliness that might reasonably be expected of one inclined to venture on so hazardous an experiment as matrimony. "The bargain with the young Captain for the hill-lot, and for a village homestead, is drawing near a close: and as the neighbors will not be backward at the stone-bee, or the raising, I see nothing to——"

"Thou deceivest thyself, observant Dudley," interrupted the girl, "if thou believest eye of thine can see that which is to be sought, ere one and the same fortune shall be the property of thee and me. Hast noted, Eben, the manner in which the cheek of the Madam hath paled, and how her eye is getting sunken, since the time when the fur trader tarried with us, the week of the storm?"

"I cannot say that there is much change in the wearing of the Madam, within the bearing of my memory," answered Dudley, who was never remarkable for minute observations of this nature, however keen he might prove in subjects more intimately connected with his daily pursuits. "She is not young and blooming as thou, Faith, nor is it often that we see——"

"I tell thee, man, that sorrow preyeth upon her form, and that she liveth but in the memory of the lost infant!"

"This is carrying mourning beyond the bounds of reason. The child is at peace; as is thy brother, Whittal, beyond all manner of question. That we have not discovered their bones, is owing to the fire, which left but little to tell of——"

"Thy head is a charnel-house, dull Dudley, but this picture of its furniture shall not suffice for me. The man who is to be my husband must have a feeling for a mother's sorrows!"

"What is now getting uppermost in thy mind, Faith! Is it for me to bring back the dead to life, or to place a child that hath been lost so many years once more in the arms of its parents?"

"It is.—Nay, open not thine eyes, as if light were first breaking into the darkness of a clouded brain! I repeat, it is!"

"I am glad that we have got to these open declarations, for too much of my life hath been already wasted in unsettled gallanting, when sound wisdom, and the example of all around me, have shown that in order to become the father of a family, and to be esteemed for a substantial settler, I should have both cleared and wived some years ago. I wish to deal justly by all, and having given thee reason to think that the day might come when we should live together, as is fitting to people of our condition, I felt it a duty to ask thee to share my chances; but now that thou dealest in impossibilities, it is needful to seek elsewhere."

"This hath ever been thy way, when a good understanding hath been established between us. Thy mind is ever getting into some discontent, and then blame is heaped on one who rarely doth anything that should in reason offend thee. What madness maketh thee dream that I ask impossibilities? Surely, Dudley, thou canst not have noted the manner in which the nature of the Madam is giving way before the consuming heat of her grief; thou canst not look into the sorrow of woman, or thou wouldst have listened with more kindness to a plan of travelling the woods for a short season, in order that it might be known whether she of whom the trader spoke is the lost one of our family, or the child of some stranger!"

Though Faith spoke with vexation, she also spoke with feeling. Her dark eye swam in tears, and the color of her brown cheek deepened, until her companion saw new reasons to forget his discontent in sympathies, which, however obtuse they might be, were never entirely dormant.

"If a journey of a few hundred miles be all thou askest, girl, why speak in parables?" he good-naturedly replied. "The kind word was not wanting to put me on such a trial. We will be married on the Sabbath, and, please Heaven, the Wednesday, or the Saturday at most, shall see me on the path of the western trader."

"No delay. Thou must depart with the sun. The more active thou provest on the journey the sooner wilt thou have the power to make me repent a foolish deed."

But Faith had been persuaded to relax a little from this severity They were married on the Sabbath, and the following day Content and Dudley left the valley, in quest of the distant tribe on which the scion of another stock was said to have been so violently engrafted.

It is needless to dwell on the dangers and privations of such an expedition. The Hudson, the Delaware, and the Susquehannah, rivers that were then better known in tales than to the inhabitants of New-England, were all crossed; and after a painful and hazardous journey, the adventurers reached the first of that collection of small interior lakes, whose banks are now so beautifully decorated with villages and farms. Here, in the bosom of savage tribes, and exposed to every danger of field and flood, supported only by his hopes, and by the presence of a stout companion that hardships or danger could not easily subdue, the father diligently sought his child.

At length a people were found, who held a captive that answered the description of the trader. We shall not dwell on the feelings with which Content approached the village that contained this little descendant of a white race. He had not concealed his errand; and the sacred character, in which he came, found pity and respect even among those barbarous tenants of the wilderness. A deputation of the chiefs received him in the skirts of their clearing. He was conducted to a wigwam, where a council-fire was lighted, and an interpreter opened the subject, by placing the amount of the ransom offered, and the professions of peace with which the strangers came, in the fairest light before his auditors. It is not usual for the American savage to loosen his hold easily, on one naturalized in his tribe. But the meek air and noble confidence of Content touched the latent qualities of those generous though fierce children of the woods. The girl was sent for, that she might stand in the presence of the elders of the nation.

No language can paint the sensation with which

Content first looked upon this adopted daughter of the savages. The years and sex were in accordance with his wishes; but, in place of the golden hair and azure eyes of the cherub he had lost, there appeared a girl in whose jet-black tresses and equally dark organs of sight, he might better trace a descendant of the French of the Canadas, than one sprung from his own Saxon lineage. The father was not quick of mind in the ordinary occupations of life, but nature was now big within him. There needed no second glance, to say how cruelly his hopes had been deceived. A smothered groan struggled from his chest, and then his self-command returned with the imposing grandeur of Christian resignation. He arose, and, thanking the chiefs for their indulgence, he made no secret of the mistake by which he had been led so far on a fruitless errand. While speaking, the signs and gestures of Dudley gave him reason to believe, that his companion had something of importance to communicate. In a private interview, the latter suggested the expediency of concealing the truth, and of rescuing the child they had in fact discovered from the hands of her barbarous masters. It was now too late to practise a deception that might have availed for this object, had the stern principles of Content permitted the artifice. But, transferring some portion of the interest which he felt for the fortunes of his own offspring, to that of the unknown parent, who, like himself, most probably mourned the uncertain fate of the girl before him, he tendered the ransom intended for Ruth, in behalf of the captive. It was rejected. Disappointed in both their objects, the adventurers were obliged to quit the village, with weary feet and still heavier hearts.

If any who read these pages have ever felt the agony of suspense in a matter involving the best of human affections, they will know how to appreciate the sufferings of the mother, during the month that her husband was absent on this holy errand. At times, hope brightened around her heart, until the glow of pleasure was again mantling on her cheek and playing in her eye. The first week of the adventure was one almost of happiness. The hazards of the journey were nearly forgotten in its anticipated results, and though occasional apprehensions quickened the pulses of one whose system answered so fearfully to the movements of the spirit, there was a predominance of hope in all her anticipations. She again passed among her maidens with a mien in which joy was struggling with the meekness of subdued habits, and her smiles once more began to beam with renovated happiness. To his dying day, old Mark Heathcote never forgot the sudden sensation that was created by the soft laugh that on some unexpected occasion came to his ear from the lips of his son's wife. Though years had elapsed between the moment when that unwonted sound was heard, and the time at which the action of the tale now stands, he had never heard it repeated. To heighten the feelings which were now uppermost in the mind of Ruth, when within a day's march of the village to which he was going, Content had found means to send the tidings of his prospects of success. It was over all these renewed wishes that disappointment was to throw its chill, and it was affections thus riveted that were to be again blighted by the cruelest of all withering influences,—that of hope defeated.

It was near the hour of the setting of the sun, when Content and Dudley reached the deserted clearing on their return to the valley. Their path led through this opening on the mountain-side, and there was one point, among the bushes, from which the buildings, that had already arisen from the ashes of the burning, might be distinctly seen. Until now, the husband and father had believed himself equal to any effort that duty might require, in the progress of this mournful service. But here he paused, and communicated a wish to his companion that he would go ahead and break the nature of the deception that had led them so far on a fruitless mission. Perhaps Content was himself ignorant of all he wished, or to what unskilful hands he had confided a commission of more than ordinary delicacy. He merely felt his own inability, and, with a weakness that may find some apology in his feelings, he saw his companion depart, without instructions or indeed without any other guide than Nature

Though Faith had betrayed no marked uneasiness during the absence of the travellers, her quick eye was the first to discover the form of her husband, as he came with a tired step across the fields, in the direction of the dwellings. Long ere Dudley reached the house, every one of its inmates had assembled in the piazza. This was no meeting of turbulent delight, or of clamorous greetings. The adventurer drew near amid a silence so oppressive, that it utterly disconcerted a studied project, by which he had hoped to announce his tidings in a manner suited to the occasion. His hand was on the gate of the little court, and still none spoke; his foot was on the low step, and yet no voice bade him welcome. The looks of the little group were rather fixed on the features of Ruth, than on the person of him who approached. Her face was pallid as death, her eye contracted, but filled with the mental effort that sustained her; and her lip scarce trembled, as, in obedience to a feeling still stronger than the one which had so long oppressed her, she exclaimed—

"Eben Dudley, where hast thou left my husband?"

"The young Captain was a-foot weary, and he tarried in the second growth of the hill; but so brave a walker cannot be far behind. We shall see him soon, at the opening by the dead beech; and it is there that I recommend the Madam——"

"It was thoughtful in Heathcote, and like his usual kindness, to devise this well-meant caution!" said Ruth, across whose countenance a smile so radiant passed, that it imparted the expression which is believed to characterize the peculiar benignancy of angels. "Still it was unnecessary; for he should have known that we place our strength on the Rock of Ages. Tell me, in what manner hath my precious one borne the exceeding weariness of thy tangled route?"

The wandering glance of the messenger had gone from face to face, until it became fastened on the countenance of his own wife, in a settled, unmeaning gaze.

"Nay, Faith hath demeaned well, both as my assistant and as thy partner, and thou mayest see that her comeliness is in no degree changed—And did the babe falter in this weary passage, or did she retard thy movements by her fretfulness? But I know thy nature, man; she hath been borne over many long miles of mountain-side and treacherous swamp, in thine own vigorous arms. Thou answerest not, Dudley!" exclaimed Ruth, taking the alarm, and laying a hand firmly on the shoulder of him she questioned, as, forcing his half-averted face to meet her eye, she seemed to read his soul.

The muscles of the sun-burnt and strong features of the borderer worked involuntarily, his broad chest swelled to its utmost expansion, big burning drops rolled out upon his brown cheeks, and then, taking the arm of Ruth in one of his own powerful hands, he compelled her to release her hold, with a firm but respectful exercise of his strength; and, thrusting the form of his own wife, without ceremony, aside, he passed through the circle, and entered the dwelling, with the tread of a giant.

The head of Ruth dropped upon her bosom, the paleness again came over her cheeks, and it was then that the inward look of the eye might first be seen, which afterwards became so constant and so painful an expression in her countenance. From that hour, to the time in which the family of the Wish-Ton-Wish is again brought immediately before the reader, no further rumors were ever heard, to lessen or increase the wasting regrets of her bosom.

CHAPTER XX.

"Sir, he hath never fed of the dainties that are bred in a book, he hath not eaten paper, as it were; he hath not drunk ink: his intellect is not replenished; he is only an animal—only sensible in the duller parts."

Love's Labor Lost.

"Here cometh Faith, to bring us tidings of the hamlet," said the husband of the woman whose character we have so feebly sketched, as he took his seat in the piazza, at the early hour and in the group already mentioned. "The Ensign hath been abroad in the hills, throughout the night, with a chosen party of our people; and perchance she hath been sent with the substance that they have gathered, concerning the unknown trail."

"The heavy-footed Dudley hath scarce mounted to the dividing ridge, where report goeth the prints of moccasons were seen," observed a young man, who in his person bore all the evidences of an active and healthful manhood. "Of what service is the scouting that faileth of the necessary distance, by the weariness of its leader?"

"If thou believest, boy, that thy young foot is equal to contend with the sinews of Eben Dudley, there may be occasion to show the magnitude of thy error, ere the danger of this Indian out-breaking shall pass away. Thou art too stubborn of will, Mark, to be yet trusted with the leading of parties that may hold the safety of all who dwell in the Wish-Ton-Wish within their keeping."

The young man looked displeased; but, fearful that his father might observe and misinterpret his humor into a personal disrespect, he turned away, permitting his frowning eye to rest, for an instant, on the timid and stolen glance of a maiden, whose cheek was glowing like the eastern sky, as she busied herself with the preparations of the table.

"What welcome news dost bring from the sign of the Whip-poor-Will?" Content asked of the woman, who had now come within the little gate of his court. "Hast seen the Ensign, since the party took the hill-paths; or is it some traveller who hath charged thee with matter for our ears?"

"Eye of man hath not seen the man since he girded himself with the sword of office," returned Faith, entering the piazza and nodding salutation to those around her; "and as for strangers, when the clock shall strike noon, it will be one month to the day that the last of them was housed within my doors. But I complain not of the want of custom, as the Ensign would never quit the bar and his gossip, to go into the mountain-lots, so long as there was one to fill his ears with the marvels of the old countries, or even to discourse of the home-stirrings of the colonies themselves."

"Thou speakest lightly, Faith, of one who merits thy respect and thy duty."

The eye of the former studied the meek countenance of her from whom this reproof came, with an intenseness and a melancholy that showed her thoughts were on other matters, and then, as if suddenly recalled to what had passed, she resumed—

"Truly, what with duty to the man as a husband, and respect to him as an officer of the colony Madam Heathcote, the task is not one of easy bearing. If the King's representative had given the colors to my brother Reuben, and left the Dudley with the halberd in his hand, the preferment would have been ample for one of his qualities, and all the better for the credit of the settlement."

"The Governor distributed his favor according to the advice of men competent to distinguish merit," said Content. "Eben was foremost in the bloody affair among the people of the Plantations, where his manhood was of good example to all in company. Should he continue as faithful and as valiant, thou mayest yet live to see thyself the consort of a Captain!"

"Not for glory gained in this night's marching, for yonder cometh the man with a sound body, and seemingly with the stomach of a Cæsar—ay, and I'll answer for it, of a regiment too! It is no trifle that will satisfy his appetite, after one of these—ha! pray Heaven the fellow be not harmed—truly, he hath our neighbor Ergot in attendance."

"There is other than he too, for one cometh in the rear whose gait and air are unknown to me—the trail hath been struck, and Dudley leadeth a captive! A savage, in his paint and cloak of skin, is taken."

This assertion caused all to rise, for the excitement of an apprehended inroad was still strong in the minds of those secluded people. Not a syllable more was uttered, until the scout and his companion were before them.

The quick glance of Faith had scanned the person of her husband, and, resuming her spirits with the certainty that he was unharmed, she was the first to greet him with words:

"How now, Ensign Dudley," said the woman, quite possibly vexed that she had unguardedly betrayed a greater interest in his welfare than she might always deem prudent. "How now, Ensign, hath the campaign ended with no better trophy than this?"

"The fellow is not a chief, nor, by his step and dull look, even a warrior; but he was, nevertheless, a lurker nigh the settlements, and it was thought prudent to bring him in;" returned the husband, addressing himself to Content, while he answered the salutation of his wife with a sufficiently brief nod. "My own scouting hath brought nothing to light, but my brother Ring hath fallen on the trail of him that is here present, and it is not a little that we are puzzled in probing, as the good Doctor Ergot calleth it, into the meaning of his errand."

"Of what tribe may the savage be?"

"There hath been discussion among us, on that matter," returned Dudley, with an oblique glance of the eye towards the physician. "Some have said he is a Narragansett, while others think he cometh of a stock still further east."

"In giving that opinion, I spoke merely of his secondary or acquired habits," interrupted Ergot; "for, having reference to his original, the man is assuredly a White."

"A White!" repeated all around him.

"Beyond a cavil; as may be seen by divers particulars in his outward conformation, viz: in the shape of the head, the muscles of the arms and of the legs, the air and gait, besides sundry other signs, that are familiar to men who have made the physical peculiarities of the two races their study."

"One of which is this!" continued Dudley, throwing up the robe of the captive, and giving his com panions the ocular evidence which had so satisfactorily removed all his own doubts. "Though the color of the skin may not be proof positive, like that named by our neighbor Ergot, it is still some, thing, in helping a man of little learning to make up an opinion in such a matter."

"Madam!" exclaimed Faith so suddenly as to cause her she addressed to start—"for the sake of Heaven's mercy! let thy maidens bring soap and water, that the face of this man may be cleansed of its paint."

"What foolishness is thy brain set upon?" rejoined the Ensign, who had latterly affected some of that superior gravity which might be supposed to belong to his official station. "We are not now under the roof of the Whip-Poor-Will, wife of mine, but in the presence of those who need none of thy suggestions to give proper forms to an examination of office."

Faith heeded no reproof. Instead of waiting for others to perform that which she had desired, she applied herself to the task, with a dexterity that had been acquired by long practice, and a zeal that seemed awakened by some extraordinary emotion. In a minute, the colors had disappeared from the features of the captive, and, though deeply tanned by exposure to an American sun and to sultry winds, his face was unequivocally that of one who owed his origin to an European ancestry. The movements of the eager woman were watched with curious interest by all present; and when the short task was nded, a murmur of surprise broke simultaneously from every lip.

'There is meaning in this masquerade," observed Content, who had long and intently studied the dull and ungainly countenance that was exposed to his scrutiny by the operation. "I have heard of Christian men who have sold themselves to gain, and who, forgetting religion and the love of their race-have been known to league with the savage in order to pursue rapine in the settlements. This wretch hath the subtlety of one of the French of the Canadas in his eye."

"Away! away!" cried Faith, forcing herself in front of the speaker, and, by placing her two hands on the shaven crown of the prisoner, forming a sort of shade to his features. "Away with all folly, about the Frenchers and wicked leagues! This is no plotting miscreant, but a stricken innocent! Whittal—my brother Whittal, dost know me?"

The tears rolled down the cheeks of the wayward woman, as she gazed into the face of her witless relative, whose eye lighted with one of its occasional gleamings of intelligence, and who indulged in a low, vacant laugh, ere he answered her earnest interrogatory.

"Some speak like men from over sea," he said, "and some speak like men of the woods. Is there such a thing as bear's meat, or a mouthful of hommony, in the wigwam?"

Had the voice of one, long known to be in the grave, broken on the ears of the family, it would scarcely have produced a deeper sensation, or have quickened the blood more violently about their hearts, than this sudden and utterly unexpected discovery of the character of their captive. Wonder and awe held them mute for a time, and then Ruth was seen standing before the restored wanderer her hands clasped in the attitude of petition, her eye contracted and imploring, and her whole person expressive of the suspense and excitement which had roused her long-latent emotions to agony.

"Tell me," said a thrilling voice, that might have quickened the intellect of one even duller than the man addressed, 'as thou hast pity in thy heart, tell me, if my babe yet live?"

"'Tis a good babe," returned the other; and ther

laughing again, in his own vacant and unmeaning manner, he bent his eyes with a species of stupid wonder on Faith, in whose appearance there was far less change, than in the speaking but wasted countenance of her who stood immediately before him.

"Give leave, dearest Madam," interposed the sister: "I know the nature of the boy, and could ever do more with him than any other."

But this request was useless. The system of the mother, in its present state of excitement, was unequal to further effort. Sinking into the watchful arms of Content, she was borne away, and, for a minute, the anxious interest of the handmaidens left none but the men on the piazza.

"Whittal—my old playfellow, Whittal Ring;" said the son of Content, advancing with a humid eye to take the hand of the prisoner. "Hast forgotten, man, the companion of thy early days? It is young Mark Heathcote that speaks."

The other looked up into his countenance, for a moment, with a reviving recollection; but shaking his head, he drew back in marked displeasure, muttering loud enough to be heard—

"What a false liar is a Pale-face! Here is one of the tall rogues, wishing to pass for a loping boy!'

What more he uttered his auditors never knew, for he instantly changed his language to some dialect of an Indian tribe.

"The mind of the unhappy youth hath even been more blunted, by exposure and the usages of a savage life, than by Nature," said Content, who with most of the others had been recalled, by his interest in the examination, to the scene they had momentarily quitted. "Let the sister deal tenderly with the lad, and, in Heaven's time, shall we learn the truth."

The deep feeling of the father clothed his words

with authority. The eager group gave place, and something like the solemnity of an official examination succeeded to the irregular and hurried interrogatories, which had first broken on the dull intellect of the recovered wanderer.

The dependants took their stations, in a circle around the chair of the Puritan, by whose side was placed Content, while Faith induced her brother to be seated on the step of the piazza, in a manner that all might hear. The attention of the brother himself, was drawn from the formality of the arrangement, by placing food in his hands.

"And now, Whittal, I would know," commenced the ready woman, when a deep silence denoted the attention of the auditors, "I would know, if thou rememberest the day I clad thee in garments of boughten cloth, from over sea; and how fond thou wast of being seen among the kine in colors so gay?"

The young man looked up in her face, as if the tones of her voice gave him pleasure; but, instead of making any reply, he preferred to munch the bread with which she had endeavored to lure him back to their ancient confidence.

"Surely, boy, thou canst not so soon have forgotten the gift I bought, with the hard earnings of a wheel that turned at night. The tail of yon peacock is not finer than thou then wast—But I will make thee such another garment, that thou mayst go with the trainers to their weekly muster."

The youth dropped the robe of skin that covered the upper part of his body, and making a forward gesture, with the gravity of an Indian, he answered—

"Whittal is a warrrior on his path; he has no time for the talk of the women!"

"Now, brother, thou forgettest the manner in which I was wont to feed thy hunger, as the frost pinched thee, in the cold mornings, and at the hour when the kine needed thy care; else thou woulds, not call me woman."

"Hast ever been on the trail of a Pequot? Know'st how to whoop among the men?"

"What is an Indian whoop, to the bleating of thy flocks, or the be lowing of cattle in the bushes? Thou rememberest the sound of the bells, as they tinkled among the second growth of an evening?"

The ancient herdsman turned his head, and seemed to lend his attention, as a dog listens to an approaching footstep. But the gleam of recollection was quickly lost. In the next moment, he yielded to the more positive, and possibly more urgent, demands of his appetite.

"Then hast thou lost the use of ears; else thou wouldst not say that thou forgettest the sound of the bells."

"Didst ever hear a wolf howl?" exclaimed the other. "That's a sound for a hunter! I saw the Great Chief strike the striped panther, when the boldest warrior of the tribe grew white as a craven Pale-face at his leaps!"

"Talk not to me of your ravenous beasts and Great Chiefs, but rather let us think of the days when we were young, and when thou hadst delight in the sports of a Christian childhood. Hast forgotten, Whittal, how our mother used to give us leave to pass the idle time in games among the snow?"

"Nipset hath a mother in her wigwam, but he sketh no leave to go on the hunt. He is a man he next snow, he will be a warrior."

"Silly boy! This is some treachery of the savage by which he has bound thy weakness with the fet ters of his craftiness. Thy mother, Whittal, was a woman of Christian belief, and one of a white race, and a kind and mourning mother was she over thy feeble-mindedness! Dost not remember, unthankful of heart! how she nursed thy sickly hours in boyhood, and how she administered to all thy bodily wants? Who was it that fed thee when a-hungered, or who had compassion on thy waywardness, when others tired of thy idle deeds, or grew impatient of thy weakness?"

The brother looked, for an instant, at the flushed features of the speaker, as if glimmerings of some faintly distinguished scenes crossed the visions of his mind; but the animal still predominated, and he continued to feed his hunger.

"This exceedeth human endurance!" exclaimed the excited Faith. "Look into this eye, weak one, and say if thou knowest her who supplied the place of that mother whom thou refusest to remember—she who hath toiled for thy comfort, and who hath never refused to listen to all thy plaints, and to soften all thy sufferings. Look at this eye, and speak—dost know me?"

"Certain!" returned the other, laughing with a half-intelligent expression of recognition; "'tis a woman of the Pale-faces, and I warrant me, one that will never be satisfied till she hath all the furs of the Americas on her back, and all the venison of the woods in her kitchen. Didst ever hear the tradition, how that wicked race got into the hunting-grounds, and robbed the warriors of the country?"

The disappointment of Faith had made her too impatient to lend a pleased attention to this tale; but, at that moment, a form appeared at her side, and by a quiet and commanding gesture directed her to humor the temper of the wanderer.

It was Ruth, in whose pale cheek and anxious eye, all the intenseness of a mother's longings might be traced, in its most touching aspect. Though so lately helpless and sinking beneath her emotions, the sacred feelings which now sustained her seemed to supply the place of all other aid; and as she glided past the listening circle, even Content himself had not believed it necessary to offer succor, or to interpose with remonstrance. Her quiet, meaning gesture seemed to say, 'proceed, and show all indulgence to the weakness of the young man.' The rising discontent of Faith was checked by habitual reverence, and she prepared to obey.

"And what say the silly traditions of which you speak?" she added, ere the current of his dull ideas had time to change its direction.

"'Tis spoken by the old men in the villages, and what is there said is gospel-true. You see all around you, land that is covered with hill and valley, and which once bore wood, without the fear of the axe, and over which game was spread with a bountiful hand. There are runners and hunters in our tribe who have been on a straight path towards the setting sun, until their legs were weary and their eyes could not see the clouds that hang over the salt lake, and yet they say, 'tis everywhere beautiful as yonder green mountain. Tall trees and shady woods rivers and lakes filled with fish, and deer and beaver plentiful as the sands on the sea-shore. All this land and water the Great Spirit gave to men of red skins; for them he loved, since they spoke truth in their tribes, were true to their friends. hated their enemies, and knew how to take scalps. Now, a thousand snows had come and melted, since this gift was made," continued Whittal, who spoke with the air of one charged with the narration of a grave tradition, though he probably did no more than relate what many repetitions had rendered familiar to his inactive mind, "and yet none but red-skins were seen to hunt the moose, or to go on the war-path. Then the Great Spirit grew angry; he hid his face from his children, because they quarrelled among themselves. Big canoes came out of the rising sun, and brought a hungry and wicked people into the land. At first, the strangers spoke soft and complaining like women. They begged room for a few wigwams, and said if the warriors would give them ground to plant, they would ask their God to look upon the red-men. But when they grew strong, they forgot their words and made liars of themselves. Oh, they are wicked knaves! A Pale-face is a panther. When a-hungered, you can hear him whining in the bushes like a strayed infant; but when you come within his leap, beware of tooth and claw!"

"This evil-minded race, then, robbed the red warriors of their land?"

"Certain! They spoke like sick women, till they grew strong, and then they out-devilled the Pequots themselves in wickedness; feeding the warriors with their burning milk, and slaying with blazing inventions, that they made out of the yellow meal."

"And the Pequods! was their great warrior dead, before the coming of the men from over sea?"

"You are a woman that has never heard a tradition, or you would know better! A Pequot is a weak and crawling cub."

"And thou—thou art then a Narragansett?"

"Don't I look like a man?"

"I had mistaken thee for one of our nearer neighbors, the Mohegan Pequods."

"The Mohicans are basket-makers for the Yengeese; but the Narragansett goes leaping through the woods, like a wolf on the trail of the deer!"

"All this is quite in reason, and now thou pointest to its justice, I cannot fail but see it. But we have curiosity to know more of the great tribe. Hast ever heard of one of thy people, Whittal, known as Miantonimoh—'tis a chief of some renown."

The witless youth had continued to eat, at intervals; but, on hearing this question, he seemed suddenly to forget his appetite. For a moment he look ed down, and then he answered slowly and not without solemnity—

"A man cannot live for ever."

"What!" said Faith, motioning to her deeply-interested auditors to restrain their impatience—"has he quitted his people? And thou lived with him, Whittal, ere he came to his end?"

"He never looked on Nipset, nor Nipset on him."

"I know nought of this Nipset; tell me of the great Miantonimoh."

"Dost need to hear twice? The Sachem is gone to the far land, and Nipset will be a warrior when the next snow comes!"

Disappointment threw a cloud on every countenance, and the beam of hope, which had been kindling in the eye of Ruth, changed to the former painful expression of deep inward suffering. But Faith still managed to repress all speech among those who listened, continuing the examination, after a short delay that her vexation rendered unavoidable.

"I had thought that Miantonimoh was still a warrior in his tribe," she said. "In what battle did he fall?"

"Mohican Uncas did that wicked deed. The Pale-men gave him great riches to murder the Sachem."

"Thou speakest of the father; but there was another Miantonimoh; he who in boyhood dwelt among the people of white blood."

Whittal listened attentively; and after seeming to rally his thoughts, he shook his head, saying before he again began to eat—

"There never was but one of the name, and there never will be another. Two eagles do not build their nests in the same tree."

"Thou sayest truly," continued Faith; well knowing that to dispute the information of her brother, was in effect to close his mouth. "Now tell me of Conanchet, the present Narragansett Sachem —he who hath leagued with Metacom, and hath of late been driven from his fastness near the sea—doth he yet live?"

The expression of the brother's countenance underwent another change. In place of the childish importance with which he had hitherto replied to the questions of his sister, a look of overreaching cunning gathered about his dull eye. The organ glanced slowly and cautiously around him, as if its owner expected to detect some visible sign of those covert intentions he so evidently distrusted. Instead of answering, the wanderer continued his meal, though less like one who had need of sustenance, than one resolved to make no communications which might prove dangerous. This change was not unobserved by Faith, or by any of those who so intently watched the means by which she had been endeavoring to thread the confused ideas of one so dull, and yet who at need seemed so practised in savage artifice. She prudently altered her manner of interrogating, by endeavoring to lead his thoughts to other matters.

"I warrant me," continued the sister, "that thou now beginnest to call to mind the times when thou led'st the cattle among the bushes, and how thou wert wont to call on Faith to give thee food, when a-weary with threading the woods in quest of the kine. Hast ever been assailed by the Narragansetts thyself, Whittal, when dwelling in the house of a Pale-face?"

The brother ceased eating. Again he appeared o muse as intently as was possible, for one of his circumscribed intellects. But shaking his head in the negative, he silently resumed the grateful office of mastication.

"What! hast come to be a warrior, and never

known a scalp taken, or seen a fire lighted in the roof of a wigwam?"

Whittal laid down the food, and turned to his sister. His face was teeming with a wild and fierce meaning, and he indulged in a low but triumphant laugh. When this exhibition of satisfaction was over, he consented to reply.

"Certain," he said. "We went on a path, in the night, against the lying Yengeese, and no burning of the woods ever scorched the 'arth as we blackened their fields! All their proud housen were turned into piles of coals."

"And where and when did you this act of brave vengeance?"

"They called the place after the bird of night as if an Indian name could save them from an Indian massacre!"

"Ha! 'Tis of the Wish-Ton-Wish thou speakest But thou wast a sufferer, and not an actor, brother in that heartless burning."

"Thou liest like a wicked woman of the Pale faces, as thou art! Nipset was only a boy on that path, but he went with his people. I tell thee, we singed the very 'arth with our brands, and not a head of them all ever rose again from the ashes."

Notwithstanding her great self-command, and the object that was constantly before the mind of Faith, she shuddered at the fierce pleasure with which her brother pronounced the extent of the vengeance, that, in his imaginary character, he believed he had taken on his enemies. Still cautious not to destroy an illusion which might aid her, in the so-long-defeated and so-anxiously-desired discovery, the woman repressed her horror, and continued—

"True—yet some were spared—surely the warriors carried prisoners back to their village. Thou didst not slay all?"

"All."

"Nay—thou speakest now of the miserables who were wrapt in the blazing block; but—but some, without, might have fallen into thy hands, ere the assailed sought shelter in the tower. Surely—surely thou didst not kill all?"

The hard breathing of Ruth caught the ear of Whittal, and for a moment he turned to regard her countenance in dull wonder. But again shaking his head, he answered in a low, positive tone—

"All;—ay, to the screeching women and crying babes!"

"Surely there is a child—I would say there is a woman, in thy tribe, of fairer skin and of form different from most of thy people. Was not such an one led a captive from the burning of the Wish-Ton-Wish?"

"Dost think the deer will live with the wolf, or hast ever found the cowardly pigeon in the nest of the hawk?"

"Nay, thou art of different color thyself, Whittal, and it well may be, thou art not alone."

The youth regarded his sister a moment with marked displeasure, and then, on turning to eat, he muttered—

"There is as much fire in snow, as truth in a lying Yengeese?"

"This examination must close," said Content, with a heavy sigh; "at another hour, we may hope to push the matter to some more fortunate result; but, yonder cometh one charged with especial service from the towns below, as would seem by the fact that he disregardeth the holiness of the day no less than by the earnest manner in which he is journeying."

As the individual named was visible to all who chose to look in the direction of the hamlet, his sudden appearance caused a general interruption to the interest which had been so strongly awakened on a subject that was familiar to every resident in the valley.

The early hour, the gait at which the stranger urged his horse, the manner in which he passed the open and inviting door of the Whip-Poor-Will, proclaimed him a messenger, who probably bore some communication of importance from the Government of the Colony to the younger Heathcote, who filled the highest station of official authority in that distant settlement. Observations to this purport had passed from mouth to mouth, and curiosity was actively alive, by the time the horseman rode into the court. There he dismounted, and, covered with the dust of the road, he presented himself, with the air of one who had passed the night in the saddle, before the man he sought.

"I have orders for Captain Content Heathcote," said the messenger, saluting all around him with the usual grave but studied courtesy of the people to whom he belonged.

"He is here to receive and to obey," was the answer.

The traveller wore a little of that mysteriousness that is so grateful to certain minds, which, from inability to command respect in any other manner, are fond of making secrets of matters that might as well be revealed. In obedience to this feeling, he expressed a desire that his communications might be made apart. Content quietly motioned for him to follow, leading the way into an inner apartment of the house. As a new direction was given by this interruption, to the thoughts of the spectators of the foregoing scene, we shall also take the opportunity to digress, in order to lay before the reader some general facts that may be necessary to the connexion of the subsequent parts of the legend.

CHAPTER XXI.

"Be certain what you do, sir; lest your justice
Prove violence."

WINTER'S TALE.

THE designs of the celebrated Metacom had been betrayed to the Colonists, by the treachery of a subordinate warrior, named Sausaman. The punishment of this treason led to inquiries, which terminated in accusations against the great Sachem of the Wampanoags. Scorning to vindicate himself before enemies that he hated, and perhaps distrusting their clemency, Metacom no longer endeavored to cloak his proceedings; but, throwing aside the emblems of peace he openly appeared with an armed hand.

The tragedy had commenced about a year before the period at which the tale has now arrived. A scene, not unlike that detailed in the foregoing pages, took place; the brand, the knife, and the tomahawk, doing their work of destruction, without pity and without remorse. But, unlike the inroad of the Wish-Ton-Wish, this expedition was immediately followed by others, until the whole of New-England was engaged in the celebrated war, to which we have before referred.

The entire white population of the Colonies of New-England had shortly before been estimated at one hundred and twenty thousand souls. Of this number, it was thought that sixteen thousand men were capable of bearing arms. Had time been given for the maturity of the plans of Metacom, he might have readily assembled bands of warriors who, aided by their familiarity with the woods, and accustomed to the privations of such a warfare, would have threatened serious danger to the growing strength of the whites. But the ordinary and selfish feelings of man were as active, among these wild tribes, as they are known to be in more artificial communities. The indefatigable Metacom, like that Indian hero of our own times, Tecumthè, ha passed years in endeavoring to appease ancient en mities and to lull jealousies, in order that all of red blood might unite in crushing a foe that promised, should he be longer undisturbed in his march to power, soon to be too formidable for their united efforts to subdue. The premature explosion in some measure averted the danger. It gave the English time to strike several severe blows against the tribe of their great enemy, before his allies had determined to make common cause in his design. The summer and autumn of 1675 had been passed in active hostilities between the English and Wampanoags, without openly drawing any other nation into the contest. Some of the Pequots, with their dependent tribes, even took sides with the whites: and we read of the Mohegans being actively employed in harassing the Sachem, on his well-known retreat from that neck of land, where he had been hemmed in by the English, with the expectation that he might be starved into submission.

The warfare of the first summer was, as might be expected, attended by various degrees of success, fortune quite as often favoring the red-men, in their desultory attempts at annoyance, as their more dis ciplined enemies. Instead of confining his operations to his own circumscribed and easily environed districts, Metacom had led his warriors to the distant settlements on the Connecticut; and it was during the operations of this season, that several of the towns on that river were first assailed and laid in ashes. Active hostilities had in some measure ceased, between the Wampanoags and the English, with the cold weather, most of the troops retiring to their homes, while the Indians apparently paused to take breath for their final effort.

It was, however, previously to this cessation of activity, that the Commissioners of the United Colonies, as they were called, met to devise the means of a concerted resistance. Unlike their former dangers from the same quarter, it was manifest, by the manner in which a hostile feeling was spreading around their whole frontier, that a leading spirit had given as much of unity and design to the movements of the foe, as could probably ever be created among a people so separated by distance and so divided in communities. Right or wrong, the Colonists gravely decided that the war on their part was just. Great preparations were therefore made to carry it on, the ensuing summer, in a manner more suited to their means, and to the absolute necessities of their situation. It was in consequence of the arrangements made for bringing a portion of the inhabitants of the Colony of Connecticut into the field, that we find the principal characters of our legend in the warlike guise in which they have just been re-introduced to the reader.

Although the Narragansetts had not at first been openly implicated in the attacks on the Colonists, facts soon came to the knowledge of the latter, which left no doubt of the state of feeling in tha nation. Many of their young men were discovered among the followers of Metacom, and arms taken from whites, who had been slain in the different encounters, were also seen in their villages. One of the first measures of the Commissioners, therefore, was to anticipate more serious opposition, by directing an overwhelming force against this people. The party collected on that occasion was probably the largest military body which the Eng lish, at that early day, had ever assembled in their Colonies. It consisted of a thousand men, of whom no inconsiderable number was cavalry—a species of troops that, as all subsequent experience has shown, is admirably adapted to operations against so active and so subtle a foe.

The attack was made in the depth of winter, and it proved fearfully destructive to the assailed. The defence of Conanchet, the young Sachem of the Narragansetts, was every way worthy of his high character for courage and mental resources, nor was the victory gained without serious loss to the Colonists. The native chief had collected his warriors, and taken post on a small area of firm land, that was situated in the centre of a densely wooded swamp; and the preparations for resistance betrayed a singular familiarity with the military expedients of a white man. There had been a palisadoed breast-work, a species of redoubt, and a regular block-house, to overcome, ere the Colonists could penetrate into the fortified village itself. The first attempts were unsuccessful, the Indians having repulsed their enemies with loss. But better arms and greater concert finally prevailed, though not without a struggle that lasted for many hours, and not until the defendants were, in truth, nearly surrounded.

The events of that memorable day made a deep impression on the minds of men who were rarely excited by any incidents of a great and moving character. It was still the subject of earnest and not unfrequently of melancholy discourse, around the fire-sides of the Colonists; nor was the victory achieved without accompaniments which, however unavoidable they might have been, had a tendency to raise doubts in the minds of conscientious religion ists concerning the lawfulness of their cause. It is said that a village of six hundred cabins was burnt and that hundreds of dead and wounded were consumed in the conflagration. A thousand warriors were thought to have lost their lives in this affair, and it was believed that the power of the nation was broken for ever. The sufferers among the Colonists themselves were numerous, and mourning came into a vast many families, with the tidings of victory.

In this expedition most of the men of the Wish-Ton-Wish had been conspicuous actors, under the orders of Content. They had not escaped with impunity; but it was confidently hoped that their courage was to meet its reward in a long continuance of peace, which was the more desirable on account of their remote and exposed situation.

In the mean time, the Narragansetts were far from being subdued. Throughout the whole continuance of the inclement season, they had caused alarms on the frontiers; and, in one or two instances their renowned Sachem had taken signal vengeance for the dire affair in which his people had so heavily suffered. As the spring advanced, the inroads became still more frequent, and the appearances of danger so far increased as to require a new call on the Colonists to arm. The messenger, introduced in the last chapter, was charged with matter that had a reference to the events of this war; and it was with an especial communication of great urgency that he had now demanded his secret audience with the leader of the military force of the valley.

"Thou hast affairs of moment to deal with, Captain Heathcote," said the hard-riding traveller, when he found himself alone with Content. "The orders of his Honor are to spare neither whip nor spur until the chief men of the borders shall be warned of the actual situation of the Colony."

"Hath aught of moving interest occurred, that

his Honor deemeth there is necessity for unusual watchfulness. We had hoped that the prayers of the pious were not in vain; and that a time of quiet was about to succeed to that violence, of which, bounden by our social covenants, we have unhappily been unwilling spectators. The bloody assault of Pettyquamscott hath exercised our minds severely—nay, it hath even raised doubts of the lawfulness of some of our deeds."

"Thou hast a commendable spirit of forgiveness Captain Heathcote, or thy memory would extend to other scenes than those which bear relation to the punishment of an enemy so remorseless. It is said on the river, that the valley of Wish-Ton-Wish hath been visited by the savage in its day, and men speak freely of the wrongs suffered by its owners on that pitiless occasion."

"The truth may not be denied, even that good should come thereof. It is certain that much suffering was inflicted on me and on mine, by the inroad of which you speak; nevertheless we have ever striven to consider it as a merciful chastisement inflicted for manifold sins, rather than as a subject that might be remembered, in order to stimulate passions that, in all reason as in all charity, should slumber as much as a weak nature will allow."

"This is well, Captain Heathcote, and in exceeding conformity with the most received doctrines," returned the stranger, slightly gaping, either from want of rest the previous night, or from disinclination to so grave a subject; "but it hath little connexion with present duties. My charge beareth especial concern with the further destruction of the Indians, rather than to any inward searchings into the condition of our own mental misgivings, concerning any right it may be thought proper to question, that hath a reference to the duty of self-protection. There is no unworthy dweller in the Connecticut Colony, sir, that hath endeavored more to cultivate a tender conscience, than the wretched sinner who standeth before you; for I have the exceeding happiness to sit under the outpourings of a spirit that hath few mortal superiors in the matter of precious gifts. I now speak of Dr. Calvin Pope; a most worthy and soul-quieting divine; one who spareth not the goad when the conscience needeth pricking, nor hesitateth to dispense consolation to him who seeth his fallen estate; and one that never faileth to deal with charity, and humbleness of spirit, and forbearance with the failings of friends, and forgiveness of enemies, as the chiefest signs of a renovated moral existence; and, therefore, there can be but little reason to distrust the spiritual rightfulness of all that listen to the riches of his discourse. But when it cometh to be question of life or death, a matter of dominion and possession of these fair lands, that the Lord hath given—why, sir, then I say that, like the Israelites dealing with the sinful occupants of Canaan, it behoveth us to be true to each other, and to look upon the heathen with a distrustful eye."

"There may be reason in that thou utterest," observed Content, sorrowfully. "Still it is lawful to mourn even the necessity which conduceth to all this strife. I had hoped that they who direct the Councils of the Colony might have resorted to less violent means of persuasion, to lead the savage back to reason, than that which cometh from the armed hand. Of what nature is thy especial errand?"

"Of deep urgency, sir, as will be seen in the narration," returned the other, dropping his voice like one habitually given to the dramatic part of diplomacy, however unskilful he might have been in its more intellectual accomplishments. "Thou wast in the Pettyquamscott scourging, and need not be reminded of the manner in which the Lord dealt with our enemies on that favor-dispensing day; but it may not be known to one so remote from the stirring and daily transactions of Christendom, in what manner the savage hath taken the chastisement. The restless and still unconquered Conanchet hath deserted his towns and taken refuge in the open woods; where it exceedeth the skill and usage of our civilized men of war, to discover, at all times the position and force of their enemies. The consequences may be easily conjectured. The savage hath broken in upon, and laid waste, in whole or in part, firstly—Lancaster, on the tenth," counting on his fingers, "when many were led into captivity· secondly, Marlborough, on the twentieth; on the thirteenth, ultimo, Groton; Warwick, on the seventeenth; and Rehoboth, Chelmsford, Andover, Weymouth, and divers other places, have been greatly sufferers, between the latter period and the day when I quitted the abode of his Honor. Pierce of Scituate, a stout warrior, and one practised in the wiles of this nature of warfare, hath been cut off with a whole company of followers; and Wadsworth and Brockleband, men known and esteemed for courage and skill, have left their bones in the woods, sleeping in common among their luckless followers."

"These are truly tidings to cause us to mourn over the abandoned condition of our nature," said Content, in whose meek mind there was no affectation of regrets on such a subject. "It is not easy to see in what manner the evil may be arrested without again going forth to battle."

"Such is the opinion of his Honor, and of all who sit with him in Council; for we have sufficient knowledge of the proceedings of the enemy, to be sure that the master-spirit of wickedness, in the person of him called Philip, is raging up and down the whole extent of the borders, awakening the tribes to what he calleth the necessity of resisting further aggression, and stirring up their vengeance, by divers subtle expedients of malicious cunning."

"And what manner of proceeding hath been ordered, in so urgent a strait, by the wisdom of our rulers?"

"Firstly, there is a fast ordained, that we come to the duty as men purified by mental struggle and deep self-examination; secondly, it is recommended that the congregations deal with more than wonted severity with all backsliders and evil-doers, in order that the towns may not fall under the divine displeasure, as happened to them that dwelt in the devoted cities of Canaan; thirdly, it is determined to lend our feeble aid to the ordering of Providence, by calling forth the allotted number of the trained bands; and, fourthly, it is contemplated to counteract the seeds of vengeance, by setting a labor-earning price on the heads of our enemies."

"I accord with the three first of these expedients, as the known and lawful resorts of Christian men," said Content. "But the latter seemeth a measure that needeth to be entertained with great wariness of manner, and some distrust of purpose."

"Fear not, since all suiting and economical discretion is active in the minds of our rulers, who have pondered sagaciously on so grave a policy. It is not intended to offer more than half the reward that is held forth by our more wealthy and elder ister of the Bay; and there is some acute question about the necessity of bidding at all for any of tender years. And now, Captain Heathcote, with the good leave of so respectable a subject, I will proceed to lay before you the details of the number and the nature of the force that it is hoped you will lead in person in the ensuing campaign."

As the result of that which followed will be seen

in the course of the legend, it is not necessary to accompany the Messenger any further in his communication. We shall therefore leave him and Content busied with the matter of their conference, and proceed to give some account of the other personages connected with our subject.

When interrupted, as already related, by the arrival of the stranger, Faith had endeavored, by a new expedient, to elicit some evidences of a more just remembrance from the dull mind of her brother. Accompanied by most of the dependants of the family, she had led him to the summit of that hill which was now crowned with the foliage of a young and thrifty orchard, and, placing him at the foot of the ruin, she tried to excite a train of recollections that should lead to deeper impressions, and, possibly, by their aid, to a discovery of the important circumstance that all so much longed to have explained.

The experiment produced no happy result. The place, and indeed the whole valley, had undergone so great a change, that one more liberally gifted might have hesitated to believe them those that have been described in our earlier pages. This rapid alteration of objects, which elsewhere know so little change in a long course of ages, is a fact familiar to all who reside in the newer districts of the Union. It is caused by the rapid improvements that are made in the first stages of a settlement. To fell the forest alone, is to give an entirely new aspect to the view; and it is far from easy to see in a village and in cultivated fields, however recent the existence of the one or imperfect the other, any traces of a spot that a short time before was known as the haunt of the wolf or the refuge of the deer.

The features, and more particularly the eye of his sister, had stirred long-dormant recollections in the mind of Whittal Ring; and though these glimp es of the past were detached and indistinct, they had sufficed to quicken that ancient confidence which was partially exhibited in their opening conference. But it exceeded his feeble powers to recall objects that would appeal to no very lively sympathies, and which had themselves undergone so material alterations. Still, the witless youth did not look on the ruin entirely without some stirrings of his nature. Although the sward around its base was lively in the brightest verdure of early summer, and the delicious odor of the wild clover saluted his senses, still there was that in the blackened and ragged walls, the position of the tower, and the view of the surrounding hills, shorn as so much of them now were, that evidently spoke to his earliest impressions. He looked at the spot, as a hound gazes at a master who has been so long lost as even to deaden his instinct; and at times, as his companions endeavored to aid his faint images, it would seem as if memory were likely to triumph, and all those deceptive opinions, which habit and Indian wiles had drawn over his dull mind, were about to vanish before the light of reality. But the allurements of a life in which there was so much of the freedom of nature mingled with the fascinating pleasures of the chase and of the woods, were not to be dispossessed so readily. When Faith artfully led him back to those animal enjoyments of which he had been so fond in boyhood, the fantasy of her brother seemed most to waver; but whenever it became apparent that the dignity of a warrior, and all the more recent and far more alluring delights of his later life, were to be abandoned ere his being could return into its former existence, his dull faculties obstinately refused to lend themselves to a change that, in his case, would have been little short of that attributed to the transmigration of souls.

After an hour of anxious, and frequently, on the part of Faith, of angry efforts to extract some evidences of his recollection of the condition of life to which he had once belonged, the attempt for the moment was abandoned. At times, it seemed as if the woman were about to prevail. He often called himself Whittal, but he continued to insist that he was also Nipset, a man of the Narragansetts, who had a mother in his wigwam, and who had reason to believe that he should be numbered among the warriors of his tribe, ere the fall of another snow.

In the mean time, a very different scene was passing at the place where the first examination had been held, and which had been immediately deserted by most of the spectators, on the sudden arrival of the Messenger. But a solitary individual was seated at the spacious board, which had been provided alike for those who owned and presided over the estate, and for their dependants to the very meanest. The individual who remained had thrown himself into a seat, less with the air of him who consults the demands of appetite, than of one whose thoughts were so engrossing as to render him indifferent to the situation or employment of his more corporeal part. His head rested on his arms, the latter effectually concealing the face, as they were spread over the plain but exquisitely neat table of cherry-wood, which, by being placed at the side of one of less costly material, was intended to form the only distinction between the guests, as, in more ancient times and in other countries, the salt was known to mark the difference in rank among those who partook of the same feast.

"Mark," said a timid voice at his elbow, "thou art weary with this night-watching, and with the scouting on the hills. Dost not think of taking food before seeking thy rest?"

"I sleep not" returned the youth, raising his

head, and gently pushing aside the basin of simple food that was offered by one whose eye looked feelingly on his flushed features, and whose suffused cheek perhaps betrayed there was secret consciousness that the glance was kinder than maiden diffidence should allow. "I sleep not, Martha, nor doth it seem to me, that I shall ever sleep again."

"Thou frightest me by this wild and unhapp eye. Hast suffered aught in the march on th mountains?"

"Dost think one of my years and strength unable to bear the weariness of a few hours' watching in the forest? The body is well, but the mind endureth grievously."

"And wilt not say what causeth this vexation? Thou knowest, Mark, that there are none in this dwelling—nay, I am certain, I might add in this valley, that do not wish thee happiness."

"'Tis kind to say it, good Martha—but, thou never hadst a sister!"

"'Tis true, I am all of my race; and yet to me it seemeth that no tie of blood could have been nearer than the love I bore to her who is lost."

"Nor mother! Thou never knew'st what 'tis to reverence a parent."

"And is not thy mother mine?" answered a voice that was deeply melancholy, and yet so soft that it caused the young man to gaze intently at his companion, for a moment, ere he again spoke.

"True, true," he said hurriedly. "Thou mus and dost love her who hath nursed thy infancy, and brought thee, with care and tenderness, to so fair and happy a womanhood." The eye of Martha grew brighter, and the color of her healthful cheek deepened, as Mark unconsciously uttered this commendation of her appearance; but as she shrunk, with female sensitiveness, from his observation, the change was unnoticed, and he continued: "Thou seest that my mother is drooping, hourly, under this sorrow for our little Ruth; and who can say what may be the end of a grief that endureth so long?"

"'Tis true that there hath been reason to fear much in her behalf; but, of late, hope hath gotten the better of apprehension. Thou dost not well, nay, I am not assured thou dost not evil, to permit this discontent with Providence, because thy mother yieldeth to a little more than her usual mourning, on account of the unexpected return of one so nearly connected with her that we have lost."

"'Tis not that, girl—'tis not that!"

"If thou refusest to say what 'tis that giveth thee this pain. I can do little more than pity."

"Listen, and I will say. It is now many years, as thou knowest, since the savage Mohawk, or Narragansett, Pequot, or Wampanoag, broke in upon our settlement, and did his vengeance. We were then children, Martha; and 'tis as a child, that I have thought of that merciless burning. Our little Ruth was, like thyself, a blooming infant of some seven or eight years; and, I know not how the folly hath beset me, but it hath been ever as one of that innocence and age, that I have continued to think of my sister."

"Surely thou knowest that time cannot stay; the greater therefore is the reason that we should be industrious to improve——"

"'Tis what our duty teacheth. I tell thee, Martha, that at night, when dreams come over me, as they sometimes will, and I see our Ruth wandering in the forest, it is as a playful, laughing child, such as we knew her; and even while waking, do I fancy my sister at my knee, as she was wont to stand when listening to those idle tales with which we lightened our childhood."

"But we had our birth in the same year and

month—dost think of me too, Mark, as one of that childish age?"

"Of thee! That cannot well be. Do I not see that thou art grown into the condition of a woman, that thy little tresses of brown have become the jet-black and flowing hair that becomes thy years, and that thou hast the stature, and, I say it not in idleness of speech, Martha, for thou knowest my tongue is no vain flatterer, but do I not see that thou hast grown into all the excellence of a most comely maiden? But 'tis not thus, or rather 'twas not thus, with her we mourn; for till this hour have I ever pictured my sister the little innocent we sported with, that gloomy night she was snatched from our arms by the cruelty of the savage."

"And what hath changed this pleasing image of our Ruth?" asked his companion, half-covering her face to conceal the still deeper glow of female gratification which had been kindled by the words just heard. "I often think of her as thou hast described, nor do I now see why we may not still believe her, if she yet live, all that we could desire to see."

"That cannot be—The delusion is gone, and in its place a frightful truth has visited me. Here is Whittal Ring, whom we lost a boy; thou seest he is returned a man, and a savage! No, no; my sister is no longer the child I loved to think her, but one grown into the estate of womanhood."

"Thou thinkest of her unkindly, while thou thinkest of others far less endowed by nature with too much indulgence; for thou rememberest, Mark, she was ever of more pleasing aspect than any that we knew."

"I know not that—I say not that—I think not that. But be she what hardships and exposure may have made her, still must Ruth Heathcote be far too good for an Indian wigwam. Oh! 'tis horrible to believe that she is the bond-woman, the servitor, the wife of a savage!"

Martha recoiled, and an entire minute passed, during which she made no reply. It was evident that the revolting idea for the first time crossed her mind, and all the natural feelings of gratified and maiden pride vanished before the genuine and pure ympathies of a female bosom.

"This cannot be," she at length murmured—"it can never be! Our Ruth must still remember the lessons taught her in infancy. She knoweth she is born of Christian lineage! of reputable name! of exalted hope! of glorious promise!"

"Thou seest by the manner of Whittal, who is of greater age, how little of that taught, can withstand the wily savage."

"But Whittal faileth of Nature's gifts; he hath ever been below the rest of men in understanding."

"And yet to what degree of Indian cunning hath he already attained!"

"But Mark," rejoined his companion, timidly, as if, while she felt all its force, she only consented to urge the argument in tenderness to the harassed feelings of the brother, "we are of equal years; that which hath happened to me, may well have been the fortune of our Ruth."

"Dost mean that being unespoused thyself, or that having, at thy years, inclinations that are free, my sister may have escaped the bitter curse of eing the wife of a Narragansett, or what is not ess frightful, the slave of his humors?"

"Truly, I mean little else than the former."

"And not the latter," continued the young man, with a quickness that showed some sudden revolution in his thoughts. "But though with opinions that are decided, and with kindness awakened in behalf of one favored, thou hesitatest, Martha, it is not like that a girl left in the fetters of savage lif would so long pause to think. Even here in the settlements, all are not difficult of judgment as thou!"

The long lashes vibrated above the dark eyes of the maiden, and, for an instant, it seemed as if she had no intention to reply. But looking timidly aside, she answered in a voice so low, that her companion scarcely gathered the meaning of that she uttered.

"I know not how I may have earned this false character among my friends," she said; "for to me it ever seemeth that what I feel and think is but too easily known."

"Then is the smart gallant from the Hartford town, who cometh and goeth so often between this distant settlement and his father's house, better assured of his success than I had thought. He will not journey the long road much oftener, alone!"

"I have angered thee, Mark, or thou wouldst not speak with so cold an eye, to one who hath ever lived with thee in kindness."

"I do not speak in anger, for 'twould be both unreasonable and unmanly to deny all of thy sex right of choice; but yet it doth seem right, that, when taste is suited and judgment appeased, there should be little motive for withholding speech."

"And wouldst thou have a maiden, of my years, in haste to believe that she was sought, when haply it may be, that he of whom you speak is in quest of thy society and friendship, rather than of my favor?"

"Then might he spare much labor and some bodily suffering, unless he finds great pleasure in the saddle; for I know not a youth in the Connecticut Colony, for whom I have smaller esteem. Others may see matter of approval in him, but, to me, he is of bold speech, ungainly air, and great disagreeableness of discourse."

"I am happy that at last we find ourselves of one

mind; for that, thou say'st of the youth, is much as I have long considered him."

"Thou! Thou thinkest of the gallant thus! Then why dost listen to his suit? I had believed thee a girl too honest, Martha, to affect such niceties of deception. With this opinion of his character, why not refuse his company?"

"Can a maiden speak too hastily?"

"And if here, and ready to ask thy favor, the answer would be——"

"No!" said the girl, raising her eyes for an instant, and bashfully meeting the eager look of her companion, though she uttered the monosyllable firmly.

Mark seemed bewildered. An entirely new and a novel idea took possession of his brain. The change was apparent by his altering countenance, and a cheek that glowed like flame. What he might have said, most of our readers over fifteen may presume; but, at that moment, the voices of those who had accompanied Whittal to the ruin were heard on their return, and Martha glided away so silently as to leave him for a moment ignorant of her absence.

CHAPTER XXII.

> "Oh! when amid the throngs of men
> The heart grows sick of hollow mirth,
> How willingly we turn us, then,
> Away from this cold earth;
> And look into thy azure breast,
> For seats of innocence and rest!"
>
> BRYANT'S *Skies*.

THE day was the Sabbath. This religious festival, which is even now observed in most of the States of the Union with a strictness that is little heeded in the rest of Christendom, was then reverenced with a severity suited to the austere habits of the Colonists. The circumstance that one should journey on such a day, had attracted the observation of all in the hamlet; but, as the stranger had been seen to ride towards the dwelling of the Heathcotes, and the times were known to teem with more than ordinary interests to the Province, it was believed that he found his justification in some apology of necessity. Still, none ventured forth to inquire into the motive of this extraordinary visit. At the end of an hour, the horseman was seen to depart as he had arrived, seemingly urged on by the calls of some pressing emergency. He had in truth proceeded further with his tidings, though the lawfulness of discharging even this imperious duty on the Sabbath had been gravely considered in the Councils of those who had sent him. Happily they had found, or thought they had found, in some of the narratives of the sacred volume, a sufficient precedent to bid their messenger proceed.

In the mean time, the unusual excitement, which

had been so unexpectedly awakened in the dwelling of the Heathcotes, began to subside in that quiet which is in so beautiful accordance with the sacred character of the day. The sun rose bright and cloudless above the hills, every vapor of the past night melting before his genial warmth into the invisible element. The valley then lay in that species of holy calm which conveys so sweet and s forcible an appeal to the heart. The world presented a picture of the glorious handywork of him who seems to invite the gratitude and adoration of his creatures. To the mind yet untainted, there is exquisite loveliness and even godlike repose in such a scene. The universal stillness permits the softest natural sounds to be heard; and the buzz of the bee, or the wing of the humming-bird, reaches the ear like the loud notes of a general anthem. This temporary repose is full of meaning. It should teach how much of the beauty of this world's enjoyments, how much of its peace, and even how much of the comeliness of nature itself, is dependent on the spirit by which we are actuated. When man reposes, all around him seems anxious to contribute to his rest; and when he abandons the contentions of grosser interests, to elevate his spirit, all living things appear to unite in worship. Although this apparent sympathy of nature may be less true than imaginative, its lesson is not destroyed, since it ufficiently shows that what man chooses to consider ood in this world is good, and that most of its strife nd deformities proceed from his own perversity.

The tenants of the valley of the Wish-Ton-Wish were little wont to disturb the quiet of the Sabbath. Their error lay in the other extreme, since they impaired the charities of life by endeavoring to raise man altogether above the weakness of his nature. They substituted the revolting aspect of a sublimated austerity, for that gracious though regulated exterior, by which all in the body may best illustrate their hopes or exhibit their gratitude. The peculiar air of those of whom we write was generated by the error of the times and of the country, though something of its singularly rigid character might have been derived from the precepts and example of the individual who had the direction of the spiritual interests of the parish. As this person will have further connexion with the matter of the legend, he shall be more familiarly introduced in its pages.

The Reverend Meek Wolfe was, in spirit, a rare combination of the humblest self-abasement and of fierce spiritual denunciation. Like so many others of his sacred calling in the Colony he inhabited, he was not only the descendant of a line of priests, but it was his greatest earthly hope that he should also become the progenitor of a race in whom the ministry was to be perpetuated as severely as if the regulated formula of the Mosaic dispensation were still in existence. He had been educated in the infant college of Harvard, an institution that the emigrants from England had the wisdom and enterprise to found, within the first five-and-twenty years of their colonial residence. Here this scion of so pious and orthodox a stock had abundantly qualified himself for the intellectual warfare of his future life, by regarding one set of opinions so steadily, as to leave little reason to apprehend he would ever abandon the most trifling of the outworks of his faith. No citadel ever presented a more hopeless curtain to the besieger, than did the mind of this zealot to the efforts of conviction; for on the side of his opponents, he contrived that every avenue should be closed by a wall blank as indomitable obstinacy could oppose. He appeared to think that all the minor conditions of argument and reason had been disposed of by his ancestors, and that it only remain ed for him to strengthen the many defences of his subject, and, now and then, to scatter by a fierce sortie the doctrinal skirmishers who might occasionally approach his parish. There was a remarkable singleness of mind in this religionist, which, while it in some measure rendered even his bigotry respectable, greatly aided in clearing the knotty subject, with which he dealt, of much embarrassing matter. In his eyes, the strait and narrow path would hold but few besides his own flock. He admitted some fortuitous exceptions, in one or two of the nearest parishes, with whose clergymen he was in the habit of exchanging pulpits; and perhaps, here and there, in a saint of the other hemisphere, or of the more distant towns of the Colonies, the brightness of whose faith was something aided, in his eyes, by distance, as this opake globe of ours is thought to appear a ball of light to those who inhabit its satellite. In short, there was an admixture of seeming charity with an exclusiveness of hope, an unweariness of exertion with a coolness of exterior, a disregard of self with the most complaisant security, and an uncomplaining submission to temporal evils with the loftiest spiritual pretensions, that in some measure rendered him a man as difficult to comprehend as to describe.

At an early hour in the forenoon, a little bell, that was suspended in an awkward belfry perched on the roof of the meeting-house, began to summon the congregation to the place of worship. The call was promptly obeyed, and ere the first notes had reached the echoes of the hills, the wide and grassy street was covered with family groups, all taking the same direction. Foremost in each little party walked the austere father, perhaps bearing on his arm a suckled infant, or some child yet too young to sustain its own weight; while at a decent distance followed the equally grave matron, casting oblique and severe glances at the little troop around her, in whom acquired habits had yet some conquests to obtain over the lighter impulses of vanity. Where there was no child to need support, or where the mother chose to assume the office of bearing her infant in person, the man was seen to carry one of the heavy muskets of the day; and when his arms were otherwise employed, the stoutest of his boys served in the capacity of armor-bearer. But in no instance was this needful precaution neglected, the state of the Province and the character of the enemy requiring that vigilance should mingle even with their devotions. There was no loitering on the path, no light and worldly discourse by the way, nor even any salutations, other than those grave and serious recognitions by hat and eye, which usage tolerated as the utmost limit of courtesy on the weekly festival.

When the bell changed its tone, Meek appeared from the gate of the fortified house, where he resided, in quality of castellan, on account of its public character, its additional security, and the circumstance that his studious habits permitted him to discharge the trust with less waste of manual labor than it would cost the village were the responsible office confided to one of more active habits. His consort followed, but at even a greater distance than that taken by the wives of other men, as if she felt the awful necessity of averting even the remotest possibility of scandal from one of so sacred a profession. Nine offspring of various ages, and one female assistant, of years too tender to be a wife herself, composed the household of the divine, and it was a proof of the salubrious air of the valley that all were present, since nothing but illness was ever deemed a sufficient excuse for absence from the common worship. As this little flock issued from the palisadoes, a female, in whose pale cheek the effects of recent illness might yet be traced, held open the gate for the entrance of Reuben Ring, and a stout youth, who bore the prolific consort of the former, with her bounteous gift, into the citadel of the village; a place of refuge that nothing but the undaunted resolution of the woman prevented her from occupying before, since more than half of the children of the valley had first seen the light within the security of its defences.

The family of Meek preceded him into the temple, and when the feet of the minister himself crossed its threshold, there was no human form visible without its walls. The bell ceased its monotonous and mournful note, and the tall, gaunt form of the divine moved through the narrow aisle to its usual post. with the air of one who had already more than half rejected the burthen of bodily encumbrance. A searching and stern glance was thrown around, as if he possessed an instinctive power to detect all delinquents; and then seating himself, the deep stillness, that always preceded the exercises, reigned in the place.

When the divine next showed his austere countenance to his expecting people, its meaning was expressive rather of some matter of worldly import, than of that absence of carnal interest with which he usually strove to draw near to his Creator in prayer.

"Captain Content Heathcote," he said with grave severity, after permitting a short pause to awaken reverence, "there has one ridden through this valley on the Lord's day, making thy habitation his halting-place. Hath the traveller warranty for this disrespect of the Sabbath, and canst thou find sufficient reason in his motive, for permitting the stranger within thy gates to neglect the solemn ordinance delivered on the mount?"

"He rideth on especial commission," answered

Content, who had respectfully arisen, when thus addressed by name; "for matter of grave interest to the well-being of the Colony is contained in the subject of his errand."

"There is nought more deeply connected with the well-being of man, whether resident in this Colony or in more lofty empires, than reverence to God's declared will," returned Meek, but half-appeased by the apology. "It would have been expedient for one, who, in common, not only setteth so good an example himself, but who is also charged with the mantle of authority, to have looked with distrust into the pretences of a necessity that may be only seeming."

"The motive shall be declared to the people, at a fitting moment; but it hath seemed more wise to retain the substance of the horseman's errand, until worship hath been offered, without the alloy of temporal concerns."

"Therein hast thou acted discreetly; for a divided mind giveth but little joy above. I hope there is equal reason why all of thy household are not with thee in the temple?"

Notwithstanding the usual self-command of Content, he did not revert to this subject without emotion. Casting a subdued glance at the empty seat where she whom he so much loved was wont to worship at his side, he said, in a voice that evidently struggled to maintain its customary equanimity—

"There has been powerful interest awakened beneath my roof this day; and it may be that the duty of the Sabbath has been overlooked by minds so exercised. If we have therein sinned, I hope he that looketh kindly on the penitent will forgive! She of whom thou speakest, hath been shaken by the violence of griefs renewed; though willing in spirit, a feeble and sinking frame is not equal to support the fatigue of appearing here, even though it be the house of God."

This extraordinary exercise of pastoral authority was uninterrupted, even by the breathings of the congregation. Any incident of an unusual character had attraction for the inhabitants of a village so remote; but here was deep, domestic interest, connected with breach of usage and indeed of law and all heightened by that secret influence that leads us to listen, with singular satisfaction, to those emotions in others, which it is believed to be natural to wish to conceal. Not a syllable that fell from the lips of the divine, or of Content, not a deep tone of severity in the former, nor a struggling accent of the latter, escaped the dullest ear in that assembly Notwithstanding the grave and regulated air that was common to all, it is needless to say there was pleasure in the little interruption of this scene; which, however, was far from being extraordinary in a community where it was not only believed that spiritual authority might extend itself to the most familiar practices, but where few domestic interests were deemed so exclusive, or individual feelings considered so sacred, that a very large proportion of the whole neighborhood might not claim a right to participate largely in both The Reverend Mr. Wolfe was appeased by the explanation, and after allowing a sufficient time to elapse, in order that the minds of the congregation hould recover their tone, he proceeded with the regular services of the morning.

It is needless to recount the well-known manner of the religious exercises of the Puritans. Enough of their forms and of their substance has been transmitted to us, to render both manner and doctrine familiar to most of our readers. We shall therefore confine our duty to a relation of such portions of the ceremonies, if that which sedulously avoided every appearance of form can thus be termed, as have an immediate connexion with the incidents.

The divine had gone through the short opening prayer, had read the passage of holy writ, had given out the verses of the psalm, and had joined in the strange nasal melody with which his flock endeavored to render it doubly acceptable, and had ended his long and fervent wrestling of the spirit in a colloquial petition of some forty minutes' duration, in which direct allusion had been made not only to the subject of his recent examination, but to divers other familiar interests of his parishioners; and all without any departure from the usual zeal on his own part, or of the customary attention and grave decorum on that of his people. But when, for the second time, he arose to read another song of worship and thanksgiving, a form was seen in the centre or principal aisle, that, as well by its attire and aspect, as by the unusual and irreverent tardiness of its appearance, attracted general observation. Interruptions of this nature were unfrequent, and even the long practised and abstracted minister paused, for an instant, ere he proceeded with the hymn, though there was a suspicion current among the more instructed of his parishioners, that the sonorous version was an effusion of his own muse.

The intruder was Whittal Ring. The witless young man had strayed from the abode of his sister, and found his way into that general receptacle, where most of the village was congregated. During his former residence in the valley, there had been no temple; and the edifice, its interior arrangements, the faces of those it contained, and the business on which they had assembled, appeared alike strangers to him. It was only when the people lifted up their voices in the song of praise, that some glimmerings of his ancient recollections were discoverable in his inactive countenance. Then, indeed, he betrayed a portion of the delight which powerful sounds can quicken, even in beings of his unhappy mental construction. As he was satisfied, however, to remain in a retired part of the aisle, listening with dull admiration, even the grave Ensign Dudley, whose eye had once or twice seemed ominous of displeasure, saw no necessity for interference.

Meek had chosen for his text, on that day, a passage from the book of Judges: "And the children of Israel did evil in the sight of the Lord; and the Lord delivered them into the hands of Midian seven years." With this text the subtle-minded divine dealt powerfully, entering largely into the mysterious and allegorical allusions then so much in vogue. In whatever manner he viewed the subject, he found reason to liken the suffering, bereaved and yet chosen dwellers of the Colonies, to the race of the Hebrews. If they were not set apart and marked from all others of the earth, in order that one mightier than man should spring from their loins, they were led into that distant wilderness, far from the temptations of licentious luxury, or the worldly-mindedness of those who built their structure of faith on the sands of temporal honors, to preserve the word in purity. As there appeared no reason on the part of the divine himself to distrust this construction of the words he had quoted, so it was evident that most of his listeners willingly lent their ears to so soothing an argument.

In reference to Midian, the preacher was far less explicit. That the great father of evil was in some way intended by this allusion, could not be doubted; but in what manner the chosen inhabitants of those regions were to feel his malign influence, was matter of more uncertainty. At times, the greedy ears of those who had long been wrought up into the impression that visible manifestations of the anger or of the love of Providence were daily presented to their eyes, were flattered with the stern joy of believing that the war which then raged around them was intended to put their moral armor to the proof, and that out of the triumph of their victories were to flow honor and security to the church. Then came ambiguous qualifications, which left it questionable whether a return of the invisible powers, that had been known to be so busy in the Provinces, were not the judgment intended. It is not to be supposed that Meek himself had the clearest mental intelligence on a point of this subtlety, for there was something of misty hallucination in the manner in which he treated it, as will be seen by his closing words.

"To imagine that Azazel regardeth the long suffering and stedfastness of a chosen people with a pleasant eye," he said, "is to believe that the marrow of righteousness can exist in the carrion of deceit. We have already seen his envious spirit raging in many tragical instances. If required to raise a warning beacon to your eyes, by which the presence of this treacherous enemy might be known, I should say, in the words of one learned and ingenious in this craftiness, that, 'when a person, having full reason, doth knowingly and wittingly seek and obtain of the Devil, or any other God besides the true God Jehovah, an ability to do or know strange things, which he cannot by his own human abilities arrive unto,' that then he may distrust his gifts and tremble for his soul. And, oh! my brethren how many of ye cling at this very moment to those tragical delusions, and worship the things of the world, instead of fattening on the famine of the desert, which is the sustenance of them that would live for ever! Lift your eyes upward, my brethren——"

"Rather turn them to the earth!" interrupted a

deep, authoritative voice from the body of the church; "there is present need of all your faculties to save life, and even to guard the tabernacle of the Lord!"

Religious exercises composed the recreation of the dwellers in that distant settlement. When they met in companies to lighten the load of life, prayer and songs of praise were among the usual indulgences of the entertainment. To them, a sermon was like a gay scenic exhibition in other and vainer communities, and none listened to the word with cold and inattentive ears. In literal obedience to the command of the preacher, and sympathizing with his own action, every eye in the congregation had been turned towards the naked rafters of the roof, when the unknown tones of him who spoke broke the momentary delusion. It is needless to say that, by a common movement, they sought an explanation of this extraordinary appeal. The divine became mute, equally with wonder and with indignation.

A first glance was enough to assure all present, that new and important interests were likely to be awakened. A stranger of grave aspect, and of a calm but understanding eye, stood at the side of Whittal Ring. His attire was of the simple guise and homely materials of the country. Still he bore about his person enough of the equipments of one familiar with the wars of the eastern hemisphere, to strike the senses. His hand was armed with a shining broadsword, such as were then used by the cavaliers of England, and at his back was slung the short carabine of one who battled in the saddle. His mien was dignified and even commanding, and there was no second look necessary to show that he was an intruder of a character altogether different from the moping innocent at his side.

"Why is one of an unknown countenance come

to disturb the worship of the temple?" demanded Meek, when astonishment permitted utterance. "Thrice hath this holy day been profaned by the foot of the stranger, and well may it be doubted whether we live not under an evil agency."

"Arm, men of the Wish-Ton-Wish! arm, and to your defences!"

A cry arose without, that seemed to circle the whole valley; and then a thousand whoops rolled out of the arches of the forest, and appeared to meet in one hostile din above the devoted hamlet. These were sounds that had been too often heard, or too often described, not to be generally understood. A scene of wild confusion followed.

Each man, on entering the church, had deposited his arms at the door, and thither most of the stout borderers were now seen hastening, to resume their weapons. Women gathered their children to their sides, and the wails of horror and alarm were beginning to break through the restraints of habit.

"Peace!" exclaimed the pastor, seemingly excited to a degree above human emotion. "Ere we go forth, let there be a voice raised to our heavenly Father. The asking shall be as a thousand men of war battling in our behalf!"

The commotion ceased as suddenly as if a mandate had been issued from that place to which their petition was to be addressed. Even the stranger, who had regarded the preparations with a stern but anxious eye, bowed his head, and seemed to join in the prayer, with a devoted and confiding heart.

"Lord!" said Meek, stretching his meagre arms, with the palms of the hands open, high above the heads of his flock, "at thy bidding, we go forth with thy aid, the gates of hell shall not prevail against us; with thy mercy, there is hope in heaven and on earth. It is for thy tabernacle that we shed blood; it is for thy word that we contend Battle in our behalf, King of Kings! send thy heavenly legions to our succor, that the song of victory may be incense at thy altars, and a foul hearing to the ears of the enemy—Amen."

There was a depth in the voice of the speaker, a supernatural calmness in the tones, and so great a confidence in the support of the mighty ally implored, that the words went to every heart. It was impossible that Nature should not be powerful within, but a high and exciting enthusiasm began to lift the people far above its influence. Thus awakened by an appeal to feelings that had never slumbered, and stimulated by all the moving interests of life, the men of the valley poured out of the temple in defence of person and fire-side, and, as they believed, of religion and of God.

There was pressing necessity, not only for this zeal, but for all the physical energies of the stoutest of their numbers. The spectacle that met the view, on issuing into the open air, was one that might have appalled the hearts of warriors more practised, and have paralyzed the efforts of men less susceptible to the impressions of a religious excitement.

Dark forms were leaping through the fields, on the hill-sides; and all adown the slopes that conducted to the valley, armed savages were seen pouring madly forward, on their path of destruction and vengeance. Behind them, the brand and the knife had been already used; for the log tenement, the stacks and the out-buildings of Reuben Ring, and of several others who dwelt in the skirts of the settlement, were sending forth clouds of murky smoke, in which forked and angry flames were already flashing fiercely. But danger most pressed still nearer. A long line of fierce warriors was even in the meadows; and in no direction could the eye be turned, that it did not meet with the appalling proof that the village was completely surrounded by an overwhelming superiority of force.

"To the garrison!" shouted some of the foremost of those who first saw the nature and imminency of the danger, pressing forward themselves in the direction of the fortified house. "To the garrison, or we are lost!"

"Hold!" exclaimed that voice which was so strange to the ears of most of those who heard it, but which spoke in a manner that by its compass and firmness commanded obedience. "With this mad disorder, we are truly lost! Let Captain Content Heathcote come to my councils."

Notwithstanding the tumult and confusion which had now in truth begun to rage fearfully around him, the quiet and self-restrained individual to whom the legal and perhaps moral right to command belonged, had lost none of his customary composure. It was plain, by the look of powerful amazement with which he had at first regarded the stranger, on his sudden interruption of the service, and by the glances of secret intelligence and of recognition they exchanged, that they had met before. But this was no time for greetings or explanations, nor was that a scene in which to waste the precious moments in useless contests about opinions.

"I am here," said he who was thus called for; "ready to lead whither thy prudence and experience shall point the way."

"Speak to the people, and separate the combatants in three bodies of equal strength. One shall press forward to the meadows, and beat back the savage, ere he encircle the palisadoed house; the second shall proceed with the feeble and tender, in their flight to its covers; and with the third—but thou knowest that which I would do with the third Hasten, or we lose all by tardiness."

It was perhaps fortunate that orders so necessary

and so urgent were given to one little accustomed to superfluity of speech. Without offering either commendation or dissent, Content obeyed. Accustomed to his authority, and conscious of the critical situation of all that was dear, the men of the village yielded an obedience more prompt and effective than it is usual to meet in soldiers who are not familiar with habits of discipline. The fighting men were quickly separated in three bodies, consisting of rather more than a score of combatants in each. One, commanded by Eben Dudley, advanced at quick time towards the meadows in the rear of the fortress, that the whooping body of savages, who were already threatening to cut off the retreat of the women and children, should be checked; while another departed in a nearly opposite direction, taking the street of the hamlet, for the purpose of meeting those who advanced by the southern entrance of the valley. The third and last of these small but devoted bodies, remained stationary, in attendance for more definite orders.

At the moment when the first of these little divisions of force was ready to move, the divine appeared in its front, with an air in which spiritual reliance on the purposes of Providence, and some show of temporal determination, were singularly united. In one hand he bore a Bible, which he raised on high as the sacred standard of his followers, and in the other he brandished a short broadsword, in a manner that proved there might be danger in encountering its blade. The volume was open, and at brief intervals the divine read, in high and excited voice, such passages as accidentally met his eye, the leaves blowing about in a manner to produce a rather remarkable admixture of doctrine and sentiment. But to these trifling moral incongruities, both the pastor and his parishioners were alike indifferent; their subtle mental exercises having given birth to a tendency of aptly reconciling all seeming discrepancies, as well as of accommodating the most abstruse doctrines to the more familiar interests of life.

"Israel and the Philistines had put their battle in array, army against army," commenced Meek, as the troop he led began its advance. Then, reading at short intervals, he continued, "Behold, I will do a thing in Israel, at which both the ears of every one that heareth it shall tingle."—"Oh house of Aaron, trust in the Lord; he is thy help and thy shield." "Deliver me, O Lord, from the evil man preserve me from the violent man."—"Let burning coals fall upon them; let them be cast into the fire; into deep pits, that they rise not again."—"Let the wicked fall into their own nets, whilst that I, withal, escape."—"Therefore doth my father love me, because I lay down my life, that I may take it again."—"He that hateth me, hateth my father also."—"Father, forgive them, for they know not what they do."—"They have heard that it hath been said, an eye for an eye, and a tooth for a tooth."—"For Joshua drew not his hand back, wherewith he stretched out the spear, until he had utterly destroyed all the inhabitants of Ai——" Thus far the words of Meek were intelligible to those who remained, but distance soon confounded the syllables. Then nought was audible but the yells of the enemy, the tramp of the men who pressed in the rear of the priest, with a display of military pomp as formidable as their limited means would allow, and those clear high tones, which sounded in the ears and quickened the blood at the hearts of his followers, as though they had been trumpet-blasts. In a few more minutes the little band was scattered behind the covers of the fields, and the rattling of fire-arms succeeded to the quaint and characteristic manner of their march.

While this movement was made in front the party ordered to cover the village was not idle. Commanded by a sturdy yeoman, who filled the office of Lieutenant, it advanced with less of religious display, but with equal activity, in the direction of the South; and the sounds of contention were quickly heard, proclaiming both the urgency of the measure and the warmth of the conflict.

In the mean time, equal decision, though tempered by some circumstances of deep personal interest, was displayed by those who had been left in front of the church. As soon as the band of Meek had got to such a distance as to promise security to those who followed, the stranger commanded the children to be led towards the fortified house. This duty was performed by the trembling mothers, who had been persuaded, with difficulty, to defer it until cooler heads should pronounce that the proper moment had come. A few of the women dispersed among the dwellings in quest of the infirm while all the boys of proper age were actively employed in transporting indispensable articles from the village, within the palisadoes. As these several movements were simultaneous, but a very few minutes elapsed between the time when the orders were issued and the moment when they were accomplished.

"I had intended that thou shouldst have had the charge in the meadows," said the stranger to Content, when nought remained to be performed, but that which had been reserved for the last of the three little bands of fighting men. "But as the work proceedeth bravely in that quarter, we will move in company. Why doth this maiden tarry?"

"Truly I know not, unless it may be of fear There is an opening for thy passage into the fort, Martha, with others of thy sex."

"I will follow the fighters that are about to

march to the rescue of them that remain in our habitation," said the girl, in a low but steady voice.

"And how know'st thou that such is the service intended for those here arrayed?" demanded the stranger, with a little show of displeasure that his military purposes should have been anticipated.

"I see it in the countenances of them that tarry," returned the other, gazing furtively towards Mark who, posted in the little line, could with difficulty brook a delay which threatened his father's house, and those whom it held, with so much jeopardy.

"Forward!" cried the stranger. "Here is no leisure for dispute. Let the maiden take wisdom, and hasten to the fort. Follow, men stout of heart! or we come too late to the succor."

Martha waited until the party had advanced a few paces, and then, instead of obeying the repeated mandate to consult her personal safety, she took the direction of the armed band.

"I fear me that 'twill exceed our strength," observed the stranger, who marched in front at the side of Content, "to make good the dwelling, at so great distance from further aid."

"And yet the visitation will be heavy, that shall drive us for a second time to the fields for a resting-place. In what manner didst get warning of this inroad?"

"The savages believed themselves concealed in the cunning place, where thou know'st that my eye had opportunity to overlook their artifices There is a Providence in our least seeming calculations: an imprisonment of weary years hath its reward in this warning!"

Content appeared to acquiesce, but the situation of affairs prevented the discourse from becoming more minute.

As they approached the dwelling of the Heathcotes, better opportunity of observing the condition of things, in and around the house, was of course obtained. The position of the building would have rendered any attempt, on the part of those in it, to gain the fort ere the arrival of assistance, desperately hazardous, since the meadows that lay between them were already alive with the ferocious warriors of the enemy. But it was evident that the Puritan, whose infirmities kept him within doors, entertained no such design; for it was shortly apparent that those within were closing and barring the windows of the habitation, and that other provisions for defence were in the course of active preparation. The feelings of Content, who knew that the house contained only his wife and father, with one female assistant, were excited to agony, as the party he commanded drew near on one side, at a distance about equal to that of a band of the enemy, who were advancing diagonally from the woods, on the other. He saw the efforts of those so dear to him, as they had recourse to the means of security provided to repel the very danger which now threatened; and, to his eyes, it appeared that the trembling hands of Ruth had lost their power, when haste and confusion more than once defeated the object of her exertions.

"We must break and charge, or the savage will be too speedy!" he said, in tones that grew thick from breathing quicker than was wont for one of his calm temperament. "See! they enter the orchard! in another minute, they will be masters of the dwelling!"

But his companion marched with a firmer step and looked with a cooler eye. There was, in hi gaze, the understanding of a man practised in scene of sudden danger, and in his mien the authority of one accustomed to command.

"Fear not," he answered; "the art of old Mark Heathcote hath departed from him, or he still knoweth how to make good his citadel against a first onset. If we quit our order, the superiority of concert will be lost, and being few in numbers, defeat will be certain; but with this front, and a fitting steadiness, our march may not be repulsed. To thee, Captain Content Heathcote, it need not be told, that he who now counsels hath seen the strif of savages ere this hour."

"I know it well—but dost not see my Ruth, laboring at the ill-fitted shutter of the chamber? The woman will be slain, in her heedlessness—for, hark! there beginneth the volley of the enemy!"

"No, 'tis he who led my troop in a far different warfare!" exclaimed the stranger, whose form grew more erect, and whose thoughtful and deeply-furrowed features assumed something like the stern pleasure which kindles in the soldier as the sounds of contention increase. "'Tis old Mark Heathcote, true to his breeding and his name! he hath let off the culverin upon the knaves! behold, they are already disposed to abandon one who speaketh so boldly, and are breaking through the fences to the left, that we may taste something of their quality. Now, bold Englishmen, strong of hand and stout of heart, you have training in your duty, and you shall not be wanting in example. You have wives and children at hand, looking at your deeds; and there is one above, that taketh note of the manner in which you serve in his cause. Here is an opening for your skill; scourge the cannibals with the hand of death! On, on to the onset, and to victory!"

CHAPTER XXIII.

Hect. "Is this Achilles?
Achil. I am Achilles.
Hect. Stand fair, I pray thee· let me look on thee.
TROILUS AND CRESSIDA.

IT may now be necessary to take a rapid glance at the situation of the whole combat, which had begun to thicken in different parts of the valley. The party led by Dudley, and exhorted by Meek, had broken its order on reaching the meadows behind the fort, and, seeking the covers of the stumps and fences, it had thrown in its fire, with good effect, on the irregular band that pressed into the fields. This decision quickly caused a change in the manner of the advance. The Indians took to covers, in their turn, and the struggle assumed that desultory but dangerous character, in which the steadiness and resources of the individual are put to the severest trial. Success appeared to vacillate; the white men at one time widening the distance between them and their friends in the dwelling, and, at another, falling back as if disposed to seek the shelter of the palisadoes. Although numbers were greatly in favor of the Indians, weapons and skill supported the cause of their adversaries. It was the evident wish of the former to break in upon the little band that opposed their progress to the village, in and about which they saw that scene of hurried exertion which has already been described—a spectacle but little likely to cool the furious ardor of an Indian onset. But the wary manner in which Dudley conducted his battle, rendered this an experiment of exceeding hazard

However heavy of intellect the Ensign might appear on other occasions, the present was one every way adapted to draw out his best and most manly qualities. Of large and powerful stature, he felt, in moments of strife, a degree of confidence in himself, that was commensurate with the amount of physical force he wielded. To this hardy assurance was to be added no trifling portion of the sort of enthusiasm that can be awakened in the most sluggish bosoms, and which, like the anger of an even-tempered man, is only the more formidable from the usually quiet habits of the individual. Nor was this the first, by many, of Ensign Dudley's warlike deeds. Besides the desperate affair already related in these pages, he had been engaged in divers hostile expeditions against the aborigines, and on all occasions had he shown a cool head and a resolute mind.

There was pressing necessity for both these essential qualities, in the situation in which the Ensign now found himself. By properly extending his little force, and yet keeping it at the same time perfectly within supporting distance, by emulating the caution of his foes in consulting the covers, and by reserving a portion of his fire throughout the broken and yet well-ordered line, the savages were finally beaten back, from stump to stump, from hillock to hillock, and fence to fence, until they had fairly entered the margin of the forest. Further the experienced eye of the borderer saw he could not follow. Many of his men were bleeding, and growing weaker as their wounds still flowed. The protection of the trees gave the enemy too great an advantage for their position to be forced, and destruction would have been the inevitable consequence of the close struggle which must have followed a charge. In this stage of the combat, Dudley began to cast anxious and inquiring looks behind him. He saw that support was not to be expected, and he also saw, with regret, that many of the women and children were still busy, transporting necessaries from the village into the fort. Falling back to a better line of covers, and to a distance that materially lessened the danger of the arrows, the weapons used by quite two-thirds of his enemies, he awaited, in sullen silence, the proper moment to effect a further retreat.

It was while the party of Dudley stood thus at bay, that a fierce yell rung in the arches of the forest. It was an exclamation of pleasure, uttered in the wild manner of those people; as if the tenants of the woods were animated by some sudden and general impulse of joy. The crouching yeomen regarded each other in uneasiness, but seeing no sign of wavering in the steady mien of their leader, each man kept close, awaiting some further exhibition of the devices of their foes. Ere another minute had passed, two warriors appeared at the margin of the wood, where they stood apparently in contemplation of the different scenes that were acting in various parts of the valley. More than one musket was levelled with intent to injure them, but a sign from Dudley prevented attempts that would most probably have been frustrated by the never-slumbering vigilance of a North American Indian.

There was however something in the air and port of these two individuals, that had its share in producing the forbearance of Dudley. They were evidently both chiefs, and of far more than usual estimation. As was common with the military leaders of the Indians, they were men also of large and commanding stature. Viewed at the distance from which they were seen, one seemed a warrior who had reached the meridian of his days, while the other had the lighter step and more flexible movement of a much briefer existence. Both were well armed, and, as was usual with people of their origin on the war-path, they were clad only in the customary scanty covering of waist-cloths and leggings. The former, however, were of scarlet, and the latter were rich in the fringes and bright colors of Indian ornaments. The elder of the two wore a gay belt of wampum around his head, in the form of a turban; but the younger appeared with a shaven crown, on which nothing but the customary chivalrous scalp-lock was visible.

The consultation, like most of the incidents that have been just related, occupied but a very few minutes. The eldest of the chiefs issued some orders. The mind of Dudley was anxiously endeavoring to anticipate their nature, when the two disappeared together. The Ensign would now have been left entirely to vague conjectures, had not the rapid execution of the mandates that had been issued to the youngest of the Indians, soon left him in no doubt of their intentions. Another loud and general shout drew his attention towards the right; and when he had endeavored to strengthen his position by calling three or four of the best marksmen to that end of his little line, the youngest of the chiefs was seen bounding across the meadow, leading a train of whooping followers to the covers that commanded its opposite extremity. In short, the position of Dudley was completely turned; and the stumps and angles of the fences, which secreted his men, were likely to become of no further use. The emergency demanded decision. Collecting his yeomen, ere the enemy had time to profit by his advantage, the Ensign ordered a rapid retreat towards the fort. In this movement he was favored by the formation of the ground, a circumstance that had been well considered on the advance; and in a very few minutes, the party found itself safely posted under the protection of a scattering fire from the palisadoes, which immediately checked the pursuit of the whooping and exulting foe. The wounded men, after a stern or rather sullen halt, that was intended to exhibit the unconquerable determination of the whites, withdrew into the works for succor, leaving the command of Dudley reduced by nearly one-half of its numbers. With this diminished force, however, he promptly turned his attention towards the assistance of those who combated at the opposite extremity of the village.

Allusion has already been made to the manner in which the houses of a new settlement were clustered near each other, at the commencement of the colonial establishments. In addition to the more obvious and sufficient motive, which has given rise to the same inconvenient and unpicturesque manner of building, over nine-tenths of the continent of Europe, there had been found a religious inducement for the inconvenient custom. One of the enactments of the Puritans said, that "no man shall set his dwelling-house, above the distance of half-a-mile, or a mile at farthest, from the meeting of the congregation where the church doth usually assemble for the worship of God." "The support of the worship of God, in church fellowship," was the reason alleged for this arbitrary provision of the law; but it is quite probable that support against danger of a more temporal character was another motive. There were those within the fort who believed the smoking piles that were to be seen, here and there, in the clearings on the hills, owed their destruction to a disregard of that protection which was thought to be yielded to those who leaned with the greatest confidence, even in the forms of earthly transactions, on the sustaining power of an all-seeing and all-directing Providence. Among this number was Reuben Ring, who submitted to the loss of his habitation, as to a merited punishment for the light-mindedness that had tempted him to erect a dwelling at the utmost limits of the prescribed distance.

As the party of Dudley retreated, that sturdy yeoman stood at a window of the chamber in which his prolific partner with her recent gift were safely lodged, for in that moment of confusion, the husband was compelled to discharge the double duty of sentinel and nurse. He had just fired his piece and he had reason to think with success, on the enemies that pressed too closely on the retiring party, and as he reloaded the gun, he turned a melancholy eye on the pile of smoking embers, that now lay where his humble but comfortable habitation had so lately stood.

"I fear me, Abundance," he said, shaking his head with a sigh, "that there was error in the measurement between the meeting and the clearing. Some misgivings of the lawfulness of stretching the chain across the hollows, came over me at the time; but the pleasant knoll, where the dwelling stood, was so healthful and commodious, that, if it were a sin, I hope it is one that is forgiven! There doth not seem so much as the meanest of its logs, that is not now melted into white ashes by the fire!"

"Raise me, husband," returned the wife, in the weak voice natural to her feeble situation; "raise me with thine arm, that I may look upon the place where my babes first saw the light."

Her request was granted, and, for a minute, the woman gazed in mute grief at the destruction of her comfortable home. Then, as a fresh yell from the foe rose on the air without, she trembled, and turned with a mother's care towards the unconscious beings that slumbered at her side.

"Thy brother hath been driven by the heathen to the foot of the palisadoes," observed the other, after regarding his companion with manly kindness for a moment, "and he hath lessened his force by many that are wounded."

A short but eloquent pause succeeded. The woman turned her tearful face upwards, and stretching out a bloodless hand, she answered—

"I know what thou wouldst do—it is not meet that Sergeant Ring should be a woman-tender, when the Indian enemy is in his neighbor's fields! Go to thy duty, and that which is to be done, do manfully! and yet would I have thee remember how many there are who lean upon thy life for a father's care."

The yeoman first cast a cautious look around him, for this the decent and stern usages of the Puritans exacted, and perceiving that the girl who occasionally entered to tend the sick was not present, he stooped, and impressing his lips on the cheek of his wife, he threw a yearning look at his offspring, shouldered his musket, and descended to the court.

When Reuben Ring joined the party of Dudley, the latter had just issued an order to march to the support of those who still stoutly defended the southern entrance of the village. The labor of securing necessaries was not yet ended, and it was on every account an object of the last importance to make good the hamlet against the enemy. The task, however, was not as difficult as the force of the Indians might, at first, have given reason to believe. The conflict, by this time, had extended to the party which was headed by Content, and, in consequence, the Indians were compelled to contend with a divided force. The buildings themselves, with the fences and out-houses, were so many breast-works, and it was plain that the assailants acted with a caution and concert, that betrayed the direction of some mind more highly gifted than those which ordinarily fall to the lot of uncivilized men.

The task of Dudley was not sc difficult as before,

since the enemy ceased to press upon his march, preferring to watch the movements of those who held the fortified house, of whose numbers they were ignorant, and of whose attacks they were evidently jealous. As soon as the reinforcement reached the Lieutenant who defended the village, he commanded the charge, and his men advanced with shouts and clamor, some singing spiritual songs, others lifting up their voice in prayer, while a few availed themselves of the downright and perhaps equally effective means of raising sounds as fearful as possible. The whole being backed by spirited and well-directed discharges of musketry, the effort was successful. In a few minutes the enemy fled, leaving that side of the valley momentarily free from danger.

Pursuit would have been folly. After posting a few look-outs in secret and safe positions among the houses, the whole party returned, with an intention of cutting off the enemy who still held the meadows near the garrison. In this design, however, their intentions were frustrated. The instant they were pressed, the Indians gave way, evidently for the purpose of gaining the protection of the woods; and when the whites returned to their works, they were followed in a manner to show that they could make no further movement without the hazard of a serious assault. In this condition, the men in and about the fort were compelled to be inefficient spectators of the scene that was taking place around the "Heathcote-house," as the dwelling of old Mark was commonly called.

The fortified building had been erected for the protection of the village and its inhabitants, an object that its position rendered feasible; but it could offer no aid to those who dwelt without the range of musketry. The only piece of artillery belonging to the settlement, was the culverin which had been discharged by the Puritan, and which served for the moment to check the advance of his enemies. But the exclamations of the stranger, and the appeal to his men, with which the last chapter closed, sufficiently proclaimed that the attack was diverted from the house, and that work of a bloody character now offered itself to those he and his companion led.

The ground around the dwelling of the Heathcotes admitted of closer and more deadly conflict than that on which the other portions of the combat had occurred. Time had given size to the orchards, and wealth had multiplied and rendered more secure the inclosures and out-buildings. It was in one of the former that the hostile parties met, and came to that issue which the warlike stranger had foreseen.

Content, like Dudley, caused his men to separate and they threw in their fire with the same guarded reservation that had been practised by the other party. Success again attended the efforts of discipline; the whites gradually beating back their enemies, until there was a probability of forcing them entirely into the open ground in their rear, a success that would have been tantamount to a victory But at this flattering moment, yells were heard behind the leaping and whooping band, that was still seen gliding through the openings of the smoke, resembling so many dark and malignant spectres acting their evil rites. Then, as a chief with a turbaned head, terrific voice, and commanding stature, appeared in their front, the whole of the wavering line received an onward impulse. The yells redoubled; another warrior was seen brandishing a tomahawk on one flank, and the whole of the deep phalanx came rushing in upon the whites, threatening to sweep them away, as the outbreaking torrent carries desolation in its course.

"Men to your square!" shouted the stranger, disregarding cover and life, together, in such a pressing emergency; "to your square, Christians and be firm!"

The command was repeated by Content, and echoed from mouth to mouth. But before those on the flanks could reach the centre, the shock had come. All order being lost, the combat was hand to hand one party fighting fiercely for victory, and the other knowing that they stood at the awful peril of their lives. After the first discharge of the musket and the twang of the bow, the struggle was maintained with knife and axe; the thrust of the former, or the descent of the keen and glittering tomahawk, being answered by sweeping and crushing blows of the musket's but, or by throttling grasps of hands that were clenched in the death-gripe. Men fell on each other in piles, and when the conqueror rose to shake off the bodies of those who gasped at his feet, his frowning eye rested alike on friend and enemy. The orchard rang with the yells of the Indians, but the Colonists fought in mute despair. Sullen resolution only gave way with life; and it happened more than once, that fearful day, that the usual reeking token of an Indian triumph was swung before the stern and still conscious eyes of the mangled victim from whose head it had been torn.

In this frightful scene of slaughter and ferocity, the principal personages of our legend were not idle. By a tacit but intelligent understanding, the stranger with Content and his son placed themselves back to back, and struggled manfully against their luckless fortune. The former showed himself no soldier of parade; for, knowing the uselessness of orders when each one fought for life, he dealt out powerful blows in silence. His example was nobly emulated by Content; and young Mark moved limb and muscle with the vigorous activity of his age. A first onset of the enemy was repelled, and for a moment there was a faint prospect of escape. At the suggestion of the stranger, the three moved, in their order, towards the dwelling, with the intention of trusting to their personal activity when released from the throng. But at this luckless instant, when hope was beginning to assume the air of probability, a chief came stalking through the horrible mêlée, seeking on each side some victim for his uplifted axe. A crowd of the inferior herd pressed at his heels, and a first glance told the assailed that the decisive moment had come.

At the sight of so many of their hated enemies still living, and capable of suffering, a common and triumphant shout burst from the lips of the Indians. Their leader, like one superior to the more vulgar emotions of his followers, alone approached in silence. As the band opened and divided to encircle the victims, chance brought him, face to face, with Mark. Like his foe, the Indian warrior was still in the freshness and vigor of young manhood. In stature, years and agility, the antagonists seemed equal; and, as the followers of the chief threw themselves on the stranger and Content, like men who knew their leader needed no aid, there was every appearance of a fierce and doubtful struggle. But, while neither of the combatants showed any desire to avoid the contest, neither was in haste to give the commencing blow. A painter, or rather sculptor, would have seized the attitudes of these young combatants for a rich exhibition of the power of his art.

Mark, like most of his friends, had cast aside all superfluous vestments ere he approached the scene of strife. The upper part of his body was naked to the shirt, and even this had been torn asunder by the rude encounters through which he had already passed. The whole of his full and heaving chest was bare, exposing the white skin and blue veins of one whose fathers had come from towards the rising sun. His swelling form rested on a leg that seemed planted in defiance, while the other was thrown in front, like a lever, to control the expected movements. His arms were extended to the rear, the hands grasping the barrel of a musket, which threatened death to all who should come within its sweep The head, covered with the short, curling, yellow hair of his Saxon lineage, was a little advanced above the left shoulder, and seemed placed in a manner to preserve the equipoise of the whole frame. The brow was flushed, the lips compressed and resolute, the veins of the neck and temples swollen nearly to bursting, and the eyes contracted, but of a gaze that bespoke equally the feelings of desperate determination and of entranced surprise.

On the other hand, the Indian warrior was a man still more likely to be remarked. The habits of his people had brought him, as usual, into the field, with naked limbs and nearly uncovered body. The position of his frame was that of one prepared to leap; and it would have been a comparison tolerated by the license of poetry, to have likened his straight and agile form to the semblance of a crouching panther. The projecting leg sustained the body, bending under its load more with the free play of muscle and sinew than from any weight, while the slightly stooping head was a little advanced beyond the perpendicular. One hand was clenched on the helve of an axe, that lay in a line with the right thigh while the other was placed, with a firm gripe, on the buck-horn handle of a knife, that was still sheathed at his girdle. The expression of the face was earnest, severe, and perhaps a little fierce, and yet the whole was tempered by the immovable and dignified calm of a chief of high qualities. The eye, however, was gazing and riveted; and, like that of the youth whose life he threatened, it appeared singularly contracted with wonder.

The momentary pause that succeeded the movement by which the two antagonists threw themselves into these fine attitudes, was full of meaning. Neither spoke, neither permitted play of muscle, neither even seemed to breathe. The delay was not like that of preparation, for each stood ready for his deadly effort, nor would it have been possible to trace in the compressed energy of the countenance of Mark, or in the lofty and more practised bearing of the front and eye of the Indian, any thing like wavering of purpose. An emotion foreign to the scene appeared to possess them both, each active frame unconsciously accommodating itself to the bloody business of the hour, while the inscrutable agency of the mind held them, for a brief interval, in check.

A yell of death from the mouth of a savage who was beaten to the very feet of his chief by a blow of the stranger, and an encouraging shout from the lips of the latter, broke the short trance. The knees of the chief bent still lower, the head of the tomahawk was a little raised, the blade of the knife was seen glittering from its sheath, and the but of Mark's musket had receded to the utmost tension of his sinews, when a shriek and a yell, different from any before heard that day, sounded near. At the same moment, the blows of both the combatants were suspended, though by the agency of very different degrees of force. Mark felt the arms of one cast around his limbs, with a power sufficient to embarrass, though not to subdue him, while the well-known voice of Whittal Ring sounded in his ears—

"Murder the lying and hungry Pale-faces! They leave us no food but air—no drink but water!"

On the other hand, when the chief turned in anger, to strike the daring one who presumed to arrest his arm, he saw at his feet the kneeling figure, the uplifted hands, and agonized features, of Martha. Averting the blow that a follower already aimed at the life of the suppliant, he spoke rapidly in his own language, and pointed to the struggling Mark. The nearest Indians cast themselves on the already half-captured youth. A whoop brought a hundred more to the spot, and then a calm as sudden, and almost as fearful, as the previous tumult, prevailed in the orchard. It was succeeded by the long-drawn, frightful, and yet meaning yell by which the American warrior proclaims his victory.

With the end of the tumult in the orchard, the sounds of strife ceased in all the valley. Though conscious of the success of their enemies, the men in the fort saw the certainty of destruction, not only to themselves, but to those feeble ones whom they should be compelled to leave without a sufficient defence, were they to attempt a sortie to that distance from their works. They were therefore compelled to remain passive and grave spectators of an evil they had not the means to avert.

CHAPTER XXIV.

"Were such things here, as we do speak about?
Or have we eaten of the insane root
That takes the reason prisoner?"
MACBETH.

An hour later presented a different scene. Bands of the enemy, that in civilized warfare would be called parties of observation, lingered in the skirts of the forest nearest to the village; and the settlers still stood to their arms, posted among the buildings, or maintaining their array at the foot of the palisadoes. Though the toil of securing the valuables continued, it was evident that, as the first terrors of alarm had disappeared, the owners of the hamlet began to regain some assurance in their ability to make it good against their enemies. Even the women were now seen moving through its grassy street with greater seeming confidence, and there was a regularity in the air of the armed men, which denoted a determination that was calculated to impose on their wild and undisciplined assailants.

But the dwelling, the out-buildings, and all the implements of domestic comfort, which had so lately contributed to the ease of the Heathcotes, were completely in the possession of the Indians. The open shutters and doors, the scattered and half-destroyed furniture, the air of devastation and waste, and the general abandonment of all interest in the protection of the property, proclaimed the licentious disorder of a successful assault. Still the work of destruction and plunder did not go on. Although here and there might be seen some warrior, decorated, according to the humors of his savage taste, with the personal effects of the former inmates of the building, every hand had been checked, and the furious tempers of the conquerors had been quieted, seemingly by the agency of some unseen and extraordinary authority. The men, who so lately had been moved by the fiercest passions of our nature, were suddenly restrained if not appeased; and, instead of that exulting indulgence of vengeance which commonly accompanies an Indian triumph, the warriors stalked about the buildings and through the adjacent grounds, in a silence which, though gloomy and sullen, was marked by their characteristic submission to events.

The principal leaders of the inroad, and all the surviving sufferers by the defeat, were assembled in the piazza of the dwelling. Ruth, pale, sorrowing, and mourning for others rather than for herself, stood a little apart, attended by Martha and the young assistant, whose luckless fortune it was to be found at her post, on this eventful day. Content, the stranger, and Mark, were near, subdued and bound, the sole survivors of all that band they had so recently led into the conflict. The gray hairs and bodily infirmities of the Puritan spared him the same degradation. The only other being present, of European origin, was Whittal Ring. The innocent stalked slowly among the prisoners, sometimes permitting ancient recollections and sympathies to come over his dull intellect, but oftener taunting the unfortunate with the injustice of their race, and with the wrongs of his adopted people.

The chiefs of the successful party stood in the centre, apparently engaged in some grave deliberation. As they were few in number, it was evident that the council only included men of the highest importance. Chiefs of inferior rank, but of great names in the limited renown of those simple tribes, conversed in knots among the trees, or paced the court at a respectful distance from the consultation of their superiors.

The least practised eye could not mistake the person of him on whom the greatest weight of authority had fallen. The turbaned warrior, already introduced in these pages, occupied the centre of the group, in the calm and dignified attitude of an Indian who hearkens to or who utters advice. His musket was borne by one who stood in waiting, while the knife and axe were returned to his girdle He had thrown a light blanket, or it might be better termed a robe of scarlet cloth, over his left shoulder, whence it gracefully fell in folds, leaving the whole of the right arm free, and most of his ample chest exposed to view. From beneath this mantle, blood fell slowly in drops, dying the floor on which he stood. The countenance of this warrior was grave, though there was a quickness in the movements of an ever-restless eye, that denoted great mental activity, no less than the disquiet of suspicion. One skilled in physiognomy might too have thought, that a shade of suppressed discontent was struggling with the self-command of habits that had become part of the nature of the individual.

The two companions nearest this chief were, like himself, men past the middle age, and of mien and expression that were similar, though less strikingly marked; neither showing those signs of displeasure, which occasionally shot from organs that, in spite of a mind so trained and so despotic, could not always restrain their glittering brightness. One was speaking, and by his glance, it was evident that the subject of his discourse was the fourth and last of their number, who had placed himself in a position that prevented his being an auditor of what was said.

In the person of the latter chief, the reader will recognise the youth who had confronted Mark and whose rapid movement on the flank of Dudley had first driven the Colonists from the meadows. The eloquent expression of limb, the tension of sinews, and the compression of muscles, as last exhibited, were now gone. They had given place to the peculiar repose that distinguishes the Indian warrior in his moments of inaction, quite as much as it marks the manner of one schooled in the forms of more polished life. With one hand he leaned lightly on a musket, while from the wrist of the other, which hung loose at his side, depended, by a thong of deer's sinew, a tomahawk from which fell drops of human blood. His person bore no other covering than that in which he had fought, and, unlike his more aged companion in authority, his body had escaped without a wound.

In form and in features, this young warrior might be deemed a model of the excellence of Indian manhood. The limbs were full, round, faultlessly straight, and distinguished by an appearance of extreme activity, without being equally remarkable for muscle. In the latter particular, in the upright attitude, and in the distant and noble gaze which so often elevated his front, there was a close affinity to the statue of the Pythian Apollo; while in the full, though slightly effeminate chest, there was an equal resemblance to that look of animal indulgence, which is to be traced in the severe representations of Bacchus. This resemblance however to a Deity that is little apt to awaken lofty sentiments in the spectator, was not displeasing, since it in some measure relieved the sternness of an eye that penetrated like the glance of the eagle, and that might otherwise have left an impression of too little sympathy with the familiar weaknesses of humanity. Still the young chief was less to be remarked by this peculiar fullness of chest, the fruit of intervals of inaction, constant indulgence of the first wants of nature, and a total exemption from toil, than most of those, who either counselled in secret near, or paced the grounds about the building. In him, it was rather a point to be admired, than a blemish; for it seemed to say, that notwithstanding the evidences of austerity which custom, and perhaps character, as well as rank, had gathered in his air, there was a heart beneath that might be touched by the charities of humanity. On the present occasion, the glances of his roving eye, though searching and full of meaning, were evidently weakened by an expression that betrayed a strange and unwonted confusion of mind.

The conference of the three was ended, and the warrior with a turbaned head advanced towards his captives, with the step of a man whose mind had come to a decision. As the dreaded chief drew near, Whittal retired, stealing to the side of the younger warrior, in a manner that denoted greater familiarity and perhaps greater confidence. A sudden thought lighted the countenance of the latter. He led the innocent to the extremity of the piazza, spoke low and earnestly, pointing to the forest, and when he saw that his messenger was already crossing the fields, at the top of his speed, he moved, with calm dignity, into the centre of the group, taking his station so near his friend, that the folds of the scarlet blanket brushed his elbow. Until this movement, the silence was not broken. When the great chief felt the passage of the other, he glanced a look of hesitation at his friends, but resuming his former air of composure, he spoke:

"Man of many winters," he commenced, in an English that was quite intelligible, while it betrayed a difficulty of speech we shall not attempt imitating, "why hath the Great Spirit made thy race like hungry wolves?—why hath a Pale-face the stomach of a buzzard, the throat of a hound, and the heart of a deer? Thou hast seen many meltings of the snow: thou rememberest the young tree a sapling. Tell me; why is the mind of a Yengeese so big, that it must hold all that lies between the rising and the setting sun? Speak, for we would know the reason, why arms so long are found on so little bodies?"

The events of that day had been of a nature to awaken all the latent energies of the Puritan. He had lifted up his spirit, with the morning, in the customary warmth with which he ever hailed the Sabbath; the excitement of the assault had found him sustained above most earthly calamities, and while it quickened feelings that can never become extinct in one who has been familiar with martial usages, it left him, stern in his manhood, and exalted in his sentiments of submission and endurance. Under such influences, he answered with an austerity that equalled the gravity of the Indian.

"The Lord hath delivered us into the bonds of the heathen," he said, "and yet his name shall be blessed beneath my roof! Out of evil shall come good; and from this triumph of the ignorant shall proceed an everlasting victory!"

The chief gazed intently at the speaker, whose attenuated frame, venerable face, and long locks, aided by the hectic of enthusiasm that played beneath a glazed and deep-set eye, imparted a character that seemed to rise superior to human weakness. Bending his head in superstitious reverence, he turned gravely to those who, appearing to possess more of the world in their natures, were more fitting subjects for the designs he meditated.

"The mind of my father is strong, but his body is like a branch of the scorched hemlock!" was the pithy declaration with which he prefaced his next remark. "Why is this?" he continued, looking severely at the three who had so lately been opposed to him in deadly contest. "Here are men with skins like the blossom of the dog-wood, and yet their hands are so dark that I cannot see them!"

"They have been blackened by toil, beneath a burning sun," returned Content, who knew how to discourse in the figurative language of the people in whose power he found himself. "We have labored, that our women and children might eat."

"No—the blood of red men hath changed their color."

"We have taken up the hatchet, that the land which the Great Spirit hath given might still be ours, and that our scalps might not be blown about in the smoke of a wigwam. Would a Narragansett hide his arms, and tie up his hands, with the war-whoop ringing in his ears?"

When allusion was made to the ownership of the valley, the blood rushed into the cheek of the warrior in such a flood, that it deepened even the natural swarthy hue; but, clenching the handle of his axe convulsively, he continued to listen, like one accustomed to entire self-command.

"What a red man does may be seen," he answered, pointing with a grim smile towards the orchard; exposing, by the movement of the blanket, as he raised his arm, two of the reeking trophies of victory attached to his belt. "Our ears are open very wide. We listen, to hear in what manner the hunting-grounds of the Indian have become the plowed elds of the Yengeese. Now let my wise men hearken, that they may grow more cunning, as the snows settle on their heads. The pale-men have a secret to make the black seem white!"

'Narragansett——"

"Wampanoag!" interrupted the chief, with the lofty air with which an Indian identifies himself with the glory of his people—then glancing a milder look at the young warrior at his elbow, he added, hastily, and in the tone of a courtier: 'tis very good—Narragansett, or Wampanoag—Wampanoag or Narragansett. The red men are brothers and friends. They have broken down the fences between their hunting-grounds, and they have cleared the paths, between their villages, of briars. What have you to say to the Narragansett?—he has not yet shut his ear."

"Wampanoag, if such be thy tribe," resumed Content, "thou shalt hear that which my conscience teacheth is language to be uttered. The God of an Englishman is the God of men of all ranks, and of all time." His listeners shook their heads doubtingly, with the exception of the youngest chief, whose eye never varied its direction while the other spoke, each word appearing to enter deep within the recesses of his mind. "In defiance of these signs of blasphemy, do I still proclaim the power of him I worship!" Content continued; "My God is thy God; and he now looketh equally on the deeds, and searcheth, with inscrutable knowledge, into the hearts of both. This earth is his footstool; yonder heaven his throne! I pretend not to enter into his sacred mysteries, or to proclaim the reason why one-half of his fair work hath been so long left in that slough of ignorance and heathenish abomination in which my fathers found it; why these hills never before echoed the songs of praise or why the valleys have been so long mute. These are truths hid in the secret designs of his sacre purpose, and they may not be known, until the last fulfilment. But a great and righteous spirit hath led hither men, filled with the love of truth and pregnant with the designs of a heavily-burthened faith, inasmuch as their longings are for things pure, while the consciousness of their transgressions bends them in deep humility to the dust. Thou bringest against us the charge of coveting thy lands, and of bearing minds filled with the corruption of riches This cometh of ignorance of that which hath been abandoned, in order that the spirit of the godly might hold fast to the truth. When the Yengeese came into this wilderness, he left behind him all that can delight the eye, please the senses, and feed the longing of the human heart, in the country of his fathers: for fair as is the work of the Lord in other lands, there is none that is so excellent as that from which these pilgrims in the wilderness have departed. In that favored isle, the earth groaneth with the abundance of its products; the odors of its sweet savors salute the nostrils, and the eye is never wearied in gazing at its loveliness.—No: the men of the Pale-faces have deserted home, and all that sweeteneth life, that they might serve God; and not at the instigations of craving minds, or of evil vanities!"

Content paused, for as he grew warm with the spirit by which he was animated, he had insensibly strayed from the closer points of his subject. His conquerors maintained the decorous gravity with which an Indian always listens to the speech of another, until he had ended; and then the Great Chief, or Wampanoag, as he had proclaimed himself to be, laid a finger lightly on the shoulder of his prisoner, as he demanded—

"Why have the people of the Yengeese lost themselves on a blind path? If the country they have left is pleasant, cannot their God hear them from the wigwams of their fathers? See—if our trees are but bushes, leave them to the red man: he will find room beneath their branches to lie in the shade. If our rivers are small, it is because the Indians are little. If the hills are low and the valleys narrow, the legs of my people are weary with much hunting, and they will journey among them the easier. Now what the Great Spirit hath made for a red man, a red man should keep. They whose skins are like the light of the morning should go back towards the rising sun, out of which they have come to do us wrong."

The chief spoke calmly, but it was like a man much accustomed to deal in the subtleties of controversy, according to the fashion of the people t whom he belonged.

"God hath otherwise decreed," said Content. "He hath led his servants hither, that the incense of praise may arise from the wilderness."

"Your Spirit is a wicked Spirit. Your ears have been cheated. The counsel that told your young men to come so far, was not spoken in the voice of the Manitou. It came from the tongue of one that loves to see game scarce, and the squaws hungry. Go—you follow the mocker, or your hands would not be so dark."

"I know not what injury may have been done the Wampanoags, by men of wicked minds, for some such there are, even in the dwellings of the well-disposed; but wrong to any hath never come from those that dwell within my doors. For these lands, a price hath been paid; and what is now seen of abundance in the valley, hath been wrought by much labor. Thou art a Wampanoag, and dost know that the hunting-grounds of thy tribe have been held sacred by my people. Are not the fences standing, which their hands placed, that not even the hoof of colt should trample the corn? and when was it known that the Indian came for justice against the trespassing ox, and did not find it?"

"The moose doth not taste the grass at the root; he liveth on the tree! He doth not stoop to feed on that which he treadeth under foot! Does the hawk look for the musketoe? His eye is too big. He can see a bird. Go—when the deer have been killed the Wampanoags will break down the fence with their own hands. The arm of a hungry man is strong. A cunning Pale-face hath made that fence: it shutteth out the colt, and it shutteth in the Indian But the mind of a warrior is too big; it will not be kept at grass with the ox."

A low but expressive murmur of satisfaction from the mouths of his grim companions, succeeded this reply of the chief.

"The country of thy tribe is far distant," returned Content, "and I will not lay untruth to my soul by presuming to say whether justice or injustice hath been done them in the partition of the lands But in this valley hath wrong never been done to the red man. What Indian hath asked for food, and not got it? If he hath been a-thirst, the cider came at his wish; if he hath been a-cold, there was a seat by the hearth; and yet hath there been reason why the hatchet should be in my hand, and why my foot should be on the war-path! For many seasons we lived on lands, which were bought of both red and white man, in peace. But though the sun shone clear so long, the clouds came at last. There was a dark night fell upon this valley, Wampanoag, and death and the brand entered my dwelling, together. Our young men were killed, and——our spirits were sorely tried."

Content paused, for his voice became thick, and his eye had caught a glimpse of the pale and drooping countenance of her who leaned on the arm of the still excited and frowning Mark for support. The young chief listened with a charmed ear. As Content had proceeded, his body was inclined a little forward, and his whole attitude was that which men unconsciously assume when intensely occupied in listening to sounds of the deepest interest.

"But the sun rose again!" said the great chief pointing at the evidences of prosperity which were everywhere apparent in the settlement, casting at the same time an uneasy and suspicious glance at his youngest companion. "The morning was clear, though the night was so dark. The cunning of a Pale-face knows how to make corn grow on a rock. The foolish Indian eats roots, when crops fail and game is scarce."

'God ceased to be angry;" returned Content meekly, folding his arms in a manner to show he wished to speak no more.

The great chief was about to continue, when his younger associate laid a finger on his naked shoulder, and, by a sign, indicated that he wished to hold communication with him apart. The former met the request with respect, though it might be discovered that he little liked the expression of his companion's features, and that he yielded with reluctance, if not with disgust. But the countenance of the youth was firm, and it would have needed more than usual hardihood to refuse a request seconded by so steady and so meaning an eye. The elder spoke to the warrior nearest his elbow, addressing him by the name of Annawon, and then, by a gesture so natural and so dignified that it might have graced the air of a courtier, he announced his readiness to proceed. Notwithstanding the habitua reverence of the aborigines for age, the others gave way for the passage of the young man, in a manner to proclaim that merit or birth, or both, had united to purchase for him a personal distinction, which far exceeded that shown, in common, to men of his years. The two chiefs left the piazza in the noiseless manner of the moccasoned foot.

The passage of these dignified warriors towards the grounds in the rear of the dwelling, as it was characteristic of their habits, is worthy of being mentioned. Neither spoke, neither manifested any womanish impatience to pry into the musings of the other's mind, and neither failed in those slight but still sensible courtesies by which the path was rendered commodious and the footing sure. They had reached the summit of the elevation so often named, ere they believed themselves sufficiently retired to indulge in a discourse which might otherwise have enlightened profane ears. When beneath the shade of the fragrant orchard which grew on the hill, the senior of the two stopped, and throwing about him one of those quick, nearly imperceptible, and yet wary glances, by which an Indian understands his precise position, as it were by instinct, he commenced the dialogue. The discourse was in the dialect of their race, but as it is not probable that many who read these pages would be much enlightened were we to record it in the precise words in which it has been transmitted to us, a translation into English, as freely as the subject requires, and the geniuses of the two languages will admit, shall be attempted.

"What would my brother have?" commenced he with the turbaned head, uttering the guttural sounds in the low, soothing tones of friendship, and even of affection. "What troubles the Great Sachem of the Narragansetts? His thoughts seem uneasy. I think there is more before his eye, than one whose sight is getting dim can see. Doth he behold the spirit of the brave Miantonimoh, who died, like a dog, beneath the blows of cowardly Pequots and false-tongued Yengeese? Or does his heart swell, with longing, to see the scalps of treacherous Pale, faces hanging at his belt? Speak, my son; the hatchet hath long been buried in the path between our villages, and thy words will enter the ears of friend."

"I do not see the spirit of my father," returned the young Sachem; "he is afar off, in the hunting-grounds of just warriors. My eyes are too weak to look over so many mountains, and across so many rivers. He is chasing the moose in grounds where there are no briars; he needeth not the sight of a young man to tell him which way the trail leadeth. Why should I look at the place where the Pequot and the Pale-face took his life? The fire which scorched this hill hath blackened the spot, and I can no longer find the marks of blood."

"My son is very wise—cunning beyond his winters! That which hath been once revenged, is forgotten. He looks no further than six moons. He sees the warriors of the Yengeese coming into his village, murdering his old women, and slaying the Narragansett girls; killing his warriors from behind, and lighting their fires with the bones of red men. I will now stop my ears, for the groans of the slaughtered make my soul feel weak."

"Wampanoag," answered the other, with a fierce flashing of his eagle eye, and laying his hand firmly on his breast, "the night the snows were red with the blood of my people, is here! my mind is dark: none of my race have since looked upon the place where the lodges of the Narragansetts stood, and yet it hath never been hid from our sight. Since that time have we travelled in the woods, bearing on our backs all that is left but our sorrow; that we carry in our hearts."

"Why is my brother troubled? There are many scalps among his people, and see, his own tomahawk is very red! Let him quiet his anger till the night cometh, and there will be a deeper stain on the axe. I know he is in a hurry, but our councils say it is better to wait for darkness, since the cunning of the Pale-faces is too strong for the hands of our young men."

"When was a Narragansett slow to leap, after the whoop was given; or unwilling to stay, when men of gray heads say 'tis better? I like your counsel; it is full of wisdom. Yet an Indian is but a man! Can he fight with the God of the Yengeese?

He is too weak. An Indian is but a man, though his skin be red!"

"I look into the clouds, at the trees, among the lodges," said the other, affecting to gaze curiously at the different objects he named, "but I cannot see the white Manitou. The pale-men were talking to him when we raised the whoop in their fields, and yet he has not heard them. Go—my son has struck their warriors with a strong hand; has he forgotten to count how many dead lie among the trees with the sweet-smelling blossoms?"

"Metacom," returned he who has been called the Sachem of the Narragansetts, stepping cautiously nearer to his friend, and speaking lower, as if he feared an invisible auditor; "thou hast put hate into the bosoms of the red men, but canst thou make them more cunning than the Spirits? Hate is very strong, but cunning hath a longer arm. See," he added, raising the fingers of his two hands before the eyes of his attentive companion, "ten snows have come and melted, since there stood a lodge of the Pale-faces on this hill. Conanchet was then a boy. His hand had struck nothing but deer. His heart was full of wishes. By day he thought of Pequot scalps, at night he heard the dying words of Miantonimoh. Though slain by cowardly Pequots and lying Yengeese, his father came with the night into his wigwam, to talk to his son. 'Does the child of so many great Sachems grow big?' would he say; 'is his arm getting strong, his foot light, his eye quick, his heart valiant? Will Conanchet be like his fathers?—when will the young Sachem of the Narragansetts become a man?' Why should I tell my brother of these visits? Metacom hath often seen the long line of Wampanoag Chiefs, in his sleep? The brave Sachems sometimes enter into the heart of their son?"

The lofty-minded, though wily Philip struck his

hand heavily upon his naked breast, as he answered—

"They are always here. Metacom has no soul but the spirit of his fathers!"

"When he was tired of silence, the murdered Miantonimoh spoke aloud," continued Conanchet, after permitting the customary courteous pause to succeed the emphatic words of his companion. "He bade his son arise, and go among the Yengeese, that he might return with scalps to hang in his wigwam; for the eyes of the dead chief liked not to see the place so empty. The voice of Conanchet was then too feeble for the council-fire; he said nothing—he went alone. An evil spirit gave him into the hands of the Pale-faces. He was a captive many moons. They shut him in a cage, like a tamed panther! It was here. The news of his ill-luck passed from the mouths of the young men of the Yengeese, to the hunters; and from the hunters it came to the ears of the Narragansetts. My people had lost their Sachem, and they came to seek him. Metacom, the boy had felt the power of the God of the Yengeese! His mind began to grow weak; he thought less of revenge; the spirit of his father came no more at night. There was much talking with the unknown God, and the words of his enemies were kind. He hunted with them. When he met the trail of his warriors in the woods, his mind was troubled, for he knew their errand. Still he saw his father's spirit, and waited. The whoop was heard that night; many died, and the Narragansetts took scalps. Thou seest this lodge of stone, over which fire has passed. There was then a cunning place above, and in it the pale-men went to fight for their lives. But the fire kindled, and then there was no hope. The soul of Conanchet was moved at that sight, for there was much honesty in them within. Though their skins were so white, they had not slain his father. But the flames would not be spoken to, and the place became like the coals of a deserted council-fire. All within were turned to ashes. If the spirit of Miantonimoh rejoiced, it was well; but the soul of his son was very heavy. The weakness was on him, and he no longer thought of boasting of his deeds at the war-post."

"That fire scorched the stain of blood from the Sachem's plain?"

"It did. Since that time I have not seen the marks of my father's blood. Gray heads and boys were in that fire, and when the timbers fell, nothing was left but coals. Yet do they, who were in the blazing lodge, stand there!"

The attentive Metacom started, and glanced a hasty look at the ruin.

"Does my son see spirits in the air?" he asked hastily.

"No, they live; they are bound for the torments. In the white head, is he who talked much with his God. The elder chief, who struck our young men so hard, was then also a captive in this lodge. He who spoke, and she, who seems even paler than her race, died that night; and yet are they now here! Even the brave youth, that was so hard to conquer, looks like a boy that was in the fire! The Yengeese deal with unknown Gods; they are too cunning for an Indian!"

Philip heard this strange tale, as a being educated in superstitious legends would be apt to listen; and yet it was with a leaning to incredulity, that was generated by his fierce and indomitable desire for the destruction of the hated race. He had prevailed, in the councils of his nation, over many similar signs of the supernatural agency that was exercised in favor of his enemies, but never before had facts so imposing come so directly and from so high a source before his mind. Even the proud resolution and farsighted wisdom of this sagacious chief were shaken by such testimony, and there was a single moment when the idea of abandoning a league that seemed desperate took possession of his brain. But true to himself and his cause, second thoughts and a firmer purpose restored his resolution, though they could not remove the perplexity of his doubts.

"What does Conanchet wish?" he said. "Twice have his warriors broke into this valley, and twice have the tomahawks of his young men been redder than the head of the woodpecker. The fire was not good fire; the tomahawk will kill surer. Had not the voice of my brother said to his young men, 'let the scalps of the prisoners alone,' he could not now say 'yet do they now stand here!'"

"My mind is troubled, friend of my father. Let them be questioned, artfully, that the truth be known."

Metacom mused an instant; then smiling, in a friendly manner, on his young and much moved companion, he made a sign to a youth who was straying about the fields, to approach. This young warrior was made the bearer of an order to lead the captives to the hill, after which the two chiefs stalked to and fro in silence, each brooding over what had passed, in a humor that was suited to his particular character and more familiar feelings.

CHAPTER XXV.

No wither'd witch shall here be seen,
No goblins lead their nightly crew;
The female fays shall haunt the green,
And dress thy grave with pearly dew.
COLLINS.

IT is rare indeed that the philosophy of a dignified Indian is so far disturbed, as to destroy the appearance of equanimity. When Content and the family of the Heathcotes appeared on the hill, they found the chiefs still pacing the orchard, with the outward composure of men unmoved, and with the gravity that was suited to their rank. Annawon, who had acted as their conductor, caused the captives to be placed in a row, choosing the foot of the ruin for their position, and then he patiently awaited the moment when his superiors might be pleased to renew the examination. In this habitual silence, there was nothing of the abject air of Asiatic deference. It proceeded from the habit of self-command, which taught the Indian to repress all natural emotions. A very similar effect was produced by the religious abasement of those whom fortune had now thrown into their power. It would have been a curious study, for one interested in the manners of the human species, to note the difference between the calm, physical, and perfect self-possession of the wild tenants of the forest, and the ascetic, spiritually sustained, and yet meek submission to Providence, that was exhibited by most of the prisoners. We say of most, for there was an exception. The brow of young Mark still retained its frown, and the angry character of his eye was only lost, when by chance it lighted on the drooping form and pallid features of his mother. There was ample time for these several and peculiar qualities to be thus silently exhibited, many minutes passing before either of the Sachems seemed inclined to recommence the conference. At length Philip, or Metacom, as we shall indifferently call him, drew near and spoke.

"This earth is a good earth," he said; "it is of many colors, to please the eyes of him who made it. In one part it is dark, and as the worm taketh the color of the leaf on which he crawls, there the hunters are black; in another part it is white, and that is the part where pale-men were born, and where they should die; or they may miss the road which leads to their happy hunting-grounds. Many just warriors, who have been killed on distant war-paths, still wander in the woods, because the trail is hid, and their sight dim. It is not good to trust so much to the cunning of——"

"Wretched and blind worshipper of Apollyon!" interrupted the Puritan, "we are not of the idolatrous and foolish-minded! It hath been accorded to us to know the Lord; to his chosen worshippers, all regions are alike. The spirit can mount, equally, through snows and whirlwinds; the tempest and the calm; from the lands of the sun, and the lands of frosts; from the depths of the ocean, from fire, from the forest——"

He was interrupted, in his turn. At the word fire, the finger of Metacom fell meaningly on his shoulder; and when he had ceased, for until then no Indian would have spoken, the other gravely asked—

"And when a man of a pale skin hath gone up in the fire, can he again walk upon earth? Is the river between this clearing and the pleasant fields of a Yengeese so narrow, that the just men can step across it when they please?"

"This is the conceit of one wallowing in the slough of heathenish abominations! Child of ignorance! know that the barriers which separate heaven from earth are impassable; for what purified being could endure the wickedness of the flesh?"

"This is a lie of the false Pale-faces," said the wily Philip; "it is told that the Indian might not learn their cunning, and become stronger than a Yengeese. My father, and those with him, were once burnt in this lodge, and now he standeth here, ready to take the tomahawk!"

"To be angered at this blasphemy, would ill denote the pity that I feel," said Mark, more excited at the charge of necromancy, than he was willing to own; "and yet to suffer so fatal an error to spread among these deluded victims of Satan, would be neglect of duty. Thou hast heard some legend of thy wild people, man of the Wampanoags, which may heap double perdition on thy soul, lest thou shouldst happily be rescued from the fangs of the deceiver. It is true, that I and mine were in exceeding jeopardy in this tower, and that to the eyes of men without we seemed melted with the heat of the flames; but the Lord put it into our spirits to seek refuge whither fire could not come. The well was made the instrument of our safety, for the fulfilment of his own inscrutable designs."

Notwithstanding the long practised and exceeding subtlety of the listeners, they heard this simple explanation of that which they had deemed a miracle, with a wonder that could not readily be concealed. Delight at the excellence of the artifice was evidently the first and common emotion of them both; nor would they yield implicit faith, until assured, beyond a doubt, that what they heard was true. The little iron door, which had permitted access to the well, for the ordinary domestic purposes of the family, was still there; and it was only after each had cast a look down the deep shaft, that he appeared satisfied of the practicability of the deed. Then a look of triumph gleamed in the swarthy visage of Philip, while the features of his associate expressed equally his satisfaction and his regret. They walked apart, musing on what they had just seen and heard; and when they spoke, it was again in the language of their people.

"My son hath a tongue that cannot lie," observed Metacom, in a soothing, flattering accent. "What he hath seen, he tells; and what he tells, is true. Conanchet is not a boy, but a chief whose wisdom is gray, while his limbs are young. Now, why shall not his people take the scalps of these Yengeese, that they may never go any more into holes in the earth, like cunning foxes?"

"The Sachem hath a very bloody mind," returned the young chief, quicker than was common for men of his station. "Let the arms of the warriors rest, till they meet the armed hands of the Yengeese, or they will be too tired to strike heavily. My young men have taken scalps, since the sun came over the trees, and they are satisfied—Why does Metacom look so hard? What does my father see?"

"A dark spot in the middle of a white plain. The grass is not green; it is red as blood. It is too dark for the blood of a Pale-face. It is the rich blood of a great warrior. The rains cannot wash it out; it grows darker every sun. The snows do not whiten it; it hath been there many winters. The birds scream as they fly over it; the wolf howls; the lizards creep another way."

"Thine eyes are getting old; fire hath blackened the place, and what thou seest is coal."

"The fire was kindled in a well; it did not burn bright. What I see, is blood."

"Wampanoag," rejoined Conanchet, fiercely, "I

have scorched the spot with the lodges of the Yengeese. The grave of my father is covered with scalps taken by the hand of his son—Why does Metacom look again? What does the chief see?"

"An Indian town burning in the midst of the snow; the young men struck from behind; the girls screaming; the children broiling on coals, and the old men dying like dogs! It is the village of the cowardly Pequots—No, I see better; the Yengeese are in the country of the Great Narragansett, and the brave Sachem is there, fighting! I shut my eyes, for smoke blinds them!"

Conanchet heard this allusion to the recent and deplorable fate of the principal establishment of his tribe, in sullen silence; for the desire of revenge, which had been so fearfully awakened, seemed now to be slumbering, if it were not entirely quelled by the agency of some mysterious and potent feeling. He rolled his eyes gloomily, from the apparently abstracted countenance of his artful companion, to those of the captives, whose fate only awaited his judgment, since the band which had that morning broken in upon the Wish-Ton-Wish was, with but few exceptions, composed of the surviving warriors of his own powerful nation. But, while his look was displeased, faculties that were schooled so highly, could not easily be mistaken, in what passed, even in the most cursory manner, be fore his sight.

"What sees my father, next?" he asked, with an interest he could not control, detecting another change in the features of Metacom.

"One who is neither white nor red. A young woman, that boundeth like a skipping fawn; who hath lived in a wigwam, doing nothing; who speaks with two tongues; who holds her hands before the eyes of a great warrior, till he is blind as the owl in the sun—I see her——"

Metacom paused, for at that moment a being that singularly resembled this description appeared before him, offering the reality of the imaginary picture he was drawing with so much irony and art.

The movement of the timid hare is scarce more hurried, or more undecided, than that of the creature who now suddenly presented herself to the warriors. It was apparent, by the hesitating and half-retreating step that succeeded the light bound with which she came in view, that she dreaded to advance, while she knew not how far it might be proper to retire. For the first moment, she stood in a suspended and doubting posture, such as one might suppose a creature of mist would assume ere it vanished, and then meeting the eye of Conanchet, the uplifted foot retouched the earth, and her whole form sunk into the modest and shrinking attitude of an Indian girl, who stood in the presence of a Sachem of her tribe. As this female is to enact no mean part in that which follows, the reader may be thankful for a more minute description of her person.

The age of the stranger was under twenty. In form she rose above the usual stature of an Indian maid, though the proportions of her person were as light and buoyant as at all comported with the fullness that properly belonged to her years. The limbs. seen below the folds of a short kirtle of bright scar let cloth, were just and tapering, even to the nicest proportions of classic beauty; and never did foot of higher instep, and softer roundness, grace a feathered moccason. Though the person, from the neck to the knees, was hid by a tightly-fitting vest of calico and the short kirtle named, enough of the shape was visible to betray outlines that had never been injured, either by the mistaken devices of art or by the baneful effects of toil. The skin was only visible at the hands, face, and neck. Its lustre having been a little dimmed by exposure, a rich, rosy tint had usurped the natural brightness of a complexion that had once been fair even to brilliancy. The eye was full, sweet, and of a blue that emulated the sky of evening; the brows, soft and arched; the nose, straight, delicate, and slightly Grecian; the forehead, fuller than that which properly belonged to a girl of the Narragansetts, but regular, delicate, and polished; and the hair, instead of dropping in long straight tresses of jet black, broke out of the restraints of a band of beaded wampum, in ringlets of golden yellow.

The peculiarities that distinguished this female from the others of her tribe, were not confined alone to the indelible marks of nature. Her step was more elastic; her gait more erect and graceful; her foot less inwardly inclined, and her whole movements freer and more decided than those of a race doomed from infancy to subjection and labor. Though ornamented by some of the prized inventions of the hated race to which she evidently owed her birth, she had the wild and timid look of those with whom she had grown into womanhood. Her beauty would have been remarkable in any region of the earth, while the play of muscle, the ingenuous beaming of the eye, and the freedom of limb and action, were such as seldom pass beyond the years of childhood, among people who, in attempting to improve, so often mar the works of nature.

Although the color of the eye was so very different from that which generally belongs to one of Indian origin, the manner of its quick and searching glance, and of the half-alarmed and yet understanding look with which this extraordinary creature made herself mistress of the more general character of the assemblage before which she had been summoned, was like the half-instinctive knowledge of one accustomed to the constant and keenest exercise of her faculties. Pointing with a finger to wards Whittal Ring, who stood a little in the background, a low, sweet voice was heard asking, in the language of the Indians—

"Why has Conanchet sent for his woman from the woods?"

The young Sachem made no reply; an ordinary spectator could not have detected about him even a consciousness of the speaker's presence. On the contrary, he maintained the lofty reserve of a chief engaged in affairs of moment. However deeply his thoughts might have been troubled, it was not easy to trace any evidence of the state of his mind in the calmness of features that appeared habitually immovable. For a single treacherous instant, only, was a glance of kindness shot towards the timid and attentive girl, and then throwing the still bloody tomahawk into the hollow of one arm, while the hand of the other firmly grasped its handle, he remained unchanged in feature, as he was rigid in limb. Not so, with Philip. When the intruder first appeared, a dark and lowering gleam of discontent gathered at his brow. It quickly changed to a look of sarcastic and biting scorn.

"Does my brother again wish to know what I see?" he demanded, when sufficient time had passed, after the unanswered question of the female, to show that his companion was not disposed to answer.

"What does the Sachem of the Wampanoags now behold?" returned Conanchet, proudly; unwilling to show that any circumstance had occurred to interrupt the subject of their conference.

"A sight that his eyes will not believe. He sees a great tribe on the war-path. There are many braves, and a chief whose fathers came from the clouds. Their hands are in the air; they strike heavy blows; the arrow is swift, and the bullet is not seen to enter, but it kills. Blood runs from the wounds that is of the color of water. Now he does not see, but he hears! 'Tis the scalp-whoop, and the warriors are very glad. The chiefs in the happy hunting-grounds are coming, with joy, to meet Indians that are killed; for they know the scalp-whoop of their children."

The expressive countenance of the young Sachem involuntarily responded to this description of the scene through which he had just passed; and it was impossible for one so tutored, to prevent the blood from rushing faster to a heart that ever beat strongly with the wishes of a warrior.

"What sees my father, next?" he asked, triumph insensibly stealing into the tones of his voice.

"A Messenger—and then he hears—the moccasons of squaws!"

"Enough;—Metacom, the women of the Narragansetts have no lodges. Their villages are in coals, and they follow the young men for food."

"I see no deer. The hunter will not find venison in a clearing of the Pale-faces. But the corn is full of milk; Conanchet is very hungry; he hath sent for his woman, that he may eat!"

The fingers of that hand, which grasped the handle of the tomahawk, appeared to bury themselves in the wood; the glittering axe itself was slightly raised; but the fierce gleaming of resentment subsided, as the anger of the young Sachem vanished, and a dignified calm again settled on his countenance.

"Go, Wampanoag," he said, waving a hand proudly, as if determined to be no longer harassed by the language of his wily associate. "My young men will raise the whoop, when they hear my voice; and they will kill deer for their women. Sachem, my mind is my own."

Philip answered to the look which accompanied these words, with one that threatened vengeance; but smothering his anger, with his accustomed wisdom, he left the hill, assuming an air that affected more of commiseration than of resentment.

"Why has Conanchet sent for a woman from the woods?" repeated the same soft voice, nearer to the elbow of the young Sachem, and which spoke with less of the timidity of the sex, now that the troubled spirit of the Indians of those regions had disappeared.

"Narra-mattah, come near;" returned the young chief, changing the deep and proud tones in which he had addressed his restless and bold companion in arms, to those which better suited the gentle ear for which his words were intended. "Fear not, daughter of the morning, for those around us are of a race used to see women at the council-fires. Now look, with an open eye—is there anything among these trees that seemeth like an ancient tradition? Hast ever beheld such a valley, in thy dreams? Have yonder Pale-faces, whom the tomahawks of my young men spared, been led before thee by the Great Spirit, in the dark night?"

The female listened, in deep attention. Her gaze was wild and uncertain, and yet it was not absolutely without gleamings of a half-reviving intelligence. Until that moment, she had been too much occupied in conjecturing the subject of her visit, to regard the natural objects by which she was surrounded: but with her attention thus directly turned upon them, her organs of sight embraced each and all, with the discrimination that is so remarkable in those whose faculties are quickened by danger and necessity. Passing from side to side, her swift glances ran over the distant hamlet, with its little fort; the buildings in the near grounds; the soft and verdant fields; the fragrant orchard, beneath whose leafy shades she stood, and the blackened tower, that rose in its centre, like some gloomy memorial, placed there to remind the spectator not to trust too fondly to the signs of peace and loveliness that reigned around. Shaking back the ringlets that had blown about her temples, the wondering female returned thoughtfully and in silence to her place.

"'Tis a village of the Yengeese!" she said, after a long and expressive pause. "A Narragansett woman does not love to look at the lodges of the hated race."

"Listen.—Lies have never entered the ears of Narra-mattah. My tongue hath spoken like the tongue of a chief. Thou didst not come of the sumach, but of the snow. This hand of thine is not like the hands of the women of my tribe; it is little, for the Great Spirit did not make it for work; it is of the color of the sky in the morning, for thy fathers were born near the place where the sun rises. Thy blood is like spring-water. All this thou knowest, for none have spoken false in thy ear. Speak—dost thou never see the wigwam of thy father? Does not his voice whisper to thee, in the language of his people?"

The female stood in the attitude which a sibyl might be supposed to assume, while listening to the occult mandates of the myterious oracle, every faculty entranced and attentive.

"Why does Conanchet ask these questions of his wife? He knows what she knows; he sees what she sees; his mind is her mind. If the Great Spirit made her skin of a different color, he made her heart the same. Narra-mattah will not listen to the lying language; she shuts her ears, for there is deceit in its sounds. She tries to forget it. One tongue can say all she wishes to speak to Conanchet; why should she look back in dreams, when a great chief is her husband?"

The eye of the warrior, as he looked upon the ingenuous and confiding face of the speaker, was kind to fondness The firmness had passed away and in its place was left the winning softness of affection, which, as it belongs to nature, is seen, at times, in the expression of an Indian's eye, as strongly as it is ever known to sweeten the intercourse of a more polished condition of life.

"Girl," he said with emphasis, after a moment of thought, as if he would recall her and himself to more important duties, "this is a war-path; all on it are men. Thou wast like the pigeon before its wing opens, when I brought thee from the nest; still the winds of many winters had blown upon thee. Dost never think of the warmth and of the food of the lodge in which thou hast past so many seasons?"

"The wigwam of Conanchet is warm; no woman of the tribe hath as many furs as Narra-mattah."

"He is a great hunter! when they hear his moccason, the beavers lie down to be killed! But the men of the Pale-faces hold the plow. Does not 'the driven snow' think of those who fenced the wigwam of her father from the cold, or of the manner in which the Yengeese live?"

His youthful and attentive wife seemed to reflect; but raising her face, with an expression of content that could not be counterfeited, she shook her head in the negative.

"Does she never see a fire kindled among the lodges, or hear the whoops of warriors as they break into a settlement?"

"Many fires have been kindled before her eyes. The ashes of the Narragansett town are not yet cold."

"Does not Narra-mattah hear her father speaking to the God of the Yengeese? Listen—he is asking favor for his child!"

"The Great Spirit of the Narragansett has ears for his people."

"But I hear a softer voice! 'Tis a woman of the Pale-faces among her children: cannot the daughter hear?"

Narra-mattah, or 'the driven snow,' laid her hand lightly on the arm of the chief, and she looked wistfully and long into his face, without an answer. The gaze seemed to deprecate the anger that might be awakened by what she was about to reveal.

"Chief of my people," she said, encouraged by his still calm and gentle brow, to proceed, "what a girl of the clearings sees in her dreams, shall not be hid. It is not the lodges of her race, for the wigwam of her husband is warmer. It is not the food and clothes of a cunning people, for who is richer than the wife of a great chief? It is not her fathers speaking to their Spirit, for there is none stronger than Manitou. Narra-mattah has forgotten all: she does not wish to think of things like these. She knows how to hate a hungry and craving race. But she sees one that the wives of the Narragansetts do not see. She sees a woman with a white skin; her eye looks softly on her child in her dreams; it is not an eye, it is a tongue! It says, what does the wife of Conanchet wish?—is she cold? here are furs—is she hungry? here is venison—is she tired? the arms of the pale woman open, that an Indian girl may sleep. When there is silence in the lodges, when Conanchet and his young men lie down, then does this pale woman speak. Sachem, she does not talk of the battles of her people, nor of the scalps that her warriors have taken, nor of the manner in which the Pequots and Mohicans fear her tribe. She does not tell how a young Narragansett should obey her husband, nor how the women must keep food in the lodges for the hunters that are wearied; her tongue useth strange words. It names a Mighty and Just Spirit it telleth of peace, and not of war; it soundeth as one talking from the clouds; it is like the falling of the water among rocks. Narra-mattah loves to listen, for the words seem to her like the Wish-Ton Wish, when he whistles in the woods."

Conanchet had fastened a look of deep and affectionate interest on the wild and sweet countenance of the being who stood before him. She had spoken in that attitude of earnest and natural eloquence that no art can equal; and when she ceased, he laid a hand, in kind but melancholy fondness, on the half-inclined and motionless head, as he answered.

"This is the bird of night, singing to its young! The Great Spirit of thy fathers is angry, that thou livest in the lodge of a Narragansett. His sight is too cunning to be cheated. He knows that the moccason, and the wampum, and the robe of fur are liars; he sees the color of the skin beneath."

"Conanchet, no;" returned the female hurriedly, and with a decision her timidity did not give reason to expect. "He seeth farther than the skin, and knoweth the color of the mind. He hath forgotten that one of his girls is missing."

"It is not so. The eagle of my people was taken into the lodges of the Pale-faces. He was young, and they taught him to sing with another tongue. The colors of his feathers were changed, and they thought to cheat the Manitou. But when the door was open, he spread his wings and flew back to hi nest. It is not so. What hath been done is good and what will be done is better. Come; there is a straight path before us."

Thus saying, Conanchet motioned to his wife to follow towards the group of captives. The foregoing dialogue had occurred in a place where the two parties were partially concealed from each other by the ruin; but as the distance was so trifling, the Sachem and his companion were soon confronted with those he sought. Leaving his wife a little without the circle, Conanchet advanced, and taking the unresisting and half-unconscious Ruth by the arm, he led her forward. He placed the two females in attitudes where each might look the other full in the face. Strong emotion struggled in a countenance which, in spite of its fierce mask of war-paint, could not entirely conceal its workings.

"See," he said in English, looking earnestly from one to the other. "The Good Spirit is not ashamed of his work. What he hath done, he hath done; Narragansett nor Yengeese can alter it. This is the white bird that came from the sea," he added, touching the shoulder of Ruth lightly with a finger, "and this the young, that she warmed under her wing."

Then, folding his arms on his naked breast, he appeared to summon his energy, lest, in the scene that he knew must follow, his manhood might be betrayed into some act unworthy of his name.

The captives were necessarily ignorant of the meaning of the scene which they had just witnessed. So many strange and savage-looking forms were constantly passing and repassing before their eyes, that the arrival of one, more or less, was not likely to be noted. Until she heard Conanchet speak in her native tongue, Ruth had lent no attention to the interview between him and his wife. But the figurative language and no less remarkable action of the Narragansett, had the effect to arouse her suddenly, and in the most exciting manner, from her melancholy.

No child of tender age ever unexpectedly came before the eyes of Ruth Heathcote, without painfully recalling the image of the cherub she had lost. The playful voice of infancy never surprised her ear without the sound conveying a pang to the heart; nor could allusion, ever so remote, be made to persons or events that bore resemblance to the sad incidents of her own life, without quickening the never-dying pulses of maternal love. No wonder, then, that when she found herself in the situation and under the circumstances described, nature grew strong within her, and that her mind caught glimpses, however dim and indistinct they might be, of a truth that the reader has already anticipated. Still, a certain and intelligible clue was wanting. Fancy had ever painted her child in the innocence and infancy in which it had been torn from her arms; and here, while there was so much to correspond with reasonable expectation, there was little to answer to the long and fondly-cherished picture. The delusion, if so holy and natural a feeling may thus be termed, had been too deeply seated to be dispossessed at a glance. Gazing long, earnestly, and with features that varied with every changing feeling, she held the stranger at the length of her two arms, alike unwilling to release her hold, or to admit her closer to a heart which might rightfully be the property of another.

"Who art thou?" demanded the mother, in a voice that was tremulous with the emotions of that sacred character. "Speak, mysterious and lovely being—who art thou?"

Narra-mattah had turned a terrified and imploring look at the immovable and calm form of the chief, as if she sought protection from him at whose hands she had been accustomed to receive it. But a different sensation took possession of her mind, when she heard sounds which had too often soothed the ear of infancy, ever to be forgotten. Struggling ceased, and her pliant form assumed the attitude of intense and entranced attention. Her head was bent aside, as if the ear were eager to drink in a repetition of the tones, while her bewildered and delighted eye still sought the countenance of her husband.

"Vision of the woods!—wilt thou not answer?" continued Ruth. "If there is reverence for the Holy One of Israel in thine heart, answer, that I may know thee!"

"Hist! Conanchet!" murmured the wife, over whose features the glow of pleased and wild surprise continued to deepen. "Come near, Sachem; the Spirit that talketh to Narra-mattah in her dreams, is nigh."

"Woman of the Yengeese!" said the husband advancing with dignity to the spot, "let the clouds blow from thy sight. Wife of a Narragansett! see clearly. The Manitou of your race speaks strong. He telleth a mother to know her child!"

Ruth could hesitate no longer; neither sound nor exclamation escaped her, but as she strained the yielding frame of her recovered daughter to her heart, it appeared as if she strove to incorporate the two bodies into one. A cry of pleasure and astonishment drew all around her. Then came the evidence of the power of nature when strongly awakened. Age and youth alike acknowledged its potency, and recent alarms were overlooked in the pure joy of such a moment. The spirit of even the lofty-minded Conanchet was shaken. Raising the hand, at whose wrist still hung the bloody tomahawk, he veiled his face, and, turning aside, that none might see the weakness of so great a warrior, he wept.

CHAPTER XXVI.

"One sees more devils than vast hell can hold;
That is, the madman:—
MIDSUMMER-NIGHT'S DREAM.

ON quitting the hill, Philip had summoned his Wampanoags, and, supported by the obedient and fierce Annawon, a savage that might, under better auspices, have proved a worthy lieutenant to Cæsar, he left the fields of Wish-Ton-Wish. Accustomed to see these sudden outbreakings of temper in their leaders, the followers of Conanchet, who would have preserved their air of composure under far more trying circumstances, saw him depart, equally without question and without alarm. But when their own Sachem appeared on the ground which was still red with the blood of the combatants, and made known his intention to abandon a conquest that seemed more than half achieved, he was not heard without murmuring. The authority of an Indian Chief is far from despotic, and though there is reason to think it is often aided, if not generated, by the accidental causes of birth and descent, it receives its main support in the personal qualities of him who rules. Happily for the Narragansett leader, even his renowned father, the hapless Miantonimoh, had not purchased a higher name for wisdom, or for daring, than that which had been fairly won by his still youthful son. The savage humors and the rankling desire for vengeance in the boldest of his subalterns, were made to quail before the menacing glances of an eye that seldom threatened without performance; nor was there one of them all, when challenged to come forth to brave the anger or to oppose the eloquence of his chief, who did not shrink from a contest which habitual respect had taught them to believe would be far too unequal for success. Within less than an hour after Ruth had clasped her child to her bosom the invaders had altogether disappeared. The dead of their party were withdrawn and concealed, with ll the usual care, in order that no scalp of a warrior might be left in the hands of his enemies.

It was not unusual for the Indians to retire satisfied with the results of their first blow. So much of their military success was dependent on surprise, that it oftener happened the retreat commenced with its failure, than that victory was obtained by perseverance.

So long as the battle raged, their courage was equal to all its dangers; but among people who made so great a merit of artifice, it is not at all surprising that they seldom put more to the hazard than was justified by the most severe discretion. When it was known, therefore, that the foe had disappeared in the forest, the inhabitants of the village were more ready to believe the movement was the result of their own manful resistance, than to seek motives that might not prove so soothing to their self-esteem. The retreat was thought to be quite in rule, and though prudence forbade pursuit, able and well-limbed scouts were sent on their trail, s well to prevent a renewal of the surprise, as to enable the forces of the Colony to know the tribe of their enemies, and the direction which they had taken.

Then came a scene of solemn ceremonies and of deep affliction. Though the parties led by Dudley and the Lieutenant had been so fortunate as to escape with a few immaterial wounds, the soldiers headed by Content, with the exception of those already named, had fallen to a man. Death had struck, at a blow, twenty of the most efficient individuals, out of that isolated and simple community Under circumstances in which victory was so barren and so dearly bought, sorrow was a feeling far stronger than rejoicing. Exultation took the aspect of humility, and while men were conscious of their well-deserving, they were the more sensible of their dependence on a power they could neither influence nor comprehend. The characteristic opinions of the religionists became still more exalted, and the close of the day was quite as remarkable for an exhibition of the peculiarly exaggerated impressions of the Colonists, as its opening had been frightful in violence and blood.

When one of the more active of the runners returned with the news that the Indians had retired through the forest with a broad trail, a sure sign that they meditated no further concealment near the valley, and that they had already been traced many miles on their retreat, the villagers returned to their usual habitations. The dead were then distributed among those who claimed the nearest right to the performance of the last duties of affection; and it might have been truly said, that mourning had taken up its abode in nearly every dwelling. The ties of blood were so general in a society thus limited, and, where they failed, the charities of life were so intimate and so natural, that not an individual of them all escaped, without feeling that the events of the day had robbed him, for ever, of some one on whom he was partially dependent for comfort or happiness.

As the day drew towards its close, the little bell again summoned the congregation to the church On this solemn occasion, but few of those who stil. lived to hear its sounds were absent. The moment when Meek arose for prayer was one of genera and intense feeling. The places so lately occupied by those who had fallen were now empty, and they resembled so many eloquent blanks in the description of what had passed, expressing far more than any language could impart. The appeal of the divine was in his usual strain of sublimated piety, mysterious insights into the hidden purposes of Providence being strangely blended with the more intelligible wants and passions of man. While h gave Heaven the glory of the victory, he spoke with a lofty and pretending humility of the instruments of its power; and although seemingly willing to acknowledge that his people abundantly deserved the heavy blow which had alighted on them, there was an evident impatience of the agents by which it had been inflicted. The principles of the sectarian were so singularly qualified by the feelings of the borderer, that one subtle in argument would have found little difficulty in detecting flaws in the reasoning of this zealot; but as so much was obscured by metaphysical mists, and so much was left for the generalities of doctrine, his hearers, without an exception, made such an application of what he uttered, as apparently rendered every mind satisfied.

The sermon was as extemporaneous as the prayer, if any thing can come extempore from a mind so drilled and fortified in opinion. It contained much the same matter, delivered a little less in the form of an apostrophe. The stricken congregation, while they were encouraged with the belief that they were vessels set apart for some great and glorious end of Providence, were plainly told that they merited far heavier affliction than this which had now befallen; and they were reminded that it was their duty to desire even condemnation, that he who framed the heavens and the earth might be glorified! Then they heard comfortable conclusions, which might reasonably teach them to expect, that though in the abstract such were the obligations of the real Christian, there was good reason to think that all who listened to doctrines so pure would be remembered with an especial favor.

So useful a servant of the temple as Meek Wolfe did not forget the practical application of his subject. It is true, that no visible emblem of the cross was shown to excite his hearers, nor were they stimulated to loosen blood-hounds on the trail of their enemies; but the former was kept sufficiently before the mind's eye by constant allusions to its merits, and the Indians were pointed at as the instruments by which the great father of evil hoped to prevent 'the wilderness from blossoming like the rose,' and 'yielding the sweet savors of godliness.' Philip and Conanchet were openly denounced, by name; some dark insinuations being made, that the person of the former was no more than the favorite tenement of Moloch; while the hearer was left to devise a suitable spirit for the government of the physical powers of the other, from among any of the more evil agencies that were named in the Bible. Any doubts of the lawfulness of the contest, that might assail tender consciences, were brushed away by a bold and decided hand. There was no attempt at justification, however; for all difficulties of this nature were resolved by the imperative obligations of duty. A few ingenious allusions to the manner in which the Israelites dispossessed the occupants of Judea, were of great service in this particular part of the subject, since it was not difficult to convince men, who so strongly felt the impulses of religious excitement, that they were stimulated rightfully. Fortified by this advantage, Mr. Wolfe manifested no desire to avoid the main question. He affirmed that if the empire of the true faith could be established by no other means, a circumstance which he assumed it was sufficiently apparent to all understandings could not be done, he pronounced it the duty of young and old, the weak and the strong, to unite in assisting to visit the former possessors of the country with what he termed the wrath of an offended Deity. He spoke of the fearful slaughter of the preceding winter, in which neither years nor sex had been spared, as a triumph of the righteous cause, and as an encouragement to persevere. Then, by a transition that was not extraordinary in an age so remarkable for religious subtleties, Meek returned to the more mild and obvious truths which pervade the doctrines of him whose church he professed to uphold. His hearers were admonished to observe lives of humility and charity, and were piously dismissed, with his benediction, to their several homes.

The congregation quitted the building with the feelings of men who thought themselves favored by peculiar and extraordinary intelligences with the author of all truth, while the army of Mahomet itself was scarcely less influenced by fanaticism than these blinded zealots. There was something so grateful to human frailty in reconciling their reséntments and their temporal interests to their religious duties, that it should excite little wonder when we add that most of them were fully prepared to become ministers of vengeance in the hands of any bold leader. While the inhabitants of the settlement were thus struggling between passions so contradictory, the shades of evening gradually fell upon their village, and then came darkness, with the rapid strides with which it follows the setting of the sun in a low latitude.

Some time before the shadows of the trees were getting the grotesque and exaggerated forms which precede the last rays of the luminary, and while the people were still listening to their pastor, a solitary individual was placed on a giddy eyrie, whence he might note the movements of those who dwelt in the hamlet, without being the subject of observation himself. A short spur of the mountain projected into the valley, on the side nearest to the dwelling of the Heathcotes. A little tumbling brook, which the melting of the snows and the occasionally heavy rains of the climate periodically increased into a torrent, had worn a deep ravine in its rocky bosom. Time, and the constant action of water, aided by the driving storms of winter and autumn, had converted many of the different faces of this ravine into wild-looking pictures of the residences of men. There was however one spot, in particular, around which a closer inspection than that which the distance of the houses in the settlement offered, might have detected far more plausible signs of the agency of human hands, than any that were afforded by the fancied resemblances of fantastic angles and accidental formations.

Precisely at that point where a sweep of the mountain permitted the best view of the valley, did the rocks assume the wildest, the most confused, and consequently the most favorable appearance for the construction of any residence which it was desirable should escape the curious eyes of the settlers, at the same time that it possessed the advantage of overlooking their proceedings. A hermit would have chosen the place as a spot suited to distant and calm observation of the world, while it was every way adapted to solitary reflection and ascetic devotion. All who have journeyed through the narrow and water-worn vineyards and meadows which are washed by the Rhone, ere that river pours its tribute into the Lake of Leman, have seen some such site, occupied by one who has devoted his life to seclusion and the altar, overhanging the village of St. Maurice, in the Canton of le Valais. But there is an air of obtrusiveness in the Swiss hermits age that did not belong to the place of which we write, since the one is perched upon its high and narrow ledge, as if to show the world in what dangerous and circumscribed limits God may be worshipped; while the other sought exemption from absolute solitude, while it courted secrecy with the most jealous caution. A small hut had been erected against the side of the rock, in a manner that presented an oblique angle. Care had been taken to surround it with such natural objects as left little reason to apprehend that its real character could be known by any who did not absolutely mount to the difficult shelf on which it stood. Light entered into this primitive and humble abode by a window that looked into the ravine, and a low door opened on the side next the valley. The construction was partly of stone and partly of logs, with a roof of bark and a chimney of mud and sticks.

One who, by his severe and gloomy brow, was a fit possessor of so secluded a tenement, was, at the hour named, seated on a stone at the most salient angle of the mountain, and at the place where the eye commanded the widest and least-obstructed view of the abodes of man in the distance. Stones had been rolled together in a manner to form a little breastwork in his front, so that, had there been any wandering gaze sweeping over the face of the mountain, it was far from probable that it would have detected the presence of a man whose whole form, with the exception of the superior parts, was so effectually concealed.

It would have been difficult to say, whether this secluded being had thus placed himself in order to indulge in some habitual and fancied communication with the little world of the valley, or whether he sat at his post in watchfulness. There was an appearance of each of these occupations in his air; for at times his eye was melancholy and softened, as if his spirit found pleasure in the charities natural to the species; and at others, the brows contracted with sternness, while the lips became more than usually compressed, like those of a man who threw himself on his own innate resolution for support.

The solitude of the place, the air of universal quiet which reigned above, the boundless leafy carpet over which the eye looked from that elevate point, and the breathing stillness of the bosom of the woods, united to give grandeur to the scene. The figure of the tenant of the ravine was as immovable as any other object of the view. It seemed, in all but color and expression, of stone. An elbow was leaning on the little screen in front, and the head was supported by a hand. At the distance of an arrow's flight, the eye might readily have supposed it no more than another of the accidental imitations which had been worn in the rock by the changes of centuries. An hour passed, and scarce a limb had been changed, or a muscle relieved. Either contemplation, or the patient awaiting of some looked-for event, appeared to suspend the ordinary functions of life. At length, an interruption occurred to this extraordinary inaction. A rustling, not louder than that which would have been made by the leap of a squirrel, was first heard in the bushes above; it was succeeded by a crackling of branches, and then a fragment of a rock came bounding down the precipice, until it shot over the head of the still motionless hermit, and fell, with a noise that drew a succession of echoes from the caverns of the place, into the ravine beneath.

Notwithstanding the suddenness of this interruption, and the extraordinary fracas with which it was accompanied, he, who might be supposed to be most affected by it, manifested none of the usual symptoms of fear or surprise. He listened intently, until he last sound had died away, but it was with expectation rather than with alarm. Arising slowly, he looked warily about him, and then walking with a quick step along the ledge which led to his hut, he disappeared through its door. In another minute, however, he was again seen at his former post; a short carabine, such as was then used by mounted warriors, lying across his knee. If doubt or perplexity beset the mind of this individual, at so palpable a sign that the solitude he courted was in danger of being interrupted, it was not of a nature sufficiently strong to disturb the equanimity of his aspect. A second time the branches rustled, and the sounds proceeded from a lower part of the precipice as if the foot that caused the disturbance was in the act of descending. Though no one was visible the nature of the noise could no longer be mistaken. It was evidently the tread of a human foot, for no beast of a weight sufficient to produce so great an impression, would have chosen to rove across a spot where the support of hands was nearly as necessary as that of the other limbs.

"Come forward!" said he who in all but the accessories of dress and hostile preparation might so well be termed a hermit—"I am already here."

The words were not given to the air, for one suddenly appeared on the ledge at the side next the settlement, and within twenty feet of the speaker. When glance met glance, the surprise which evidently took possession of the intruder and of him who appeared to claim a better right to be where they met, seemed mutual. The carabine of th atter, and a musket carried by the former, fell into the dangerous line of aim at the same instant, and in a moment they were thrown upwards again, as if a common impulse controlled them. The resident signed to the other to draw nigher, and then every appearance of hostility disappeared in that sort of familiarity which confidence begets.

"How is it," said the former to his guest, when both were calmly seated behind the little screen of stones, "that thou hast fallen upon this secret place? The foot of stranger hath not often trod these rocks, and no man before thee hath ever descended the precipice."

"A moccason is sure," returned the other with Indian brevity. "My father hath a good eye. He can see very far from the door of his lodge."

"Thou knowest that the men of my color speak often to their Good Spirit, and they do not love to ask his favor in the highways. This place is sacred to his holy name."

The intruder was the young Sachem of the Narragansetts, and he who, notwithstanding this plausible apology, so palpably sought secrecy rather than solitude, was the man that has often been introduced into these pages under the shade of mystery. The instant recognition and the mutual confidence require no further explanation, since enough has already been developed in the course of the narrative, to show that they were no strangers to each other. Still the meeting had not taken place without uneasiness on the one part, and great though admirably veiled surprise on the other. As became his high station and lofty character, the bearing of Conanchet betrayed none of the littleness of a vulgar curiosity He met his ancient acquaintance with the calm dignity of his rank, and it would have been difficult for the most inquiring eye to have detected a wandering glance, a single prying look, or any other sign that he deemed the place at all extraordinary for such an interview. He listened to the little explanation of the other, with grave courtesy, and suffered a short time to elapse before he made any reply.

"The Manitou of the pale-men," he then said "should be pleased with my father. His words are often in the ears of the Great Spirit! The trees and the rocks know them."

"Like all of a sinful and fallen race," returned the stranger with the severe air of the age, "I have much need of my askings. But why dost thou think that my voice is so often heard in this secret place?"

The finger of Conanchet pointed to the worn rock at his feet, and his eye glanced furtively at the beaten path which led between the spot and the door of the lodge.

"A Yengeese hath a hard heel, but it is softer than stone. The hoof of the deer would pass many times, to leave such a trail."

"Thou art quick of eye, Narragansett, and yet thy judgment may be deceived. My tongue is not the only one that speaketh to the God of my people."

The Sachem bent his head slightly, in acquiescence, as if unwilling to press the subject. But his companion was not so easily satisfied, for he felt the consciousness of a fruitless attempt at deception goading him to some plausible means of quieting the suspicions of the Indian.

"That I am now alone, may be matter of pleasure or of accident," he added; "thou knowest that this hath been a busy and a bloody day among the pale-men, and there are dead and dying in their lodges. One who hath no wigwam of his own may have found time to worship by himself."

"The mind is very cunning," returned Conanchet; "it can hear when the ear is deaf—it can see when the eye is shut. My father hath spoken to the Good Spirit, with the rest of his tribe."

As the chief concluded, he pointed significantly towards the distant church, out of which the excited congregation we have described was at that moment pouring into the green and little-trodden street of the hamlet. The other appeared to understand his meaning, and, at the same instant, to feel the folly, as well as the uselessness, of attempting any longer to mislead one that already knew so much of his former mode of life.

"Indian, thou sayest true," he rejoined gloomily "the mind seeth far, and it seeth often in the bitterness of sorrow. My spirit was communing with the spirits of those thou seest, when thy step was first heard; besides thine own, the feet of man never mounted to this place, except it be of those who minister to my bodily wants. Thou sayest true; the mental sight is keen; and far beyond those distant hills, on which the last rays of the setting sun are now shining so gloriously, doth mine often bear me in spirit. Thou wast once my fellow-lodger, youth, and much pleasure had I in striving to open thy young mind to the truths of our race, and to teach thee to speak with the tongue of a Christian; but years have passed away—hark! There cometh one up the path. Hast thou dread of a Yengeese?"

The calm mien with which Conanchet had been listening, changed to a cold smile. His hand had felt for the lock of the musket, some time before his companion had betrayed any consciousness of the approaching footstep; but until questioned, no change of countenance was visible.

"Is my father afraid for his friend?" he asked, pointing in the direction of him who approached. "Is it an armed warrior?"

"No: he cometh with the means of sustaining a burthen that must be borne, until it pleaseth him who knoweth what is good for all his creatures to ease me of it. It may be the parent of her thou hast this day restored to her friends, or it may be the brother; for, at times, I owe this kindness to different members of that worthy family."

A look of intelligence shot across the swarthy features of the chief. His decision appeared taken. Arising, he left his weapon at the feet of his companion, and moved swiftly along the ledge, as if to meet the intruder. In another instant he returned, bearing a little bundle closely enveloped in belts of richly-beaded wampum. Placing the latter gently by the side of the old man, for time had changed the color of the solitary's hair to gray, he said, in a low, quick voice, pointing with significance at what he had done—

"The Messenger will not go back with an empty hand. My father is wise; he will say what is good."

There was little time for further explanation. The door of the hut had scarcely closed on Conanchet, before Mark Heathcote appeared at the point where the path bent around the angle of the precipice.

"Thou knowest what hath passed, and wilt suffer me to depart with brief discourse," said the young man, placing food at the feet of him he came to seek; "ha! what hast here?—didst gain this in the fray of the morning?"

"It is booty that I freely bestow; take it to the house of thy father. It is left with that object. Now tell me of the manner in which death hath dealt with our people, for thou knowest that necessity drove me from among them, so soon as liberty was granted."

Mark showed no disposition to gratify the other's wish. He gazed on the bundle of Conanchet, as if his eye had never before looked on a similar object, and keenly contending passions were playing about a brow that was seldom as tranquil as suited the self-denying habits of the times and country.

"It shall be done, Narragansett!" he said, speaking between his clenched teeth; "it shall be done!" Then turning on his heel, he stalked along the giddy path with a rapidity of stride that kept the other in fearful suspense for his safety, until his active form had disappeared.

The recluse arose, and sought the occupant of his humble abode.

"Come forth," he said, opening the narrow door for the passage of the Chief. "The youth hath departed with thy burthen, and thou art now alone with an ancient associate."

Conanchet reappeared at the summons, but it was with an eye less glowing and a brow less stern than when he entered the little cabin. As he moved slowly to the stone he had before occupied, his step was arrested for a moment, and a look of melancholy regret seemed to be cast at the spot where he had laid the bundle. Conquering his feelings, however, in the habitual self-command of his people, he resumed his seat, with the air of one that was grave by nature, while he appeared to exert no effort in order to preserve the admirable equanimity of his features. A long and thoughtful silence succeeded, and then the solitary spoke.

"We have made a friend of the Narragansett Chief," he said, "and this league with Philip is broken?"

"Yengeese," returned the other, "I am full of the blood of Sachems."

"Why should the Indian and the white do each other this violence? The earth is large, and there is place for men of all colors and of all nations on its surface."

"My father hath found but little," said the other, bestowing such a cautious glance at the narrow limits of his host, as at once betrayed the sarcastic purport of his words, while it equally bespoke the courtesy of his mind.

"A light-minded and vain prince is seated on the throne of a once-godly nation, Chief, and darkness has again come over a land which of late shone with a clear and shining light! The just are made to flee from the habitations of their infancy, and the temples of the elect are abandoned to the abominations of idolatry. Oh England! England! when will thy cup of bitterness be full?—when shall this judgment pass from thee? My spirit groaneth over thy fall—yea, my inmost soul is saddened with the spectacle of thy misery!"

Conanchet was too delicate to regard the glazed eye and flushed forehead of the speaker, but he listened in amazement and in ignorance. Such expressions had often met his ear before, and though his tender years had probably prevented their producing much effect, now, that he again heard them in his manhood, they conveyed no intelligible meaning to his mind. Suddenly laying a finger on the knee of his companion, he said—

"The arm of my father was raised on the side of the Yengeese, to-day; yet they give him no seat at their council-fire!"

"The sinful man, who ruleth in the island whence my people came, hath an arm that is long as his mind is vain. Though debarred from the councils of this valley, Chief, time hath been, when my voice was heard in councils that struck heavily at the power of his race. These eyes have seen justice done on him who gave existence to the double-tongued instrument of Belial, that now governeth a rich and glorious realm!"

"My father hath taken the scalp of a great chief!"

"I helped to take his head!" returned the solitary, a ray of bitter exultation gleaming through the habitual austerity of his brow.

"Come.—The eagle flies above the clouds, that he may move his wings freely. The panther leaps longest on the widest plain; the biggest fish swim in the deep water. My father cannot stretch himself between these rocks. He is too big to lie down in a little wigwam. The woods are wide; let him change the color of his skin, and be a gray head at the council-fire of my nation. The warriors will listen to what he says, for his hand hath done a strong deed!"

"It may not be—it may not be, Narragansett That which hath been generated in the spirit, must abide, and it would be 'easier for the blackamoor to become white, or for the leopard to change his spots,' than for one who hath felt the power of the Lord, to cast aside his gifts. But I meet thy proffers of amity in a charitable and forgiving spirit. My mind is ever with my people; yet is there place for other friendships. Break then this league with the evil-minded and turbulent Philip, and let the hatchet be for ever buried in the path between thy village and the towns of the Yengeese."

"Where is my village? There is a dark place near the islands on the shores of the Great Lake; but I see no lodges."

"We will rebuild thy towns, and people them anew. Let there be peace between us."

"My mind is ever with my people;" returned the Indian, repeating the other's words, with an emphasis that could not be mistaken.

A long and melancholy pause succeeded; and when the conversation was renewed, it had reference to those events which had taken place in the fortunes of each, since the time when they were both tenants of the block-house that stood amid the ancient habitations of the Heathcotes. Each appeared too well to comprehend the character of the other, to attempt any further efforts towards producing a change of purpose; and darkness had gathered about the place, before they arose to enter the hut of the solitary.

CHAPTER XXVII.

"Sleep, thou hast been a grandsire, and begot
A father to me: and thou hast created
A mother and two brothers."

CYMBELINE

THE short twilight was already passed, when old Mark Heathcote ended the evening prayer. The mixed character of the remarkable events of that day had given birth to a feeling, which could find no other relief than that which flowed from the usual zealous, confiding, and exalted outpouring of the spirit. On the present occasion, he had even resorted to an extraordinary, and, what one less devout might be tempted to think, a supererogatory offering of thanksgiving and praise. After dismissing the dependants of the establishment, supported by the arm of his son, he had withdrawn into an inner apartment, and there, surrounded only by those who had the nearest claims on his affections, the old man again raised his voice to laud the Being, who, in the midst of so much general grief, had deigned to look upon his particular race with the eyes of remembrance and of favor. He spoke of his recovered grand-child by name, and he dealt with the whole subject of her captivity among the heathen, and her restoration to the foot of the altar, with the fervor of one who saw the wise decrees of Providence in the event, and with a tenderness of sentiment that age was far from having extinguished. It was at the close of this private and peculiar worship, that we return into the presence of the family.

The spirit of reform had driven those, who se

violently felt its influence, into many usages that, to say the least, were quite as ungracious to the imagination, as the customs they termed idolatrous were obnoxious to the attacks of their own unaccommodating theories. The first Protestants had expelled so much from the service of the altar, that little was left for the Puritan to destroy, without incurring the risk of leaving it naked of its loveliness. By a strange substitution of subtlety for humility, it was thought pharisaical to bend the knee in public, lest the great essential of spiritual worship might be supplanted by the more attainable merit of formula; and while rigid aspects, and prescribed deportments of a new character, were observed with all the zeal of converts, ancient and even natural practices were condemned, chiefly, we believe, from that necessity of innovation which appears to be an unavoidable attendant of all plans of improvement, whether they are successful or the reverse. But though the Puritans refused to bow their stubborn limbs when the eye of man was on them, even while asking boons suited to their own sublimated opinions, it was permitted to assume in private an attitude which was thought to admit of so gross an abuse, inasmuch as it infers a claim to a religious vitality, while in truth the soul might only be slumbering in the security of mere moral pretension.

On the present occasion, they who worshipped in secret had bent their bodies to the humblest posture of devotion. When Ruth Heathcote arose from her knees, it was with a hand clasped in that of the child whom her recent devotion was well suited to make her think had been rescued from a condition far more gloomy than that of the grave. She had used a gentle violence to force the wondering being at her side to join, so far as externals could go, in the prayer; and, now it was ended, she sought the countenance of her daughter, in order to read the impression the scene had produced, with all the solicitude of a Christian, heightened by the tenderest maternal love.

Narra-mattah, as we shall continue to call her, in air, expression, and attitude, resembled one who had a fancied existence in the delusion of some exciting dream. Her ear remembered sounds which had so often been repeated in her infancy, and her memory recalled indistinct recollections of most of the objects and usages that were so suddenly replaced before her eyes; but the former now conveyed their meaning to a mind that had gained its strength under a very different system of theology, and the latter came too late to supplant usages that were rooted in her affections by the aid of all those wild and seductive habits that are known to become nearly unconquerable in those who have long been subject to their influence. She stood, therefore, in the centre of the grave, self-restrained group of her nearest kin, like an alien to their blood, resembling some timid and but half-tamed tenant of the air, that human art had endeavored to domesticate, by placing it in the society of the more tranquil and confiding inhabitants of the aviary.

Notwithstanding the strength of her affections, and her devotion to all the natural duties of her station, Ruth Heathcote was not now to learn the manner in which she was to subdue any violence in their exhibition. The first indulgence of joy and gratitude was over, and in its place appeared the never-tiring, vigilant, engrossing, but regulated watchfulness, which the events would naturally create. The doubts, misgivings, and even fearful apprehensions, that beset her, were smothered in an appearance of satisfaction; and something like gleamings of happiness were again seen playing about a brow that had so long been clouded with an unobtrusive but corroding care.

"And thou recallest thine infancy, my Ruth?" asked the mother, when the respectful period of silence, which ever succeeded prayer in that family, was passed; "thy thoughts have not been altogether strangers to us, but nature hath had its place in thy heart. Tell us, child, of thy wanderings in the forest, and of the sufferings that one so tender must have undergone among a barbarous people. There is pleasure in listening to all thou hast seen and felt, now that we know there is an end to unhappiness."

She spoke to an ear that was deaf to language like this. Narra-mattah evidently understood her words, while their meaning was wrapped in an obscurity that she neither wished to nor was capable of comprehending. Keeping a gaze, in which pleasure and wonder were powerfully blended, on that soft look of affection which beamed from her mother's eye, she felt hurriedly among the folds of her dress, and drawing a belt that was gaily ornamented after the most ingenious fashion of her adopted people, she approached her half-pleased, half-distressed parent, and, with hands that trembled equally with timidity and pleasure, she arranged it around her person in a manner to show its richness to the best advantage. Pleased with her performance, the artless being eagerly sought approbation in eyes that bespoke little else than regret. Alarmed at an expression she could not translate, the gaze of Narra-mattah wandered, as if it sought support against some sensation to which she was a stranger. Whittal Ring had stolen into the room, and missing the customary features of her own cherished home, the looks of the startled creature rested on the countenance of the witless wanderer. She pointed eagerly at the work of her hands, appealing by an eloquent and artless gesture to the taste of one who should know whether she had done well.

"Bravely!" returned Whittal, approaching nearer to the subject of his admiration—"'tis a brave belt, and none but the wife of a Sachem could make so rare a gift!"

The girl folded her arms meekly on her bosom, and again appeared satisfied with herself and with the world.

"Here is the hand of him visible who dealeth in all wickedness," said the Puritan. "To corrupt the heart with vanities, and to mislead the affections by luring them to the things of life, is the guile in which he delighteth. A fallen nature lendeth but too ready aid. We must deal with the child in fervor and watchfulness, or better that her bones were lying by the side of those little ones of thy flock, who are already inheritors of the promise."

Respect kept Ruth silent; but, while she sorrowed over the ignorance of her child, natural affection was strong at her heart. With the tact of a woman and the tenderness of a mother, she both saw and felt that severity was not the means to effect the improvement they desired. Taking a seat herself, she drew her child to her person, and, first imploring silence by a glance at those around her, she proceeded, in a manner that was dictated by the mysterious influence of nature, to fathom the depth of her daughter's mind.

"Come nearer, Narra-mattah;" she said, using the name to which the other would alone answer. "Thou art still in thy youth, my child; but it hath pleased him whose will is law, to have made thee the witness of many changes in this varying life. Tell me if thou recallest the days of infancy, and if thy thoughts ever returned to thy father's house, during those weary years thou wast kept from our view?"

Ruth used gentle force to draw her daughter nearer while speaking, and the latter sunk into that posture from which she had just arisen, kneeling, as she had often done in infancy, at her mother's side. The attitude was too full of tender recollections not to be grateful, and the half-alarmed being of the forest was suffered to retain it during most of the dialogue that followed. But while she was thus obedient in person, by the vacancy or rather wonder of an eye that was so eloquent to express all the emotions and knowledge of which she was the mistress, Narra-mattah plainly manifested that little more than the endearment of her mother's words and manner was intelligible. Ruth saw the meaning of her hesitation; and, smothering the pang it caused, she endeavored to adapt her language to the habits of one so artless.

"Even the gray heads of thy people were once young," she resumed; "and they remember the lodges of their fathers. Does my daughter ever think of the time when she played among the children of the Pale-faces?"

The attentive being at the knee of Ruth listened greedily. Her knowledge of the language of her childhood had been sufficiently implanted before her captivity, and it had been too often exercised by intercourse with the whites, and more particularly with Whittal Ring, to leave her in any doubt of the meaning of what she now heard. Stealing a timid look over a shoulder, she sought the countenance of Martha, and, studying her lineaments for near a minute with intense regard, she laughed aloud in the contagious merriment of an Indian girl.

"Thou hast not forgotten us! That glance at her who was the companion of thy infancy assures me, and we shall soon again possess our Ruth in affection, as we now possess her in the body. I will not speak to thee of that fearful night when the vio lence of the savage robbed us of thy presence, nor of the bitter sorrow which beset us at thy loss; but there is one who must still be known to thee, my child; He who sitteth above the clouds, who holdeth the earth in the hollow of his hand, and who looketh in mercy on all that journey on the path to which his own finger pointeth. Hath he yet a place in thy thoughts? Thou rememberest His Holy Name, and still thinkest of his power?"

The listener bent her head aside, as if to catch the full meaning of what she heard, the shadows of deep reverence passing over a face that had so lately been smiling. After a pause, she audibly murmured the word—

"Manitou."

"Manitou, or Jehovah; God, or King of Kings, and Lord of Lords! it mattereth little which term is used to express his power. Thou knowest him then, and hast never ceased to call upon his name?"

"Narra-mattah is a woman. She is afraid to speak to the Manitou aloud. He knows the voices of the chiefs, and opens his ears when they ask help."

The Puritan groaned, but Ruth succeeded in quelling her own anguish, lest she should disturb the reviving confidence of her daughter.

"This may be the Manitou of an Indian," she said, "but it is not the Christian's God. Thou art of a race which worships differently, and it is proper that thou shouldst call on the name of the Deity of thy fathers. Even the Narragansett teacheth this truth! Thy skin is white, and thy ears should hearken to the traditions of the men of thy blood."

The head of the daughter drooped at this allusion to her color as if she would fain conceal the mortifying truth from every eye; but she had not time for answer ere Whittal Ring drew near, and pointing to the burning color of her cheeks, that were deepened as much with shame as with the heats of an American sun, he said—

"The wife of the Sachem hath begun to change. She will soon be like Nipset, all red—See," he added, laying a finger on a part of his own arm where the sun and the winds had not yet destroyed the original color; "the Evil Spirit poured water into his blood too, but it will come out again. As soon as he is so dark that the Evil Spirit will not know him, he will go on the war-path; and then the lying Pale-faces may dig up the bones of their fathers, and move towards the sun-rise, or his lodge will be lined with hair of the color of a deer!"

"And thou, my daughter! canst thou hear this threat against the people of thy nation—of thy blood—of thy God—without a shudder?"

The eye of Narra-mattah seemed in doubt; still it regarded Whittal with its accustomed look of kindness. The innocent, full of his imaginary glory, raised his hand in exultation, and by gestures that could not easily be misunderstood, he indicated the manner in which he intended to rob his victims of the usual trophy. While the youth was enacting the disgusting but expressive pantomime, Ruth watched the countenance of her child in nearly breathless agony. She would have been relieved by a single glance of disapprobation, by a solitary movement of a rebellious muscle, or by the smallest sign that the tender nature of one so lovely, and otherwise so gentle, revolted at so unequivocal evidence of the barbarous practices of her adopted people. But no Empress of Rome could have witnessed the dying agonies of the hapless gladiator, no consort of a more modern prince could read the bloody list of the victims of her husband's triumph, nor any betrothed fair listen to the murderous deeds of him her imagination had painted as a hero, with less indifference to human suffering, than that with which the wife of the Sachem of the Narragansetts looked on the mimic representation of those exploits which had purchased for her husband a renown so highly prized. It was but too apparent that the representation, rude and savage as it was, conveyed to her mind nothing but pictures in which the chosen companion of a warrior should rejoice. The varying features and answering eye too plainly proclaimed the sympathy of one taught to exult in the success of the combatant; and when Whittal, excited by his own exertions, broke out into an exhibition of a violence more ruthless even than common, he was openly rewarded by another laugh. The soft, exquisitely feminine tones of this involuntary burst of pleasure, sounded in the ears of Ruth like a knell over the moral beauty of her child. Still subduing her feelings, she passed a hand thoughtfully over her own pallid brow, and appeared to muse long on the desolation of a mind that had once promised to be so pure.

The colonists had not yet severed all those natural ties which bound them to the eastern hemisphere. Their legends, their pride, and in many instances their memories, aided in keeping alive a feeling of amity, and it might be added of faith, in favor of the land of their ancestors. With some of their descendants, even to the present hour, the *beau ideal* of excellence, in all that pertains to human qualities and human happiness, is connected with the images of the country from which they sprung. Distance is known to cast a softening mist, equally over the moral and physical vision. The blue outline of mountain which melts into its glowing background of sky, is not more pleasing than the pictures which fancy sometimes draws of less material things; but, as he draws near, the disappointed traveller too often finds nakedness and deformity, where he so fondly imagined beauty only was to be seen. No wonder then that the dwellers of the simple provinces of New-England blended recollections of the country they still called home, with most of their poetical pictures of life. They retained the language, the books, and most of the habits, of the English. But different circumstances, divided interests, and peculiar opinions, were gradually beginning to open those breaches which time has since widened, and which promises soon to leave little in common between the two people, except the same forms of speech and a common origin: it is to be hoped that some charity may be blended with these ties.

The singularly restrained habits of the religionists, throughout the whole of the British provinces, were in marked opposition to the mere embellishments of life. The arts were permitted only as they served its most useful and obvious purposes. With them, music was confined to the worship of God, and, for a long time after the original settlement, the song was never known to lead the mind astray from what was conceived to be the one great object of existence. No verse was sung, but such as blended holy ideas with the pleasures of harmony; nor were the sounds of revelry ever heard within their borders. Still, words adapted to their particular condition had come into use, and though poetry was neither a common nor a brilliant property of the mind, among a people thus disciplined in ascetic practices, it early exhibited its power in quaint versification, that was always intended, though with a success it is almost pardonable to doubt, to redound to the glory of the Deity. It was but a natural enlargement of this pious practice, to adapt some of these spiritual songs to the purposes of the nursery.

When Ruth Heathcote passed her hand thoughtfully across her brow, it was with a painful conviction that her dominion over the mind of her child was sadly weakened, if not lost for ever. But the efforts of maternal love are not easily repulsed. An idea flashed upon her brain, and she proceeded to try the efficacy of the experiment it suggested. Nature had endowed her with a melodious voice, and an ear that taught her to regulate sounds in a manner that seldom failed to touch the heart. She possessed the genius of music, which is melody, unweakened by those exaggerated affectations with which it is often encumbered by what is pretendingly called science. Drawing her daughter nearer to her knee, she commenced one of the songs then much used by the mothers of the Colony, her voice scarcely rising above the whispering of the evening air, in its first notes, but gradually gaining, as she proceeded, the richness and compass that a strain so simple required.

At the first low breathing notes of this nursery song, Narra-mattah became as motionless as if her rounded and unfettered form had been wrought in marble. Pleasure lighted her eyes, as strain succeeded strain; and ere the second verse was ended, her look, her attitude, and every muscle of her ingenuous features, were eloquent in the expression of delight. Ruth did not hazard the experiment without trembling for its result. Emotion imparted feeling to the music, and when, for the third time in the course of her song, she addressed her child, the saw the soft blue eyes that gazed wistfully on her face swimming in tears. Encouraged by this unequivocal evidence of success, nature grew still more powerful in its efforts, and the closing verse was sung to an ear that nestled near her heart, as it had often done during the early years of Narra-mattah while listening to its melancholy melody.

Content was a quiet but an anxious witness of this touching evidence of a reviving intelligence between his wife and child. He best understood the look that beamed in the eyes of the former, while her arms were, with extreme caution, folded around her who still leaned upon her bosom, as if fearful one so timid might be frightened from her security by any sudden or unaccustomed interruption. A minute passed in the deepest silence. Even Whittal Ring was lulled into quiet, and long and sorrowing years had passed since Ruth enjoyed moments of happiness so pure and unalloyed. The stillness was broken by a heavy step in the outer room; a door was thrown open by a hand more violent than common, and then young Mark appeared, his face flushed with exertion, his brow seemingly retaining the frown of battle, and with a tread that betrayed a spirit goaded by some fierce and unwelcome passion. The burthen of Conanchet was on his arm. He laid it upon a table; then pointing, in a manner that appeared to challenge attention, he turned, and left the room as abruptly as he had entered.

A cry of joy burst from the lips of Narra-mattah, the instant the beaded belts caught her eye. The arms of Ruth relaxed their hold in surprise, and before amazement had time to give place to more connected ideas, the wild being at her knee had flown to the table, returned, resumed her former posture, opened the folds of the cloth, and was holding before the bewildered gaze of her mother the patient features of an Indian babe.

It would exceed the powers of the unambitious pen we wield, to convey to the reader a just idea of the mixed emotions that struggled for mastery in the countenance of Ruth. The innate and never-dying sentiment of maternal joy was opposed by all those feelings of pride, that prejudice could not fail to implant even in the bosom of one so meek. There was no need to tell the history of the parentage of the little suppliant, who already looked up into her face, with that peculiar calm which renders his race so remarkable. Though its glance was weakened by infancy, the dark glittering eye of Conanchet was there; there were also to be seen the receding forehead and the compressed lip of the father; but all these marks of his origin were softened by touches of that beauty which had rendered the infancy of her own child so remarkable.

"See!" said Narra-mattah, raising the infant still nearer to the riveted gaze of Ruth; "'tis a Sachem of the red men! The little eagle hath left his nest too soon."

Ruth could not resist the appeal of her beloved. Bending her head low, so as entirely to conceal her own flushed face, she imprinted a kiss on the forehead of the Indian boy. But the jealous eye of the young mother was not to be deceived. Narra-mattah detected the difference between the cold salute and those fervent embraces she had herself received, and disappointment produced a chill about her own heart. Replacing the folds of the cloth with quiet dignity, she arose from her knees, and withdrew in sadness to a distant corner of the room. There she took a seat, and with a glance that might almost be termed reproachful, she commenced a low Indian song to her infant.

"The wisdom of Providence is in this, as in all its dispensations;" whispered Content over the shoulder of his nearly insensible partner. "Had we received her as she was lost, the favor might have exceeded our deservings. Our daughter is grieved that thou turnest a cold eye on her babe."

The appeal was sufficient for one whose affections had been wounded rather than chilled. It recalled Ruth to recollection, and it served at once to dissipate the shades of regret that had been unconsciously permitted to gather around her brow. The displeasure, or it would be more true to term it sorrow, of the young mother was easily appeased A smile on her infant brought the blood back to her heart in a swift and tumultuous current; and Ruth, herself, soon forgot that she had any reason for regret, in the innocent delight with which her own daughter now hastened to display the physical excellence of the boy. From this scene of natural feeling, Content was too quickly summoned by the intelligence that some one without awaited his presence, on business of the last importance to the welfare of the settlement.

CHAPTER XXVIII.

"It will have blood; they say, blood
Will have blood!"

MACBETH.

THE visiters were Dr. Ergot, the Reverend Meek Wolfe, Ensign Dudley, and Reuben Ring. Content found these four individuals seated in an outer room, in a grave and restrained manner, that would have done no discredit to the self-command of an Indian council. He was saluted with those staid and composed greetings which are still much used in the intercourse of the people of the Eastern States of this Republic, and which have obtained for them a reputation, where they are little known, of a want of the more active charities of our nature. But that was peculiarly the age of sublimated doctrines, of self-mortification, and of severe moral government, and most men believed it a merit to exhibit, on all occasions, the dominion of the mind over the mere animal impulses. The usage, which took its rise in exalted ideas of spiritual perfection, has since grown into a habit, which, though weakened by the influence of the age, still exists to a degree that often leads to an erroneous estimate of character.

At the entrance of the master of the house, there was some such decorous silence as that which is known to precede the communications of the aborigines. At length Ensign Dudley, in whom matter, most probably in consequence of its bulk, bore more than an usual proportion to his less material part, manifested some evidences of impatience that the divine should proceed to business. Thus admonished, or possibly conceiving that a sufficient concession had been made to the dignity of man's nature, Meek opened his mouth to speak.

"Captain Content Heathcote," he commenced, with that mystical involution of his subject which practice had rendered nearly inseparable from all his communications; "Captain Content Heathcote, this hath been a day of awful visitations, and of gracious temporal gifts. The heathen hath been smitten severely by the hand of the believer, and the believer hath been made to pay the penalty of his want of faith, by the infliction of a savage agency. Azazel hath been loosened in our village, the legions of wickedness have been suffered to go at large in our fields, and yet the Lord hath remembered his people, and hath borne them through a trial of blood as perilous as was the passage of his chosen nation through the billows of the Red Sea. There is cause of mourning, and cause of joy, in this manifestation of his will; of sorrow that we have merited his anger, and of rejoicing that enough of redeeming grace hath been found to save the Gomorrah of our hearts. But I speak to one trained in spiritual discipline, and schooled in the vicissitudes of the world, and further discourse is not necessary to quicken his apprehension. We will therefore turn to more instant and temporal exercises. Have all of thy household escaped unharmed throughout the strivings of this bloody day?"

"We praise the Lord that such hath been his pleasure," returned Content. "Other than as sorrow hath assailed us through the mourning of friends the blow hath fallen lightly on me and mine."

"Thou hast had thy season; the parent ceaseth to chastise, while former punishments are remembered. But here is Sergeant Ring, with matter to communicate, that may still leave business for thy courage and thy wisdom."

Content turned his quiet look upon the yeoman, and seemed to await his speech. Reuben Ring, who was a man of many solid and valuable qualities, would most probably have been exercising the military functions of his brother-in-law, at that very moment, had he been equally gifted with a fluent discourse. But his feats lay rather in doing than in speaking, and the tide of popularity had in consequence set less strongly in his favor than might have happened had the reverse been the case. The present, however, was a moment when it was necessary to overcome his natural reluctance to speak, and it was not long before he replied to the inquiring glance of his commander's eye.

"The Captain knows the manner in which we scourged the savages at the southern end of the valley," the sturdy yeoman began, "and it is not necessary to deal with the particulars at length. There were six-and-twenty red-skins slain in the meadows, besides as many more that left the ground in the arms of their friends. As for the people, we got a few hurts, but each man came back on his own limbs."

"This is much as the matter hath been reported."

"Then there was a party sent to brush the woods on the trail of the Indians," resumed Reuben, without appearing to regard the interruption. "The scouts broke off in pairs in the duty, and finally men got to searching singly, of which number I was one. The two men of whom there is question——"

"Of what men dost speak?" demanded Content.

"The two men of whom there is question," returned the other, continuing the direct course of his own manner of relating events, without appearing to see the necessity of connecting the threads of his communication; "the men of whom I have spoken to the Minister and the Ensign——"

"Proceed," said Content, who understood his man

"After one of these men was brought to his end I saw no reason for making the day bloodier than it already was, the more especially as the Lord had caused it to begin with a merciful hand which shed its bounties on my own dwelling. Under such an opinion of right-doing, the other was bound and led into the clearings."

"Thou hast made a captive?"

The lips of Reuben scarce severed as he muttered a low assent; but the Ensign Dudley took upon himself the duty of entering into further explanations, which the point where his kinsman left the narrative enabled him to do with sufficient intelligence.

"As the Sergeant hath related," he said, "one of the heathen fell, and the other is now without, waiting a judgment in the matter of his fortune."

"I trust there is no wish to harm him," said Content, glancing an eye uneasily around at his companions. "Strife hath done enough in our settlement this day. The Sergeant hath a right to claim the scalp-bounty, for the man that is slain; but for him that liveth, let there be mercy!"

"Mercy is a quality of heavenly origin," replied Meek Wolfe, "and it should not be perverted to defeat the purposes of heavenly wisdom. Azazel must not triumph, though the tribe of the Narragansetts should be swept with the besom of destruction. Truly, we are an erring and a fallible race, Captain Heathcote; and the greater, therefore, the necessity that we submit, without rebellion, to the inward monitors that are implanted, by grace, to teach us the road of our duty——"

"I cannot consent to shed blood, now that the strife hath ceased," hastily interrupted Content, "Praised be Providence! we are victors; and it is time to lean to councils of charity."

"Such are the deceptions of a short-sighted wisdom!" returned the divine, his dim, sunken eye shining with the promptings of an exaggerated and subtle spirit. "The end of all is good, and we may not, without mortal danger, presume to doubt the suggestions of heavenly gifts. But there is not question here concerning the execution of the captive, since he proffereth to be of service in far greater things than any that can depend on his life or death. The heathen rendered up his liberty with little struggle, and hath propositions that may lead us to profitable conclusion of this day's trials."

"If he can aid in aught that shall shorten the perils and wantonness of this ruthless war, he shall find none better disposed to listen than I."

"He professeth ability to do that service."

"Then, of Heaven's mercy! let him be brought forth, that we counsel on his proposals."

Meek made a gesture to Sergeant Ring, who quitted the apartment for a moment, and shortly after returned followed by his captive. The Indian was one of those dark and malignant-looking savages that possess most of the sinister properties of their condition, with few or none of the redeeming qualities. His eye was lowering and distrustful, bespeaking equally apprehension and revenge; his form of that middling degree of perfection which leaves as little to admire as to condemn, and his attire such as denoted him one who might be ranked among the warriors of a secondary class. Still, in the composure of his mien, the tranquillity of his step, and the self-possession of all his movements, he displayed that high bearing, his people rarely fail to exhibit, ere too much intercourse with the whites begins to destroy their distinctive traits.

"Here is the Narragansett," said Reuben Ring, causing his prisoner to appear in the centre of the room; "he is no chief, as may be gathered from his uncertain look."

"If he effect that of which there hath been question, his rank mattereth little. We seek to stop the currents of blood that flow like running water, in these devoted Colonies."

"This will he do," rejoined the divine, "or we shall hold him answerable for breach of promise."

"And in what doth he profess to aid in stopping the work of death?"

"By yielding the fierce Philip, and his savage ally, the roving Conanchet, to the judgment. Those chiefs destroyed, our temple may be entered in peace, and the voice of thanksgiving shall again rise in our Bethel, without the profane interruption of savage shrieks."

Content started, and even recoiled a step, as he listened to the nature of the proposed peace-offering.

"And have we warranty for such a proceeding, should this man prove true?" he asked, in a voice that sufficiently denoted his own doubts of the propriety of such a measure.

"There is the law, the necessities of a suffering

nature, and God's glory, for our justification," drily returned the divine.

"This outsteppeth the discreet exercise of a delegated authority. I like not to assume so great power, without written mandates for its execution."

"The objection hath raised a little difficulty in my own mind," observed Ensign Dudley; "and as it hath set thoughts at work, it is possible that what I have to offer will meet the Captain's good approbation."

Content knew that his ancient servitor was, though often uncouth in its exhibition, at the bottom a man of humane heart. On the other hand, while he scarce admitted the truth to himself, he had a secret dread of the exaggerated sentiments of his spiritual guide; and he consequently listened to the interruption of Eben, with a gratification he scarcely wished to conceal.

"Speak openly," he said; "when men counsel in a matter of this weight, each standeth on the surety of his proper gifts."

"Then may this business be dispatched without the embarrassment the Captain seems to dread. We have an Indian, who offers to lead a party through the forests to the haunts of the bloody chiefs, therein bringing affairs to the issue of manhood and discretion."

"And wherein do you propose any departure from the suggestions that have already been made?"

Ensign Dudley had not risen to his present rank, without acquiring a suitable portion of the reserve which is so often found to dignify official sentiments. Having ventured the opinion already placed, however vaguely, before his hearers, he was patiently awaiting its effects on the mind of his superior, when the latter, by his earnest and unsuspecting countenance, no less than by the question just given, showed that he was still in the dark as to the expedient the subaltern wished to suggest.

"I think there will be no necessity for making more captives," resumed Eben, "since the one we have appears to create difficulties in our councils. If there be any law in the Colony, which says that men must strike with a gentle hand in open battle, it is a law but little spoken of in common discourse. and though no pretender to the wisdom of legislators, I will make bold to add, it is a law that may as well be forgotten until this outbreaking of the savages shall be quelled."

"We deal with an enemy that never stays his hand at the cry of mercy," observed Meek Wolfe, "and though charity be the fruit of Christian qualities, there is a duty greater than any which belongeth to earth. We are no more than weak and feeble instruments in the hands of Providence, and as such our minds should not be hardened to our inward promptings. If evidence of better feeling could be found in the deeds of the heathen, we might raise our hopes to the completion of things; but the Powers of Darkness still rage in their hearts, and we are taught to believe that the tree is known by its fruits."

Content signed to all to await his return, and left the room. In another minute, he was seen leading his daughter into the centre of the circle. The half-alarmed young woman clasped her swaddled boy to her bosom, as she gazed timidly at the grave faces of the borderers; and her eye recoiled in fear, when its hurried glance met the sunken, glazed, excited, and yet equivocal-looking organ of the Reverend Mr. Wolfe.

"Thou hast said that the savage never hearkens to the cry of mercy," resumed Content; "here is living evidence that thou hast spoken in error. The misfortune that early befell my family, is not unknown to any in this settlement; thou seest in this trembling creature the daughter of our love—her we have so long mourned. The wept of my household is again with us; our hearts have been oppressed, they are now gladdened. God hath returned our child!"

There was a deep, rich pathos in the tones of the father, that affected most of his auditors, though each manifested his sensibilities in a manner suited to his particular habits of mind. The nature of the divine was touched, and all the energies of his severe principles were wanting to sustain him above the manifestation of a weakness that he might have believed derogatory to his spiritual exaltation of character. He therefore sat mute, with hands folded on his knee, betraying the struggles of an awakened sympathy only by a firmer compression of the interlocked fingers, and an occasional and involuntary movement of the stronger muscles of the face. Dudley suffered a smile of pleasure to lighten his broad, open countenance; and the physician, who had hitherto been merely a listener, uttered a few low syllables of admiration of the physical perfection of the being before him, with which there was mingled some evidence of natural good feeling.

Reuben Ring was the only individual who openly betrayed the whole degree of the interest he took in the restoration of the lost female. The stout yeoman arose, and, moving to the entranced Narra-mattah, he took the infant into his large hands, and for a moment the honest borderer gazed at the boy with a wistful and softened eye. Then raising the diminutive face of the infant to his own expanded and bold features, he touched its cheek with his lips, and returned the babe to its mother, who witnessed the whole proceeding in some such tribulation as the startled wren exhibits when the foot of the urchin is seen to draw too near the nest of its young.

"Thou seest that the hand of the Narragansett hath been stayed," said Content, when a deep silence had succeeded this little movement, and speaking in a tone which betrayed hopes of victory.

"The ways of Providence are mysterious!" returned Meek; "wherein they bring comfort to the heart, it is right that we exhibit gratitude; and wherein they are charged with present affliction, it is meet to bow with humbled spirits to their orderings. But the visitations on families are merely—"

He paused, for at that moment a door opened, and a party entered bearing a burthen, which they deposited, with decent and grave respect, on the floor, in the very centre of the room. The unceremonious manner of the entrance, the assured and the common gravity of their air, proclaimed that the villagers felt their errand to be a sufficient apology for this intrusion. Had not the business of the past day naturally led to such a belief, the manner and aspects of those who had borne the burthen would have announced it to be a human body.

"I had believed that none fell in this day's strife, but those who met their end near my own door," said Content, after a long, respectful, and sorrowing pause. "Remove the face-cloth, that we may know on whom the blow hath fallen."

One of the young men obeyed. It was not easy to recognise, through the mutilations of savage barbarity, the features of the sufferer. But a second and steadier look showed the gory and still agonized countenance of the individual who had, that morning, left the Wish-Ton-Wish on the message of the colonial authorities. Even men as practised as those present, in the horrible inventions of Indian cruelty, turned sickening away from a spectacle that was calculated to chill the blood of all who had not become callous to human affliction. Content made a sign to cover the miserable remnants of mortality, and hid his face, with a shudder.

It is not necessary to dwell on the scene that followed. Meek Wolfe availed himself of this unexpected event, to press his plan on the attention of the commanding officer of the settlement, who was certainly far better disposed to listen to his proposals, than before this palpable evidence of the ruthless character of their enemies was presented to his view. Still Content listened with reluctance, nor was it without the intention of exercising an ulterior discretion in the case, that he finally consented to give orders for the departure of a body of men, with the approach of the morning light. As much of the discourse was managed with those half-intelligible allusions that distinguished men of their habits, it is probable that every individual present had his own particular views of the subject: though it is certain, one and all faithfully believed that he was solely influenced by a justifiable regard to his temporal interest, which was in some degree rendered still more praiseworthy by a reference to the service of his Divine Master.

As the party returned, Dudley lingered a moment, alone, with his former master. The face of the honest-meaning Ensign was charged with more than its usual significance; and he even paused a little, after all were beyond hearing, ere he could muster resolution to propose the subject that was so evidently uppermost in his mind.

"Captain Content Heathcote," he at length commenced, "evil or good comes not alone in this life. Thou hast found her that we sought with so much pain and danger, but thou hast found with her more than a Christian gentleman can desire. I am a man of humble station, but I may make bold to know what should be the feelings of a father, whose child is restored, replenished by such an over-bountiful gift."

"Speak plainer," said Content, firmly.

"Then I would say, that it may not be grateful to one who taketh his place among the best in this Colony, to have an offspring with an Indian cross of blood, and over whose birth no rite of Christian marriage hath been said. Here is Abundance, a woman of exceeding usefulness in a newly-settled region, hath made Reuben a gift of three noble boys this very morning. The accession is little known, and less discoursed of, in that the good wife is accustomed to such liberality, and that the day hath brought forth still greater events. Now a child, more or less, to such a woman, can neither raise question among the neighbors, nor make any extraordinary difference to the household. My brother Ring would be happy to add the boy to his stock; and should there be any remarks concerning the color of the younker, at a future day, it should give no reason of surprise, had the whole four been born, on the day of such an inroad, red as Metacom himself!".

Content heard his companion to the end, without interruption. His countenance, for a single instant, as the meaning of the Ensign became unequivocal, reddened with a worldly feeling to which he had long been a stranger; but the painful expression as quickly disappeared, and in its place reigned the meek submission to Providence that habitually characterized his mien.

"That I have been troubled with this vain thought, I shall not deny," he answered; "but the Lor hath given me strength to resist. It is his will tha. one sprung of heathen lineage shall come beneath my roof, and let his will be done! My child, and all that are hers, are welcome."

Ensign Dudley pressed the point no further, and they separated.

CHAPTER XXIX.

"'Tarry a little;—there is something else."
MERCHANT OF VENICE.

WE shift the scene. The reader will transport himself from the valley of the Wish-Ton-Wish, to the bosom of a deep and dark wood.

It may be thought that such scenes have been too often described to need any repetition. Still, as it is possible that these pages may fall into the hands of some who have never quitted the older members of the Union, we shall endeavor to give them a faint impression concerning the appearance of the place to which it has become our duty to transfer the action of the tale.

Although it is certain that inanimate, like animate nature, has its period, the existence of the tree has no fixed and common limit. The oak, the elm, and the linden, the quick-growing sycamore and the tall pine, has each its own laws for the government of its growth, its magnitude, and its duration. By this provision of nature, the wilderness, in the midst of so many successive changes, is always maintained at the point nearest to perfection, since the accessions are so few and gradual as to preserve its character.

The American forest exhibits in the highest degree the grandeur of repose. As nature never does violence to its own laws, the soil throws out the plant which it is best qualified to support, and the eye is not often disappointed by a sickly vegetation. There ever seems a generous emulation in the trees, which is not to be found among others or different families, when left to pursue their quiet existence in the solitude of the fields. Each struggles towards the light, and an equality in bulk and a similarity in form are thus produced, which scarce belong to their distinctive characters. The effect may be easily imagined. The vaulted arches beneath are filled with thousands of high, unbroken columns, which sustain one vast and trembling canopy of leaves. A pleasing gloom and an imposing silence have their interminable reign below, while an outer and another atmosphere seems to rest on the cloud of foliage.

While the light plays on the varying surface of the tree-tops, one sombre and little-varied hue colors the earth. Dead and moss-covered logs; mounds covered with decomposed vegetable substances, the graves of long-past generations of trees; cavities left by the fall of some uprooted trunk; dark fungi, that flourish around the decayed roots of those about to lose their hold, with a few slender and delicate plants of a minor growth, and which best succeed in the shade, form the accompaniments of the lower scene. The whole is tempered, and in summer rendered grateful, by a freshness which equals that of the subterranean vault, without possessing any of its chilling dampness. In the midst of this gloomy solitude, the foot of man is rarely heard. An occasional glimpse of the bounding deer or trotting moose, is almost the only interruption on the earth itself; while the heavy bear or leaping panther, is, at long intervals, met seated on the branches of some venerable tree. There are moments, too, when troops of hungry wolves are found hunting on the trail of the deer; but these are seen rather as exceptions to the stillness of the place, than as accessories that should properly be introduced into the picture. Even the birds are, in common, mute, or when they do break the silence, it is in a discordance that suits the character of their wild abode.

Through such a scene two men were industriously journeying, on the day which succeeded the inroad last described. They marched as wont, one after the other, the younger and more active leading the way through the monotony of the woods, as accurately and as unhesitatingly as the mariner directs his course by the aid of the needle over the waste of waters. He in front was light, agile, and seemingly unwearied; while the one who followed was a man of heavy mould, whose step denoted less practice in the exercise of the forest, and possibly some failing of natural vigor.

"Thine eye, Narragansett, is an unerring compass by which to steer, and thy leg a never-wearied steed;" said the latter, casting the but of his musket on the end of a mouldering log, while he leaned on the barrel for support. "If thou movest on the war-path with the same diligence as thou usest in our errand of peace, well may the Colonists dread thy enmity."

The other turned, and without seeking aid from the gun which rested against his shoulder, he pointed at the several objects he named, and answered—

"My father is this aged sycamore; it leans against the young oak—Conanchet is a straight pine. There is great cunning in gray hairs," added the chief stepping lightly forward until a finger rested on the arm of Submission; "can they tell the time when we shall lie under the moss like a dead hemlock?"

"That exceedeth the wisdom of man. It is enough, Sachem, if when we fall, we may say with truth, that the land we shadowed is no poorer for our growth. Thy bones will lie in the earth where thy fathers trod, but mine may whiten in the vault of some gloomy forest"

The quiet of the Indian's face was disturbed. The pupils of his dark eyes contracted, his nostrils dilated, and his full chest heaved; and then all reposed, like the sluggish ocean, after a vain effort to heave its waters into some swelling wave, during a general calm.

"Fire hath scorched the prints of my father's moccasons from the earth," he said, with a smile that was placid though bitter, "and my eyes cannot find them. I shall die under that shelter," pointing through an opening in the foliage to the blue void; "the falling leaves will cover my bones."

"Then hath the Lord given us a new bond of friendship. There is a yew-tree and a quiet church-yard in a country afar, where generations of my race sleep in their graves. The place is white with stones, that bear the name of——"

Submission suddenly ceased to speak, and when his eye was raised to that of his companion, it was just in time to detect the manner in which the curious interest of the latter changed suddenly to cold reserve, and to note the high courtesy of the air with which the Indian turned the discourse.

"There is water beyond the little hill," he said. "Let my father drink and grow stronger, that he may live to lie in the clearings."

The other bowed, and they proceeded to the spot in silence. It would seem, by the length of time that was now lost in taking the required refreshment, that the travellers had journeyed long and far. The Narragansett ate more sparingly, however, than his companion, for his mind appeared to sustain a weight that was far more grievous than the fatigue which had been endured by the body. Still his composure was little disturbed outwardly, for during the silent repast he maintained the air of a dignified warrior, rather than that of a man whose air could be much affected by inward sorrow When nature was appeased, they both arose, and continued their route through the pathless forest.

For an hour after quitting the spring, the progress of our two adventurers was swift, and uninterrupted by any passing observation or momentary pause. At the end of that time, however, the speed of Conanchet began to slacken, and his eye, instead of maintaining its steady and forward direction, was seen to wander with some of the appearance of indecision.

"Thou hast lost those secret signs by which we have so far threaded the woods," observed his companion; "one tree is like another, and I see no difference in this wilderness of nature; but if thou art at fault, we may truly despair of our object."

"Here is the nest of the eagle," returned Conanchet, pointing at the object he named perched on the upper and whitened branches of a dead pine; "and my father may see the council-tree in this oak—but there are no Wampanoags!"

"There are many eagles in this forest, nor is that oak one that may not have its fellow. Thine eye hath been deceived, Sachem, and some false sign hath led us astray."

Conanchet looked at his companion attentively. After a moment, he quietly asked—

"Did my father ever mistake his path, in going from his wigwam to the place where he looked upon the house of his Great Spirit?"

"The matter of that often-travelled path was different, Narragansett. My foot had worn the rock with many passings, and the distance was a span. But we have journeyed through leagues of forest, and our route hath lain across brook and hill, through brake and morass, where human vision hath not been able to detect the smallest sign of the presence of man."

"My father is old," said the Indian, respectfully.

"His eye is not as quick as when he took the scalp of the Great Chief, or he would know the print of a moccason—see," making his companion observe the mark of a human foot that was barely discernible by the manner in which the dead leaves had been displaced; "his rock is worn, but it is harder than the ground. He cannot tell by its signs who passed, or when."

"Here is truly that which ingenuity may portray as the print of man's foot; but it is alone, and may be some accident of the wind."

"Let my father look on every side; he will see that a tribe hath passed."

"This may be true, though my vision is unequal to detect that thou wouldst show. But if a tribe hath passed, let us follow."

Conanchet shook his head, and spread the fingers of his two hands in a manner to describe the radii of a circle.

"Hugh!" he said, starting even while he was thus significantly answering by gestures, "a moccason comes!"

Submission, who had so often and so recently been arrayed against the savages, involuntarily sought the lock of his carbine. His look and action were menacing, though his roving eye could see no object to excite alarm.

Not so Conanchet. His quicker and more practised vision soon caught a glimpse of the warrior who was approaching, occasionally concealed by the trunks of trees, and whose tread on the dried leaves had first betrayed his proximity. Folding his arms on his naked bosom, the Narragansett chief awaited the coming of the other, in an attitude of calmness and dignity. Neither did he speak nor suffer a muscle to play, until a hand was placed on one of his arms, and he who had drawn near said, in tones of amity and respect—

"The young Sachem hath come to look for his brother?"

"Wampanoag, I have followed the trail, that your ears may listen to the talk of a Pale-face."

The third person in this interview was Metacom He shot a haughty and fierce glance at the stranger, and then turned to his companion in arms, with recovered calmness, to reply.

"Has Conanchet counted his young men since they raised the whoop?" he asked, in the language of the aborigines. "I saw many go into the fields, that never came back. Let the white men die."

"Wampanoag, he is led by the wampum of a Sachem. I have not counted my young men; but I know that they are strong enough to say that what their chief hath promised shall be done."

"If the Yengeese is a friend of my brother, he is welcome. The wigwam of Metacom is open; let him enter it."

Philip made a sign for the others to follow, and led the way to the place he had named.

The spot chosen by Philip for his temporary encampment, was suited to such a purpose. There was a thicket, denser than common, on one of its sides; a steep and high rock protected and sheltered its rear; a swift and wide brook dashed over fragments that had fallen, with time, from the precipice in its front; and towards the setting sun, a whirlwind had opened a long and melancholy glade through the forest. A few huts of brush leaned against the base of the hill, and the scanty implements of their domestic economy were scattered among the habitations of the savages. The whole party did not number twenty; for, as has been said, the Wampanoag had acted latterly more by the agency of his allies, than with the materials of his own proper force.

The three were soon seated on a rock whose foot

was washed by the rapid current of the tumbling water. A few gloomy-looking and fierce Indians watched the conference, in the back-ground.

"My brother hath followed my trail, that my ears may hear the words of a Yengeese," Philip commenced, after a sufficient period had elapsed to escape the imputation of curiosity. "Let him speak."

"I have come singly into the jaws of the lion, restless and remorseless leader of the savages," returned the bold exile, "that you may hear the words of peace. Why hath the son seen the acts of the English so differently from the father? Massassoit was a friend of the persecuted and patient pilgrims who have sought rest and refuge in this Bethel of the faithful; but thou hast hardened thy heart to their prayers, and seekest the blood of those who wish thee no wrong. Doubtless thy nature is one of pride and mistaken vanities, like that of all thy race, and it hath seemed needful to the vain-glory of thy name and nation to battle against men of a different origin. But know there is one who is master of all here on earth, as he is King of Heaven! It is his pleasure that the sweet savor of his worship should arise from the wilderness. His will is law, and they that would withstand do but kick against the pricks. Listen then to peaceful counsels, that the land may be parcelled justly to meet the wants of all, and the country be prepared for the incense of the altar."

This exhortation was uttered in a deep and almost unearthly voice, and with a degree of excitement that was probably increased by the intensity with which the solitary had lately been brooding over his peculiar opinions, and the terrible scenes in which he had so recently been an actor. Philip listened with the high courtesy of an Indian prince. Unintelligible as was the meaning of the speaker, his countenance betrayed no gleaming of impatience, his lip no smile of ridicule. On the contrary, a noble and lofty gravity reigned in every feature; and ignorant as he was of what the other wished to say, his attentive eye and bending head expressed every wish to comprehend.

"My pale friend hath spoken very wisely," he said, when the other ceased to speak. "But he doth not see clearly in these woods; he sits too much in the shade. His eye is better in a clearing. Metacom is not a fierce beast. His claws are worn out, his legs are tired with travelling. He cannot jump far. My pale friend wants to divide the land. Why trouble the Great Spirit to do his work twice? He gave the Wampanoags their hunting-grounds, and places on the salt lake to catch their fish and clams, and he did not forget his children the Narragansetts. He put them in the midst of the water, for he saw that they could swim. Did he forget the Yengeese? or did he put them in a swamp, where they would turn into frogs and lizards!"

"Heathen, my voice shall never deny the bounties of my God! His hand hath placed my fathers in a fertile land, rich in the good things of the world, fortunate in position, sea-girt and impregnable. Happy is he who can find justification in dwelling within its borders!"

An empty gourd lay on the rock at the side of Metacom. Bending over the stream, he filled it to the brim with water, and held the vessel before the eyes of his companions.

"See," he said, pointing to the even surface of the fluid: "so much hath the Great Spirit said it shall hold. "Now," he added, filling the hollow of the other hand from the brook, and casting its contents into the gourd, "now my brother knows that some must come away. It is so with his country There is no longer room in it for my pale friend."

"Did I attempt to deceive thine ears with this

tale, I should lay falsehood to my soul. We are many, and sorry am I to say that some among us are like unto them that were called "Legion." But to say that there is not still place for all to die where they are born, is to utter damning untruth."

"The land of the Yengeese is then good—very good," returned Philip; "but their young men like one that is better."

"Thy nature, Wampanoag, is not equal to comprehend the motives which have led us hither, and our discourse is getting vain."

"My brother Conanchet is a Sachem. The leaves that fall from the trees of his country, in the season of frosts, blow into my hunting-grounds. We are neighbors and friends," slightly bending his head to the Narragansett. "When a wicked Indian runs from the islands to the wigwams of my people, he is whipt and sent back. We keep the path between us open, only for honest red men."

Philip spoke with a sneer, that his habitual loftiness of manner did not conceal from his associate chief, though it was so slight as entirely to escape the observation of him who was the subject of his sarcasm. The former took the alarm, and for the first time during the dialogue did he break silence.

"My pale father is a brave warrior," said the young Sachem of the Narragansetts. "His hand took the scalp of the Great Sagamore of his people!"

The countenance of Metacom changed instantly In place of the ironical scorn that was gathering about his lip, its expression became serious and respectful. He gazed steadily at the hard and weather beaten features of his guest, and it is probable that words of higher courtesy than any he had yet used would have fallen from him, had not, at that moment, a signal been given, by a young Indian set to watch on the summit of the rock, that one approached. Both Metacom and Conanchet appeared to hear this cry with some uneasiness. Neither however arose, nor did either betray such evidence of alarm as denoted a deeper interest in the interruption, than the circumstances might very naturally create A warrior was shortly seen entering the encampment, from the side of the forest which was known to lie in the direction of the Wish-Ton-Wish.

The moment Conanchet saw the person of the newly-arrived man, his eye and attitude resumed their former repose, though the look of Metacom still continued gloomy and distrustful. The difference in the manner of the chiefs was not however sufficiently strong to be remarked by Submission, who was about to resume the discourse, when the new-comer moved past the cluster of warriors in the encampment, and took his seat near them, on a stone so low, that the water laved his feet. As usual there was no greeting between the Indians for some moments, the three appearing to regard the arrival as a mere thing of course. But the uneasiness of Metacom prompted a communication sooner than common.

"Mohtucket," he said, in the language of their tribe, "hath lost the trail of his friends. We thought the crows of the pale-men were picking his bones!"

"There was no scalp at his belt, and Mohtucket was ashamed to be seen among the young men with an empty hand."

"He remembered that he had too often come back without striking a dead enemy," returned Metacom, about whose firm mouth lurked an expression of ill-concealed contempt. "Has he now touched a warrior?"

The Indian, who was merely a man of the inferior class, held up the trophy which hung at his girdle to the examination of his chief. Metacom looked at the disgusting object with the calmness and nearly with the interest, that a virtuoso would lavish on an antique memorial of some triumph of former ages. His finger was thrust through a hole in the skin, and then, while he resumed his former position, he observed drily—

"A bullet hath hit the head. The arrow of Mohtucket doth little harm!"

"Metacom hath never looked on his young man like a friend, since the brother of Mohtucket was killed."

The glance that Philip cast at his underling, though it was not unmingled with suspicion, was one of princely and savage scorn. Their white auditor had not been able to understand the discourse, but the dissatisfaction and uneasiness of the eyes of both were too obvious not to show that the conference was far from being amicable.

"The Sachem hath discontent with his young man," he observed, "and from this may he understand the nature of that which leadeth many to quit the land of their fathers, beneath the rising sun, to come to this wilderness in the west. If he will now listen, I will touch further on the business of my errand, and deal more at large with the subject we have but so lightly skimmed."

Philip manifested attention. He smiled on his guest, and even bowed his assent to the proposal; still his keen eye seemed to read the soul of his subordinate, through the veil of his gloomy visage. There was a play of the fingers of his right hand, when the arm fell from its position across his bosom to his thigh, as if they itched to grasp the knife whose buck-horn handle lay within a few inches of their reach. Yet his air to the white man was composed and dignified. The latter was again about to speak, when the arches of the forest suddenly rung with the report of a musket. All in and near the encampment sprung to their feet at the well-known sound, and yet all continued as motionless as if so many dark but breathing statues had been planted there. The rustling of leaves was heard, and then the body of the young Indian, who had been posted on the rock, rolled to the edge of the precipice, whence it fell, like a log, on the yielding roof of one of the lodges beneath. A shout issued from the forest behind, a volley roared among the trees, and glancing lead was whistling through the air, and cutting twigs from the undergrowth on every side. Two more of the Wampanoags were seen rolling on the earth, in the death-agony.

The voice of Annawon was heard in the encampment, and at the next instant the place was deserted.

During this startling and fearful moment, the four individuals near the stream were inactive. Conanchet and his Christian friend stood to their arms, but it was rather as men cling to the means of defence in moments of great jeopardy, than with any intention of offensive hostilities. Metacom seemed undecided. Accustomed to receive and inflict surprises, a warrior so experienced could not be disconcerted; still he hesitated as to the course he ought to take. But when Annawon, who was nearer the scene, sounded the signal of retreat, he sprung towards the returned straggler, and with a single blow of his tomahawk brained the traitor. Glances of fierce revenge, and of inextinguishable though disappointed hatred, were exchanged between the victim and his chief, as the former lay on the rock gasping for breath; and then the latter turned in his tracks, and raised the dripping weapon over the head of the white man.

"Wampanoag, no!" said Conanchet, in a voice of thunder. "Our lives are one".

Philip hesitated. Fierce and dangerous passions were struggling in his breast, but the habitual self-command of the wily politician of those woods prevailed. Even in that scene of blood and alarm, he smiled on his powerful and fearless young ally; then pointing to the deepest shades of the forest, he bounded towards them with the activity of a deer.

CHAPTER XXX.

"But, peace be with him!
That life is better life, past fearing death,
Than that which lives to fear."
MEASURE FOR MEASURE.

COURAGE is both a comparative and an improvable virtue. If the fear of death be a weakness common to the race, it is one that is capable of being diminished by frequent exposure, and even rendered extinct by reflection. It was therefore with sensibilities entirely changed from their natural course, that the two individuals who were left alone by the retreat of Philip, saw the nature and the approach of the danger that now beset them. Their position near the brook had so far protected them from the bullets of the assailants; but it was equally obvious to both, that in a minute or two the Colonists would enter an encampment that was already deserted. Each, in consequence, acted according to those opinions which had been fostered by the habits of their respective lives.

As Conanchet had no act of vengeance, like that which Metacom had performed, immediately before his eyes, he had, at the first alarm, given all his faculties to the nature of the attack. The first minute was sufficient to understand its character and the second enabled him to decide.

"Come," he said hastily, but with perfect self-possession, pointing as he spoke to the swift-running stream at his feet; "we will go with the water; let the marks of our trail run before."

Submission hesitated. There was something like haughty military pride in the stern determination of his eye, which seemed reluctant to incur th disgrace of a flight so unequivocal, and, as he might have believed, so unworthy of his character.

"No, Narragansett!" he answered; "flee for thy life, but leave me to reap the harvest of my deeds. They can but leave my bones by the side of those of this traitor at my feet."

The mien of Conanchet was neither excited nor displeased. He quietly drew the corner of his light robe over a shoulder, and was about to resume his seat on the stone from which he had but a minute before arisen, when his companion again urged him to fly.

"The enemies of a chief must not say that he led his friend into a trap, and that when his leg was fast he ran away himself, like a lucky fox. If my brother stays to be killed, Conanchet will be found near him."

"Heathen, heathen!" returned the other, moved nearly to tears by the loyalty of his guide; "many a Christian man might take lessons from thy faith. Lead on—I will follow, at the utmost of my speed."

The Narragansett sprung into the brook, and took its downward course—a direction opposite to that which Philip had chosen. There was wisdom in this expedient, for though their pursuers might see that the water was troubled, there was no certainty as to the direction of the fugitives. Conanchet had foreseen this little advantage, and, with the instinctive readiness of his people, he did not fail to make it of service. Metacom had been influenced by the course taken by his warriors, who had retired under shelter of the rocks.

Ere the two fugitives had gone any great distance, they heard the shouts of their enemies in the encampment; and soon after, scattering shot announced that Philip had already rallied his people to resistance. There was an assurance of safety in the latter circumstance, which caused them to relax their speed.

"My foot is not as active as in days that are past," said Submission; "we will therefore recover strength while we may, lest we be yet taken at emergency. Narragansett, thou hast ever kept thy faith with me, and come of what race or worship in what manner thou mayst, there is one to remember it."

"My father looked with the eye of a friend on the Indian boy, that was kept like a young bear in a cage. He taught him to speak with the tongue of a Yengeese."

"We passed weary months together in our prison, Chief; and Apollyon must have been strong in a heart, to resist the opportunity of friendship in such a situation. But, even there, my confidence and care were repaid, for without thy mysterious hints, gathered from signs thou hadst gleaned thyself during the hunt, it would not have been in my power to warn my friends that thy people contemplated an attack, the unhappy night of the burning. Narragansett, we have done many acts of kindness, each in his own fashion, and I am ready to confess this last not to be the least of thy favors Though of white blood and of Christian origin, I can almost say that my heart is Indian."

"Then die an Indian's death!" shouted a voice, within twenty feet of the spot where they were wading down the stream.

The menacing words were rather accompanied

than seconded by a shot, and Submission fell. Conanchet cast his musket into the water, and turned to raise his companion.

"It was merely age dealing with the slippery stones of the brook;" said the latter, as he recovered his footing. "That had well-nigh been a fatal discharge! but God, for his own purpose, hath still averted the blow."

Conanchet did not speak. Seizing his gun, which lay at the bottom of the stream, he drew his friend after him to the shore, and plunged into the thicket that lined its banks. Here they were momentarily protected from missiles. But the shouts that succeeded the discharge of the muskets, were accompanied by yells that he knew to proceed from Pequots and Mohegans, tribes that were in deadly hostility to his own people. The hope of concealing their trail from such pursuers was not to be indulged, nd for his companion to escape by flight he knew .o be impossible. There was no time to lose. In such emergencies, with an Indian, thought takes the character of instinct. The fugitives stood at the foot of a sapling, whose top was completely concealed by masses of leaves, which belonged to the under-brush that clustered around its trunk. Into this tree he assisted Submission to ascend, and then, without explaining his own views, he instantly left the spot, rendering his own trail as broad and perceptible as possible, by beating down the bushes as he passed.

The expedient of the faithful Narragansett wa completely successful. Before he had got a hundred yards from the place, he saw the foremost of the hostile Indians hunting like blood-hounds on his footsteps. His movement was slow, until he saw that, having his person in view, all of the pursuers had passed the tree. Then, the arrow parting from the bow was scarce swifter than his flight.

The pursuit now partook of all the exciting incidents and ingenious expedients of an Indian chase. Conanchet was soon hunted from his cover, and obliged to trust his person in the more open parts of the forest. Miles of hill and ravine, of plain, of rocks, of morass and stream, were crossed, and still the trained warrior held on his way, unbroken in spirit and scarce wearied in limb. The merit of a savage, in such an employment, rests more on his bottom than on his speed. The three or four Colonists, who had been sent with the party of amicable Indians to intercept those who might attempt to escape down the stream, were early thrown out; and the struggle was now entirely between the fugitive and men equally practised in limb and ingenious in expedient.

The Pequots had a great advantage in their number. The frequent doublings of the fugitive kept the chase within the circle of a mile, and as each of his enemies tired, there were always fresh pursuers to take his place. In such a contest, the result could not be questionable. After more than two hours of powerful exertion, the foot of Conanchet began to fail, and his speed very sensibly to flag. Exhausted by efforts that had been nearly supernatural, the breathless warrior cast his person prostrate on the earth, and lay for several minutes as if he were dead.

During this breathing-time, his throbbing pulses grew more calm, his heart beat less violently, and the circulation was gradually returning to the tranquil flow of nature in a state of rest. It was at this moment, when his energies were recruited by rest, that the chief heard the tread of the moccasons on his trail. Rising, he looked back on the course over which he had just passed with so much pain. But a single warrior was in view. Hope for an instant regained the ascendency, and he raised his musket to fell his approaching adversary. The aim was cool, long, and it would have been fatal, had not the useless tick of the lock reminded him of the condition of the gun. He cast the wet and unserviceable piece away, and grasped his tomahawk; but a band of Pequots rushed in to the rescue, rendering resistance madness. Perceiving the hopelessness of his situation, the Sachem of the Narragansetts dropped his tomahawk, loosened his belt, and advanced unarmed, with a noble resignation, to meet his foes. In the next instant, he was their prisoner.

"Bring me to your chief," said the captive, haughtily, when the common herd into whose hands he had fallen would have questioned him on the subject of his companions and of his own fate. "My tongue is used to speak with Sachems."

He was obeyed, and before an hour had passed, the renowned Conanchet stood confronted with his most deadly enemy.

The place of meeting was the deserted encampment of the band of Philip. Here most of the pursuers had already assembled, including all of the Colonists who had been engaged in the expedition. The latter consisted of Meek Wolfe, Ensign Dudley, Sergeant Ring, and a dozen private men of the village.

The result of the enterprise was, by this time, generally known. Though Metacom, its principal object, had escaped; yet, when it was understood that the Sachem of the Narragansetts had fallen into their hands. there was not an individual of the party who did not think his personal risk more than amply compensated. Though the Mohegans and Pequots restrained their exultation, lest the pride of their captive should be soothed by such an evidence of his importance, the white men drew around the prisoner with an interest and a joy they did not care to conceal. Still, as he had yielded to an Indian, there was an affectation of leaving the chief to the clemency of his conquerors. Perhaps some deeply-pondered scheme of policy had its influence in this act of seeming justice.

When Conanchet was placed in the centre of the curious circle, he found himself immediately in presence of the principal chief of the tribe of the Mohegans. It was Uncas, son of that Uncas whose fortunes had also prevailed, aided by the whites, in the conflict with his father, the hapless but noble Miantonimoh. Fate had now decreed, that the same evil star, which had governed the destinies of the ancestor, should extend its influence to the second generation.

The race of Uncas, though weakened of its power, and shorn of much of its peculiar grandeur, by a vicious alliance with the English, still retained most of the fine qualities of savage heroism. He, who now stood forth to receive his captive, was a warrior of middle age, of just proportions, of a grave though fierce aspect, and of an eye and countenance that expressed all those contradictory traits of character which render the savage warrior almost as admirable as he is appalling. Until this moment, the rival chieftains had never met, except in the confusion of battle. For a few minutes, neither spoke. Each stood regarding the fine outlines, the eagle eye, the proud bearing, and the severe gravity, of the other, in secret admiration, but with a calmness so immovable, as entirely to conceal the workings of his thoughts. At length, they began to assume miens suited to the part each was to enact in the coming scene. The countenance of Uncas became ironical and exulting, while that of his captive grew still more cold and unconcerned.

"My young men," said the former, "have taken a fox skulking in the bushes. His legs were very long; but he had no heart to use them."

Conanchet folded his arms on his bosom, and the glance of his quiet eye seemed to tell his enemy, that devices so common were unworthy of them both. The other either understood its meaning, or loftier feelings prevailed; for he added, in a better taste—

"Is Conanchet tired of his life, that he comes among my young men?"

"Mohican," said the Narragansett chief, "he has been there before; if Uncas will count his warriors, he will see that some are wanting."

"There are no traditions among the Indians of the islands!" said the other, with an ironical glance at the chiefs near him, "They have never heard of Miantonimoh; they do not know such a field as the Sachem's plain!"

The countenance of the prisoner changed. For a single instant, it appeared to grow dark, as if a deep shadow were cast athwart it; and then every feature rested, as before, in dignified repose. His conqueror watched the play of his lineaments, and when he thought nature was getting the ascendancy, exultation gleamed about his own fierce eye; but when the self-possession of the Narragansett returned, he affected to think no more of an effort that had been fruitless.

"If the men of the islands know little," he continued, it is not so with the Mohicans. There was once a great Sachem among the Narragansetts; he was wiser than the beaver, swifter than the moose, and more cunning than the red fox. But he could not see into to-morrow. Foolish counsellors told him to go upon the war-path against the Pequots and Mohicans. He lost his scalp; it hangs in the smoke of my wigwam. We shall see if it will know the hair of its son. Narragansett, here are wise men of the Pale-faces; they will speak to you. If they offer a pipe, smoke: for tobacco is not plenty with your tribe."

Uncas then turned away, leaving his prisoner to the interrogatories of his white allies.

"Here is the look of Miantonimoh, Sergeant Ring," observed Ensign Dudley to his wife's brother, after he had contemplated for a reasonable time the features of the prisoner. "I see the eye and the tread of the father, in this young Sachem. And more, Sergeant Ring; the chief favors the boy we picked up in the fields some dozen years agone, and kept in the block for the matter of many months, caged like a young panther. Hast forgotten the night, Reuben, and the lad, and the block? A fiery oven is not hotter than that pile was getting, before we dove into the earth. I never fail to think of it, when the good Minister is dealing powerfully with the punishments of the wicked, and the furnaces of Tophet!"

The silent yeoman comprehended the disconnected allusions of his relative, nor was he slow in seeing the palpable resemblance between their prisoner and the Indian boy whose person had once been so familiar to his eye. Admiration and surprise were blended, in his honest face, with an expression that appeared to announce deep regret. As neither of these individuals, however, was the principal personage of their party, each was fain to remain an attentive and an interested observer of that which followed.

"Worshipper of Baal!" commenced the sepulchral voice of the divine; "it has pleased the King of Heaven and earth to protect his people! The triumph of thy evil nature hath been short, and now cometh the judgment!"

These words were uttered to ears that affected deafness. In the presence of his most deadly foe, and a captive, Conanchet was not a man to suffer his resolution to waver. He looked coldly and vacantly on the speaker, nor could the most suspicious or the most practised eye have detected in his mien his knowledge of the English language. Deceived by the stoicism of the prisoner, Meek muttered a few words, in which the Narragansett was strangely dealt by, denunciations and petitions in his favor being blended in the quaint and exaggerated fashions of the times; and then he submitted to the interference of those present, who were charged with the duty of deciding on the fate of the Indian.

Although Eben Dudley was the principal and the efficient military man in this little expedition from the valley, he was accompanied by those whose authority was predominant in all matters that did not strictly appertain to the executive portion of the duty. Commissioners, named by the Government of the Colony, had come out with the party, clothed with power to dispose of Philip, should that dreaded chief, as was expected, fall into the hands of the English. To these persons the fate of Conanchet was now referred.

We shall not detain the narrative to dwell on the particulars of the council. The question was gravely considered, and it was decided with a deep and conscientious sense of the responsibility of those who acted as judges. Several hours were passed in deliberation, Meek opening and closing the deliberations by solemn prayers. The judgment was then announced to Uncas, by the divine himself.

"The wise men of my people have consulted together in the matter of this Narragansett," he said, "and their spirits have wrestled powerfully with the subject. In coming to their conclusion, if it wear the aspect of time-serving, let all remember, the Providence of Heaven hath so interwoven the interests of man with its own good purposes, that to the carnal eye they may outwardly seem to be inseparable. But that which is here done is done in good faith to our ruling principle, which is good faith to thee and to all others who support the altar in this wilderness. And herein is our decision: We commit the Narragansett to thy justice, since it is evident that while he is at large, neither thou, who art a feeble prop to the church in these regions, nor we, who are its humble and unworthy servitors, are safe. Take him, then, and deal with him according to thy wisdom. We place limits to thy power, in only two things. It is not meet that any born of humanity, and having human sensibilities, should suffer more in the flesh than may be necessary to the ends of duty; we therefore decree that thy captive shall not die by torture; and, for the better security of this our charitable decision, two of our number shall accompany thee and him to the place of execution; it being always supposed, it is thy intention to inflict the pains of death. Another condition of this concession to a foreordered necessity, is, that a Christian minister may be at hand, in order that the sufferer may depart with the prayers of one accustomed to lift his voice in petitions to the footstool of the Almighty."

The Mohegan chief heard this sentence with deep attention. When he found he was to be denied the satisfaction of proving, or perhaps of overcoming, the resolution of his enemy, a deep cloud passed across his swarthy visage. But the strength of his tribe had long been broken, and to resist would have been as unprofitable as to repine would have been unseemly. The conditions were therefore accepted, and preparations were accordingly made among the Indians to proceed to judgment.

These people had few contradictory principles to appease, and no subtleties to distract their decision. Direct, fearless, and simple in all their practices, they did little more than gather the voices of the chiefs, and acquaint their captive with the result. They knew that fortune had thrown an implacable enemy into their hands, and they believed that self-preservation demanded his life. To them it mattered little whether he had arrows in his hands, or had yielded himself an unarmed prisoner. He knew the risk he ran in submitting, and he had probably consulted his own character, rather than their benefit, in throwing away his arms. They therefore pronounced the judgment of death against their captive merely respecting the decree of their white allies, which had commanded them to spare the torture.

So soon as this determination was known, the Commissioners of the Colony hastened away from the spot with consciences that required some aid from the stimulus of their subtle doctrines, in order to render them quiet. They were, however, ingenious casuists; and as they hurried along their return path, most of the party were satisfied that they had rather manifested a merciful interposition, than exercised any act of positive cruelty.

During the two or three hours which had passed in these solemn and usual preparations, Conanchet was seated on a rock, a close but apparently an unmoved spectator of all that passed. His eye was mild, and at times melancholy; but its brightness and its steadiness remained unimpaired. When his sentence was announced, it exhibited no change; and he saw all the pale-men depart, with the calm ness he had maintained throughout. It was only as Uncas, attended by the body of his party and the two white superintendents who had been left, approached, that his spirit seemed to awaken.

"My people have said that there shall be no more wolves in the woods," said Uncas; "and they have commanded our young men to slay the hungriest of them all."

"It is well!" coldly returned the other

A gleaming of admiration, and perhaps of humanity, came over the grim countenance of Uncas, as he gazed at the repose which reigned in the firm features of his victim. For an instant, his purpose wavered.

"The Mohicans are a great tribe!" he added; "and the race of Uncas is getting few. We will paint our brother so that the lying Narragansetts shall not know him, and he will be a warrior on the main land."

This relenting of his enemy had a corresponding effect on the generous temper of Conanchet. The lofty pride deserted his eye, and his look became milder and more human. For a minute, intense thought brooded around his brow; the firm muscles of his mouth played a little, though scarcely enough to be seen, and then he spoke.

"Mohican," he said, "why should your young men be in a hurry? My scalp will be the scalp of a Great Chief to-morrow. They will not take two, should they strike their prisoner now."

"Hath Conanchet forgotten any thing, that he is not ready?"

"Sachem, he is always ready—But"——he paused, and spoke in tones that faltered,—"does a Mohican live alone?"

"How many suns doth the Narragansett ask?"

"One: when the shadow of that pine points towards the brook, Conanchet will be ready. He will then stand in the shade, with naked hands."

"Go," said Uncas, with dignity; "I have heard the words of a Sagamore."

Conanchet turned, and passing swiftly through the silent crowd, his person was soon lost in the surrounding forest.

CHAPTER XXXI.

"Therefore, lay bare your bosom."
MERCHANT OF VENICE.

THE night that succeeded was wild and melancholy. The moon was nearly full, but its place in the heavens was only seen, as the masses of vapor which drove through the air occasionally opened, suffering short gleams of fitful light to fall on the scene below. A south-western wind rather moaned than sighed through the forest, and there were moments when its freshness increased, till every leaf seemed a tongue, and each low plant appeared to be endowed with the gift of speech. With the exception of these imposing and not unpleasing natural sounds, there was a solemn quiet in and about the village of the Wish-Ton-Wish. An hour before the moment when we resume the action of the legend, the sun had settled into the neighboring forest, and most of its simple and laborious inhabitants had already sought their rest.

The lights however still shone through many of the windows of the "Heathcote house," as, in the language of the country, the dwelling of the Puritan was termed. There was the usual stirring industry in and about the offices, and the ordinary calm was reigning in the superior parts of the habitation. A solitary man was to be seen on its piazza. It was young Mark Heathcote, who paced the long and narrow gallery, as if impatient of some interruption to his wishes.

The uneasiness of the young man was of short continuance; for, ere he had been many minutes at his post, a door opened, and two light and timid forms glided out of the house.

"Thou hast not come alone, Martha," said the youth, half-displeased. "I told thee that the matter I had to say was for thine own ear."

"It is our Ruth. Thou knowest, Mark, that she may not be left alone, for we fear her return to the forest. She is like some ill-tamed fawn, that would be apt to leap away at the first well-known sound from the woods. Even now, I fear that we are too much asunder.

"Fear nothing; my sister fondles her infant, and she thinketh not of flight; thou seest I am here to intercept her, were such her intention. Now speak with candor, Martha, and say if thou meanest in sincerity that the visits of the Hartford gallant were less to thy liking than most of thy friends have believed?"

"What I have said cannot be recalled."

"Still it may be repented of."

"I do not number the dislike I may feel for the young man among my failings. I am too happy, here, in this family, to wish to quit it. And now that our sister——there is one speaking to her at this moment, Mark!"

"'Tis only the innocent," returned the young man, glancing his eye to the other end of the piazza. "They confer often together. Whittal hath just come in from the woods, whither he is much inclined to pass an hour or two, each evening. Thou wast saying that now we have our sister—?"

"I feel less desire to change my abode."

"Then why not stay with us for ever, Martha?"

"Hist!" interrupted his companion, who, though conscious of what she was about to listen to, shrunk, with the waywardness of human nature, from the very declaration she most wished to hear, "hist—there was a movement. Ah! our Ruth and Whittal are fled!"

"They seek some amusement for the babe--they are near the out-buildings. Then why not accept a right to remain for ever——"

"It may not be, Mark," cried the girl wresting her hand from his grasp; "they are fled!"

Mark reluctantly released his hold, and followed to the spot where his sister had been sitting. She was, in truth, gone; though some minutes passed before even Martha seriously believed that she had disappeared without an intention of returning. The agitation of both rendered the search ill-directed and uncertain, and there was perhaps a secret satisfaction in prolonging their interview even in this vague manner, that prevented them for some time from giving the alarm. When that moment did come, it was too late. The fields were examined, the orchards and out-houses thoroughly searched, without any traces of the fugitives. It would have been useless to enter the forest in the darkness, and all that could be done in reason, was to set a watch during the night, and to prepare for a more active and intelligent pursuit in the morning.

But, long before the sun arose, the small and melancholy party of the fugitives threaded the woods at such a distance from the valley, as would have rendered the plan of the family entirely nugatory. Conanchet had led the way over a thousand forest knolls, across water-courses, and through dark glens, followed by his silent partner, with an industry that would have baffled the zeal of even those from whom they fled. Whittal Ring, bearing the infant on his back, trudged with unwearied step in the rear. Hours had passed in this manner, and not a syllable had been uttered by either of the three. Once or twice, they had stopped at some spot where water, limpid as the air, gushed from the rocks; and, drinking from the hollows of their hands, the march had been resumed with the same speechless industry as before.

At length Conanchet paused. He studied the position of the sun, gravely, and took a long and anxious look at the signs of the forest, in order that he might not be deceived in its quarter. To an unpractised eye, the arches of the trees, the leaf-covered arth, and the mouldering logs, would have seemed everywhere the same. But it was not easy to deceive one so trained in the woods. Satisfied equally with the progress he had made, and with the hour the chief signed to his two companions to place themselves at his side, and took a seat on a low shelf of rock, that thrust its naked head out of the side of a hill.

For many minutes, after all were seated, no one broke the silence. The eye of Narra-mattah sought the countenance of her husband, as the eye of wo man seeks instruction from the expression of features that she has been taught to revere; but still she spoke not. The innocent laid the patient babe at the feet of its mother, and imitated her reserve.

"Is the air of the woods pleasant to the Honeysuckle, after living in the wigwam of her people?" asked Conanchet, breaking the long silence. "Can a flower, which blossomed in the sun, like the shade?"

"A woman of the Narragansetts is happiest in the lodge of her husband."

The eye of the chief met her confiding look with affection, and then it fell, mild and full of kindness, on the features of the infant that lay at their feet. There was a minute, during which an expression of bitter melancholy gathered about his brow.

"The Spirit that made the earth," he continued, is very cunning. He has known where to put the hemlock, and where the oak should grow. He has left the moose and the deer to the Indian hunter, and he has given the horse and the ox to a Pale-face.

Each tribe hath its hunting-grounds, and its game. The Narragansetts know the taste of a clam, while the Mohawks eat the berries of the mountains. Thou hast seen the bright bow which shines in the skies, Narra-mattah, and knowest how one color is mixed with another, like paint on a warrior's face The leaf of the hemlock is like the leaf of th sumach; the ash, the chestnut; the chestnut, th linden; and the linden, the broad-leaved tree whic bears the red fruit, in the clearing of the Yengeese; but the tree of the red fruit is little like the hemlock! Conanchet is a tall and straight hemlock, and the father of Narra-mattah is a tree of the clearing, that bears the red fruit. The Great Spirit was angry when they grew together."

The sensitive wife understood but too well the current of the chief's thoughts. Suppressing the pain she felt, however, she answered with the readiness of a woman whose imagination was quickened by her affections.

"What Conanchet hath said is true. But the Yengeese have put the apple of their own land on the thorn of our woods, and the fruit is good!"

"It is like that boy," said the chief, pointing to his son; "neither red nor pale. No, Narra-mattah; what the Great Spirit hath commanded, even a Sachem must do."

"And doth Conanchet say this fruit is not good?" asked his wife, lifting the smiling boy with a mother's 'oy before his eyes.

The heart of the warrior was touched. Bending his head, he kissed the babe, with such fondness as parents less stern are wont to exhibit. For a moment, he appeared to have satisfaction in gazing at the promise of the child. But, as he raised his head, his eye caught a glimpse of the sun, and the whole expression of his countenance changed. Motioning to his wife to replace the infant on the earth, he turned to her with solemnity, and continued—

"Let the tongue of Narra-mattah speak without fear. She hath been in the lodges of her father, and hath tasted of their plenty. Is her heart glad?"

The young wife paused. The question brought with it a sudden recollection of all those reviving sensations, of that tender solicitude, and of those soothing sympathies, of which she had so lately been the subject. But these feelings soon vanished; for, without daring to lift her eyes to meet the attentive and anxious gaze of the chief, she said firmly, though with a voice that was subdued by diffidence—

"Narra-mattah is a wife."

"Then will she listen to the words of her husband. Conanchet is a chief no longer. He is a prisoner of the Mohicans. Uncas waits for him in the woods!"

Notwithstanding the recent declaration of the young wife, she heard of this calamity with little of the calmness of an Indian woman. At first, it seemed as if her senses refused to comprehend the meaning of the words. Wonder, doubt, horror, and fearful certainty, each in its turn prevailed; for she was too well schooled in all the usages and opinions of the people with whom she dwelt, not to understand the jeopardy in which her husband was placed.

"The Sachem of the Narragansetts a prisoner f Mohican Uncas!" she repeated in a low tone, s if the sound of her voice were necessary to dispel some horrible illusion. "No! Uncas is not a warrior to strike Conanchet!"

"Hear my words," said the chief, touching the shoulder of his wife, as one arouses a friend from nis slumbers. "There is a Pale-face in these woods who is a burrowing fox. He hides his head from the Yengeese When his people were on the trail, barking like hungry wolves, this man trusted to a Sagamore. It was a swift chase, and my father is getting very old. He went up a young hickory, like a bear, and Conanchet led off the lying tribe. But he is not a moose. His legs cannot go like running water, for ever!"

"And why did the great Narragansett give his life for a stranger?"

"The man is a brave;" returned the Sachem, proudly: "he took the scalp of a Sagamore!"

Again Narra-mattah was silent. She brooded, in nearly stupid amazement, on the frightful truth.

"The Great Spirit sees that the man and his wife are of different tribes," she at length ventured to rejoin. "He wishes them to become the same people. Let Conanchet quit the woods, and go into the clearings with the mother of his boy. Her white father will be glad, and Mohican Uncas will not dare to follow."

"Woman, I am a Sachem and a warrior among my people!"

There was a severe and cold displeasure in the voice of Conanchet, that his companion had never before heard. He spoke in the manner of a chief to his woman, rather than with that manly softness with which he had been accustomed to address the scion of the Pale-faces. The words came over her heart like a withering chill, and affliction kept her mute. The chief himself sate a moment longer in a stern calmness, and then rising in displeasure, he pointed to the sun, and beckoned to his companions to proceed. In a time that appeared to the throbbing heart of her who followed his swift footsteps, but a moment, they had turned a little eminence, and, in another minute, they stood in the presence of a party that evidently awaited their coming

The grave group consisted only of Uncas, two of his fiercest-looking and most athletic warriors, the divine, and Eben Dudley.

Advancing rapidly to the spot where his enemy stood, Conanchet took his post at the foot of the fatal tree. Pointing to the shadow, which had not yet turned towards the east, he folded his arms on his naked bosom, and assumed an air of haughty unconcern. These movements were made in the midst of a profound stillness.

Disappointment, unwilling admiration, and distrust, all struggled through the mask of practised composure, in the dark countenance of Uncas. He regarded his long-hated and terrible foe, with an eye that seemed willing to detect some lurking signs of weakness. It would not have been easy to say whether he most felt respect, or regret, at the faith of the Narragansett. Accompanied by his two grim warriors, the chief examined the position of the shadow with critical minuteness, and when there no longer existed a pretext for affecting to doubt the punctuality of their captive, a deep ejaculation of assent issued from the chest of each. Like some wary judge, whose justice is fettered by legal precedents, as if satisfied there was no flaw in the proceedings, the Mohegan then signed to the white men to draw near.

"Man of a wild and unreclaimed nature!" commenced Meek Wolfe, in his usual admonitory and ascetic tones, "the hour of thy existence draws to its end! Judgment hath had rule; thou hast been weighed in the balances, and art found wanting. But Christian charity is never weary. We may not resist the ordinances of Providence, but we may temper the blow to the offender. That thou art here to die, is a mandate decreed in equity, and rendered awful by mystery; but further, submission to the will of Heaven doth not exact. Heathen, thou hast a soul, and it is about to leave its earthly tenement for the unknown world——"

Until now, the captive had listened with the courtesy of a savage when unexcited. He had even gazed at the quiet enthusiasm, and singularly contradictory passions, that shone in the deep lines of the speaker's face, with some such reverence as he might have manifested at an exhibition of one of the pretended revelations of a prophet of his tribe. But when the divine came to touch upon his condition after death, his mind received a clear, and to him an unerring, clue to the truth. Laying a finger suddenly on the shoulder of Meek, he interrupted him, by saying—

"My father forgets that the skin of his son is red. The path to the happy hunting-grounds of just Indians lies before him."

"Heathen, in thy words hath the Master Spirit of Delusion and Sin uttered his blasphemies!"

"Hist!—Did my father see that which stirred the bush?"

"It was the viewless wind, idolatrous and idle-minded infant, in the form of adult man!"

"And yet my father speaks to it," returned the Indian, with the grave but cutting sarcasm of his people. "See," he added, haughtily, and even with ferocity; "the shadow hath passed the root of the tree. Let the cunning man of the Pale-faces tand aside; a Sachem is ready to die!"

Meek groaned audibly, and in real sorrow; for, notwithstanding the veil which exalted theories and doctrinal subtleties had drawn before his judgment, the charities of the man were grounded in truth. Bowing to what he believed to be a mysterious dispensation of the will of Heaven, he withdrew to a short distance, and, kneeling on a rock, his voice was heard, during the remainder of the ceremonies, lifting its tones in fervent prayer for the soul of the condemned.

The divine had no sooner quitted the place, than Uncas motioned to Dudley to approach. Though the nature of the borderer was essentially honest and kind, he was, in opinions and prejudices, but a creature of the times. If he had assented to the judgment which committed the captive to the mercy of his implacable enemies, he had the merit of having suggested the expedient that was to protect the sufferer from those refinements in cruelty which the savages were known to be too ready to inflict. He had even volunteered to be one of the agents to enforce his own expedient, though, in so doing, he had committed no little violence to his natural inclinations. The reader will therefore judge of his conduct, in this particular, with the degree of lenity that a right consideration of the condition of the country and of the usages of the age may require There was even a relenting and a yielding of purpose in the countenance of this witness of the scene, that was favorable to the safety of the captive, as he now spoke. His address was first to Uncas.

"A happy fortune, Mohegan, something aided by the power of the white men, hath put this Narragansett into thy hands," he said. "It is certain that the Commissioners of the Colony have consented that thou shouldst exercise thy will on his life; but there is a voice in the breast of every human being, which should be stronger than the voice of revenge, and that is the voice of mercy. It is not yet too late to hearken to it. Take the promise of the Narragansett for his faith—take more, take a hostage in this child, which with its mother shall be guarded among the English, and let the prisoner go."

"My brother asketh with a big mind!" said Uncas, drily.

"I know not how nor why it is I ask with this earnestness," resumed Dudley, "but there are old recollections and former kindnesses, in the face and manner of this Indian! And here, too, is one, in the woman, that I know is tied to some of our settlements, with a bond nearer than that of common charity—Mohegan, I will add a goodly gift of powde and of muskets, if thou wilt listen to mercy, and take the faith of the Narragansett."

Uncas pointed with ironical coldness to his captive, as he said—

"Let Conanchet speak!"

"Thou hearest, Narragansett. If the man I begin to suspect thee to be, thou knowest something of the usages of the whites. Speak; wilt swear to keep peace with the Mohegans, and to bury the hatchet in the path between your villages?"

"The fire that burnt the lodges of my people turned the heart of Conanchet to stone," was the steady answer.

"Then can I do no more than see the treaty respected," returned Dudley, in disappointment. "Thou hast thy nature, and it will have way. The Lord have mercy on thee, Indian, and render thee such judgment as is meet for one of savage opportunities."

He made a gesture to Uncas that he had done, and fell back a few paces from the tree, his honest features expressing all his concern, while his eye did not refuse to do its duty by closely watching each movement of the adverse parties. At the same instant, the grim attendants of the Mohegan chief, in obedience to a sign, took their stations on each side of the captive. They evidently waited for the last and fatal signal, to complete their unrelenting purpose. At this grave moment there was a pause, as if each of the principal actors pondered serious matter in his inmost mind.

"The Narragansett hath not spoken to his woman," said Uncas, secretly hoping that his enemy might yet betray some unmanly weakness, in a moment of so severe trial. "She is near."

"I said my heart was stone;" coldly returned the Narragansett.

"See—the girl creepeth like a frightened fowl among the leaves. If my brother Conanchet will look, he will see his beloved."

The countenance of Conanchet grew dark, but it did not waver.

"We will go among the bushes, if the Sachem is afraid to speak to his woman with the eyes of a Mohican on him. A warrior is not a curious girl, that he wishes to see the sorrow of a chief!"

Conanchet felt, hurriedly, for some weapon that might strike his enemy to the earth, and then a low murmuring sound at his elbow stole so softly on his ear, as suddenly to divert the tempest of passion.

"Will not a Sachem look at his boy?" demanded the suppliant. "It is the son of a great warrior: why is the face of his father so dark on him?"

Narrah-mattah had drawn near enough to her husband, to be within reach of his hand. With extended arms she held the pledge of their former happiness towards the chief, as if to beseech a last and kindly look of recognition and love.

"Will not the great Narragansett look at his boy?" she repeated, in a voice that sounded like the lowest notes of some touching melody. "Why is his face so dark, on a woman of his tribe?"

Even the stern features of the Mohegan Sagamore showed that he was touched. Beckoning to his grim attendants to move behind the tree, he turned and walked aside, with the noble air of a savage, when influenced by his better feelings. Then light shot into the clouded countenance of Conanchet. His eyes sought the face of his stricken and grieved consort, who mourned less for his danger than she grieved for his displeasure. He received the boy from her hands, and studied his features long and intently. Beckoning to Dudley, who alone gazed on the scene, he placed the infant in his arms.

"See!" he said, pointing to the child; "it is a blossom of the clearings. It will not live in th shade."

He then fastened a look on his trembling partner There was a husband's love in the glance. "Flower of the open land!" he said; "the Manitou of thy race will place thee in the fields of thy fathers. The sun will shine upon thee, and the winds from beyond the salt lake will blow the clouds into the woods. A Just and Great Chief cannot shut his ear to the Good Spirit of his people. Mine calls his son to hunt among the braves that have gone on the long path; thine points another way. Go, hear his voice, and obey. Let thy mind be like a wide clearing; let all its shadows be next the woods; let it forget the dream it dreamt among the trees. 'Tis the will of the Manitou."

"Conanchet asketh much of his wife; her sou is only the soul of a woman!"

"A woman of the Pale-faces; now let her seek her tribe. Narra-mattah, thy people speak strange traditions. They say that one just man died for all colors. I know not. Conanchet is a child among the cunning, and a man with the warriors. If this be true, he will look for his woman and boy in the happy hunting-grounds, and they will come to him. There is no hunter of the Yengeese that can kill so many deer. Let Narra-mattah forget her chief till that time, and then, when she calls him by name, let her speak strong, for he will be very glad to hear her voice again. Go; a Sagamore is about to start on a long journey. He takes leave of his wife with a heavy spirit. She will put a little flower of two colors before her eyes, and be happy in its growth. Now let her go. A Sagamore is about to die."

The attentive woman caught each slow and measured syllable, as one trained in superstitious legends would listen to the words of an oracle. But, accustomed to obedience and bewildered with her grief, she hesitated no longer. The head of Narra-mattah sunk on her bosom, as she left him, and her face was buried in her robe. The step with which she passed Uncas was so light as to be inaudible; but when he saw her tottering form, turning swiftly, he stretched an arm high in the air. The terrible mutes just showed themselves from behind the tree, and vanished. Conanchet started, and it seemed as if he were about to plunge forward; but, recovering himself by a desperate effort, his body sunk back against the tree, and he fell in the attitude of a chief seated in council. There was a smile of fierce triumph on his face, and his lips evidently moved. Uncas did not breathe, as he bent forward to listen:—

"Mohican, I die before my heart is soft!" uttered firmly, but with a struggle, reached his ears. Then came two long and heavy respirations. One was the returning breath of Uncas, and the other the dying sigh of the last Sachem of the broken and dispersed tribe of the Narragansetts.

CHAPTER XXXII.

> "Each lonely scene shall thee restore;
> For thee the tear be duly shed:
> Beloved till life could charm no more,
> And mourn'd till pity's self be dead."
>
> COLLINS.

AN hour later, and the principal actors in the foregoing scene had disappeared. There remained only the widowed Narra-mattah, with Dudley, the divine, and Whittal Ring.

The body of Conanchet still continued, where he had died, seated like a chief in council. The daughter of Content and Ruth had stolen to its side, and she had taken her seat, in that species of dull woe, which so frequently attends the first moments of any unexpected and overwhelming affliction. She neither spoke, sobbed, nor sorrowed in any way that grief is wont to affect the human system. The mind seemed palsied, though a withering sense of the blow was fearfully engraven on every lineament of her eloquent face. The color had deserted her cheeks, the lips were bloodless, while, at moments, they quivered convulsively, like the tremulous movement of the sleeping infant; and, at long intervals, her bosom heaved, as if the spirit within struggled heavily to escape from its earthly prison. The child lay unheeded at her side, and Whittal Ring had placed himself on the opposite side of the corpse.

The two agents, appointed by the Colony to witness the death of Conanchet, stood near, gazing mournfully on the piteous spectacle. The instant the spirit of the condemned man had fled, the prayers of the divine had ceased, for he believed that then the soul had gone to judgment. But there was more of human charity, and less of that exaggerated severity in his aspect, than was ordinarily seated in the deep lines of his austere countenance. Now that the deed was done, and the excitement of his exalted theories had given way to the more positive appearance of the result, he might even have moments of harassing doubts concerning the lawfulness of an act that he had hitherto veiled under the forms of a legal and necessary execution of justice. The mind of Eben Dudley vacillated with none of the subtleties of doctrine or of law. As there had been less exaggeration in his original views of the necessity of the proceeding, so was there more steadiness in his contemplation of its fulfilment. Feelings, they might be termed emotions, of a different nature troubled the breast of this resolute but justly-disposed borderer.

"This hath been a melancholy visitation of necessity, and a severe manifestation of the foreordering will," said the Ensign, as he gazed at the sad spectacle before him. "Father and son have both died, as it were, in my presence, and both have departed for the world of spirits, in a manner to prove the inscrutableness of Providence. But dost not see, here, in the face of her who looketh like a form of stone, traces of a countenance that is familiar?"

"Thou hast allusion to the consort of Captain Content Heathcote?"

"Truly, to her only. Thou art not, reverend sir, of sufficient residence at the Wish-Ton-Wish, to remember that lady in her youthfulness. But to me, the hour when the Captain led his followers into the wilderness, seemeth but as a morning of the past season. I was then active in limb, and something idle in reflection and discourse; it was in that journey, that the woman who is now the mother of my children and I first made acquaintance. I have seen many comely females in my time, but never did I look on one so pleasant to the eye, as was the consort of the Captain until the night of the burning. Thou hast often heard the loss she then met, and, from that hour, her beauty hath been that of the October leaf rather than its loveliness in the season of fertility. Now look on the face of this mourner, and say if there be not here such an image as the water reflects from the overhanging bush. In verity, I could believe it was the sorrowing eye and bereaved look of the mother herself!"

"Grief hath struck its blow heavily on this unoffending victim," uttered Meek, with great and subdued softness in his manner. "The voice of petition must be raised in her behalf, or——"

"Hist!—there are some in the forest; I hear the rustling of leaves!"

"The voice of him, who made the earth, whispereth in the winds; his breath is the movement of nature!"

"Here are living men!—But, happily, the meeting is friendly, and there will be no further occasion for strife. The heart of a father is sure as ready eye and swift foot."

Dudley suffered his musket to fall at his side, and both he and his companion stood in attitudes of decent composure, to await the arrival of those who approached. The party that drew near, arrived on the side of the tree opposite to that on which the death of Conanchet had occurred. The enormous trunk and swelling roots of the pine concealed the group at its feet, but the persons of Meek and the Ensign were soon observed. The instant they were discovered, he who led the new-comers bent his footsteps in that direction.

"If, as thou hast supposed, the Narragansett hath again led her thou hast so long mourned into the forest," said Submission, who acted as guide to those who followed, "here are we, at no great distance from the place of his resort. It was near yon rock that he gave the meeting with the bloody-minded Philip, and the place where I received the boon of an useless and much-afflicted life from his care, is within the bosom of that thicket which borders the brook. This minister of the Lord, and our stout friend the Ensign, may have further matter to tell us of his movements."

The speaker had stopped within a short distance of the two he named, but still on the side of the tree opposite to that where the body lay. He had addressed his words to Content, who also halted to await the arrival of Ruth, who came in the rear, supported by her son, and attended by Faith and the physician, all equipped like persons engaged in a search through the forest. A mother's heart had sustained the feeble woman for many a weary mile, but her steps had begun to drag, shortly before they so happily fell upon the signs of human beings, near the spot where they now met the two agents of the Colony.

Notwithstanding the deep interest which belonged to the respective pursuits of the individuals who composed these two parties, the interview was opened with no lively signs of feeling on either side. To them a journey in the forest possessed no novelties, and after traversing its mazes for a day, the newly-arrived encountered their friends, as men meet on more beaten tracks, in countries where roads unavoidably lead them to cross each other's paths. Even the appearance of Submission in front of the travellers, elicited no marks of surprise in the unmoved features of those who witnessed his approach. Indeed, the mutual composure of one who had so long concealed his person, and of those who had more than once seen him in striking and mysterious situations, might well justify a belief that the secret of his presence near the valley had not been confined to the family of the Heathcotes. This fact is rendered still more probable, by the recollection of the honesty of Dudley, and of the professional characters of the two others.

"We are on the trail of one fled, as the truant fawn seeketh again the covers of the woods," said Content. "Our hunt was uncertain, and it might have been vain, so many feet have lately crossed the forest, were it not that Providence hath cast our route on that of our friend, here, who hath had reason to know the probable situation of the Indian camp. Hast seen aught of the Sachem of the Narragansetts, Dudley? and where are those thou led'st against the subtle Philip? That thou fell upon his party, we have heard; though further than thy general success, we have yet to learn. The Wampanoag escaped thee?"

"The wicked agencies that back him in his designs, profited the savage in his extremity. Else would his fate have been that which I fear a far worthier spirit hath been doomed to suffer."

"Of whom dost speak?—but it mattereth not. We seek our child; she, whom thou hast known, and whom thou hast so lately seen, hath again left us. We seek her in the camp of him who hath been to her—Dudley, hast seen aught of the Narragansett Sachem?"

The Ensign looked at Ruth, as he had once before been seen to gaze on the sorrowing features of the woman; but he spoke not. Meek folded his arms on his breast, and seemed to pray inwardly. There was, however, one who broke the silence, though his tones were low and menacing.

"It was a bloody deed!" muttered the innocent. "The lying Mohican hath struck a Great Chief, from behind. Let him dig the prints of his moccason from the earth, with his nails, like a burrowing fox; for there'll be one on his trail, before he can hide his head Nipset will be a warrior the next snow!"

"There speaks my witless brother!" exclaimed Faith, rushing ahead—she recoiled, covered her face with her hands, and sunk upon the ground, under the violence of the surprise that followed.

Though time moved with his ordinary pace, it appeared to those who witnessed the scene which succeeded, as if the emotions of many days were collected within the brief compass of a few minutes. We shall not dwell on the first harrowing and exciting moments of the appalling discovery.

A short half-hour served to make each person acquainted with all that it was necessary to know. We shall therefore transfer the narrative to the end of that period.

The body of Conanchet still rested against the tree. The eyes were open, and though glazed in death, there still remained about the brow, the compressed lips, and the expansive nostrils, much of that lofty firmness which had sustained him in the last trial of life. The arms were passive at its sides, but one hand was clenched in the manner with which it had so often grasped the tomahawk, while the other had lost its power in a vain effort to seek the place in the girdle where the keen knife should have been. These two movements had probably been involuntary, for, in all other respects, the form was expressive of dignity and repose. At its side, the imaginary Nipset still held his place menacing discontent betraying itself through the ordinary dull fatuity of his countenance.

The others present were collected around the mother and her stricken child. It would seem that all other feelings were, for the moment, absorbed in apprehensions for the latter. There was much reason to dread, that the recent shock had suddenly deranged some of that fearful machinery which links the soul to the body. This dreaded effect, however, was more to be apprehended by a general apathy and failing of the system, than by any violent and intelligible symptom.

The pulses still vibrated, but it was heavily, and like the irregular and faltering evolutions of the mill, which the dying breeze is ceasing to fan. The pallid countenance was fixed in its expression of anguish. Color there was none, even the lips resembling the unnatural character which is given by images of wax. Her limbs, like her features, were immovable; and yet there was, at moments, a working of the latter, which would seem to imply not only consciousness, but vivid and painful recollections of the realities of her situation.

"This surpasseth my art," said Doctor Ergot, raising himself from a long and silent examination of the pulse; "there is a mystery in the construction of the body, which human knowledge hath not yet unveiled. The currents of existence are sometimes frozen in an incomprehensible manner, and this I conceive to be a case that would confound the most learned of our art, even in the oldest countries of the earth. It hath been my fortune to see many arrive and but few depart from this busy world, and yet do I presume to foretell that here is one destined to quit its limits ere the natural number of her days has been filled!"

"Let us address ourselves, in behalf of that which shall never die, to Him who hath ordered the event from the commencement of time," said Meek, motioning to those around him to join in prayer.

The divine then lifted up his voice, under the arches of the forest, in an ardent, pious, and eloquent petition. When this solemn duty was performed, attention was again bestowed on the sufferer. To the surprise of all, it was found that the blood had revisited her face, and that her radiant eyes were lighted with an expression of brightness and peace. She even motioned to be raised, in order that those near her person might be better seen.

"Dost know us?" asked the trembling Ruth. "Look on thy friends, long-mourned and much-suffering daughter! 'Tis she who sorrowed over thy infant afflictions, who rejoiced in thy childish happiness, and who hath so bitterly wept thy loss, that craveth the boon. In this awful moment, recall the lessons of youth. Surely, surely, the God that bestowed thee in mercy, though he hath led thee on a wonderful and inscrutable path, will not desert thee at the end! Think of thy early instruction, child of my love; feeble of spirit as thou art, the seed may yet quicken, though it hath been cast where the glory of the promise hath so long been hid."

"Mother!" said a low struggling voice in reply The word reached every ear, and it caused a general and breathless attention. The sound was soft and low, perhaps infantile, but it was uttered without accent, and clearly.

"Mother—why are we in the forest?" continued the speaker. "Have any robbed us of our home, that we dwell beneath the trees?"

Ruth raised a hand imploringly, for none to interrupt the illusion.

"Nature hath revived the recollections of her youth," she whispered. "Let the spirit depart, if such be his holy will, in the blessedness of infant nnocence!"

"Why do Mark and Martha stay?" continued

the other. "It is not safe, thou knowest, mother, to wander far in the woods; the heathen may be out of their towns, and one cannot say what evil chance might happen to the indiscreet."

A groan struggled from the chest of Content, and the muscular hand of Dudley compressed itself on the shoulder of his wife, until the breathlessly attentive woman withdrew, unconsciously, with pain.

"I've said as much to Mark, for he doth not always remember thy warnings, mother; and those children do so love to wander together!—but Mark is, in common, good; do not chide, if he stray too far—mother, thou wilt not chide!"

The youth turned his head, for even at that moment, the pride of young manhood prompted him to conceal his weakness.

"Hast prayed to-day, my daughter?" said Ruth, struggling to be composed. "Thou shouldst not forget thy duty to His blessed name, even though we are houseless in the woods."

"I will pray now, mother," said the creature of this mysterious hallucination, struggling to bow her face into the lap of Ruth. Her wish was indulged, and for a minute, the same low childish voice was heard distinctly repeating the words of a prayer adapted to the earliest period of life. Feeble as were the sounds, none of their intonations escaped the listeners, until near the close, when a species of holy calm seemed to absorb the utterance. Ruth raised the form of her child, and saw that the features bore the placid look of a sleeping infant. Life played upon them, as the flickering light lingers on the dying torch. Her dove-like eyes looked up into the face of Ruth, and the anguish of the mother was alleviated by a smile of intelligence and love. The full and sweet organs next rolled from face to face, recognition and pleasure accompanying each change. On Whittal they became perplexed and doubtful, but when they met the fixed, frowning, and still commanding eye of the dead chief, their wandering ceased for ever. There was a minute, during which, fear, doubt, wildness, and early recollections, struggled for the mastery. The hands of Narra-mattah trembled, and she clung convulsively to the robe of Ruth.

"Mother!—mother!—" whispered the agitated victim of so many conflicting emotions, "I will pray again—an evil Spirit besets me."

Ruth felt the force of her grasp, and heard the breathing of a few words of petition; after which the voice was mute, and the hands relaxed their hold. When the face of the nearly insensible parent was withdrawn, to the others the dead appeared to gaze at each other with a mysterious and unearthly intelligence. The look of the Narragansett was still, as in his hour of pride, haughty, unyielding, and filled with defiance; while that of the creature who had so long lived in his kindness was perplexed, timid, but not without a character of hope. A solemn calm succeeded, and when Meek raised his voice again in the forest, it was to ask the Omnipotent Ruler of Heaven and Earth to sanctify his dispensation to those who survived.

The changes which have been wrought, on this continent, within a century and a half, are very wonderful. Cities have appeared where the wilderness then covered the ground, and there is good reason to believe that a flourishing town now stands on, or near, the spot where Conanchet met his death. But, notwithstanding so much activity has prevailed in the country, the valley of this legend remains but little altered. The hamlet has increased to a village; the farms possess more of the air of cultivation; the dwellings are enlarged, and are somewhat more commodious; the churches are increased to three; the garrisoned houses, and all other signs of apprehension from violence, have long since disappeared; but still the place is secluded, little known, and strongly impressed with the marks of its original sylvan character.

A descendant of Mark and Martha is, at this hour, the proprietor of the estate on which so many of the moving incidents of our simple tale were enacted. Even the building which was the second habitation of his ancestor, is in part standing, though additions and improvements have greatly changed its form. The orchards, which in 1675 were young and thrifty, are now old and decaying. The trees have yielded their character for excellence, to those varieties of the fruit which the soil and the climate have since made known to the inhabitants. Still they stand, for it is known that fearful scenes occurred beneath their shades, and there is a deep moral interest attached to their existence.

The ruins of the block-house, though much dilapidated and crumbling, are also visible. At their foot is the last abode of all the Heathcotes who have lived and died in that vicinity, for near two centuries. The graves of those of later times are known by tablets of marble: but nearer to the ruin are many, whose monuments, half-concealed in the grass, are cut in the common coarse free-stone of the country.

One, who took an interest in the recollection of days long gone, had occasion a few years since to visit the spot. It was easy to trace the births and deaths of generations, by the visible records on the more pretending monuments of those interred within a hundred years. Beyond that period, research became difficult and painful. But his zeal was not to be easily defeated.

To every little mound, one only excepted, there was a stone, and on each stone, illegible as it might be, there was an inscription. The undistinguished grave, it was presumed, by its size and its position, was that which contained the bones of those who fell in the night of the burning. There was another, which bore, in deep letters, the name of the Puritan. His death occurred in 1680. At its side there was an humble stone, on which, with great difficulty, was traced the single word 'Submission.' It was impossible to ascertain whether the date was 1680, or 1690. The same mystery remained about the death of this man, as had clouded so much of his life. His real name, parentage, or character, further than they have been revealed in these pages, was never traced. There still remains, however, in the family of the Heathcotes, an orderly-book of a troop of horse, which tradition says had some connexion with his fortunes. Affixed to this defaced and imperfect document, is a fragment of some diary or journal, which has reference to the condemnation of Charles I. to the scaffold.

The body of Content lay near his infant children, and it would seem that he still lived in the first quarter of the last century. There was an aged man, lately in existence, who remembers to have seen him, a white-headed patriarch, reverend by his years, and respected for his meekness and justice. He had passed nearly, or quite, half-a-century unmarried. This melancholy fact was sufficiently shown by the date on the stone of the nearest mound. The inscription denoted it to be the grave of "Ruth, daughter of George Harding of the Colony of Massachusetts Bay, and wife of Capt. Content Heathcote." She died in the autumn of 1675, with, as the stone reveals, "a spirit broken for the purposes of earth, by much family affliction, though with hopes justified by the covenant, and her faith in the Lord."

The divine, who lately officiated, if he do not now officiate, in the principal church of the village, is called the reverend Meek Lamb. Though claiming a descent from him who ministered in the temple at the period of our tale, time and intermarriages have produced this change in the name, and happily some others in doctrinal interpretations of duty. When this worthy servant of the church found the object which had led one born in another state, and claiming descent from a line of religionists who had left the common country of their ancestors to worship in still another manner, to take an interest in the fortunes of those who first inhabited the valley, he found a pleasure in aiding the inquiries. The abodes of the Dudleys and Rings were numerous in the village and its environs. He showed a stone, surrounded by many others that bore these names, on which was rudely carved, "I am Nipset, a Narragansett; the next snow, I shall be a warrior!" There is a rumor, that though the hapless brother of Faith gradually returned to the ways of civilized life, he had frequent glimpses of those seducing pleasures which he had once enjoyed in the freedom of the woods.

Whilst wandering through these melancholy remains of former scenes, a question was put to the divine concerning the place where Conanchet was interred. He readily offered to show it. The grave was on the hill, and distinguished only by a headstone that the grass had concealed from former search. It merely bore the words—"the Narragansett."

"And this at its side?" asked the inquirer. "Here is one also, before unnoted."

The divine bent in the grass, and scraped the moss from the humble monument. He then pointed to a line, carved with more than usual care. The inscription simply said—

"The Wept of Wish-Ton-Wish."

www.ingramcontent.com/pod-product-compliance
Lightning Source LLC
LaVergne TN
LVHW020925110826
845150LV00004B/768

9781425554200